ALAN ROLAND

In Search of Self in India and Japan

Toward a Cross-Cultural Psychology

PRINCETON UNIVERSITY PRESS

Copyright © 1988 by Princeton University Press

Published by Princeton University Press, 41 William Street, Princeton, New Jersey 08540
In the United Kingdom: Princeton University Press, Guildford, Surrey

All Rights Reserved

This book has been composed in Linotron Sabon and Gill Sans
by Vail-Ballou Press of the Maple-Vail Book Group.

Clothbound editions of Princeton University Press books are printed on acid-free paper,
and binding materials are chosen for strength and durability. Paperbacks, although satisfactory
for personal collections, are not usually suitable for library rebinding.

Printed in the United States of America by Princeton University Press, Princeton, New Jersey

Designed by Laury A. Egan

Library of Congress Cataloging-in-Publication Data

Roland, Alan, 1930–
  In search of self in India and Japan.
  Bibliography: p.   Includes index.
  1. Self—Cross-cultural studies.   2. Personality and culture—
Cross-cultural studies.   3. East Indians—Psychology.   4. Japanese—Psychology.
5. Psychoanalysis—Cross-cultural studies.   I. Title.
BF697.R637   1988   155.2′0952   88-9985
ISBN 0-691-08617-6 (alk. paper)

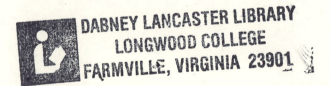

To Jackie, Tika, and Ariel,
who journeyed with me
through India and Japan

C O N T E N T S

P R E F A C E

Beginnings and Belongings

No one undertakes a journey, particularly one of the psyche, without taking along a lot of personal baggage. This is even more true when investigating the psyche of persons from vastly different cultures from one's own, such as India and Japan. Some of the baggage involves conscious, well-planned preparations, anticipating contingencies of the trip, but some of one's belongings are taken inadvertently, and still other items may not even be known to exist until you are in the midst of your travels. Moreover, every journey has its beginnings, that is, its reasons and motives for going. We do not go just anywhere, but rather are pulled to very specific places and studies. What will be looked for, what will be perceived, how one will proceed, how the study is shaped, and what meanings are derived from it are all strongly influenced by the beginnings and belongings. The subjectivity of the psychoanalytic observer is thus an integral part of the field.

I could well say that the beginning of this entire research project occurred with a totally unexpected event in March 1971. A gaunt, intense-looking Indian man stopped me at the door in the later hours of the evening after I had just finished teaching a class at The New School. "Dr. Roland, I saw in The New School catalogue that you have been to India and are teaching a course on Identity, Identification, and Self-Image. My own identity is extremely fragmented. I would like to see you for therapy." Thus began a several month collaborative therapy with an Indian novelist, Ashis, whom I describe at length in Chapter Two. I was immediately struck in those therapy sessions that the quality of his mind was of a different cast than that of any American patient I had ever worked with. Slowly, indeed, an enormous fracture in his identity did emerge between Indian and Western values and modes of being—both anchored, to be sure, within familial relationships, but nevertheless relating to profound civilizational issues. It was from this therapeutic relationship with an artistically gifted Indian that I first formulated my psychoanalytic research on "Identity Conflicts and Resolutions in Urban Indians," in which I proposed working in short-term psychoanalytic therapy with urban Indian patients exposed to a high degree of Westernization. This was the beginning of my psychoanalytic odyssey to India.

Or was it? Some years previously, in 1964, my wife and I had spent six weeks of a summer vacation in India, touring major cities and centers. The trip turned out to be richly laden with interesting and unexpected experiences and relationships.[1] I arranged for lectures and meetings with various psychologists and psychoanalysts that would lay the groundwork for future clinical psychoanalytic research. My wife and I vowed to return for a year's research—which then materialized thirteen years and two children later. Such were the initial seeds for this psychoanalytic research in India.

Is there, however, any one true beginning? Beginnings are often, in fact, journeys themselves, antecedents to new explorations not originally anticipated or even directly related. In 1950, after emerging from a year's experience in the Marine Corps and while in the throes of a late adolescent identity crisis, I came upon the writings of Vivekananda and Vedanta philosophy in my search for values and life meaning. I transferred to Antioch College to study Indian philosophy and culture with Professor M. N. Chatterjee,[2] and then took the few courses on India and the Far East, did a senior thesis on Gandhi, and arranged work periods at two Vedanta centers, a Theosophical printing press, and a mountain retreat of Meher Baba in California.[3] I seriously contemplated graduate work in South Asian studies, but it was the early 1950s, when graduate programs in South Asian studies were still few and far between. Instead, I headed off into clinical psychology to deal more directly with the therapeutics of both others and myself, and to fashion a career.

Why one is drawn to another culture or civilization, or resonates to a different historical era even in one's own civilization, is something

---

[1] One such unexpected experience occurred when my wife became ill in Aurangabad and I was invited to give a lecture on Rapid Eye Movement Dream Research to the local Rotary Club by the physician who was taking care of her. This led to my meeting Dr. Christian, the first American-trained physician in Aurangabad, who talked at length of his clairvoyant dreams and practice of kundalini yoga.

[2] Professor Chatterjee, chairman of the Social Science Department, was a philosopher in the traditional Indian sense. He was accounted to be the most influential professor at Antioch over a span of some thirty years by an alumni poll in the early 1950s.

[3] The Vedanta Centers in Boston and in La Crescenta, California, were started by Swami Paramananda, a disciple of Swami Vivekananda, as part of the Ramakrishna movement in the United States. By the time I worked there, these centers were being run by Srimati Gayatri Devi, Swami Paramananda's niece. The Theosophical press still publishes *Manas*, a philosophical weekly.

about which contemporary psychoanalysis and psychology have little to say.[4] Perhaps we find in other cultures and eras aspects of our inner life that have relatively little place in contemporary society. Or perhaps there are even earlier beginnings. . . .

Other important antecedents to this research project lie in the kinds of psychoanalytic identity and theoretical orientations that have shaped the study. In the 1960s, when American Freudian psychoanalysis was with rare exceptions medical and highly traditional in theory and technique, I became trained at and associated with the National Psychological Association for Psychoanalysis (N.P.A.P.).[5] Given the marginality of N.P.A.P., I could develop professionally in a milieu where I did not have to adhere to any psychoanalytic party line, but could make my own integrations of theory and technique from the complexities of the broad Freudian mainstream. Even in the 1960s, Freudian psychoanalysis was by no means monolithic, and even in my early training, I was drawn to a multi-model approach to Freudian psychoanalysis.[6] My theoretical orientation thus differs from others in cross-cultural psychoanalytic work in its emphasis and use of multiple psychoanalytic models.

I have always staked claims to whatever intensely interested and excited me, but have never felt the need continually to mine the same vein. I later found that what had initially seemed to be disparate interests

[4]Self psychology is beginning to have something to say about this issue in terms of cultural selfobjects; that is, that aspects of culture with which one resonates help to sustain a cohesive sense of self.

[5]The American Psychoanalytic Association and the American Academy of Psychoanalysis, the major Freudian and neo-Freudian psychoanalytic organizations, respectively, are completely dominated by the medical psychoanalytic establishment, and have excluded nonmedical psychoanalysts from their membership with but rare exceptions since the 1930s. The N.P.A.P. was founded by Theodor Reik in the late 1940s, preserving Freud's original idea of training suitable candidates from any discipline. It is now the largest organization of its kind in the United States, maintaining a training institute heterogeneous in its courses, as well as publishing *The Psychoanalytic Review*, a foremost journal of psychoanalysis and culture. The N.P.A.P. is a member neither of the American Psychoanalytic Association nor of the American Academy of Psychoanalysis, and has been in opposition to a growing psychology establishment that has wanted to restrict psychoanalysis to the three disciplines of psychiatry, Ph.D. psychology, and social work (with the inclusion sometimes of psychiatric nurses with a masters degree). The N.P.A.P. is, however, a member of two umbrella organizations furthering multi-discipline psychoanalysis: the National Association for the Advancement of Psychoanalysis and the Council of Psychoanalytic Psychotherapists.

[6]A multi-model approach is closer to the actual clinical work of psychoanalysts than is their narrative discourse in papers, where they usually strive for a rigorous consistency. A recent work espousing such an approach theoretically is Pine (1984).

frequently coming together at unexpected levels of integration in new journeys.

One of the most relevant theoretical paths for this study was an investigation of the internalization process which I developed in a course at The New School (Roland 1972) involving issues of identity and self.[7] A comprehensive approach to the personal internalization of social and cultural reality seems to me an area of psychoanalytic theory that affords a far more pertinent and workable basis for integrating psychoanalytic work with the social sciences and cross-cultural research than does classical Freudian psychosexual theory, or even much of Freudian structural theory when it does not sufficiently account for cultural differences in peoples' consciences. This exploration into the internalization process almost immediately led to an interdisciplinary course on psychoanalysis and the social sciences team-taught with social scientists at The New School Senior College; and soon after it led to an interdisciplinary book on *Career and Motherhood: Struggles for a New Identity* (Roland and Harris 1978). The multi-faceted integrations of psychoanalysis with both social science and history were central to this study.

Another relevant psychoanalytic beginning that involved extensive interdisciplinary collaboration started with a clinical paper on dreams, and another on dreams and art (Roland 1971, 1972). Work on these led me to understand the fundamental reductionism psychoanalysts frequently invoke when analyzing literature and the arts, and to envision a new basis for more valid interdisciplinary investigations (Roland 1974a, 1974b, 1978b). This pathway soon led to intensive collaborative work on Pirandello with Gino Rizzo, a noted Pirandello scholar and critic at City University (Roland and Rizzo 1978).

This work not only impressed me with the necessity of considering fully the complexities of other fields when doing interdisciplinary work, but also showed me that serious interdisciplinary collaboration necessitates a tolerance for threats to one's self-esteem where one must willingly apprentice oneself to the other's field—as indeed the other must do to the complexities of psychoanalysis—and function simultaneously as specialist and student. I soon came to realize that when psychoanalysts ply their trade in disregard for the ecology of another discipline, little of substance can be accomplished.

I further realized that my insight into the relationship between the dream and art—that the unconscious personal elements in art are embedded in and fuel a larger artistic vision that in important ways

---

[7] All of these psychoanalytic concepts are defined in the Glossary.

transcends psychoanalytic viewpoints—has to be extended to issues raised by the juxtaposition of psychoanalysis and cross-cultural research or the study of historical change. I came to see the psychological makeup of persons in societies so civilizationally different as India, Japan, and America as embedded in the fundamentally distinct cultural principles of these civilizations and the social patterns and child rearing that these principles shape.[8] This is quite different from the many psychoanalysts, who tend to assume the primacy of psychic reality, and believe that psychology determines culture and society—another form of psychoanalytic reductionism.

Two other major parts of my theoretical framework acquired from past psychoanalytic explorations became highly relevant to this study along the way. The first is my orientation to the real relationship in psychoanalytic therapy (Roland 1967), which stood me in good stead in India and Japan, where the real relationship is central to the psychoanalytic relationship; some therapists in these relationship-centered cultures are highly critical of the Western tendency to ignore the importance of relationship—outside of transference—in psychoanalytic therapy (Neki 1976a; Nishizono 1980; Surya and Jayaram 1964). The second is the use of the psychoanalyst's awareness of his or her own emotional reactions and attitudes toward patients for understanding the transferences of the patient (Roland 1981). Again, I found myself at home in both India and Japan, where one must constantly rely on one's empathy, inner reactions, and intuitions in the predominant modes of communication.

From the very beginning of this research project I was strongly impelled to go to Japan as well as India (these are the only two Asian countries with a psychoanalytic movement). This impulse was later confirmed by two Japanese psychoanalysts who commented that much of what I had to say about the Indian familial self was generally true of Japanese as well.[9] The need to grasp the similarities as well as important differentiating factors resulted in a journey to Japan in the summer of 1982.

[8] I am using a civilizational perspective as Singer (1972, 39–80, 250–259) has delineated it in his synthesis of the formulations of Alfred Kroeber and Robert Redfield. From their historical-anthropological viewpoint, civilization is conceptualized as distinctive, enduring overall patterns or styles of social and cultural structures and elements that have attained consistency even with the borrowing and incorporating of foreign elements. In other words, there are recognizable organizing principles to the social and cultural patterns of any given civilization, as well as a shared cultural consciousness.

[9] Dr. Masahisa Nishizono and Dr. Mikihachiro Tatara were on panels with me at which I discussed some of my ideas.

But this journey to Japan, like the Indian one, also had earlier roots. In 1969 my wife and I had spent eight weeks in Japan, where I met major Japanese psychoanalysts with whom I renewed contact thirteen years later for this research project. But my overwhelming involvement then was as an artist. We stayed four weeks in Kyoto, where I did a series of etchings and watercolors of Zen gardens, and studied wood-block printing.[10] Even before journeying to Japan, my landscapes frequently seemed to many to be Far Eastern in sensibility. These artistic beginnings have undoubtedly still earlier ones involving my father, a commercial artist by profession and a recognized water-colorist by aspiration, who on occasion was mistaken for being Japanese. Thus, my initial great attraction for Japanese culture was not through philosophy, as in India, but rather through art and aesthetics.

This intense involvement with art has also played a major role in shaping this study. Most salient is the trust developed through art in my own imagination and vision of reality, which has helped me in formulating new concepts and frameworks for the Indian and Japanese selves. Simultaneously there is a striving to be perceptive in a closely detailed way, rather than a demand for rigorous theoretical consistency.

The Journey

What I had originally thought would be an interesting journey in clinical psychoanalytic research in India and Japan turned out to be a much longer odyssey with a far greater rethinking of psychoanalysis and myself than I had anticipated. A psychological journey through India and Japan is also a voyage of self-discovery. I do not mean this simply as an inner spiritual quest. As a gradual understanding of the major contours of the inner landscape of the Indian psyche came into focus from my clinical work in India, I found myself looking back over my shoulder at the American psyche, including my own. It is not that the details changed in any significant way from what I had known before. Rather, as when ascending steeply to a Himalayan hill station or pilgrimage site far above the towns below, the perspective sharply changes and the patterns of the town become clear in a way they hadn't been while walking its streets, similarly, certain patterns implied by my Americanness as well

[10] I became a member of the Ruth Leaf Etching Workshop from 1968 to 1978 (leaving it to work on this research), exhibiting in a variety of juried shows and galleries. I have now resumed doing etchings.

as by my ethnic Jewish background become distinct in a way they hadn't been while I was immersed in American relationships.

I realized that being Jewish was central to my understanding of the emotionality and relationships of the Indian extended family. Having grown up on the periphery of a traditional Jewish extended family in Brooklyn, where innumerable relatives were living in close proximity to each other, I experienced from frequent visits a joint household and intimate, interdependent, extended family relationships, although my parents had already opted for the more individualized American mode of the nuclear family. I felt my Jewish roots have enabled me to be psychologically half way to India; nor was I surprised to learn that many of my Indian friends and colleagues, when they had studied in the United States, had mostly Jews as their close friends. The emotionality and intellectuality are at times strikingly similar.

Just as Indians and Japanese who have headed West frequently search for their own roots and identity as they encounter a totally different culture and life style, I went in the opposite direction.[11] As we were coming in for a landing to Bombay, the plane banked so sharply that when I supposedly looked down all I could see were the stars, while if I looked up, there were the lights of the city. It was as if the world was turned upside down. India, I found, is indeed on the other side of the world from America, a mirror reflecting many of the antitheses between the two societies and psyches. It dawned on me that it is not simply that we view things differently, coming from varied cultures (Hall 1959: 128–164), but that our very inner emotional-cognitive makeup is of another order. I had to question much that I had come to assume was normal and natural.

As I wrestled with psychoanalytic formulations that would capture the makeup of the Indian self as I was observing it, I began an increasingly searching reexamination of the theoretical models of psychoanalysis I carried with me. From my reflections on the current psychoanalytic theories, ranging from developmental models—especially the psychosocial ones of Erikson (1950) and Mahler (Mahler et al. 1975)—to our present norms of mental health and adult functioning, to various aspects of classical structural theory (particularly involving superego and

[11] "Almost certainly, one of the motives for becoming a traveller in my own psychosocial country has been my experience, shared by many other Indians, of studying, working, and living for long stretches of time in Europe and in the United States. At some time during this self-chosen exile, a more or less protracted cultural confrontation with the self as the battleground becomes almost inevitable" (Kakar 1978, 12–13).

ego functioning), to the more current issues of narcissism and the self (Kohut 1971, 1977), and even to Rank's interesting work on the will and individuation (Menaker 1982), I realized that the whole elaboration of the psychoanalytic theory of personality in its many variations is Western-centric. Much of it is clearly related to the clinical data of Western personality in societies emphasizing individualism. Although psychoanalysis repeatedly claims to deal with the universals of psychological makeup and ideal norms of mature human functioning, yet these universals, ideals, and norms were frequently contradicted in India and Japan. And when these norms of development and functioning have been applied by psychoanalysts to Asians, Africans, and others, the inevitable results are that they are seen as inferior or psychopathological[12]— a theoretical position that is tenable only if one assumes the inherent superiority of Western civilization and psyche. When not used normatively, the central developmental constructs are simply not very relevant to persons from these other cultures.

Only much later in my reflections did I realize that not only did the norms and values of psychological functions, and psychological makeup itself, differ but that the very categories in which I was thinking as a psychoanalyst differed from Indian cultural categories of thought about human nature. Such Indian assumptions include the constant emphasis on contextuality, from time to space to ethics to human nature to groups; the subtle interrelatedness of the divine and the mundane; the flows and exchanges of substances within and between persons, with minimal outer boundaries. I could accept that empirical reality itself might be varied, but I was less prepared for questioning my basic way of thinking.

Only now have I begun to appreciate how much of the theoretical structure of psychoanalysis is based on Western philosophical thought— for example, the fundamental split between self and object, and between self-representation and object-representation—and flows directly from Cartesian dualistic assumptions. Thus our very way of conceptualizing human nature is deeply rooted within Western culture. More than this: when we universalize our findings and assume that everyone has essentially the same nature (Ramanujan 1980), we take for granted the Western cultural premise of universalization. It finally dawned on me that there are profound intrinsic interrelationships between cultural conceptualizations of human nature (even when philosophically and scientifi-

---

[12]See Muensterberger (1969) for an excellent example of this in his summation of the literature on separation-individuation in psychoanalytic-anthropological studies.

cally based), actual psychological makeup, and the nature of interpersonal relationships in a given culture.[13] But this is anticipating much of what this book is about.

I was further struck by the overwhelming orientation of Freudian psychoanalysis to intrapsychic phenomena, generally ignoring how historical, social, and cultural patterns shape the inner world (with certain exceptions such as the ego-ideal and superego)—another manifestation of Western individualistic assumptions. I began thinking of Freud's statement of the narcissistic wounds suffered by man, first in his realization that the earth is not in the center of the universe, then that he is an evolutionary descendent of the primates, and finally that man is governed far more by unconscious processes than he is aware (Freud 1917, 139–141). Perhaps we should now add a further blow to the self-esteem of Western man: the realization that the prevailing psychological maps and norms assumed to be universal are in fact Western-centric.

It was only after these reflections that I saw the necessity for a significant reorientation and restructuring of psychoanalytic theory to take into account the Indian and Japanese experiences. As a Freudian analyst deeply committed to the psychoanalytic endeavor, I began a profound search for the essentials of psychoanalytic therapy and theory. I found that psychoanalytic therapy was indeed helpful to my Indian patients, that the various dimensions of human nature that psychoanalysis addresses were all relevant, but that how the content of these dimensions are spelled out in psychoanalytic theory is Western-centric.

I gradually worked out a theoretical strategy to integrate both Western universalizing and Indian contextualizing modes of thinking (Ramanujan 1980) wherein broad psychoanalytic categories from the major models of Freudian psychoanalysis are used as universals,[14] but are elaborated upon contextually from the observations of actual clinical psychoanalytic work with Indians and Japanese rather than from their present content in psychoanalysis. I also formulated new concepts to delineate psychological and psychosocial realities in Indians and Japanese that are minimally present in Western cultures. Thus I decontextualize various psychoanalytic categories of their Western content before recontextualizing them with the clinical data of Indians and Japanese. Such

[13] I had in effect rediscovered what Hallowell (1955) had earlier formulated.

[14] The major Freudian models in America currently include drive theory and structural theory (often referred to as classical psychoanalysis), ego psychology, object-relations theory, and self psychology.

analyses of content have rarely entered psychoanalytic theorizing even in relation to patients from greatly differing ethnic groups in the West.[15]

For instance, I deliberately avoid setting up current psychoanalytic elaborations of certain structures (such as the superego) as yardsticks to measure Indian and Japanese psyches. Rather I first endeavor to elaborate the universal category of conscience in its Indian and Japanese forms on the basis of clinical psychoanalytic therapy. Then I compare the Indian ego-ideal and superego with the Japanese and American ones to show how each is oriented toward functioning only within its own social and cultural contexts. I therefore interrelate psychoanalytic theorizing about Indians and Japanese with historical, cultural, and social patterns far more than Freudian psychoanalysts generally do.[16]

Only much later did I learn that this whole comparative psychoanalytic enterprise has been anticipated by a revolution in the social sciences and philosophy of science.[17] Psychoanalysts, in a positivistic mode, usually assume they are free of the interplay of culture in making their observations and formulating them into theories. In contrast, anthropologists in their shift to symbolic analyses have realized that embedded in the very foundations of theory are a variety of cultural assumptions; that, in effect, the social scientist is very much part of a sociocultural field in his basic mode of thinking and values, and therefore must relate to another culture in terms of its own symbolic systems and meanings

---

[15] As a result, Hispanics, Blacks, and Italians are often viewed pejoratively in their development and functioning.

[16] I have been greatly helped in developing the sociohistorical and cultural contexts necessary to understand the Indian and Japanese selves by various specialists in the United States. The most valuable have been the South Asian Studies Program at the University of Chicago, where I became influenced by the work of ethnosociologists (Marriott 1976; Marriott and Inden 1977; Inden and Nicholas 1977), with its implications for developing a comparative psychoanalysis, as well as by the significant work on social change (Singer 1972; Rudolph and Rudolph 1967) and cultural analyses (Ramanujan 1980); the interdisciplinary seminar on "The Indian Self in Its Social and Cultural Contexts" at the Southern Asian Institute, Columbia University, which I have co-chaired; and the Van Leer Project at Harvard University, with two week-long interdisciplinary workshops on India and Japan, where an overall vision of human potential as being developed in very different ways in varying cultures has been highly congruent with and supportive of my own views. I found specialists on India to be unusually receptive to a psychoanalytic perspective.

[17] In terms of this shift in the philosophy of science, see Thomas S. Kuhn (1962); for the social sciences, there are a number of anthropologists who have changed to this new perspective, perhaps the most important one being Clifford Geertz (1973). Very recently, Heinz Kohut (1984) has incorporated some of Kuhn's perspective in endeavoring to formulate a new psychoanalytic theoretical paradigm.

without imposing his own on it. It is evident that these realizations and endeavors are central to evolving a comparative psychoanalysis.

Indians and Japanese

In both India and Japan the patients and colleagues I worked with are well educated, urban, and from the middle and upper middle classes. My access to the world of the Indian patients was particularly helped by the fact that of all Asian groups—far more than the urban Japanese I worked with—urban Indians such as these have been the most exposed to Westernizing influences through two centuries of British colonial rule, and since Independence through relatives in one Western country or another who visit home at least every other year. Although rooted within their Indian milieu and culture, these urban Indians have assimilated Western culture to a great extent both socially and psychologically. Firmly grounded in at least two Indian languages, they also speak and write fluent English—an English that has evolved along distinctly Indian lines.[18] It was thus possible for an English-speaking Western psychoanalyst such as myself to conduct psychoanalytic therapy with them with only a minimum of language difficulties.

Both men and, increasingly, women are college-educated, with a sizable number having postgraduate degrees. Though obviously still a small percentage of India's total population (some estimate them to be as much as 15 percent of India's 700,000,000 + population), these urban, educated persons nevertheless now include the third-largest national group of scientists and technologists in the world. Undoubtedly, these urban, educated Indians are the largest group in the world who have extensively bridged two vastly different civilizations. This book is a clinical psychoanalytic study of the inner world of such persons, who are still in the process of effecting an integration into an expanding self.

Most of my psychoanalytic work in India was done in Bombay, where I conducted short-term psychoanalytic therapy with some thirteen Indian patients for periods of one to six months, two to five times a week. The number of sessions for various patients ranged from ten to the seventies. Patients were encouraged to speak as freely as possible whatever was on their mind or whatever came to mind, and I focused consistently on various resistances and transferences, the hallmark of psychoanalytic work.

---

[18] Indian English is now looked upon as a distinct form of English, as different from English in Great Britain as American English.

The patients came from highly heterogeneous regional and religious backgrounds, reflecting the cosmopolitan nature of Bombay, where people from all over India have come to live. They were from five different religious communities: six were Hindu upper-caste persons, three were Parsees, two were Muslims from the Borah and Ismaili communities, one was Christian, and another Jewish. Their heterogeneity was further reflected in the fact that seven were Maharastrian, three were Gujerati, two Punjabi, and one Goan. Ten of the thirteen were college graduates, eight of these with postgraduate work and specialization, mostly with master's degrees, and one each in law and medicine. Two patients have achieved recognition in the arts and one more is obviously artistically talented. Their age range was from nineteen to sixty-three, with the majority in their middle to late twenties and thirties—much like my patients in New York City. Seven of the thirteen were married, four had children, and one and possibly still another were homosexual. I have naturally disguised the true identity of all of my patients for reasons of confidentiality, but in a way that is not incongruent with their real background.

With only one exception, all of these patients were functioning in a range from reasonably competent to highly creative in their work and/or family. They were thus very much like others of the educated urban middle and upper middle classes, and could by no means be considered deviants or significantly disturbed members of Indian society. They were rather similar to what is sometimes humorously termed the "normal neurotic" of American society.

This intensive psychoanalytic work in Bombay was supplemented by other clinical data from various sources: supervision of psychoanalysts, students in psychoanalytic training, and psychoanalytically oriented social workers and psychiatrists—some of whose patients were from the lower and scheduled castes. I co-counseled with two women social workers from the Indian Council of Mental Health female college students from three colleges in Bombay whose student bodies' life styles range from traditional to moderately modern; and I sat in on individual counseling sessions at St. Xavier's College.[19] Still other data came from my participation in case conferences at a variety of institutions.[20]

---

[19] This opportunity to sit in at St. Xavier's—one of two colleges in Bombay with students from the most modernized sectors—was afforded to me by Mr. Chinwalla, a psychoanalyst who was Head of the Counseling Department.

[20] In Bombay, I heard cases from the students of the Indian Psychoanalytic Society, the staff of the Indian Council of Mental Health, the Social Service Department of the Atomic Energy Commission, and the Tata Institute for Social Services.

Throughout my clinical experiences in Bombay and elsewhere, I had continuous opportunity for discussion with other psychoanalytic therapists, mental health professionals, and various social scientists. This became an integral part of my methodology. I also had occasion to give a large number of lectures at various institutions.[21] I sometimes requested an informal discussion of questions and topics emerging from my own clinical work in exchange for lecturing. Some of the comments and critiques from discussion periods were highly apropos and helpful, as were examples cited to illustrate further some of the formulations I had made. Sometimes the group dynamics at these meetings were themselves significant to observe.

My journey also took me to three other Indian cities. In New Delhi I was affiliated with the Centre for the Study of Developing Societies in Delhi, the leading interdisciplinary group of social scientists and psychologists in India. Lengthy luncheon discussions enabled me to develop a broader sociocultural and historical view of India.

I spent only two weeks in Ahmedabad at the B. M. Institute of Mental Health, the outstanding psychoanalytic mental health center in India at that time, but this part of my experience was very significant. Dr. B. K. Ramanujam, then Associate Director, in collaboration with the Director, Mrs. Kamalini Sarabhai, planned a program in which I attended case conferences and gave some lectures. But most valuable was a period every day for four days in which I was given the opportunity to raise any issue I wanted with the senior staff. During the second week there, during a Conference of the International Study Group of Child Psychiatry, I was able to present some of my initial formulations on Indian identity as related to attitudes toward psychoanalysis, which are incorporated into Chapter Three.

My third city of clinical work was Bangalore, where I was affiliated for a month in the summer of 1980 with the National Institute for Mental Health and Neuro Sciences (N.I.M.H.A.N.S.). I wanted to ascertain whether my observations and formulations of the familial self and how it is expanding through Westernization/modernization, could be extended to south Indian patients living in a more traditional life style than the highly cosmopolitan west and north Indian urbanites I had seen in Bombay.[22] N.I.M.H.A.N.S. afforded clinical experience in-

[21] One was given as the seventh Girindrasekhar Memorial Lecture to the Indian Psychoanalytic Society in Calcutta, January 1978: "Psychoanalytic Perspectives on Personality Development in India," later published.

[22] I am using the term Westernization/modernization rather than Westernization as M. N. Srinivas (1966) does, or modernization as Milton Singer (1972) uses it. Westernization/

volving supervision, short-term therapy, case conferences, and Family Institute group therapy, as well as lengthy exchanges with staff members on south Indian patients. Many of the latter were from the urban middle and lower classes, and some came from villages through the Community Psychiatry Program. I found that many of my formulations are relevant to these south Indian patients and to those from rural areas, as well. The significant differences between rural and urban patients are attributable to the psychological effects of Westernization/modernization, which I discuss in Chapters Two through Five.

My clinical experience in India has been supplemented since returning by short-term psychoanalytic therapy in New York City with five Indian patients. Four of these patients have been women, two from a north Indian background (Himachal Pradesh and Uttar Pradesh), one from south India, and still another from Bengal. All have doctorates in different fields, and two of them have returned to India to stay. The fifth patient has been a Punjabi man with a college degree. All are upper-caste, three coming from distinguished families.

It is relevant to acknowledge the limitations of such a psychoanalytic sample, even when it has been extended through discussions with other Indian analysts. Like anthropological samples, it cannot be held to be entirely representative of the overall population, or even of the patient's community or class. Nevertheless, clinical observations of a number of patients do convey a picture of the Indian self and its reactions to social change that is undoubtedly relevant to other similarly educated urbanites.

For a month in Hiroshima, I had the unusual experience for a foreigner of becoming part of a working group of up to thirty-five psychoanalytically oriented therapists from many cities in the Inland Sea area, including the graduate students of Dr. Mikihachiro Tatara, who headed the group.[23] I supervised in depth five cases seen in once-a-week psychoanalytic therapy. Process notes of all sessions had been carefully kept

---

modernization connotes that there are always varying degrees of Western values, life styles, technology, and other cultural contributions in modernization in India, even when Western innovations are totally assimilated into Indian society and traditionalized. Westernization and modernization are thus intertwined in highly varying, complex ways and cannot be easily or readily separated.

[23] Dr. Tatara is now Chairman of the Clinical Psychology Department at Hiroshima University. He was trained at the William Alanson White Institute in New York City, as were two other members of his group, Drs. Yoshiko Idei and Totaro Ichimaru. Dr. Tatara had further training at the Austen Riggs Foundation in Stockbridge, Massachusetts.

and translated into English. Three of the persons I supervised, Drs. Idei and Ichimaru, and one graduate student, Miss Yuko Takenori, all spoke fluent English; Dr. Tatara, a gifted simultaneous translator, translated my comments to the other members of the group and their remarks to me. Since the supervisory sessions were all held in a group, this enabled lengthy exchanges and discussions to go on both within the formal sessions and afterward at one or another local snack place to which we always retired. Our meetings also included a two-day seminar on self psychology, where there were lengthy exchanges on differing narcissistic structures in Japanese and Americans.

The patients I supervised included a middle-aged traditional woman with marital problems, two teen-age boys with school problems, and a young man and woman in their mid-twenties who were seen in a mental hospital, but who did not seem to be schizophrenic. All were from cities in the Inland Sea area, the former three being from an educated, middle-class background, and the latter two coming from unstable, lower middle-class families. This case material was supplemented by two other sets of material: a young man and woman in their early twenties from upper middle-class Tokyo families seen in psychoanalysis by Miss Chizuko Yamagami, and cases of schizophrenic patients seen by Professor Moses Burg.[24] Supervision of patients seen in psychoanalytic therapy was supplemented by intensive discussions with a number of Japanese psychoanalysts on Japanese psychological makeup, in which I used the same methodology as I had in India.

I was relatively quickly attuned to the Japanese familial-group self, the psychosocial dimensions of Japanese hierarchical relationships, and the Japanese reactions to Westernization/modernization thanks to my prior work in India. The Indian experience also enabled me to see the Japanese from a perspective different from the usual comparison with Westerners.

Methodological and Theoretical Orientations

My central methodology is to use the disciplined subjectivity or trained empathy of the psychoanalyst in actual psychoanalytic therapy with In-

---

[24] Miss Yamagami was trained for seven years as a child analyst in the Tavistock group in England and is currently affiliated with Dr. Okonogi's group in Tokyo. Professor Burg has been a psychoanalytic psychologist since the early 1950s in Tokyo, and is Professor of Psychology at Toyo University.

dian patients and in supervision of Indian and Japanese psychoanalytic therapists. Integral to the methodology have been on-the-spot dialogues with psychoanalytic therapists and social scientists from within their own culture, enabling me to understand a number of puzzling observations, to become sensitive to certain phenomena in my patients that I was unaware of, and to see things from an Indian and Japanese viewpoint. These discussions also helped to expand my data base by ascertaining whether my observations on a very limited number of patients seen over a short period of time are generalizable for a more comprehensive picture of the Indian and Japanese selves. The fact that five of my Indian patients were actively working as therapists themselves, so that they were able to reflect with considerable awareness on what aspects of their own conflicts, psychological makeup, and situations were representative of others in the culture and what were idiosyncratic to themselves and their own families, was often of enormous assistance. I use the clinical data from psychoanalytic therapy to formulate the inner workings of the Indian and Japanese psyches, to evaluate how they have been affected by Westernization/modernization, and to conceptualize a comparative psychoanalysis rooted within its social and cultural contexts. This endeavor differs from the usual interests of psychoanalysts, who wish to elaborate different kinds of psychopathology and their therapeutic resolutions, or to frame a new universal theory of personality or a new developmental model.

In doing psychoanalytic therapy, there is an implicit or even hidden methodology that is constantly employed by analysts but is rarely articulated. Psychoanalysts assume an implicit understanding of more or less normal modes of psychological functioning, relationships, and development in assessing psychopathology in their patients. Analysts are always juxtaposing the figure of the problems patients are struggling with and their developmental genesis with the ground of what is more or less normal. Theoretical arguments to the contrary—that psychoanalysts are or should be neutrally objective and value-free—do not take into account how a psychoanalyst must actually function.[25] These understandings are rarely articulated in ongoing clinical work, but enter psychoanalytic theory primarily through its developmental models of normality and psychopathology. In doing clinical psychoanalytic work in societies so different from America as India and Japan, I have frequently had to

[25] An important stance of psychoanalysts toward patients is to be neutral, that is, not to impose one's values or ideology on patients, but rather to respect their autonomy and right to choose their own values. Part of this attitude of neutrality reflects positivistic assumptions of objectivity and the belief that the analyst can be value-free.

struggle with understanding basic relationships and courses of development that are the assumed ground for any analyst working there. Articulating these understandings thus became a methodological cornerstone in formulating a comparative psychoanalysis of the Indian and Japanese selves.

Why, then, has such psychoanalytic research rarely been used by Indian and Japanese psychoanalysts in a formulation of their own psyches? Or for that matter, by European and American analysts on theirs? For one thing, formulating a comparative psychoanalysis of persons within one's own culture has not been the approach of practicing psychoanalysts anywhere. Psychoanalysis as constituted today is largely an elaborate ethnopsychoanalysis of Western man (and to varied degrees Western women),[26] but implicitly rather than explicitly. A comparative psychoanalytic orientation has not developed because it is extremely difficult to focus one's mind in this way without functioning as an analyst in two cultures that are *civilizationally* different, in order to observe the constant dramatic contrasts. Indeed, the only Indian psychoanalysts who have written about the Indianness of psychological phenomena are men who have trained abroad; in Japan, again, the major contributors of theories about the Japanese psyche have also trained abroad.[27] These analysts have also commented on the Westernness of certain psychoanalytic formulations, something Western analysts could not do because they lacked experience in Asian or African cultures.

A second reason may be that most Indian psychoanalysts do not feel quite comfortable in challenging or modifying psychoanalytic theory when the data call for it—a hazardous enterprise throughout the history of psychoanalysis.[28] Rather, they respond in an importantly characteristic

[26] Trenchant criticisms have been raised in recent years about Freud's understanding of the psychology of women in a growing psychoanalytic literature on women. Two efforts to formulate a more distinct psychoanalytic psychology of women are papers by Doris Bernstein (1983) and Esther Menaker (Roland and Harris 1978, 87–102).

[27] In India, there are Sudhir Kakar (1978, 1979), trained at the Frankfurt Psychoanalytic Institute, and B. K. Ramanujam (1979, 1986) trained at the Menninger Foundation. In Japan, two of the major psychoanalytic theorists have been Dr. Kosawa, who was trained in Vienna in the 1930s and formulated the Ajase Complex, and Dr. Takeo Doi (1973), who trained at the Menninger Foundation and the San Francisco Psychoanalytic Institute.

[28] Over the years it has become evident that psychoanalysts easily welcome new clinical observation as long as they are put within the accepted theoretical paradigms. Whenever new theoretical structures are formulated on the basis of clinical observations, considerable controversy is generated. A case in point is Kohut's (1971, 1977) clinical observations of developmental arrests and deficits as they are manifested in the transference. When he formulated a new theory of narcissism to contain these observations, diatribes quickly ensued.

Indian cognitive style: they contextualize the formal theory into one compartment, and their own frequently more astute clinical and cultural understandings, informally elaborated, into another. This problem has been handled in a completely different way in the seminal work of the Japanese psychoanalyst Takeo Doi (1973), who jettisoned the formal theoretical structure of psychoanalysis and relied on a psychodynamic exposition of Japanese linguistic terms to delineate the Japanese psyche.

A third cause relates to psychological issues of identity that I discuss in Chapter Two: exposure to Western denigration has been (and still can be) so severe that there is a reluctance to express openly their Indianness. I hope that this work will be a stimulus to the greater publication by Indian psychoanalysts of their own frequently astute observations and cogent informal formulations. They, after all, have much more to say about the subtleties of the Indian self and its development than I have.

How is this work different from other related psychoanalytic efforts, particularly in the burgeoning field of psychoanalytic anthropology? This study is the first to examine the self from the dual perspectives of historical change and sociocultural analysis. It is also the first to be based on actual psychoanalytic therapy with several cases. Psychoanalytic anthropological studies are usually made in rural areas in the context of cohesive cultures that have maintained many of their indigenous social and cultural patterns. In these cases, the researchers apply a Western psychoanalytic framework to their ethnographic observations. This direct or indirect use of ethnographic material within a Western psychoanalytic framework, which on occasion may also include the use of autobiography, biography, and oral history, is for instance characteristic of *every* psychoanalytically oriented book on India to date (Carstairs 1957; Kakar 1978, 1982; Spratt 1966).

These works are thus primarily based on observational, cultural, and interview data, but not on actual psychoanalytic therapeutic work. The advantages of the methodology used in this study of actual clinical psychoanalytic work in another culture is that it can contribute a much greater level of psychic depth to our understanding; through this, one can reformulate the contents of the various psychoanalytic categories to be more congruent with the indigenous psyche, and less Western-centric.

In recent years a new trend has developed in psychoanalytic anthropology that focuses on personal, subjective experience through observation, long-term interviewing, or even quasi-psychoanalytic or therapeutic interviews over extended periods of time with villagers (Boyer

1979; Crapanzano 1980; LeVine 1979; Parin et al. 1980). In effect, some researchers are using depth psychological interviews as a new ethnographic method. Their efforts to integrate the inner worlds of their subjects with the predominant sociohistorical and sociocultural patterns of the community go far beyond the reductionistic stance of much of applied psychoanalysis. The differences between this new psychoanalytic-ethnographic methodology and the one employed in this work are first, that my subjects are part of a highly sophisticated, cosmopolitan urban culture that has partially integrated two civilizationally distinct cultures; and second, that these urban Indians and Japanese are genuinely in psychoanalytic therapy, sometimes desperately and at times painfully struggling with inner problems that they are highly motivated to resolve—rather than being paid interviewees. A greater depth of psychoanalytic understanding can thus ensue.

There remains the critical question as to which psychoanalytic framework to use to encompass either ethnographic interview data or that of psychoanalytic therapy. The actual theoretical orientations of psychoanalytic anthropology have ranged from classical drive theory (Devereux 1980) to structural theory, to ego psychology and its developmental models (Boyer 1979; Hallowell 1955; S. LeVine 1979; Obeyesekere 1981, 1984; Parin et al. 1980), object-relations theory (Lindholm 1982), the Eriksonian model (Kakar 1978), and even a Lacanian analysis (Crapanzano 1980); but these researchers have usually restricted themselves to one or another of these theoretical orientations, or at most to the first three.

I am trying to cast as large a net as possible to catch Indian and Japanese psychological experience by using a Freudian multi-model approach that encompasses all of the above theories (with the exception of a Lacanian analysis) and includes self psychology. Simultaneously I rely considerably on my own empathic and intuitive judgment as essential, regardless of what the theory says. I firmly believe that all of these models of the mind—including Rank's innovative contributions around individuation and immortality, and neo-Freudian and Jungian positions—if approached critically and integratively contribute to varying extents to understanding one or another aspect of the human animal; nevertheless, all these theories commit the usual blind man's error of considering an ear, leg, or tail of the psyche to be the whole beast.[29]

[29] It should be noted, however, that one or even several of these Freudian viewpoints can be used in either a reductionistic or an integrative manner. Breadth of psychoanalytic viewpoint is no guarantee for avoiding reductionism once one is dealing with historical or social or cultural phenomena in conjunction with the psychological.

What is true for the psychoanalytic theory of personality is also true for the methodology of clinical psychoanalytic work.[30] There is, for instance, a great deal of complexity and more than a little controversy over the psychoanalytic theory of technique, particularly involving the nature of transference and the psychoanalytic relationship. The stance one takes on these issues becomes very relevant to clinical psychoanalytic work in India and Japan. Again, my approach is to consider transference from a multi-model orientation, while assessing the nature of the real relationship between analyst and patient in these societies and its relation to the transference. I believe these principles are essential to attain the needed flexibility for psychoanalytic work in India and Japan.

One final point on theoretical orientation, an issue that is enmeshed in continual controversy. To what extent is human nature universal, and to what extent is it a manifestation of varying cultures and societies? Like many other critical questions and issues, this is too easily posed in terms of a fundamental dichotomy, whereas the truth resides in various paradoxical interrelationships between these seemingly polar opposites. Certainly, I could work psychoanalytically in India and then Japan—as Indian and Japanese psychoanalysts work in America— only by being able to be empathically in touch with the common threads of humanity in all of us. Likewise, a sensitive Indian, Japanese, or American can grasp and feel the other's cultural nuances. I have further found that many if not most of the basic psychoanalytic categories that structure the psychoanalytic theory of personality also seem to catch these common aspects of humanity within their net. But when I have reexamined the elaboration of the content of these categories as they now constitute a psychoanalytic theory of personality, I find our view of so-called common humanity to be overwhelmingly Western-centric. It is only now, with the early advances of ethnopsychoanalysis and psychoanalytic anthropology, that there is any orientation that even begins to address the issues of our common humanity and the profound variations that are socioculturally and sociohistorically related. From my psychoanalytic sojourns in India and Japan as well as my work in New York City, it becomes obvious that different chords of human potential are played fortissimo in certain cultures and pianissimo in others, and some are completely differently orchestrated into highly contrasting life styles and inner psychological configurations. It is to the issue of evolving a psychoanalytic framework to encompass our common humanity and its

[30] Robert A. LeVine (1982a, 171–304), for instance, convincingly asserts the value of a psychoanalytic orientation to culture and personality studies, but conveys a much more monolithic picture of psychoanalytic theory and methodology than is presently warranted.

profound variations in cultures that are civilizationally distinct that I address the concluding chapter of this work.

Tales and Readers

When journeys are completed and travelers return, tales are told and retold. Which tales are told and how they are related depends greatly on your listeners' interests. Which stories will grip some and bore others? How should the tale be told to involve those who have not traversed the same terrain? What fillers are needed for those for whom some tales are completely foreign territory?

Readers of this work may encompass many kinds, ranging from urban Indians and Japanese to South Asian and East Asian specialists, psychoanalysts and Indian and Japanese mental health professionals, psychoanalytic social scientists and psychohistorians, those involved in comparative religion and mysticism, specialists in modernization in Asian countries, and simply the interested intellectual and intelligent layman who wishes to know more about Indians and Japanese. It is a rare person who would be familiar with the diversity of terms from the many fields drawn on in this work, including psychoanalysis and anthropology, let alone those of Indian and Japanese culture. I have therefore included a glossary to cover concepts from all of these areas. Moreover, I have spelled out some of the theoretical positions of psychoanalysis, and of anthropology and history in India and Japan, that may be elementary to specialists in these fields but unknown to those relatively unfamiliar with these disciplines.

These are cautionary tales for Western psychoanalysts, particularly those interested in cross-cultural psychoanalytic research where there are "more things in heaven and earth . . . than are dreamt of" in contemporary psychoanalysis.[31] Erik Erikson in the keynote address at the International Congress of Psycho-Analysis in 1979 called for a future meeting of the congress to devote itself to the issues and findings of psychoanalysis from Eastern countries. It is hoped that this book, and especially the final chapter—where I use the lever of my Indian and Japanese psychoanalytic experiences to move psychoanalysis into a comparative perspective—will help to open discussion among Western analysts, with a view to interesting them in such a perspective.

[31] "There are more things in heaven and earth, Horatio, / than are dreamt of in your philosophy" *Hamlet*, Act I, Scene V, ll. 166–167.

I am well aware that telling tales to diverse audiences will result in criticism from a number of sides. Psychoanalysts could well question my methodology of short-term psychoanalytic work in India and Japan: that until one sees a number of patients through a full analysis, such conclusions as I have drawn are only tentative ones. Indians and Japanese may well feel I have missed important subtleties or not understood others. South Asia and Japan specialists, on the other hand, could easily criticize me for not being sufficiently grounded in all of the literature in these fields; whereas psychoanalytic anthropologists could certainly express similar views regarding their specialty. This kind of interdisciplinary work inevitably generates problems of this sort. But it is also apparent that there is as yet no one psychoanalytically trained who has worked extensively in psychoanalytic therapy in India, Japan, and a Western country, and who is also a specialist in South Asian and Japanese studies, as well as in psychoanalytic anthropology and psychohistory. Despite all of the problems and perils attending this kind of work, I expect that there is much that I have to tell that will be of real significance to all of my audiences.

Helpers and Guides

This journey was not taken alone. I received generous financing, organizational affiliation and support, the collaboration of colleagues abroad, the cooperation of my family, and by no means least, guides to unfamiliar inner landscapes.

The necessary financial support came from a Professional Development Grant from the American Institute of Indian Studies for 1977-1978, and a Senior Research Grant from them in the summer of 1980. I owe my deepest gratitude to Dr. Pradeep Mehendiratta and his staff at the A.I.I.S. office in New Delhi for making all kinds of arrangements for us that went far beyond financial support. Organizational support came from various affiliating agencies who cooperated in this research, and more particularly from certain persons who paved the way for my work. In New York City, my sponsoring institution was the National Psychological Association for Psychoanalysis. For my research work in India, I am most deeply indebted to the indefatible energies and good will of Mrs. Freny Mehta, Director, and her staff of the Indian Council of Mental Health in Bombay, who effectively arranged for most of my clinical work upon which this study is based. I am also indebted to the Bombay Branch of the Indian Psychoanalytic Society, and particularly to Mr. Udayan Patel, who helped me to organize case discussions and seminars.

In Delhi, I feel particularly grateful to Professor Ashis Nandy, who not only introduced me to members and meetings of the Centre for the Study of Developing Societies, but to other major social scientists and psychologists as well, such as Professors Anandalakshmi and Veena Das, and Dr. Shib Mitra.[32] I was graciously given the opportunity to sit in on intake conferences at the All-India Institutes of Medical Sciences by Professor Neki,[33] where I had discussions with a psychoanalytic psychologist, Dr. Shakuntala Dube. I am very thankful to Dr. Sudhir Kakar (1978, 1979), who generously let me read his as yet unpublished manuscripts. In Bangalore, I am particularly indebted to Dr. Ravi Kapur, then Head of Psychiatry, for arranging my one-month stay at the National Institute for Mental Health and Neuro Sciences, and to psychiatrists Drs. C. Shamasunder, Usha Sundaram, and Illana Cariappa, as well as the Head of Psychology, Dr. Satyavatha, who all contributed to my clinical work there.

I feel deeply grateful to Dr. Mikihachiro Tatara and his group in Hiroshima, who not only arranged for my clinical work but who also effectively took care of our various family needs. In Tokyo, I am very thankful to Professor Moses Burg for illuminating discussions and access to a psychiatric hospital and other meetings he was involved in. I had further lengthy discussions in Tokyo with other senior psychoanalysts such as Drs. Takeo Doi, Akihisa Kondo, and Keigo Okonogi, as well as with younger analysts such as Drs. Osamu Kitayama and Minakawa, and Miss Yamagami, who spent a great deal of time translating her process notes of psychoanalytic sessions. In Fukuoka, I met with Dr. Masahisa Nishizono, a senior psychoanalyst, and some of his staff. As in India, I also met with anthropologists, including Professors Sumiko Iwao, Chie Nakane (our discussions being oriented toward a Japan-India comparison), and Hiroshi Wagatsuma.

Along this journey, many have served as guides to the unfamiliar terrain of the Indian and Japanese selves and societies. Undoubtedly, my most important guide and mentor for India is Dr. B. K. Ramanujam, the most

---

[32] Professor Anandalakshmi was Head of the postgraduate program in Child Development, and is now Director of Lady Irwin College; Professor Veena Das is an anthropologist at Delhi University. Dr. Shib Mitra is a psychoanalyst who was then Director of the National Council for Educational Research and Training.

[33] Professor Neki was then Head of Psychiatry at the All-India Institutes of Medical Sciences and President of the Indian Psychiatric Association.

astute psychoanalytic clinician I encountered in India. My initial contact with Ram was in Ahmedabad in 1977, but I have since been able to continue our intensive discussions and collaboration in New York City. In a metaphorical sense, Ram journeyed with me through India.

In Japan, Dr. Tatara was a constant guide for our month in Hiroshima, he and others of his group tactfully pointing out a number of the subtle nuances of relating within the work group, as well as many of the inner workings of the Japanese psyche.

Then there were my companions to India and Japan, my wife, Jackie, and two children, Tika and Ari, six and five when we first set off. The sharing of diverse experiences, relating to Indians and Japanese as a family as well as individually, all contributed to the enrichment of these journeys.

No work such as this could have reached its present state without helpful critiques and comments from a number of persons who have read the manuscript for substance and style at various stages along the way. I am grateful for comments from a variety of anthropologists who are South Asia and Japan specialists, including Veena Das, Charles Leslie, Owen Lynch, McKim Marriott, Ralph Nicholas, Gananath Obeyesekere, Manisha Roy (also a Jungian analyst), Milton Singer, and Hiroshi Wagatsuma. From the historical side, I am equally indebted to South Asian historians Geraldine Forbes and Leonard Gordon. From the vantage point of psychoanalysis, psychology, and psychiatry, I have profited from comments and critiques from Stephen Aaron, Anandalakshmi, Takeo Doi, Fred Feirstein, Sudhir Kakar, Ravi Kapur, Nobuko Meaders, Kanwel and Birgitte Mehra, Masao Miyamoto, Ashis Nandy, Joel Newman, Loveleen Posmentier, Roberta Satow, Mikihachiro Tatara, and Yasuhiko Taketomo. There have also been the helpful comments of the poet and linguist A. K. Ramanujan. There is the unknown reader of this manuscript for a university press who sagaciously suggested that I put my case data more in the forefront of this work. Finally, I am extremely grateful to Margaret Case, my editor, for her sound judgment and enthusiastic support all along the way; and to her and Edith Kurzweil for helping trim the sails of a lengthy work for a tauter, more focused reading. I am very thankful to Vikram Seth, who graciously granted permission to use his poem, "Divali." As an important aid to writing this manuscript, I received a grant from the American Council of Learned Societies and the Social Science Research Council Joint Committee on South Asia in 1980–1981.

IN SEARCH OF SELF IN INDIA AND JAPAN

C H A P T E R   O N E

Introduction: The Familial Self, the Individualized Self, and the Spiritual Self

The Self in Civilizational Perspective

In this work I investigate profound changes in the structure of the self that take place when persons are in intense contact with both Eastern and Western cultures; to do this I examine the nature of the self from a cross-civilizational perspective.[1] I intend to work on as broad a canvas as possible, encompassing civilizational issues as they are manifested psychologically in cultures as radically different as those of India, Japan, and the United States. I juxtapose and contrast the development, inner structures, and functioning of the self in these three societies so that they serve as figure and ground for each other, thus highlighting each and putting the others into more accurate perspective, while delineating the expanding nature of the Indian and Japanese selves. In effect, I try to step onto an imaginary platform in psychological space to survey the

[1] I am carrying the historical-anthropological viewpoint referred to in the Preface, note 8, a step further by postulating that the self of persons from different civilizations varies significantly according to the civilization the person is living in. That is, the psychological dimension is also profoundly affected by the major organizing principles of different civilizations as they are manifested through social and cultural patterns.

panorama of radically different selves in the process of change. By highlighting this relativity, one can see the changing self in truer perspective.

I have found from my work in India, Japan, and America that the intrapsychic self varies significantly if not radically according to the social and cultural patterns of societies so civilizationally different. I find that people have a different experiential, affective sense of self and relationships, as well as vastly different internalized world views that give profoundly different meanings to everyday experiences and relationships. From these observations, I have come to realize the need for a framework to integrate psychoanalytic observations on the intra-psychic self developed through the familial relationships of childhood and adolescence with views of the psychosocial dimensions of the self involved in adult relationships patterned by a particular culture. In effect, if we are to understand individuals in different cultures, psychoanalysis and the social sciences must become partners in an intricate dance whose steps vary considerably, and become even more complex with inter-civilizational encounters.

In trying to observe the self from a civilizational point of view, I consider it more helpful to use whatever perspectives will shed light on the self than to strive for consistency at this stage. I thus draw from a variety of Freudian psychoanalytic models. Indeed, the psychoanalytic field at this point is far from reaching a consensus on any unified theory of the self, and meanwhile various conceptualizations of the self shed light on different clinical data. I also draw from concepts of the self in social science as well as some Hindu ones. I then formulate overarching conceptualizations of the self that are more oriented toward cross-civilizational studies than are those current in psychoanalysis.

From a psychoanalytic standpoint, I use the concept of the self as a supraordinate organizing principle of the psyche, as initially conceptualized by Hartmann (1964) in Freudian psychoanalysis but later developed in far more sophisticated fashion by both Erikson (1963) and Lichtenstein (1977) from their work on identity. In line with this conceptualization, I also view the self as having its own organizational schema or suborganizations, as elaborated in the work of Klein (1976) and Gedo (Gedo and Goldberg 1973; Gedo 1979, 1981).[2] I prefer the term "self" to Erikson's (1963) concept of "self-identity," as his elaboration of the latter is far too rooted in Western individualistic personality and culture to be an accurate representation of the Indian or Japanese self. Never-

---

[2] Klein and Gedo based their work on the self in good part on Erikson's and Lichtenstein's contributions, respectively, on identity as the major organizer of the psyche.

4

theless, Erikson's concept of self-identity is enormously useful in other respects in its focus on self experience and continuity, and its linking of the intra-psychic with the social, cultural, and historical; and the idea of identity conflicts are quite relevant to Indians and Japanese struggling with Westernization.

I utilize still another psychoanalytic perspective on the self that derives from an object-relations viewpoint, in which social relationships and cultural symbols are filtered through and internalized into the psyche in affect-laden inner images of self and other(s) in complex interrelationships (Grinker 1957; Jacobson 1964; Kahn 1974; Kernberg 1975; Segal 1964; Winnicott 1965). I also consider self as related to authenticity in terms of Winnicott's (1960) true and false self, and to related concepts of Kohut (1980), Loewald (1960), and the Menakers (1965). A third psychoanalytic use of self is related to Kohut's (1971, 1977) seminal contributions on the self as developing through bipolar internalization processes, intrinsically related to issues of self-regard and cohesiveness. Rank's perspectives on the self as encompassing individuation, will, and self-creation (Menaker 1982) are also useful. It goes without saying that I also make use of the varying developmental models inherent in these psychoanalytic perspectives on the self.

From sociological and anthropological perspectives, I am using self in terms of social roles, presentations, and modes of communication (Goffman 1959; LeVine 1982a; Parsons 1964), taking into account those aspects of the self directly and consciously related to differing patterns of interpersonal relationships.[3] I particularly elaborate the idea of a public versus a private self for Indians and Japanese, where the former as well as the latter self are deeply internalized into the psyche. My perspective on the self is related to Hallowell's (1955) contributions on the self as profoundly interrelated with its social and cultural environment. One of his important orientations—the use of indigenous conceptions of the self—is closely related to my own psychoanalytic observations, and I shall consider how these conceptions, when internalized, affect psychological development and functioning.

Finally, I view the self through the Hindu categories of *jiva* (finite) and *Atman* (Infinite), with highly differing experiential components of consciousness and being in each (Bon Maharaj 1963). This is to take into account spiritual practices and experiences that are not formulated in Freudian psychoanalysis.

[3] Erikson (1963) also tried to integrate the self and social roles through his concept of self-identity as the intrapsychic representation of the person's place in the interpersonal configurations in a given culture.

I am now convinced that we must speak of three overarching or su-praordinate organizations of the self: the familial self, the individualized self, and the spiritual self, as well as an expanding self.[4] The concepts of the familial self and individualized self are born out of my cross-cultural experience rather than current psychoanalytic theory. Each forms a total organization of the self in Eastern and Western (particularly Northern European/American) societies, respectively, with varying sub-organizations. Each suborganization of the familial self, indeed, en-compasses one or another category of psychoanalytic theory, but in a way that reflects the clinical data of Indians and Japanese rather than of Westerners. The suborganizations of the individualized self are those same categories and contents currently constituting psychoanalytic the-ory, but given different meanings. Such meanings can only be affixed through a comparative perspective.

The spiritual self, on the other hand, involves a major dimension of human experience that is ignored or treated reductively by most of Freudian psychoanalysis. This self is relevant to anyone involved in spir-itual pursuits, but forms quite different psychological integrations in those having a familial self and those with an individualized self.

The expanding self represents a growing individuation of the self. Its attendant conflicts derive primarily from the experience of inter-civili-zational contacts and the social change that is generated in the process.[5] A tripartite framework helps clarify the psychological processes involved in this expanding self. Both Indians and Japanese in their inter-civiliza-tional encounters utilize various facets of their familial self to modern-ize, while simultaneously they assimilate certain aspects of the individ-ualized self of Westerners; some Americans, on the other hand, have become involved in the spiritual self through a large influx of Eastern spiritual teachers, utilizing a new paradigm from outside contemporary Western secular culture. A basic thesis of this work, then, is that in urban Indians, Japanese, and Americans the expanding self incorporates

[4] It has long been recognized that any conceptual definition of spiritual experiences is totally inadequate. From lack of any adequate terms, I am simply calling this self the spiritual self, to highlight experiential states of consciousness and being that are not usu-ally experienced in everyday relationships. These states are nevertheless immanent within the person, and at a highly realized state of consciousness, within the phenomenal world as well.

[5] This self is most closely related to Erikson's (1950, 1968) concept of self-identity syntheses and to Rank's and the Menakers' work on individuation as involving the social process (Menaker 1982; Menaker and Menaker 1965). Erikson, the Menakers, and Rank are among the very few psychoanalysts in the Freudian tradition to give important psycho-logical weight to historical experience.

new basic organizational structures and paradigms from another civilization, or from certain profound changes generated by their own cultural principles. In terms of indigenous social change, for example, the women's movement in America can be seen as an effort to realize important dimensions of the individualized self, previously overwhelmingly reserved for Western men, as well as legitimitizing certain values of the familial self; women's psychological conflicts are frequently between these two selves.

From a cross-cultural perspective, the distinctions between the three broad categories of the self are of value in various ways. First, when the organizational cores of the individualized and familial selves are delineated, each highlights the other. Second, by formulating the various suborganizations of the familial self, it not only becomes more feasible to compare the various facets of the Indian and Japanese familial selves but it will also become possible to make comparisons with the familial self of persons from different cultures. These categories also allow comparisons among the differing integrations of the familial with the spiritual self in persons from India, Japan, and other cultures where some kind of familial self predominates. An analysis through contrast sheds light on a new integration Americans are effecting in realizing the spiritual self in the context of their individualized selves. Finally, such an analysis clarifies the inner emotional experience of Indians—and others with a familial self—who have emigrated and are living in American-style relationships in which the individualized self predominates. A tripartite analysis should also be of considerable value for understanding the psychological makeup of persons coming to psychoanalysis in America from various Mediterranean cultures—such as Hispanics, Italians, and Greeks—where some of the norms and functioning of the familial self are dominant, however individualized these patients may seem to be.

A brief outline of the familial self, the individualized self, and the spiritual self may help orient the reader for the rest of this work. By the familial self of Indians and Japanese, I mean a basic inner psychological organization that enables women and men to function well within the hierarchical intimacy relationships of the extended family, community, and other groups. The familial self encompasses several important suborganizations: *symbiosis-reciprocity* that involves intensely emotional intimacy relationships, with their emotional connectedness and interdependence, in relationship-centered cultures where there is a constant affective exchange through permeable outer ego boundaries, where a highly private self is maintained, where high levels of empathy and receptivity to others are cultivated, and where the experiential sense of self is of a "we-self" that is felt to be highly relational in different social contexts;[6] *narcissistic configurations of we-self regard* that denote self-esteem derived from strong identification with the reputation and honor of the family and other groups, as well as with the others in hierarchical relationships, from nonverbal mirroring throughout life, and from culturally encouraged idealization of elders; a *socially contextual ego-ideal* that carefully observes traditionally defined reciprocal responsibilities and obligations, and through a public self the social etiquette of diverse hierarchical relationships, in complexly varying interpersonal contexts and situations; a *superego* that structures aggression and sexuality according to the exingencies of hierarchical extended family and group relationships, with congruent unconscious defensive functions; *modes of communication* that are always on at least two different levels; and *modes of cognition and ego functioning* that are highly contextual and oriented toward symbols, signs, and influences. These inner psychological organizations, structures, and processes of the familial self underlie the great variety of group character throughout the Indian subcontinent, and are not meant as an elaboration of national character or modal personality. Similar suborganizations of the familial self are equally present in the Japanese, but assume a somewhat different form as well as at times, content.

The individualized self, on the other hand, is the predominant inner psychological organization of Americans, enabling them to function in a highly mobile society where considerable autonomy is granted if not imposed on the individual. The individual must thus choose from a variety of social options in contractual, egalitarian relationships (even within an organizational hierarchy), governed by a predominant cultural principle of individualism. The individualized self is characterized by inner representational organizations that emphasize: an *individualistic "I-ness"* with relatively self-contained outer ego boundaries, sharp differentiation between inner images of self and other, and considerable social individuation orienting the person toward relatively autonomous functioning, inner separateness, and initiative; individualistic *narcissistic structures of self-regard* that are again relatively self-contained and more independent of mirroring and idealization in adulthood; a *superego* highly differentiated and oriented around relatively abstract principles of behavior

---

[6] The phrase, "we-self" was coined by Drs. Al Collins and Prakash Desai, Sanskritist-psychologist and psychiatrist, respectively. It contrasts with the self of Westerners, which is implicitly always an I-self.

suited to a variety of situations; an *ego-ideal* that incorporates differing balances of varying aspects of individualism in men and increasingly in women—from competitive individualism to self-actualization—while functioning within the norms of a great variety of extra-familial groups; and *modes of cognition and ego-functioning* that are strongly oriented toward rationalism, self-reflection, efficiency, mobility, and adaptability to extra-familial relationships. All of these substructures are oriented toward the ongoing self-creation of one's own self-identity in the adolescent and adult years through the exploration and realization of inner potentials in various activities and relationships.

The spiritual self is the inner spiritual reality that is within everyone and is realized and experienced to varying extents by a very limited number of persons through a variety of spiritual disciplines. The spiritual self, usually expressed in India through a complex structure of gods and goddesses as well as through rituals and meditation, is a basic assumption in Hindu culture and is psychologically deeply engraved in the preconscious of all Indians, even if they make no particular effort to realize it. In Japan, the avenues toward realization of the spiritual self are different, tending toward more aesthetic modes such as the tea ceremony, flower arranging, calligraphy, and communion with nature. In both societies the spiritual self is usually confined to a highly private self, but by no means defines the latter, which is a basic constituent of the familial self.

It is my strong impression that the traditional psychological makeup of Indians and Japanese consists of varying integrations of a familial self with a spiritual self with very little of the more individualized self I have outlined above—which is not to deny the considerable individuality of Indians and the more subtle individuality of Japanese. This contrasts dramatically with predominant modes of American psychological makeup, where the individualized self is the dominant note, with background chords of the familial self.[7] Only the most muted measures of the spiritual self have traditionally been sounded in modern Western culture, with occasional loud echoes coming from certain artistic and philosophical quarters, as well as from religious groups on the margin of Catholicism, Protestantism, and Judaism.[8] From a Hindu philosophic-psychological standpoint, both the familial and individualized selves are viewed

---

[7] Partial exceptions are those persons from ethnic and national backgrounds originally from southern Europe, Asia, and Africa. The familial self also manifests itself much more in Western women than in men.

[8] These groups include meditative monastic orders in Catholicism such as the Carthusians, the Quakers and Shakers in Protestantism, and Kabbalists and Hasidim in Judaism.

as jiva-atman, both being the consciousness of finite or phenomenological selves in contrast to the realization and inner experience of Atman or Spirit.

A Comparative Civilizational Frame

To work on as broad a canvas of the self as I envisage, I must first outline in broad strokes a civilizational frame for comparing India, Japan, and America. Only then can the contexts be established for filling in the highlights and shadings of the differing selves with their contrasts, nuances, and appropriate colorations.

From a philosophic standpoint, there are two clearly defined structures of consciousness, or modes of being in the world, in the East and West that are intrinsically antithetical to each other—though in a given person they can sometimes be integrated. In Indian culture, the ultimate goal of life is the pursuit of subjective, pure consciousness through readily defined disciplines, with the gradual dismantling of mental phenomena into consciousness. By contrast, the structure of consciousness in the West is essentially the pursuit of mentation: conceptual thought that unifies reality, objectivization of all phenomena, cognition of the objects of consciousness, and behind everything a view of reality as an abundance of phenomena (Haas 1956, 159–184; Vollrath, Mohanty, and Dove 1974, 1–18).

Central to these differing forms of consciousness is the relationship of subjects to objects (meaning both material objects and persons). In the West, the fundamental dualism between subject and object reflects the overwhelming dualism of Western cultural categories—such as mind-body, spirit-matter—and assumes their universal validity. Knowledge is pursued to ascertain the conceptual unity behind diverse phenomena, with the goal of mastering or controlling the object but not fundamentally changing the subject. By contrast, in the Asian context knowledge is traditionally sought with the aim of transforming subjective consciousness rather than controlling the environment. In a philosophical tradition of monistic thinking, man is fundamentally of the same substance as the rest of nature, and thus persons tend to identify with the diversity of phenomena rather than feeling separate. The subject-object relationship is much closer, and nature is to be intimately lived in and expressed through poetry and painting, as in China and Japan, rather than to be observed, judged, and analyzed (Haas 1956, 205, 208–209).

One aspect of this close relationship is the magic-cosmic sense of the world, where subject and object influence each other through affinities involving intense exchanges and emanations, correspondances of visible and invisible realms involving dynamic relationships between the two, and transmutations of the self affecting the object. Objective causality does not exist in this world, but rather only juxtapositions, identities, and synchronicities. Although the magic world has become more or less obliterated in the overt world of the contemporary scientific West, except for occasional remaining pockets or in forms such as science fiction (pers. com. Gananath Obeyesekere) and commercialized pseudo magic (pers. com. Manisha Roy), it has survived to a far greater extent in the East (Haas 1956). What better example is there of the difference between the scientific and magic-cosmic relationship to objects than the investigation of planetary bodies, as in astronomy, and the study of these same objects as intrinsically related to human destiny, as in astrology?

In relation to time, the West has developed linear, historical theories of social events; in Hindu culture time is essentially ahistorical and mythological: in recurrent cycles through festivals, holidays, rituals, and such there is a repetition and reintegration into life of the mythological and divine presence. Space in the contemporary West is essentially profane, or homogeneous, neutral, and mathematical in conception; in Asia, sacred space such as pilgrimage spots and temples connect the earth with the divine (Eliade 1959).

The Oriental artist aspires to evoke spiritual and other emotional states in the onlooker, rather than trying to express beauty or individuality directly. In pursuing a search for hidden meanings in objects, the Oriental artist paradoxically reveals an inner consciousness. By contrast, Western art has become increasingly individualistic over the centuries, and the last century has seen the development of a creative subjectivity through the poetic use of the imagination and intuitive reason. Paradoxically, in this contemporary search for subjectivity, the Western artist inadvertantly reveals hidden meanings in the object—thus traveling the opposite direction from the traditional Oriental artist (Maritain 1953, 9–34).

From a sociocultural point of view, Indians and Japanese may be described as "collective man" (Dumont 1970) or "dividuals" (Marriott 1976)—in contrast to the Western individual—emotionally and socially enmeshed primarily within the extended kinship group and secondarily in caste or community in India (Yalman 1969), and in the family and work or other groups in Japan. In Indian culture, there is a highly particularistic view of persons as having differing natures from each other through their qualities (*guna*), powers (*shakti*), and inclinations from past actions (*karma*) and attachments (*samskara*) in other lives. Persons are thus not equal to each other, but rather interact in hierarchical relationships through myriad transactions and exchanges of gross and subtle substances, which have a transforming effect on both superior and subordinate (Marriott 1976, 1980). Different strategies of giving and receiving are integral to these inner transformations, and vary according to the particular familial hierachical relationship, the hierarchical relationship between castes, and the traditional stages of the life cycle, as well as the four traditional goals of life.

In contrast, Western society may be culturally defined as composed of a collection of individuals who as the ultimate unit of society are equal to each other and are essentially similar in nature. They have absolute rights in society and are a kind of monad obliged by society to be free (Dumont 1970). Individualism is based not only on social equality—which is also present in Muslim society—but also on permissive kinship arrangments that started in northwestern Europe (Yalman 1969). Somewhat related to the Western individual is the renouncer in Indian society, who is free of the social hierarchy of caste and extended family (Dumont 1970).[9]

From a social-psychological standpoint, personal emotional needs for sociability, dependence, security, and status are fulfilled much more through strongly affective intimacy relationships in the extended family and to some extent in the *jati* (community) in India and the group in Japan than is true in the West. In contrast, in the West and in America in particular, the individual tries to fulfil these needs through friends and extra-familial social groups in a highly mobile society where emotional ties tend to be temporary. Thus, intimate relationships in America are far more unstable and precarious than in India or Japan, and dependency needs are suppressed, especially in the male world, because of competition. Further social contrasts encompass the moral code: contractual social relationships with abstract standards of behavior in the West versus mutual, interdependent obligations governed by contextual norms in the East; marriage: freely chosen pairings based on romantic love and equality of the sexes, with the marital relationship exclusive and central to the kinship structure versus arranged marriages in which the marital relationship is subordinate to the hierarchical relationships

[9] The dualism between the dividual and the renouncer in Indian society is mitigated by the Brahmin who traditionally mediates between the social and spiritual realms (Das 1977).

of the extended family; and child rearing: education for rights and freedom versus duties and obligations (Hsu 1963, 1971).

In summary, the basic cultural conceptions of human nature and relationships, and the actual social patterns, are profoundly different in Eastern societies from those of the West. Although this is an overly brief and much simplified comparative analysis, it will nevertheless provide an orienting compass for my platform in psychological space, enabling me to maintain a better balance and perspective as I describe the differing and changing selves in Indians and Japanese.

PART ONE

The Indian and Japanese Self and Social Change

CHAPTER TWO

Indian Identity and Colonialism

Sociohistorical Perspective

It has usually been the prerogative of social scientists and historians to study the cascading effect of social change in Asian countries and cultures such as India and Japan, including the dynamic interactions of traditional, Westernizing, and modernizing influences. Although this wider perspective on the dynamics of social change is essential, our understanding may well need a complementary investigation in depth of individuals caught in the swirling eddies of change. It is to the problem of evolving a psychoanalytic psychology of social change relevant to the Indian and Japanese experience that I address these next five chapters. By probing the individual through depth psychoanalytic work, I assume that his or her psychological makeup, resolutions, and conflicts are not simply idiosyncratic, but in important ways reflect prevailing and changing sociocultural patterns, thus shedding light on social change and how it is internalized in new integrations or in ongoing conflicts and challenges within the psyche.

Central to a psychological analysis of Indian identity conflicts and resolutions are the effects of the colonial experience with the British, which are of a whole other order than those incurred by the Japanese rush to modernize after the Meiji Restoration (1868) and the American Occupation—which underlie Japanese identity issues (see Chapter Four). The Indian experience thus merits a separate discussion. From the beginning of the British colonial presence, radically new types of political, economic, legal, social, and educational institutions were gradually introduced, including a secular government and a British legal code; contractual economic relationships, with a market and a monetary economy; Western science and higher-level technology, with radically new means of communication and transportation; and context-free principles—in terms of time, modes of relationship, and conscience—in contrast to the Indian stress on contextualization (Ramanujan 1980). These powerful Westernizing influences created a whole new urban elite intelligentsia,[1] drawn from the literate upper castes of the rural areas to coastal trading cities, where they increased family and *jati* (caste) income and position in society.[2] These elite groups together with upperclass Muslims who followed suit, spread Westernizing influences and eventually entered the political framework established by the British, though the rural masses remained largely untouched.

As the point is central to issues of Indian identity, it is imperative to note that Western innovations and ideas were not simply fostered for assimilation in a natural give-and-take atmosphere. British administrative, educational, and missionary attitudes all conveyed intense attitudes of British superiority and Indian inferiority in numerous shades and ways over the two centuries of the colonial presence. This had enormous psychological impact, particularly on the Western-educated elite who were most closely associated with the raj.[3] These attitudes started among the late eighteenth- and early nineteenth-century British Orientalists and administrators. Although the Orientalists performed an invaluable function in making known to the West the major Hindu and Buddhist scriptures and in reconstructing Indian history—thus influencing a variety of Western thinkers as well as furnishing an historical perspective to Indian intellectuals—they viewed Indian society and culture in their era as totally debased and degenerate, and compared it unfavorably with both a past golden age and contemporary European culture (see Kopf 1969). There was little recognition of any current vital, living tradition. This Orientalist deprecation was supplemented by Unitarian and later Christian attitudes that condemned most Hindu rituals and worship as

---

[1] Srinivas (1965) uses the term Westernization, whereas Singer (1972) and the Rudolphs (1967) refer to these changes as modernization; Lannoy (1971) calls the process Westernization under the British and modernization after Independence.

[2] In Bengal this elite was formed primarily of primarily Brahmins and Kayasthas; in Madras they were mainly Brahmins, and in Bombay, Brahmins, Kshatriyas, and Vaishyas.

[3] Since the men were far more exposed to British attitudes than women, they were much more affected by colonial denigration.

idolatrous and barbarian, and severely criticized a number of social practices.

From the 1820s on, Utilitarians and Anglicists increasingly viewed Indian culture so disparagingly that they believed reform and modernization could take place only by completely anglicizing Indians (Kopf 1969). Thomas Macaulay, and Anglicist adherents to Macaulayism, further developed these highly denigrating attitudes, contemptuously seeing Indians as deceitful, cowardly, unclean, conceited, and totally inferior to Europeans. Macaulay's remedy was to turn Indians into Englishmen through English-medium education in European subjects, and conversion to English values and life style. The reverberating effects of this educational system are still felt today, and greatly affect Indian identity.

By the time the British Crown affixed India to its empire after the uprising of 1857, the British public, influenced by missionary tracts, Macaulayism, and the Utilitarians, had an image of India as the epitome of depravity.[4] As the nineteenth century progressed, chauvanistic nationalism, together with doctrines of Social Darwinism, served to intensify British attitudes of racial and cultural superiority. It became the rule, for example, for middle-class salaried civil servants to keep totally aloof from Indian society, living an aristocratic life among themselves quite different from the style of the earlier Orientalists.

Attitudes of racial superiority were particularly well developed and embedded in the military after 1857, for the British instituted a policy of refusing to accept enlistees from the literate upper castes who had almost caused their overthrow. They turned to Punjabi Sikhs, Muslims, lower-caste Hindus, and Nepalis, keeping them in close-knit groups to promote communal rather than nationalist feelings. This colonial military stratagem became ideologically laden with racism when the British accorded these new groups the status of the "martial races of India," equal in manliness to Europeans; whereas the remaining disarmed Indians—especially the upper-caste, educated Bengalis—were considered effete, weak, and timid nonmartial races (Chaudhuri 1930–1931). The strong nineteenth- and twentieth-century British-European emphasis on male chauvanism thus expressed itself by projecting the rejected parts of British male personality onto those Indians who had most challenged the raj (Nandy 1983). These deprecating attitudes have by no means

---

[4] The Sepoy Mutiny of 1857 was a full-fledged rebellion led by upper-caste Hindu officers in the Bengal Army to rid India of the British. The rebellion, after almost succeeding, was self-righteously and ruthlessly suppressed by the British, thereby insuring their total control of India. See Hutchins 1967.

19

completely subsided even to this day. The intense denigration of Indian culture and Indians under the colonial regime resulted in profound consequences to the Western-educated Hindu upper castes and upper-class Muslims, and complicated the processes of acculturation and assimilation of foreign elements into the Indian framework (Rudolphs 1967; Singer 1972; Srinivas 1966).

Identity Theory and
the Indian Experience

To formulate a psychoanalytic psychology of social change in India necessitates a reexamination of Erik Erikson's (1950, 1968) multi-faceted, seminal concept of identity, which involves both self-identity and ego-identity. The former alludes to the contents and self-experience of identity, the latter to the process of identity formation. Self-identity, from one perspective, is an important psychosocial concept that indicates personal identity as it relates to the person's place within a group and its values and norms, and can thus be used in a general way for persons in any culture. But as Erikson elaborated upon the concepts of self-identity and ego-identity, he assumed in both cases the act of self-creation that is central to contemporary Western and particularly American personality.[5]

Contemporary American culture has granted to, if not imposed on, the individual an enormous degree of autonomy in the adolescent and young adult years to choose who will be a mate or love partner, what kind of educational or vocational training to get and then what kind of work to do, what social affiliations to make, where to live, and what kind of ideology or value system to develop and become committed to. The frequently enormously difficult intrapsychic task of the individual adolescent and young adult in American society to integrate these adult role commitments with the intrapsychic identifications and self-images developed within the family is the crux of Erikson's elaboration of self-identity and ego-identity. His work perceptively charts the stormy seas that are more often than not encountered in this prolonged act of self-creating—the identity conflicts, confusions and crises, the frequent need for a moratorium, the occasional synthesis around negative identities,

---

[5] Otto Rank (Menaker 1982) also formulated this self-creation of personality in his emphasis on the will and individuation; like Erikson, he did not realize to what extent this is rooted within Western sociocultural contexts and psychology.

and eventually, it is hoped, the resolution of a positive identity synthesis. Even in his elaboration of the childhood psychosocial stages of development—such as autonomy and initiative—he treats them as two early building blocks for the adolescent and young adult struggle for a self-created identity. Although this psychological description may not fully apply to all segments of society, it is clearly the dominant mode of psychological development in youth in contemporary America.

Erikson's brilliant elaboration of identity is not, however, the experience of childhood, youth, and young adulthood in traditional Indian society, nor does it hold true for middle and upper middle-class urban circles to any significant extent. Traditional and even contemporary urban Indian culture grants neither the kind of autonomy nor the various social and cultural options to the person that American culture does. Marriages are still arranged, educational and occupational choices are still chosen with predominating parental guidance, social affiliations or friends usually become absorbed by the extended family with no separation of age groups, and a highly integrated Hindu world view, with certain variations and nuances, is still pervasively present and operative. In essence, psychological development and functioning in Hindu India does not involve the self-creation of identity as it occurs among Americans. Rather, it involves processes of the familial self and self-transformation.

Does this mean that identity in youth and adulthood has no meaning in contemporary urban India? Not at all. Here, the work of the Japanese psychoanalyst Masahisa Nishizono (1969) is pertinent. He points out that contemporary Japanese have, as it were, a two-layered personality: a deeper core personality associated with traditional Japanese culture, and an upper layer associated with acculturation to American and Western influences in Japan. I would suggest an Indian analogy to this. Identity conflicts and resolutions in urban Indians invariably involve reactions of a core Indian self to the enormous social and cultural changes brought about by some two hundred years of British colonial rule, some forty years of accelerated contacts with the West since Independence, and a Western-oriented educational system. Acculturation to these changes involves exposure to frequently conflicting value systems and world views, to significantly different ways of social relatedness and life styles, and to equally different modes of psychological functioning. Since British rule lasted infinitely longer than the American occupation of Japan, the Indian acculturation process has undoubtedly progressed much further than it has in Japan.

But vastly complicating the acculturation process with its concom-

21

mitant identity integrations for Indians was the incorporation of the constant British deprecation of everything Indian. Thus the need for an identity synthesis is not within the core self, as it is for Westerners, but rather between the core self and various aspects of acculturation to Western culture, tremendously conflicted by British devaluation of the indigenous self.

The painfulness of this kind of identity conflict in Indian men has resulted in three identifiable and understandable directions of identity resolution. In extreme form, they are: identification with the aggressor, where there is an almost total identification with a British or Western way of life and values, with a corresponding denigration of Indian culture, values, and life style, even though the core self remains very much Indian; the opposite reaction of total rejection and criticism of everything Western and the idealization of all things Indian, usually involving identification with Indian spiritual culture as opposed to Western materialism; and reassertion of an Indian identity over against a Western one to regain an inner sense of esteem and parity, initially through efforts to reinterpret and reform various aspects of Indian culture and society, countering British rule and criticism, while incorporating Western innovations into a new synthesis. In actuality, these three ideal types more often occur in various admixtures than in pure form.

So powerful have been these kinds of identity struggles generated by British colonial rule that they continue even some forty years after Independence. Sudhir Kakar has remarked that beneath the guise of many overtly held value positions, deep down, Western-educated Indian men must to this day make a decisive choice between being Indian in identity or Western.[6] Whenever the identity investment is more Western, there is inevitably a subtle or open denigration of many things Indian.

The third identity resolution gave rise to formidable nineteenth- and twentieth-century reform movements, varying considerably in their efforts to reassert an Indian identity, gain a measure of parity with the British, and incorporate various aspects of Western culture. Highly charismatic, venerated leaders led these movements, reinterpreting traditional Hindu culture and reasserting its legitimacy. Simultaneously they tried to reform the more glaring social injustices and modernize various aspects of the society in new syntheses within the syncretistic tradition of Hinduism. Since Bengal was the late eighteenth- and nineteenth-cen-

[6] Remark made in a discussion at a symposium at the Asia Society, "The Indian Psyche Today: Wounded Civilization or Renaissance?" New York City, April 1980.

tury hub of the British colonial presence in India, the earliest reformers and movements originated there.

The most significant movement among the *bhadralok*—the educated elite of Bengal, who settled in many other parts of India and spread their ideas widely—was the Brahmo Samaj, founded by Ram Mohun Roy in the early nineteenth century (Kopf 1979). Stung by increasingly trenchant British criticism of Hindu devotional and ritual idol worship as well as of a variety of social practices, especially related to the position of women, Roy developed an ideological and social posture to counteract this pervasive deprecation. He reasserted the part of Hinduism that was admired by the Orientalists—the monism of Advaita Vedanta—thus anchoring religious belief in indigenous scriptures such as the Vedas. He also sided with British criticism by completely shunning idol worship and rituals, downgrading the powerful mother goddesses of Bengali Shaktoism, and asserting a more masculine theistic principle to his monism. This enabled Western-educated Hindu men in constant contact with the British to develop a new indigenous image of masculine authority and assertiveness unconnected to the ritual powers of Shaktoism, to cope better with British organizational authority and competitive individualism (Nandy 1980b). Similarly, new identity syntheses were effected by incorporating a strong ethic for social reform and social service, improving women's position by better education, increasing the age of marriage, permitting widow remarriage, and by adopting various aspects of Western culture such as rationalism, liberalism, humanism, and science.

Brahmo women became increasingly well educated as the nineteenth century progressed, and used Western forms of organization to pursue social reform themselves, gradually becoming politicized in their own organization and ultimately joining Gandhi's National Movement. The Brahmo Samaj was thus enormously influential on the identity of both men and women of the *bhadralok,* eventually spawning most of the early nationalist political leaders. It had little if any influence, however, over the rest of the people.

Another powerful Bengali movement that more strongly reasserted Hindu religion and culture as a basis for nationalist aspirations and parity with the British, while incorporating various Westernizing aspects, was the Ramakrishna Mission founded by Swami Vivekananda. Vivekananda not only asserted the indigenous religious principle of multiple paths to the realization of the spiritual self as primary to religion, but also reaffirmed Hindu devotional and ritual worship (downgraded by the Brahmo Samaj). Thus Evangelical Christianity, which figured so strongly in colonial denigration of Hinduism, was reduced to one of many paths, and one that had by and large lost its primary religious function. At the same time, Vivekananda adopted Brahmo Westernized principles of social service and education, and countered British deprecation of Indians as effete by calling upon the more traditional Kshatriya values of manliness.

Other highly influential Bengalis who endeavored to develop a new identity synthesis were the strongly charismatic, political-religious leader Sri Aurobindo, who initially gave a powerful ideological, religious basis to Indian nationalism and in his later, more spiritual, phase synthesized Western civilizational influences with a reinterpretation and reassertion of Hinduism; the internationally noted poet, Rabindranath Tagore, who came from a Brahmo background and played a major role in the revival of Indian arts through founding Santiniketan, a college of the arts; and the important nationalist leader, Subhash Chandra Bose, a political activist who drew upon Bengali Shaktoism to fight the British.

Simultaneously, the Punjab experienced a renaissance of Vedic Hinduism and social reform and education through the Arya Samaj founded by Swami Dayananda. In the Madras area, the Theosophical movement created in the latter part of the nineteenth century also strongly reaffirmed the legitimacy of Hinduism; this was the only major movement in which Westerners—including Madame Blavatsky, Annie Besant, and Colonel Olcott—played important roles. All of these movements eventually became overshadowed by Gandhi and the National Movement, which was the first to draw in large numbers of the rural and urban masses.

Another example of the third kind of identity resolution occurred when the British introduced a scientific world view and the ideology of rationalism. Major religious and philosophical leaders such as Vivekananda and Aurobindo, among others, asserted that the scientific approach and rationalism could easily be incorporated within the religio-philosophic orientation of Hinduism, particularly in the context of the Upanishads. Highly creative scientists such as the physicist Jagadis Chandra Bose and the mathematician Srinivasa Ramanujan actively used basic Hindu philosophical postulates concerning the pervasiveness of *shakti* and emanations from the Godhead or Brahman in their scientific work. The assertion of Hindu principles in science became part of a major identity struggle for Bose (Nandy 1980a). By the mid-twentieth century, the research of Edward Shils (1961) on Indian intellectuals and a project conducted by Professor Sinari at the Indian Institute of Technology (pers. com.) both indicated no basic ideological conflict in many

Indian intellectuals and scientists between the Hindu and scientific world views; the latter is simply seen as a legitimate type of investigation into one of the multi-layered realities of the cosmos. Contemporary India has thus been able to train legions of scientists and technologists with surprisingly little intellectual conflict over differing views of reality.

Case Study—Ashis

The encounter on an evening in March 1971 with a gaunt, intense-looking man at The New School in New York led to a three-and-a-half month collaborative psychoanalytic therapy with Ashis, an Indian writer and intellectual, which was to continue six years later in Bombay for another few months. He explained that he was desperately caught between extreme Westernization in his upbringing as a child and youth by a highly dominating father, and a 180–degree turn to Hinduism in his early twenties when he had rejected much of his Westernized upbringing. Now, however, at age thirty-six, he felt semi-paralyzed in his work and deeply inhibited and despairing of developing a career in India, in spite of being extremely well connected socially and with ample financial resources. He experienced these two sides of himself to be at complete odds with each other—he felt that one could not be Western in outlook and mode of being and also Hindu. He thought this fractured identity was responsible for his current psychological paralysis, as well as for his stomach upsets and other physical problems. He thus turned to me in desperation to heal the clash of warring identity elements within his self.

Ashis, who was from a north Indian *jati* ranked as Kshatriya, illustrates the profound psychological effects of Westernization on some of the Indian upper middle-class, upper-caste, urban, educated elite, and the identity conflicts engendered in them. His badly fractured identity is on the extreme end of the continuum, to be sure. Yet from others' reactions to his writings, it is evident that his conflicts and inner struggles reflect those of a significant group of Indian men brought up by their fathers to be highly Westernized—significant not so much in their numbers as in the important positions they now hold and the influence they wield in contemporary India.

Ashis explained that he was on an extremely tight budget, since the regulations of the Indian government had tied up his funds in India. He was just barely able to scrape by while working toward a graduate degree in a well-known writers' program at City University. His wife and two daughters had to stay behind in India while he was here, a not unusual arrangement for many Indians who study abroad. We agreed that he would come twice a week at a fee low by New York City standards, but appropriate when paid in rupees; the fee was to be collected when and if I ever returned to India. I should add parenthetically that I generally do not see patients on this kind of highly uncertain financial basis, nor in my experience would most American patients agree to do so even if I offered, as I have on very rare occasions. But I felt strongly that the problems Ashis presented were most unusual for an American analyst to encounter, and were ones I was obviously very interested in.

What I did not realize until years later is that Ashis had set up with me some of the fundamental psychosocial dimensions of Indian hierarchical relationships, ones fundamentally different from the more usual contractual relationships I was used to. By openly expressing his dependency needs, that he wanted and needed help from me even though payment could be made only in the uncertain future, he subtly accorded me a superior position in the relationship, where my gratification and esteem would derive from helping him.[7] Contractual exchanges of assistance for payment, the overt American mode of the psychoanalytic relationship, were minimal in this case.

While Ashis expressed considerable despair over his current situation and state of mind, usually in a whining voice, he also conveyed that he had a real ray of hope. Just the previous year his wife had gone to Brighu, a temple in the Punjab, for an astrological reading on Ashis from one of the Brighu *shastras*. His horoscope predicted that at around this time—the time that Ashis was beginning to see me—his career would turn around and take a sharp turn for the better. He explained to me that the Brighu *shastras* are horoscopes written on palm leaves by a sage several hundred years ago at this temple in the Punjab. One goes there with the exact minute of one's birth and the temple priests will fetch the relevant horoscope, which will reveal not only one's future but one's past as well.

Again, it wasn't until much later that I realized that Ashis felt there

[7] I realized this years later after I returned from my work in India to the United States while I was discussing with Professor Moses Burg, an American psychoanalytic therapist who had worked for many years in Japan, the *amae* theory of the Japanese psychoanalyst Takeo Doi. Burg emphasized the subtle exchange in Japanese hierarchical relationships between dependency needs on the junior's part and narcissistic gratification on the superior's part. Further conversations on this topic with Dr. B. K. Ramanujam greatly clarified this essential psychosocial dimension of hierarchical relationships within the Indian setting, including the much more open expression of dependency needs than Americans feel comfortable with.

was a confluence between the prediction of his horoscope and his coming for psychoanalytic therapy. What Americans usually experience as discrete happenings or coincidences Indians approach through more metonymic thinking (Ramanujan 1980). That is, predictions made in a magic-cosmic orientation to reality (Haas 1956) are experienced as being played out in everyday life situations, so that there is a profound congruence between the two rather than any discrete duality.

Ashis took the readings from his Brighu horoscope quite seriously, which psychologically gave him a distinct ray of hope in what was then an enveloping gloom. (Such predictions played a very similar psychological role in an Indian woman patient in her middle thirties, who desperately wanted to get married. Veena had developed an excellent career as a professional with a doctorate, but despaired of getting married because her father had already died and her older brothers were not making the kinds of efforts to find a suitable husband that she felt they should. The only thing that kept her hopes alive was repeated readings by astrologers and palmists that consistently predicted a very late but excellent marriage—which eventually occurred.) This assumption of a personal destiny that would have its very particular turns, twists, and cycles is very different from the current American ethos in which the individual feels it is almost totally up to himself or herself to bring things about. I should add that both Ashis and Veena made every effort possible to advance career and marriage, respectively, but each assumed that what would eventually happen would be related to their destiny.

Ashis generally came to session either railing against his father for foisting a Westernized upbringing and values upon him or, in a most unusual way, bringing with him notes or books of three great South Asian figures he profoundly revered—Rabindranath Tagore, Ananda K. Coomaraswamy, and Mohandas K. Gandhi—and then discussing his thoughts about certain of their passages in session.[8] He revealed that for him Tagore stood for feelings, Coomaraswamy for the life of the mind, and Gandhi for action; or more precisely and profoundly, they embodied the three major forms of yoga: *bhakti yoga* or the path of devotion, *jñana yoga* or the path of philosophical discrimination, and *karma yoga* or the path of selfless action. This trinity thus symbolized for Ashis all sides of himself and a complete synthesis of yoga.[9] But I

---

[8] A. K. Coomaraswamy wrote some of the finest aesthetic exposition and criticism of Indian art, comparing it with Western art, while Curator of Asiatic Art at the Boston Museum of Fine Arts.

[9] The most similar psychoanalytic perspective appears in Freud's (1931) paper, "Libidinal Types." Milton Singer (1981) has written on the Indian self and identity, relating

also realized from readings in my student days that Tagore, Coomaraswamy, and Gandhi were key figures in the reassertion of a Hindu world view vis-à-vis British colonialism, incorporating in various ways and to varying degrees differing aspects of Western culture. Ashis was obviously using them to try to heal his fractured identity.

In his associations, Ashis's mind worked very differently from that of any of my American patients, and I thus felt less than self-assured as an analyst with him. It is one thing to have some background in Indian culture and history; but it is quite another to know how Indians function psychologically. I remember musing how my Freudian colleagues would respond to a patient constantly associating to Hindu yoga and spiritual goals and their clash with Western ideals of achievement and success—not to mention astrology and the Brighu *shastras*. Would they have evaluated his strivings as disturbed or regressed fantasies?

My therapeutic sense at the time was not to analyze his intense, obsessional preoccupation with these three great men as some kind of resistance to a freer flow of associations—as one senior colleague had suggested—but rather to respond on an empathic level, discussing and accepting what he was presenting on the level he was presenting it.[10] I mainly interpreted to Ashis that he couldn't simply sweep all of his Westernized upbringing under the rug, since it was too much a part of him through unconscious identifications with his father and incorporation of his father's expectations; that he would gradually have to integrate this major identity element with his Hinduism. I further conveyed that I understood that this would not be easy and might take considerable time, but that my impression was that this was taking place on a larger cultural scale.

What I did not understand at the time was that Ashis's railing so openly at his father was highly unusual for an Indian man. I took it at face value and didn't investigate it. I was used to American male patients excoriating their fathers at one or another stage of the analysis, sometimes at the very beginning. This is an example, of course, of how a psychoanalyst must know the basic patterns and range of more or less normal reactions and relationships in a society to proceed with analysis.

As the weeks wore on, Ashis felt appreciably better, was more involved in his graduate work, and enthusiastically wrote and directed a

---

Charles Pierce's theories of signs and symbols involving feeling, thinking, and action to the Indian notions of *bhakti yoga, jñana yoga,* and *karma yoga.*

[10] This was just before Kohut's (1971) seminal work on idealizing and mirroring transferences appeared, work that is highly relevant to Ashis, so I was going completely on my own intuitions.

play with Indian dance. He discussed in some detail a novel he had resumed working on after some years, dealing with the whole issue of the forced Westernization of Indian sons like himself and its disastrous effects on India. He gradually became involved with one of the Ramakrishna Order swamis at one of the Vedanta Centers in New York City in a particular kind of *bhakti yoga*. One day, he exclaimed that he felt he would do better through the practice of this form of yoga than through psychoanalysis. I in turn indicated that I saw no particular conflict between the two, but this did not prevent him from terminating the therapy. What I had not realized at the time was that his urge to terminate came just at the point that he revealed that his father had committed suicide by jumping into a well when Ashis was nineteen. I had no idea then of the profound cultural and psychological meanings of such a suicide within the Indian family context.[11] I did not see Ashis again until six years later in Bombay.

Before delineating our further work together in Bombay, I would like to present Ashis's background and development from material I gathered in sessions both in New York City and Bombay. It throws considerable light on the complex interrelationship of sociohistorical and sociocultural factors with personal psychological makeup and the idiosyncratic in men of Ashis's generation and milieu.

Ashis had been raised with overwhelming Western values by a dominant father who completely identified with the British and their life style, and who sent Ashis at one period to an English boarding school in India attended primarily by English children. This step exemplified his father's extreme Westernization, as Westernized Indian fathers would characteristically send their children, especially their sons, to convent schools or other English-language schools attended mainly by Indians, to advance them educationally for the available careers in the civil service and professions. At all of these kinds of schools, Indian boys such as Ashis are exposed only to Western learning and anything Indian is denigrated to varying degrees.

What is striking about Ashis's father is his own background. Not

---

[11]I did not know how profoundly an Indian son's inner sense of esteem is so closely interwoven with the father and family reputation in a sense of we-ness, and thus how utterly shaken Ashis was by the father's suicide. His turn to *bhakti* meditation and a relationship with the swami helped compensate for the enormous inner shame and narcissistic mortification that welled up in him upon revealing the suicide—which were too intense for him to remain in therapy with me. At the time I was too unfamiliar with Indian psychological makeup to interpret it.

infrequently, an upper-caste Indian family that was still quite traditional, if not orthodox, might send a son to an English-language school and college for greater career advancement that would reflect well on and be of assistance to the family. But Ashis's father came from an extended family in which some illustrious men had already become important, at times renowned, leaders of one of the major Hindu reform movements, one that reasserted the value of Hinduism and Indian nationalism vis-à-vis British colonialism and that called for a simple, almost ascetic life style. What led his father to break with this tradition and opt for a Westernized identity I never learned. In any case, having the inclinations, ambition, and potentialities to fulfill British colonial expectations and needs, his father successfully made his way to a high position in the Indian Civil Service, a very elite position for any Indian to attain within the British raj. Indian members of the I.C.S., through their identification with the British, were noted for their arrogance, insolence, and irritability. Ashis described his father as being aggressively and ambitiously career-minded, tremendously talented in organizational skills, and authoritarian in the sense of being domineering, bullying, critical, and inconsiderate of anyone under him.

The point is that Ashis was subjected to strong Westernized values, attitudes, and life style *within* the Indian familial father-son relationship, resulting in far more profound identity conflicts than if he had simply attained a Western education. The influence of Ashis's mother remained shadowy throughout the therapy; but in contrast to most Indian women, who tended to remain traditional, Ashis described her as going along with her dominant husband's values and ways of doing things, and as unable to protect Ashis from his father's dominance. Ashis perceived his father as tending to bully and exploit her by having her constantly entertain to further his career. In sharp contrast to his grandfather's generation, Ashis's family lived in a unitary household, so that he had no other extended family members to turn to.

There was a basic temperamental clash between Ashis, the oldest of three sons, and his father. Ashis was artistic, imaginative, and meditative, all of which his father completely denigrated. As an instance, his father dismissed the considerable distinction Ashis attained in winning first prize in English poetry in the English boarding school, and then chided him for doing only moderately well in math—a subject that really counts for a career. In spite of this fundamental clash, Ashis went along with his father's values and plans for a highly scientific education and career throughout his adolescence, and succeeded in acquiring an engineering degree from an American university. There was absolutely none of the typical American adolescent's rebellion against parental or other authorities' values and wishes through association with peer groups in trying to find oneself and one's identity.

To understand this is to recognize that while Ashis's father's values, life style, and even manner of authority were overwhelmingly Westernized, the inner emotional structure of the father-son hierarchical relationship was totally Indian. That is, throughout childhood and adolescence, Ashis had been typically deferential, obedient, and subordinate to his father, trying to gain his father's (and family's) respect as well as to reflect well on his father and family by doing his best in society to meet his father's expectations—essential elements of a boy's familial self. Thus a multi-layered psychological organization developed, in which the values and life goals belonged to those of another culture, in Ashis's case Western, but the inner emotional structuring remained highly Indian. The values, however, became deeply internalized because they were taken in through the traditional emotional structuring of the father-son relationship.

I would like to touch upon other aspects of the Indian father-son relationship here to give more of a framework for Ashis's development and reactions. In the traditional father-son hierarchical relationship, the father is usually characterized as being overtly distant and aloof, an authoritative disciplinarian toward the son, as well as being responsibly concerned; the son in turn shows the proper deference and subordination to his father with a strong curbing of any direct expression of anger or hostility, and with relatively little effort at any autonomous self-assertion, even in adolescence. Sons tend to idealize strongly and respect fathers and elders—the idealizations sometimes serving as unconscious defenses against angry feelings—and intensely need to have the father respond positively to the inner core of heightened self-regard originally derived from early maternal relationships. While the overt nature of the father's distant, authoritative attitudes have been emphasized by writers such as Carstairs (1957) in his psychological ethnography and Kakar (1978) in his psychoanalytic commentary on ethnographic work, it is evident from my own clinical work with Ashis and other Indian patients, as well as from intensive discussions with Indian psychiatrists, B. K. Ramanujam and Ravi Kapur, that covertly there is an intense father-son emotional attachment. However, because the father in the overt relationship is so aloof because of extended-family hierarchical considerations, the son is constantly striving to gain evidence of his father's respect and recognition, as well as to reflect well on him. I have heard of Indian men in their sixties, whose fathers are no longer living, still intensely seeking their fathers' respect and recognition for what they are doing. The intensity of this need tends to transcend the parallel need in Western father-son relationships, based on intergenerational strivings and conflict. Thus his father's respect becomes paramount to an Indian son's self-worth, and if gaining it means, as in Ashis's case, to become Westernized, the son will surely do this.

Given his father's firm direction for him, his mother's willingness to abandon her traditions for her husband's Westernized values, and Ashis's typical, deferential responses as a son, Ashis might well have simply become one more of the Indian upper middle-class educated elite strongly identified with Western values. That is, he could have become overwhelmingly preoccupied with his career and getting ahead, identifying with characteristic British colonial condescension to Hindu religion and culture, becoming alienated from Hindu culture, and looking to the West for all models and theories.[12] For Ashis, this whole development was not fated to be. Just a few years after Indian Independence, when Ashis was about nineteen and was completing college, his father became enmeshed in a scandal and, upon learning that he was on the verge of being arrested, committed suicide by jumping into a well. To understand what had befallen his father is to delve into the profound differences between Indian and Western psychosocial modes of hierarchical relationships and authority.

In contrast to Western hierarchical relationships—which tend to be based on a fixed status and power relationship, governed by contractual agreements and an ideology of essential equality—Indian hierarchical relationships are oriented toward firmly internalized expectations in both superior and subordinate for reciprocity and mutual obligations in a more closely emotionally connected relationship. Where traditionally there are few if any contractual agreements, the superior in particular is profoundly assumed to be concerned, giving, and responsible for his or her subordinates, and the subordinate to be loyal and deferential to the superior. Obviously, superiors and/or subordinates may fail to live up to these reciprocal responsibilities, but when this occurs, clinical data amply indicate tremendous hurt, bitterness, and anger, thus showing the strength of the internalized expectations. In a colonial setting, the authority not only reacts along more Western lines but becomes highly authoritarian, since there are few contractual controls and an ideology of superiority offsets any views of equality, while the subordinates still

[12] Many Western-educated men tend to become overwhelmingly engaged in their career while the sensitive few begin a prolonged search for their cultural roots (pers. com. Kapilya Vatsyayan).

respond along traditional Indian lines, especially to an Indian in a position of authority.

This is exactly what happened to Ashis's father. Having identified with a British colonial mode of hierarchical relationship and authority, he was apparently perceived by his Indian subordinates to have failed them seriously in their strong expectations of a responsibly concerned, hierarchical authority. They must have harbored bitter resentment, because not long after Independence, these subordinates seized upon a quite usual and acceptable mode of corruption to create a scandal and a legal investigation. Ashis's father then committed suicide.

Ashis's world fell apart. All that his father stood for came into question. At age nineteen, his whole sense of life purpose went up in smoke. The idealized figure fell and shattered into a thousand pieces. Ashis's sense of self-worth—so tied in for an Indian son with his father and family—became shaky, his judgment questionable, and an inner sense of shame and secretiveness swept over him in relation to his father's suicide and its enormous blot on the family reputation and himself, essential elements to an Indian. Ashis then moved to another part of India, keeping his father's suicide secret from even his closest friends and associates. Thus Ashis's blatant, overt anger at his father, so unusual for an Indian man, was not simply the surfacing of suppressed childhood ambivalence toward his father, but rather was rage at the father with whom he was so closely connected for profoundly letting him down.

Ashis tried to put his world together again by seeing his father's problem as a suicidal identification with British and Western values, and by searching for new idealized hierarchical figures as selfobjects to bolster his shattered sense of self-worth. He rejected everything Western and became completely absorbed in Hinduism, initially with his grandfather's generation—the illustrious reform leaders of his extended family who reasserted their Hindu identity, including one uncle who had been a noted swami. According to reports of someone who had known Ashis in his early twenties, he led an extremely serious, ascetic life in Bombay, characteristic of those from this movement. But what was meaningful and suitable for his grandfather's generation was not entirely so for him. He eventually left this movement and was formally initiated by the then head swami of the Ramakrishna Order, becoming regularly involved in spiritual practices. He later turned to the writings of three great idealized leaders of the modern Indian renaissance—Tagore, Coomaraswamy, and Gandhi—leaders who had stood the test of time. His obsessional preoccupation with their writings in his therapy bespoke the enormous inner strain he was under to contain his anxieties and inner self-fragmentation.

Although Ashis's profound disillusionment with Westernization and his about-face turn to Hinduism was extreme, there is no question that similar reversals occur in other Indians as well. This important direction of change from Westernization to indigenous culture has not been sufficiently dealt with by prevailing theories of modernization, but it is increasingly evident and important today in Asian and African countries.

The only problem was that in the process Ashis had become semi-paralyzed in his functioning. In psychodynamic terms, since Ashis had strongly identified with his father and his father's Westernized expectations, the turn to Hindu values for realizing the spiritual self profoundly clashed with this more deeply etched Westernization. His new idealized images were at war with the older shattered ones, resulting in a seriously fractured identity.

Two factors have gradually enabled Ashis to heal partially this enormous fracture in his identity. One has been psychoanalytic therapy, in which the unconscious relationship to his father has been extensively explored in terms of his bitterly angry feelings toward his father and the profound psychological effects of the suicide, and in which it was made apparent that he would gradually have to integrate some of the Western identity elements related to his father with his involvement with Hinduism and idealized leaders of the Hindu renaissance. In this sense, although the particular idiosyncratic familial circumstances vary, Ashis has had to accomplish through his own identity integration a task that Indians, particularly the urban educated elite, are still struggling with: the monumental civilizational integration of various aspects of Westernization within the broad syncretistic framework of Hinduism.

This relates to his other means of identity resolution through assertion of the literary talents that his father so despised. As Otto Rank (1932), Margaret Brenman-Gibson (1981), and Esther Menaker (1982) have discussed in their work on artistic creativity, it is common for the artist to make new identity integrations through art, communicating and articulating his identity struggles to an audience that is wrestling with the same issues in a far less conscious manner. This is precisely what Ashis has done. He has written novels and short stories in Hindi, all dealing with the father-son relationship and the conflicts between Westernization and Hinduism. In effect, his struggle with his own warring identity elements became the basis for his work, while his writing helped him to resolve this struggle by transcending his self through this form of individuation; in the process, he gained important recognition from others for a new identity integration, while articulating for them many of the same struggles he was going through.

When I arrived in Bombay in the summer of 1977, six years after our work together in New York City, Ashis occupied a rather significant position in an important organization related to the film industry and communication. Soon after he had terminated therapy with me in New York City, some of his writings had come to the attention of an Indian man of international stature and nationwide respect who was then at the United Nations. He thereupon gave Ashis an important position in his organization in India, after Ashis completed his graduate work in the summer of 1971. Ashis worked for him, by report, in a highly productive, creative manner, but this man suddenly and tragically died a few years later. Further journal and newspaper articles brought Ashis to the attention of another man of nationally recognized stature, who then hired him for his current position. By the time of my arrival, Ashis's novel was finally complete and was about to be published. He immediately requested that I write an introduction to it and help him with the design of the jacket. I was taken aback at the time; no American patient had ever asked anything like this. Only later did I realize that his request was not only a transference—to have an authority figure to counter the father who so denigrated his literary aspirations—but also expressed a common expectation of Indians for a more involved connection and relationship than American patients anticipate. Ashis's request and those of other Indian patients made far more sense to me when I realized from Ramanujam (1980a) that Indians expect their therapists to fulfill the role of a missing extended family elder when there was no one responsibly concerned and attuned to the son or daughter.

Even though his career had skyrocketed and he had become recognized as a writer, Ashis was quite depressed and seemed once again semi-paralyzed in his work. He was therefore eager to resume psychoanalytic therapy. His depression seemed immediately related to the resignation of the head of his agency some few months previously because of changes in the political climate of Maharasthra. The former director was apparently a man greatly revered by all and deeply respected by Ashis, who spoke of his high level of creativity and abilities and his strong spiritual presence, quite similar to that of Ashis's previous benefactor. Both men had taken a personal interest in Ashis, recognizing his rather special combination of literary, technological, and organizational skills together with his strong commitment to Indian culture and his spiritual inclinations. Both had given Ashis a free hand in his work while being responsive to Ashis's ideas and initiatives. Ashis, deeply respecting both and feeling that he was in their personal orbits, was assiduously loyal and devoted, and had turned out some extraordinarily creative work, accomplishing for his present organization in one year a major task that a number of men had been unable to do over ten previous years. He was able to get twenty-two others to work under him in an atmosphere of creative expression, while constantly prodding them to produce.

Ashis complained he didn't have anyone now to whom he could look up, and thus he had lost interest in his work. The new director is far too bureaucratic, quantitative, and unimaginative for Ashis to be involved with in any way comparable to his former quasi guru/father relationships at work. Moreover, although the new director is apparently aware that Ashis is a highly creative person, he shows little appreciation, considering him immature and something of an oddball—an oddball for writing office memos in verse, and immature because Ashis openly expresses and asserts himself in meetings. This is simply not done in traditional hierarchical relationships.

To work psychoanalytically with this level of Ashis's depression is to understand that in traditional as well as contemporary Indian work settings it is well nigh impossible for a highly intelligent Indian man or woman to work creatively without being promoted and protected by a benefactor. I have talked with several Indians who assert that as a junior person even with a relatively high position in an organization—whether a government agency, corporation, or university—you are simply not listened to by those senior in the hierarchy unless there is a benefactor, usually the head of the organization, who takes a special interest in you. Congruent with this hierarchical framework is an inner psychological structure of the familial self, whereby Indian men or women profoundly need the active support, respect, and involvement of senior authority figures in the hierarchy to work productively and creatively. The superior is experienced as an important selfobject to their self-regard and is someone they must feel closely connected to emotionally; any attempt at self-assertive strivings in their work without such a supportive hierarchical figure is extremely difficult.[13] Thus it was crucial for me to

---

[13] Another example is a brilliant Indian woman who expressed how difficult it is for her to do her own highly creative work in an American university with the current head of her department, who is unappreciative of her considerable abilities. She registered surprise over her American colleague who handled the same situation by saying, in effect, "To hell with him, I'll do what I please."

acknowledge the difficulties at work, where the departure of the former head of the agency truly made Ashis's position rather bleak.

There was, however, a further factor in Ashis's work situation highly relevant to his depression, a factor also central to modernizing tendencies in contemporary India. Indians who have been college-educated in the West or who have worked there and have been exposed to relationships oriented around individualism have developed a more individualized life style and functioning at work than is typical in India. Upon returning to a traditional hierarchical work situation, these men find that the stifling of their more individualized self rankles a great deal (Kakar 1978, 120).

I have encountered some of the same reactions from Japanese psychoanalysts trained in the United States. There, too, the junior person is culturally directed not to assert or express himself openly: "the nail that stands out gets hammered in." Each of these persons finds it extremely trying for some time to readapt to traditional Japanese hierarchical group relationships after they had become used to more open, creative self-expression.

Ashis, through his Western education, is actually far more individualized than most Indian men in his work patterns, so that he becomes extremely annoyed by any kind of hierarchical, bureaucratic procedure. (Another sign of his greater individuation was his arranging his own marriage though newspaper advertisements—unusual for an Indian man.) On the other hand, his core familial self is still predominant, so that he must function with an appreciative, involved benefactor in a close, reciprocal relationship. Thus Ashis was unable to work creatively without an appreciative head of his agency even though he was given an unusual amount of freedom for an employee of an Indian organization.

To understand more fully Ashis's responses within an Indian context, I should point out that within the formal structures of hierarchical relationships, there is not only far greater emotional connectedness among Indians than among Westerners but important distinctions are made as to whether or not the person in the superior position is a superior person. Since self-regard and the sense of self are deeply tied to the other(s) in hierarchical relationships—either superior or subordinate—it can become deeply troubling to be with a superior whom one neither respects nor is respected by.

I concluded that the valid psychoanalytic goal with Ashis was not for him to function independently, in the way one would tend to work with most American patients, that is, he should *not* have to learn to be on his own with an unappreciative director whom he deprecated. The problem for our psychoanalytic work together was why he was staying on with his current director, which was clearly a masochistic adaptation unconsciously equated with remaining with the father who so denigrated his creative talents, whereas a move elsewhere to a hierarchical relationship of mutual respect where he could be far more appreciated would be more growth-enhancing.

When I conveyed this to Ashis and encouraged him to move on to a more supportive director, he responded by saying that this was exactly what Professor Mukerjee[14] at the Indian Institute of Technology in Powaii had told him just the previous week. Professor Mukerjee, it turned out, was an internationally noted scientist who was also a palmist of considerable local repute. Over the years, upon having to reach any major career decision or in the midst of any important difficulties in life, Ashis would dash off in his organization car with his driver to Powaii to consult with Professor Mukerjee. On more than this one occasion, Ashis reacted to one or another of my hard-earned psychoanalytic interpretations by responding that this was just what Professor Mukerjee had conveyed to him recently.[15] Professor Mukerjee would then tell Ashis more or less what was in store for him and what to do about it. It became evident that palmistry as another important dimension of the Hindu magic-cosmic orientation to reality played a major ongoing role in Ashis's life, a dimension much more important than astrology.

Like some of my other Indian patients, Ashis's orientation toward the magic-cosmic world went beyond anything I have yet encountered with American patients. In the Hindu view, it is assumed that everyone has an unfolding destiny and inner evolution, and since everyone is profoundly related to the cosmos as the microcosm is to the macrocosm, one can derive a better picture of oneself and one's destiny in major life relationships and situations through readings of the cosmos through astrology, palmistry, clairvoyant dreams, and such. It is further assumed that one's life does not progress in any linear way but that there are ups and downs or, perhaps more accurately, changing cycles of good and bad times. Like the Biblical Joseph, one can do a great deal to cope with destiny; it is not to be taken passively—as Western stereotypes would have it.

I particularly wanted to meet Professor Mukerjee because of the congruence of his interpretations from palmistry with my own from a psychoanalytic understanding—not an everyday occurrence for an Ameri-

---

[14] This is not his real name.

[15] Freud freely acknowledged that poets easily arrived at psychological insights he had labored to achieve; but not palmists.

can psychoanalyst to encounter. When we eventually met, I asked whether his understanding and predictions came directly from reading Ashis's and others' palms or from some kind of telepathic or other psychic powers. He said from both. When he holds someone's palm, ideas immediately come to mind. On the other hand, there are not only the distinct lines and mounts common to palmistry everywhere, but also very small signs on the palm that are only used in Hindu palmistry, which he sees as being crucial. From a few remarks Professor Mukerjee made, it seemed apparent that he himself was personally involved in the practice of yoga, and was further intent on researching various aspects of psychic phenomena, the spirit world, and yogic *siddhis* or powers. He did not convey any surprise over the congruence between his own insights and mine. Interestingly enough, although Ashis and Professor Mukerjee have had a long-term relationship, I could tell from what each said independently of the other that they did not know each other well personally, and that Ashis's psychobiography did not figure in the other man's advice. It seems apparent that Ashis's use of the magic-cosmic world of astrology and particularly of palmistry has been primarily in the service of furthering his career and trying to fulfill his own inner inclinations toward individuation and spiritual realization.

Although I recognized and discussed with Ashis his depression and semi-paralysis as related to difficult hierarchical work relationships, I nevertheless saw that there was a deeper level to his depression. I sensed a great inner sadness in Ashis as we met for those initial sessions in Bombay. I gradually realized that although Ashis was still vibrantly railing at his father with trenchant attacks, he could never have evolved such positive working relationships with his two major benefactors nor have become such an astute administrator and organizer himself if there weren't a far more positive father-son relationship than Ashis was aware of. I assumed that he could only form a close relationship with a male hierarchical figure if he had had a prototype that he had internalized, and that he could only perform with such a high level of organizational skill by deeply identifying with his father's unusual organizational abilities.

I pointed out to Ashis his inner feelings of sadness, which he confirmed, and interpreted that the loss of his director evoked unfinished feelings of mourning around the death of his father. I further pointed out from what he had previously told me that his father had obviously taken an enormous interest in him, and no matter how disillusioned Ashis had become after his father's death, there must have been an earlier intense attachment and idealization of him. The interpretation of his unfinished mourning rang true to him, and he associated that all he has wanted to do since the director resigned is to be by himself—something very unusual for him. He then recalled that when his former benefactor had suddenly died, he had become similarly depressed for months, and ten years before then, when he had had still another benefactor, an Englishman, who suddenly had to return to England, he also became depressed in the same way. He had responded to all of these losses through some creative effort as if to heal these losses: when his father died, he began his novel; when the Englishman left, he began some other writing; when his benefactor of the early 1970s suddenly died, Ashis wrote a spate of articles; and now he had started a screenplay of the novel that was about to be published.

Psychodynamically, Ashis's depression mainly derived from an unconsciously displaced, unfinished mourning of a consciously hated father onto three different benefactors. As these three benefactors each had suddenly left Ashis by leaving their jobs or through death, the separation unconsciously evoked profound feelings around the sudden death and loss of his father. Since the childhood and adolescent ambivalence was so great toward his father the collapse of the idealizations so painful and enraging, the separation so emotionally upsetting, and the shame over the father's suicide so intense, the mourning process had never been worked through. His unrelenting antagonism toward his father thus served unconsciously to defend against positive feelings toward him, painful feelings of loss, and wounded we-self esteem.

Ashis came to the following session almost completely free of depression, a recovery his friends had commented about in the meantime, and agilely began talking about how to find a suitable work situation for himself and better models to follow. He expressed how difficult it was to be creative in India without a benefactor who could really appreciate you, how any creative self-assertion and expression are simply not countenanced without such a benefactor. He suggested that he might go abroad temporarily to write until such a benefactor turned up, or perhaps found his own organization with international support to assist Indian creative artists; he felt there was a great need for such an organization. These two solutions—going abroad temporarily or starting his own organization—are exactly what a few other creative men whom I have met in my short stay in India have done.

He finished the session by talking about possible models to follow. He returned to the idealized figures he first mentioned in New York City. Coomaraswamy combined Indian and Western thought as he, himself, was trying to do, but could never function in India. Gandhi,

Tagore, and Vivekananda followed a traditional Indian pattern of taking vows of poverty and greatly reducing their wants so as to be in a position to affect society, but he himself felt that he was too aristocratic in his tastes to be able to go that way, and that going abroad periodically might be his only solution until suitable benefactors turned up in India. In effect, these older idealized models didn't meet his current needs. But he ended on an upbeat note: he felt that his career and his creativity were coming closer together.

As Ashis shed his depression and became more mobilized, he began to articulate a subtle, longstanding, intense inner conflict between strong urges to write in terms of literary and spiritual aspirations associated with Hinduism and equally strong efforts to further his organizational career, associated with his father and his more Westernized, career-oriented values. Ashis told of starting to write the screenplay for his novel rather than just handing it over to the film producers to do; of possibly doing a book on film policy as well as to restructure the film industry and distribution in India to give greater opportunity for art films to be shown than is now the case; and of possibly starting another novel or screenplay dealing with Partition at the time of Independence in four different cities, incorporating the Hindu metaphysical idea of the outgoingness of the soul and its return to its inner source. As he would talk of these literary aspirations, he simultaneously mentioned that they would put him in a new orbit in his career. His previous leaps to high organizational positions had come, after all, only after his two previous benefactors had read his ideas. He then commented that his writing was similar to Tagore's: that writing is a *sadhana* or spiritual discipline oriented toward inner transformation. But immediately afterwards he indicated how useful his books or screenplay might be in furthering his career, subtly conveying an inner tension between the two aspirations.

These dual meanings that Ashis ascribed to his writing and the conflict between them is something I have never found in my psychoanalytic work with recognized American artists and writers. Rather, they inevitably struggled with how to make their artistic career more viable and successful. Here was still another arena in which Ashis's identity conflict between Hindu and Westernized identifications and values was being played out.

I at first pointed out that it is possible to have literary creativity and a spiritual life on one hand, and to be involved in a career of creative organizational work on the other—that the two could be discrete activities and not have to be constantly intertwined. He experienced some relief at this, but then commented that his father had consistently denigrated the poetic and literary side of himself, and recalled the incident of receiving first prize in English poetry in the boarding school for English children. I began interpreting to him that he must experience this whole creative, literary side of himself with considerable tension and conflict, since he must have internalized his father's hostile attitudes toward these talents. He acknowledged this. But much more to the point was my final interpretation of the session, that his view of literary creativity as a way of putting himself into a new career orbit was actually an unconscious compromise: he could use his poetic talents, but only in the service of fulfilling his father's career-oriented expectations. Ashis strongly assented that always having to give a pound of flesh when he creates was an important insight.

I had been seeing Ashis on a more or less twice-a-week basis for approximately two months, but now he had to leave Bombay for his work for three weeks; and then, after a couple of sessions, he would have to leave again for two and half months. In those two sessions at the end of September, he continued the theme of his conflict over his literary life. He said he was very upset after realizing that he was still constantly placating his father by using his literary work to further his career. When he associated this with his anxiety over how his novel would be received, I conveyed that his anxiety went further than the normal author's concern. My interpretation that his anxiety was related to an inner fear that his assertion of his artistic identity would cause him to lose his father's love and respect was confirmed when Ashis immediately associated that he wouldn't show his boss the book because the latter would think less of Ashis and possibly fire him. I realized that his inner fear of the loss of his father's respect and love were major factors in his masochistically staying in his current position, and in his constant struggle to assert the artistic side of himself. I suggested that he needed an environment in which people would appreciate his artistic, creative side, his more authentic self.[16] He responded that Professor Mukerjee had recently told him the same thing. The next morning he ex-

---

[16] My suggestion derived from work with masochistic dynamics, where it is apparent that the person clings to highly rejecting and/or exploitative relationships because he or she inwardly believes that if there weren't this type of relationship, there would be nothing—which is far more painful to contemplate. These adult masochistic relationships inevitably derive from childhood familial ones, where if there weren't a rejecting, sadistic, or exploitative relationship with the parent, there would indeed be no relationship at all. In adult life, however, there is usually the choice of moving into more supportive relationships. For the psychoanalytic delineation of this type of masochistic dynamics from an ego psychological and object-relations viewpoint, in contrast to the classical analysis by Freud and others, see the work of Menaker (1952) and Berliner (1947).

pressed his feeling that the whole problem of the loss of love and respect from his father was too much for him to cope with. We had reached an important core conflict around the assertion of his literary self and his relationship with his father, which now had to be interrupted by his leaving Bombay for two and a half months.

After he returned in December, I saw him for four sessions before we left India the first time. The theme of his intense inner conflict over literary creativity and spiritual aspirations as against aggressive career advancement and the placation of his father continued to be played out in a number of variations. He was now able to write every day, something he could not do before, but with considerable inner tension. However, as he promoted his novel, he was totally self-assured and relaxed— quite different from the usual writer or artist—as he symbolically fulfilled his father's practical, career-oriented expectations.

In another variation, he was in a quandry over which of two books to start, since he had just finished the screenplay of the novel. It emerged that once again one of the books, about film criticism, was related to his literary-spiritual interests and aspirations, while the other book, concerned with broader policy decisions, was perceived by him as being far more oriented toward advancing his career. Over a month's time, he had indeed opted for the book that would contribute the most in his eyes to his career advancement, and had already completed six chapters. On the other hand, he was now able to write in his office at work, something he could never do before, and was writing this more technical book in fine, literary style. Thus, he had given in to his father's expectations in terms of the choice of the book, but now had invaded the father's organizational domain with his own literary aspirations.

In our final session in January 1978, he told of a large seminar held in Bombay on the subject of his novel; many intellectuals came who talked of their own similar identity struggles over being Westernized and searching for their own cultural roots. This recognition was extremely important to Ashis. Since his director was still as unresponsive and unappreciative of him as ever, Ashis was seriously entertaining the possibility of going to the writers program at Iowa University, or to McGill University, or to work with UNESCO. I encouraged this temporary move abroad. I then learned that Professor Mukerjee had encouraged him to do the same thing, telling Ashis that if he now went abroad for awhile, he would have a whole new career, one much more consonant with his literary aspirations—that the more involved he became with his writing, the more it would become a career in itself.

In this final session, he also said he was feeling physically worse, that his stomach was bothering him more—which was probably in part a reaction to the separation engendered by my leaving the country. As is quite customary, he had already seen allopathic and homeopathic doctors, and had just seen someone from the Islamic Ullanic tradition. Indians are generally extremely pragmatic in the choice of a doctor, and may go to a number from radically different schools of medicine. Ashis was also quite aware that his stomach problems, not uncommon in India, could well be emotionally related; he was aware of this not from his psychoanalytic sophistication but from common Indian cultural notions of the continuity between mind and body.

He further told me that besides his stomach ailments, he was very irritable and unpleasant to everyone around him, particularly his subordinates at work and his wife and children at home. I interpreted to him that his writing, although it was an expression of a more authentic self, aroused tremendous inner conflict because of the father's inner presence; that to cope with the punitive and bullying father, he unconsciously identified with him and began bullying those around him at the office and at home—which his father used to do. I later learned, on our next trip to India, that this interpretation of an unconscious identification with the aggressor alleviated his intense irritability when others were around.

When I next saw Ashis, in July of 1980, I learned he had stayed on in his current position, waiting for a promotion to a higher position in the organization, where he would have had more control and influence. Both the professor and Ashis's wife had constantly urged him to leave. I found, to my surprise, a rather remarkable shift in his attitudes toward his father, probably signaling that the mourning had been lived through. For the first time, Ashis spoke kindly of his father, presenting him in a positive light. And for the very first time in session, he revealed that while his father was in the Indian Civil Service he had actually started some sixty different businesses, but his father's brothers had been unable to run them. Ashis deeply felt that if his father could only have resigned from the Indian Civil Service, he could have built up one of the great business-industrial empires in India with his considerable entreprenurial skills and spirit, and could have avoided the disaster that befell him. This was poignantly said, however, in the context of his own continuing struggle to leave his own organization to further his writing. Ashis seemed to have strongly identified with his father's need for position and importance, and in his partial failure to realize his own self, he was able to empathize with his father's unsuccessful struggles to be a major entrepreneur. He did not, however, express any of the former unrelenting railing at his father, so that it was obvious that a major inner change had taken place.

On the other hand, Ashis was continuing with his writing, particularly on film, art, literature, and other traditional modes of communication in India. His thesis was that development was based far too much on Western models and didn't sufficiently take into account Indian modes and models. Ashis was well enough grounded in Western aesthetic theories and Western media to be able to show their significant differences from Indian culture. In his view, the wholesale adherence to Western models held by many Westernized Indians was in various ways highly inappropriate to Indian development.

Psychodynamically, although Ashis's conflict between the literary-meditative side of himself and his more Westernized career goals of organizational position and power was partially worked out in this last phase of psychoanalytic therapy, in my judgment it would have taken some months more to work it through thoroughly, and it might not have been finally resolved until the mourning process itself was completed. The problem was that although the literary-meditative inclinations were more in keeping with his own individuation and with traditional Indian culture, his father's more Westernized values were far more emotionally anchored in Ashis's familial self through a traditional Indian father-son hierarchical relationship. Ashis decided not to pursue analysis with any of the other psychoanalysts in Bombay, as he knew some of them too personally and didn't feel comfortable with others.

The illumination of Ashis's struggles, conflicts, and partial resolutions through psychoanalytic therapy seems to throw light in one way or another on the situation of a large number of urban Western-educated Indian men. Ashis's main identity conflict is a civilizational one, firmly set within the Indian sociohistorical experience of British colonialism and of Indian reassertion of indigenous culture and nationalism. His identity struggle is shared with others of the urban educated elite who are trying to reassert Indian religious and philosophical culture over a secular Westernization/modernization that stresses deculturation and alienation from the indigenous cultures of India. In other Indians there is usually a stronger sublayering of maternally connected Hindu ideals and values than is present in Ashis but these are, similarly, profoundly denigrated by the father's overt identification with Western values and attitudes. The crisis in Ashis's identity came about much earlier in life than is characteristic for other sensitive Indian men, however, because of the idiosyncratic circumstance of his father's suicide. It was Ashis's literary creativity that enabled him to see that his own personal struggle was part of a much greater Indian one—the return to and reassertion of indigenous culture—which then oriented him toward using his literary efforts to resolve his identity struggles both for himself and others.

There is, however, another dimension to Ashis's identity struggles that is related to the situation of a sizable number of urban Indians being educated abroad. Ashis, like them, is far more individualized in his work patterns than most Indians, so that there is conflict with the more traditional, hierarchical work relationships in which subordinates frequently gain little recognition for their creative efforts. Yet strong aspects of the core familial self remain, so that these men still need an appreciative benefactor who will recognize and promote their more individualized self.

In concluding, I would like to comment in greater depth on the nature of our psychoanalytic relationship in terms of cross-cultural psychoanalytic work. First, it is obvious that this was short-term psychoanalytic therapy and not a full analysis. In a fuller analysis I would expect that as we got closer to resolving Ashis's intense individuation struggles between his literary aspirations and his father's depreciation of them, issues around the mother-son relationship would gradually surface. I have sometimes worked with American men for two or three years around a highly problematic father-son relationship and transferences before the maternal one comes into focus.

The nature of the transference throughout was that I was an empathic selfobject frequently though not always in tune with his identity struggles and his efforts to individuate as a creative writer. Where the narcissistic dimension is so intensely strong in terms of his father's suicide and its effects on Ashis, a selfobject empathic transference is not unusual. There was some idealization of me, but his main idealizations were obviously directed to some of the great figures of the Indian national and cultural renaissance. Moreover, this kind of selfobject transference is not unusual where one works with masochistic dynamics, the masochistic transference usually being played out in outside relationships such as Ashis's with his current director (Berliner 1947; Menaker 1952).

From Kohut's (1971) self psychological perspective derived from work with Americans, Ashis's search for new idealized figures in his late teens would be seen as a result of an earlier developmental deficit or arrest, with the implication that he should be more autonomous by then and not need an idealized figure quite so much. In terms of Indian narcissistic structures, however, there is a much more prolonged need for idealized figures to be associated with, a need which lasts throughout life. This is emotionally related not to childhood deficits and arrests, but rather to a plethora of early childhood mirroring relationships and idealizations, as well as to profound adult goals for individuation. The choice of Ashis's idealized figures were all profoundly tied to his individuation strivings.

That there was little of the more classical conflict around superego and drive derivatives in our work does not, of course, mean it might not be present. In most patients seen in a long-term analysis, issues of early object relationships, structural conflicts, ego developmental struggles, and narcissism involving selfobjects sooner or later surface. However, any individual patient may be far more involved with a particular one of these four major dimensions of psychoanalysis over a prolonged period of time. With Ashis, our work primarily involved issues of identity and self, with strong aspects of a struggle toward individuation, a masochistic relationship at work, and reactive depressions involving an unfinished mourning process.[17]

Identity, Autobiography, and Biography

A question may be raised at this point: to what extent is the psychoanalytic study of any person relevant to others in the same society, because of the idiosyncratic nature of the particular person's conflicts and family background? That is, how representative is that person of others from his milieu—in Ashis's case, from an upper middle-class, upper-caste, highly Westernized background? By discussing some additional data to compare with Ashis's story, I hope to show that although the particular chords may be different from those of Ashis, the theme will be quite similar. Further, although there is always a complex mixture of the idiosyncratic personal and familial background with sociohistorical and cultural factors, it is possible for the psychoanalyst to separate these dimensions out and use the case to comment on larger themes.

Although contacts with the British raj varied in both quality and quantity from the late eighteenth to the middle of the twentieth century, an examination of autobiographies of men of the Westernized elite from

[17] Thus, the contributions of Berliner (1947), Erikson (1950, 1968), Freud (1914), Kohut (1971, 1977), Lichtenstein (1977), Menaker (1952), E. and W. Menaker (1965), Rank (Menaker 1982), and Winnicott (1965) were most relevant to psychoanalytic therapy with Ashis; but the theories of each had to be significantly altered to fit the Indian context.

a variety of periods and regions suggest important identity issues related to generational involvement with the raj (Walsh 1982). The first generation of these men had often to contend with the opposition of orthodox members of their own extended families and communities—witness Gandhi's conflict with his community over being educated in England—but many persevered and pressed their own sons into a Western education, and administrative, teaching, or professional roles. Although they also fostered education of their daughters, these women usually remained firmly rooted in traditional Hindu practices and rituals, the tradition varying from region to region.

These Western-educated men functioned not only within British-defined education and work roles, but increasingly within the social values of a colonial ruler who, throughout the latter half of the nineteenth and twentieth centuries, arrogantly claimed superiority. Esteemed in their own Indian families and communities as men who had become successful and prosperous, they were openly denigrated by their British teachers and supervisors. No matter how they strove to emulate values of achievement, manliness, and universal principles, they were generally considered by the British to have the qualities of servility, indolence, effeminacy, weakness, and unprincipled and litigious behavior. Nor were they ever granted acceptance by the British into their society. If the first generation of Western-educated Indian men sometimes faced social isolation from their own communities, the second generation was faced with a fractured identity, in which the values of being Western came from their own fathers as well as the British, but a core self with traditional Hindu cultural and religious values was derived from intense, earlier relationships with their mothers, aunts, grandmothers, and servants. What was Indian in them was devalued, while what was Western enabled them to attain good positions, economic advancement, and often recognition by their own communities—never acceptance by the British. It is not surprising that these men sometimes gave evidence of being torn by warring identity elements, and occasionally became paralyzed in their functioning.

In the biographies of the innovators we find what direction was taken to resolve this impasse: to seek parity with the British, to restore some semblance of self-esteem and remove doubts of civilizational inferiority, and to deal intellectually with social theories deriving from neo-Darwinism and Comtean positivism, not to mention Christian ideology as expounded by the missionaries—all extolling the superior nature of Western civilization. The Indian innovator, whether in science, politics, or religion, searched for sources of self-esteem in the broader national arena, finding a way to live that would have its roots in indigenous cultural forms while using Western systems of organization, political institutions, and technology.

One of the more innovative identity syntheses emerged in the life of Jagadis Chandra Bose, the world-renowned Bengali physicist and plant physiologist (Nandy 1980a). Bose took giant strides in legitimatizing professional science within the framework of indigenous Hindu values, developing in the process an alternative world view of science to the predominant Western one. He formulated a view of science around Vedantic monism and the experimental inquiry into *prakriti* or *shakti* in all forms, while he changed the value orientation of science from the Western cultural ones of the control and subjugation of nature to the more sympathetic, traditional Hindu viewpoint of knowledge used for self-transformation and contemplation. As a result, Indians could subsequently be comfortably involved within the scientific enterprise without crushing feelings of inferiority. Although Bose's quest for an identity of parity with the British eventually resulted in a rigid approach and a decline in his scientific work, this does not in the least negate the importance of his synthesis for Indians of a modern scientific role within the basic Hindu traditions.

Although Gandhi eventually formulated the most politically relevant identity for Indians in the National Movement, another heroic attempt at a new kind of political identity was that of Subhas Chandra Bose (Gordon 1974, 223–264). Bose strove to combine indigenous religious ideals with Western values: Bengali ideals of *shakti* or the mother goddess with nationalism and, more importantly, the religious activism of Vivekananda with British and Indian Kshatriya values of self-assertion, manliness, and bravery. This type of identity model again legitimatized traditional Indian religious strivings while incorporating certain British values, subsuming the latter to the former.

Lest it be imagined that the major identity models have all reasserted a Hindu world view, one has only to turn to the brilliantly scathing writings of V. S. Naipaul (1977), who stridently asserts a position that is also present in India to varying degrees. When all of the bombast and rhetoric are stripped away, a clear image emerges of a British-educated Indian raised in a traditional Hindu community, who has opted for the individualized self of the West and Western intellectual culture in his identity as a writer. Swinging with both arms in *India: A Wounded Civilization,* he delivers roundhouse rights to the "underdeveloped ego" of the familial self, without autonomy, and repeated left jabs to the traditional culture of the spiritual self and the magic-cosmic world, with its lack of critical intellectual inquiry and reflection.[18] In a less belligerent and more humorous short story, Naipaul (1971) details the movement of an Indian servant in America from a hierarchically oriented familial self to that of a more American individualized self—associating the latter with open rebellion and a freer style of sexuality. The very virulence of *India: A Wounded Civilization* gives evidence of the profound presence, and equally profound rejection, of identity elements of the familial and spiritual selves within the writer—in part confirmed by his feelings of equal alienation from the British society in which he lives.

In another medium, a poem by Vikram Seth (1980, 17) is poignant evidence of an educated Indian's personal struggle with his identification with British colonial values.

DIVALI

Three years of neurotic
Guy Fawkes Days—I recall
That lonely hankering—
But I am home after all.

Home. These walls, this sky
Splintered with wakes of light,
These mud-lamps beaded round
The eaves, this festive night,

These streets, these voices . . . yet
The old insensate dread,
Abeyant as that love,
Once more shifts in my head.

Five? six? generations ago
Somewhere in the Punjab
My father's family, farmers,
Perhaps had a small shop

And two generations later
Could send a son to school

---

[18] Naipaul was raised in a traditional Brahmin family that had emigrated to a village in Trinidad in the West Indies. In *India: A Wounded Civilization* (1977, 107–109, 118–119), he mainly quoted from letters from Sudhir Kakar, using Kakar's status as a psychoanalyst to lend authoritativeness and credence to his own position. But Naipaul quoted just that area of Kakar's work that clearly evidences Kakar's own partial identification with Western values in his evaluation of Indian psychological functioning.

To gain the conqueror's
Authoritarian seal:

English! Six-armed god,
Key to a job, to power,
Snobbery, the good life,
This separateness, this fear.

English: beloved language
of Jonson, Wordsworth's tongue—
These my "meridian names"
Whose grooves I crawl along.

The Moghuls fought and ruled
And settled. Even while
They hungered for musk-melon,
Rose, peach, nightingale,

The land assumed their love.
At sixty they could not
Retire westwards. The British
Made us the Orient.

How could an Englishman say
About the divan-e-khas
"If there is heaven on earth
It is this; it is this; it is this."

Macaulay the prophet of learning
Chewed at his pen: one taste
Of Western wisdom "surpasses
All the books of the East,"

And Kalidas, Shankaracharya,
Panini, Bhaskar, Kabir,
Surdas sank, and we welcomed
The reign of Shakespeare.

The undigested Hobbes,
The Mill who later ground
(Through talk of liberty)
The Raj out of the land . . .

O happy breed of Babus,
I march on with your purpose;

We will have railways, common law
And a good postal service—

And as I twist along
Those grooves from image to image,
Violet, elm-tree, swan,
Pork-pie, gable, scrimmage

And as we title our memoirs
"Roses in December"
Though we well know that here
Roses *grow* in December

And as we import songs
Composed in the U.S.
For Vietnam (not even
Our local horrors grip us)

And as, over gin at the Club,
I note that egregious member
Strut just perceptibly more
When with a foreigner,

I know that the whole world
Means exile for our breed
Who are not home at home
And are abroad abroad,

Huddled in towns, while around:
"He died last week. My boys
Are starving. Daily we dig
The ground for sweet potatoes."

"The landlord's hirelings broke
My husband's ribs—and I
Grow blind in the smoke of the hearth."
"Who will take care of me

When I am old? No-one
Is left." So it goes on,
The cyclic shadow-play
Under the sinister sun;

That sun that, were there water,
Could bless the dispirited land,

Coaxing three crops a year
From this same yieldless ground.

Yet would these parched wraiths still
Starve in their ruins, while
"Silkworms around them grow
Into fat cocoons?" Sad soil,

This may as well be my home.
Because no other nation
Moves me thus? What of that?
Cause for congratulation?

This may as well be my home;
I am too used to the flavour
Of tenuous fixity;
I have been brought to savour

Its phases: the winter wheat—
The flowers of Har-ki-Doon—
The sal forests—the hills
Inflamed with rhododendron—

The first smell of the Rains
On the baked earth—the peaks
Snow-drowned in permanence—
The single mountain lakes.

What if my tongue is warped?
I need no words to gaze
At Ajanta, those flaked caves,
Or at the tomb of Mumtaz;

And when an alap of Marwa
Swims on slow flute-notes over
The neighbours' roofs at sunset
Wordlessly like a lover

It holds me—till the strain
Of exile, here, or there,
Subverts the trance, the fear
Of fear found everywhere.

"But freedom?" the notes would sing . . .
Parole is enough. Tonight

Below the fire-crossed sky
Of the Festival of Light

Give your soul leave to feel
What distilled peace it can;
In lieu of joy, at least
This lapsing anodyne.

"The world is a bridge. Pass over it,
Building no house upon it."
Acceptance may come with time;
Rest, then disquieted heart.

Psychoanalysis in India and Japan

Identity and Psychoanalysis in India

The discipline of psychoanalysis—a Western import in India—frequently engenders identity conflicts in Indian mental health practitioners around questions of the fundamental nature of the Indian self and social change. By delving into these reactions to psychoanalysis, we can see more clearly contemporary Indian tendencies to assimilate or reject certain Westernizing/modernizing influences.

The Indian Psychoanalytic Society is one of the older members of the International Psychoanalytic Association; it was officially affiliated in 1922 (Nandi 1979; Ramana 1964). Its inception was entirely due to the pioneering work of its founder, Girindrasakhar Bose, a highly gifted Bengali physician who quite independently set himself on a course of clinical exploration similar to Freud's. In 1920, on something of a dare from some close friends, he formulated his own unique ideas on repression into a thesis, *Concept of Repression* (Bose 1966), for which he was awarded the coveted doctoral degree from the University of Calcutta and a lectureship in the Department of Psychology, University College of Science and Technology. Psychoanalysis thus became ensconced in Calcutta academia in the early 1920s, which was not to occur in many Western countries until decades later. Bose then began a lifelong correspondence with Freud in 1921, sending him his book and later papers on his elaborate theory of opposite wishes.

At the present time, the Indian Psychoanalytic Society is centered in

Calcutta, where there are some fifteen psychoanalysts as well as students and a sizable group of associates from other fields. At one time it included the noted social anthropologist the late Nirmal Kumar Bose. It also has its own mental hospital, Lumbini Park. There is now a dynamic branch of the society in Bombay, with a Psychoanalytic Therapy and Research Center and the Indian Council of Mental Health. The former is run by members and students of the Psychoanalytic Society, whereas the latter is a psychoanalytically oriented school and college counseling center organized by one of the psychoanalysts. There is also a very small handful of psychoanalysts, students, and psychoanalytically oriented theoreticians in New Delhi. In Ahmedabad, there has been an excellent, comprehensive, psychoanalytically oriented mental health center, the B. M. Institute of Mental Health, originally cofounded by Gardner and Lois Murphy, American psychologists, with the Sarabhai family in the early 1950s, and continued with intimate contacts with some members of the British Psychoanalytic Society, particularly Jock Sutherland.[1] There is an occasional psychoanalyst or analytically oriented therapist in other Indian cities, as well, where there are strong Westernizing influences. The National Institute of Mental Health and Neuro Sciences (N.I.M.H.A.N.S.) in Bangalore, for instance, the leading mental health center in south India, has a small group of psychodynamically oriented psychiatrists and psychologists on their staff who are involved in doing psychotherapy.

Of more central concern here is the theoretical stance of psychoanalysis in India. The overwhelming orientation of the Indian Psychoanalytic Society in Calcutta is what is commonly referred to as "classical Freudian," with emphases on the early topological and libido theories and the later structural theory, with relatively little mention of object-relations theory, ego psychological stages of development, or self psychology and identity theory. In Bombay, largely through the influence of one of two senior psychoanalysts, M. V. Amrith, now retired, the orientation is far more toward the work of Melanie Klein (Segal 1964) and object-relations theory, with considerable influence from Wilfred Bion (1977). In New Delhi, there is a strong Eriksonian cast to the writings of Sudhir Kakar (1978, 1979, 1982) and Ashis Nandy (1980a, 1980b, 1983), who have endeavored to integrate psychoanalysis with social science work

---

[1] Kamalini Sarabhai was trained at the British Psychoanalytic Society and had been director of the B. M. Institute since its inception. At the present time, with Kamalini Sarabhai's untimely death and the departure of the clinical director, B. K. Ramanujam, the psychoanalytic emphasis at the B. M. Institute has seriously declined.

on India.[2] This integration is missing from the work of the Indian psychoanalysts in Calcutta and Bombay (as well as from that of most Western analysts); the classical Freudian and Kleinian perspectives are based on the assumption of the primacy of intrapsychic reality, and tend to ignore complex cultural, social, and historical factors as they are internalized within the psyche. Drawing on broad Freudian theory as well as his extensive clinical experience at the B. M. Institute of Mental Health at Ahmedabad, B. K. Ramanujam (1979, 1980a, 1980b, 1981a, 1981b, 1986), the former clinical director, has made strides in formulating Indian psychological makeup and functioning within extended family relationships and Indian culture. His writings are based on extensive psychoanalytic work with individuals, families, and children afforded by the ample funding of the Sarabhai family and under the directorship of the psychoanalyst Kamalini Sarabhai.

Provocative questions may be asked here both as to why psychoanalysis developed so early in India, and why it has not grown there as it has, for instance, in America or even in France since the late 1960s. Although Hindu culture has never developed a theory of unconscious psychological processes, it has certainly stressed a variety of dimensions of psychological functioning. These range from the extraordinary interpersonal sensitivity needed for extended family and other group relationships to the culture's highly particularlistic emphasis on a person's development through the combination of their qualities (*gunas*), powers (*shakti*), effects of familial and individual actions (*karma*), and attachments (*samskaras*) carried over from past lives. A theory of unconscious motivation and structures could rather easily be integrated into a culture that in certain ways so stresses the psychological.

On the other hand, it is obvious that psychoanalysis has not taken off in India. There may be a number of factors involved in this, not the least being the absence of a sizable number of well-trained practicioners and the inhibiting factor of economics. In Ahmedabad, where the Sarabhai family fortune had enabled the B. M. Institute of Mental Health to offer low-cost psychoanalytically oriented treatment to anyone who came, and where high standards of treatment by an interdisciplinary team of workers was implemented, the community came in droves from all castes and classes, from the most traditional to the most Westernized. Nevertheless, we are faced with the question of why the psychoanalytic movements of Calcutta and Bombay have not developed to any

---

[2] Ashis Nandy is a psychologist who is a psychoanalytic theoretician rather than a practicing psychoanalyst.

extent, though both are presently expanding, the latter in an apparently more dynamic way. One answer to this question may be derived from the work of Phillip Rieff (1968), and as applied to French society from Sherry Turkle (1978). Psychoanalysis has flourished in the United States over the past several decades, and in the late 1960s exploded in France after a period of being an alienated, miniscule movement; Rieff and Turkle relate this burgeoning to important sociocultural factors and changes in both societies. They particularly emphasize the "deconversion" from the belief systems and symbols of traditional "positive communities" to a less culturally and socially integrated society that shares only the symbols of science, where each individual must create his or her own personal world view of symbols and meaning. This, of course, has been the prevailing situation in the United States, where there has not been any integrated national culture and where a militant individualism has been combined with enormous social mobility oriented initially around the frontier and then around the acceptance of large waves of immigration. In France, a unique synthesis of state, society, and the individual has only recently crumbled, a deconversion that has thrown the person back upon himself, thus enabling a psychoanalytic orientation to become enormously influential.

In India, although there are indeed small highly Westernized elites in the major cities who tend to be alienated from Indian culture, and although Indian culture has been profoundly affected by the impact of Western culture, even in the urban areas there is a strong continuity of Hindu, Moslem, Christian, and Parsee cultural and social institutions. Indigenous mental health healers are still important in the society.[3] Deconversion of positive social and cultural communities has simply not occurred, even in Bombay, to nearly the extent it has in America and France. A psychoanalytic world view that guides the individual and family in a world of crumbling supports is not, therefore, at this point appropriate enough to the Indian scene for psychoanalysis to become a major factor in Indian culture. On the other hand, where greater individualization is slowly developing and being incorporated within the core Indian self in the urban areas, and where social relationships are often less traditional and ritually grounded, it can reasonably be expected that there will be a continued and sustained growth of some kind of psychoanalytic orientation and therapy.

[3] For information on north India, there is the work of Hoch (1977) and Kakar (1982). In south India, this tradition has been investigated by Dr. R. L. Kapur, formerly head of psychiatry, National Institute for Mental Health and Neuro Sciences, Bangalore.

To return to the major theme of Indian identity: the attitudes toward psychoanalysis of some major leaders of the psychiatric community are very significant. Indian psychiatrists commonly use various forms of Western therapies first introduced into India by the British: the current armementarium of drugs,[4] electric shock treatment, psychiatric history-taking and diagnosis, and certain forms of psychotherapy usually of a more supportive and directive type, when time allows. A variety of techniques and theories originating from the West are thus utilized in a nonconflictual way. Psychoanalysis, however, has been something of a fishbone in their throats. Some of the negative attitudes toward psychoanalysis can certainly be laid at the doorstep of a common psychiatric ambivalence toward psychoanalysis. A more penetrating analysis of these psychiatrists' writings (Neki 1973, 1975, 1976a, 1976b, 1977; Pande 1968; Surya 1966; Surya and Jayaram 1964), however, brings to light fundamental conflicts and integrations of Westernizing/modernizing influences in an Indian mental health professional's identity.

The central issue is that, unlike other Western forms of therapy, psychoanalysis is a *Weltanschauung,* with a whole value-laden sociocultural orientation. An important aspect of this orientation is the ideal of rational man (Meltzer 1978), and correspondingly negative attitudes toward religion. With but rare exceptions, psychoanalysts have approached religion and religious experience unrelentingly in terms of compensations and psychopathology. Any type of spiritual experience has usually been reduced either to problems of the oedipal stage or, more usually to a reliving of the original infant-mother relationship—originally called the oceanic feeling and now in more contemporary, sophisticated terms, symbiosis (Masson 1980). Some of the major leaders of psychiatry who most vociferously reject psychoanalysis are profoundly involved in the Indian spiritual tradition and in their own meditation. It is clear that the religious factor involved in the realization of the spiritual self is for them a central issue. Rejection of psychoanalysis in many Indians' professional identity can thus be seen as echoing a strong need to reassert a basic Indian identity around the spiritual self, in contrast to Western values antagonistic to their own—a variation on the theme of the reassertion of Hindu identity and culture vis-à-vis the British.

But the issues involving psychoanalysis in India are far more complex and profound than this simple conflict between religious and antireligious viewpoints. Central to the psychoanalytic value system, especially

---

[4] It should be noted that although tranquilizers have largely been developed in the West, the original tranquilizer, reserpine, first came from India, where Buddhist monks were known to have used it for centuries.

in the United States, is the stress laid on a mental-health model of individual autonomy, of highly developed intrapsychic structures in which the individual develops a strong inner separation from others and sharply differentiates between inner images of self and other, of norms of self-reliance, self-assertion, self-actualization, and a high degree of relatively open, verbal self-expression. In the American urban middle and upper-middle classes, it is usually expected that a youth will develop the intrapsychic structures and integrated identity necessary to function independently in a variety of social groups and situations apart from the family, eventually leaving the family nest.

Many Indian psychiatric leaders view these mental health norms as inappropriate to Indian psychological development and functioning in the extended family and culture, and thus as not at all universal (Neki 1976a; Surya 1966). They rather emphasize the emotional bonding of kinship that enables the Indian person to live in emotionally close and responsibly interdependent relationships, where the sense of self is deeply involved with others, where relationships are governed by reciprocal hierarchical principles, and where there is a constant need for approval to maintain and enhance self-regard. Their ideal of mental health is not a rational, socially autonomous and self-actualizing person, but rather that of a person centered in a spiritual consciousness and being, so that there is an inner calm amid the stresses and pulls of close familial and other group hierarchical relationships. They view the psychoanalytic values inherent in the individualized self of the West, therefore, as profoundly out of tune with an Indian milieu, particularly a traditional one.

Further contributing to their rejection of psychoanalysis as an unsuitable Western import is the theoretical emphasis, or in Indian terms overemphasis, that a Western classical psychoanalyst puts on the curative nature of cognitive processes such as interpretation, to the detriment of the real relationship, as distinguished from the transference relationship, between analyst and analysand. To be sure, there are notable rumblings of dissent within the Western psychoanalytic community on this issue (Alexander 1950; Greenson and Wexsler 1969; Menaker 1942; Roland 1967; Szaz 1957), but the Indians are responding to the dominant model of the traditional psychoanalytic relationship. As many Indian therapists have noted, an Indian patient usually relates to a therapist as to a family elder, or possibly a guru, but always expects a real involvement from the therapist.

If these psychiatric leaders represent one end of a continuum in their rejection of the ideology of psychoanalysis in their professional identity, then the other end is occupied by a number of Bombay psychoanalysts—

a few of them also important psychiatrists—who closely identify with psychoanalytic values around the individualized self.[5] Closely associated with Westernizing/modernizing values, they tend to see Indian child rearing and familial hierarchical relationships as implicitly opposed to modernization (Bassa 1978). Such analysts relate to the Indian psyche and relationships through the lens of their more Westernized psychoanalytic framework.

The culture hero of the Bombay psychoanalytic group is W. Bion (1977), undoubtedly the most mystically oriented of any Western Freudian psychoanalyst, and possibly the only Western analyst who grew up in India. Many of these analysts seem best able to approach Indian spiritual life through identifying with a Westerner like Bion, who partially embodies it; simultaneously they have profound ambivalence toward indigenous Indian religious culture. A study of a number of analysands in Bombay, many of whom are in the arts, shows that although almost all felt they were appreciably helped by their analysis, a minority were quite angry over the rejecting attitudes of the Bombay psychoanalysts toward their spiritual aspirations (N. Seth 1980). A couple of analysts, like a number of other highly educated urbanites, have high regard for the late J. Krishnamurti. He was a major Indian spiritual leader to be sure, but one who emphasized an unusual degree of autonomy and independence in the spiritual search, and thus was more in tune with Westernized values of the individualized self than is the usual Indian guru.

In summary, these analysts try to synthesize a professional psychoanalytic identity around more Westernized values of the individualized self with an ambivalent orientation to the spiritual self. This type of identity synthesis in part confirms Singer's (1972) observations in Madras of cultural changes in religious orientation accommodating more modernizing practices. Undoubtedly, these analysts mirror aspects of the current sociocultural milieu of Bombay, the most cosmopolitan of Indian cities, with a window wide open to the flow of Western influences.

The middle ground of the continuum is occupied by a very small group of psychoanalysts and psychoanalytically oriented psychiatrists and psychologists who have endeavored to work out a different type of professional and personal identity synthesis. They have on the whole been trained in the West—in contrast to most Indian analysts and psychiatrists—and have struggled with their own inner identity integra-

---

[5] I am omitting from this discussion the psychoanalysts in Calcutta, as I am not sufficiently familiar with their attitudes on these issues.

tions. Well versed in contemporary psychoanalytic theory, they are trying to understand the Indian psyche on its own ground, evolving theoretical constructs to describe it and modified modes of psychoanalytic therapy to render assistance to the Indian patient. This is not to say that other Indian psychoanalysts are not of considerable help to their patients; but my impression is that their therapeutic methods and their understanding of Indian psychological makeup and modes of relationship are informal, and may at times be considerably different from their formal theoretical framework.

The analysts of the middle ground are frequently similar to several psychologists and social scientists in that they are well trained in excellent Western graduate programs. They see the need to evolve new theoretical paradigms for psychology and the social sciences in India, ones more related to the data of Indian society. These psychoanalysts, psychologists, and social scientists are also trying to integrate a new professional identity around Westernizing influences on theory and practice, but largely within the frameworks of Indian cultural and social patterns, and the familial and spiritual selves.

Psychoanalytic Therapy in India

We are still left with the substantive question as to the goals and practice of psychoanalytic therapy in India. If there is any legitimacy to the assertion of certain major psychiatrists that Western normative goals of psychoanalysis around autonomy, and separation are profoundly incompatible with the ability to function within the Indian extended family, then how suitable is psychoanalysis for India? Is it simply a Western import incongruously imitated by a miniscule group of analysts and patients whose identity is highly Westernized; or is it rather a Western innovation that can be altered and integrated within the framework of Indian culture and society? To answer these questions is to delve into the nature of the psychoanalytic relationship and process in India and to reexamine the essentials of psychoanalytic therapy.

In the contemporary United States, when a young urban adult who comes for analysis is living in a family situation fraught with difficulties, the psychoanalyst frequently works initially on emotional difficulties that keep this person tied to pathological familial relationships. However, the real crux of psychoanalytic therapy emerges later when, through the transferences the patient makes onto the analyst and others, the deeply internalized patterns of familial relationships from childhood and adolescence are gradually relived, understood, and resolved, or developmental deficits are repaired. At that point, the patient is able to relate to current family members and others in a more dispassionate, appropriate way, without being disturbed or overwhelmed by them. It is thus the working out or working through of past internalized relationships with their concommitant defenses in the patient's psyche, through reexperiencing them in the transference and/or having a transference that repairs deficits in structure, that constitute the essence of psychoanalysis.

In the Indian setting, the fundamental goal for a man who remains in his parents' family or for a woman with basic responsibilities to her in-laws is to enable each to function in a less disturbed and more fulfilling way, freer of anxiety and other symptoms, within the context of the complex interdependencies and reciprocal responsibilities of the extended family and other hierarchical relationships. This frequently means to understand and resolve transference reactions within extended family relationships, which then enables the patient to handle current relationships in a more appropriate and happier way. I have found, for instance, in the case of Saida (see Chapter Five) that even where realistic difficulties with a mother-in-law are considerable, by resolving transference reactions displaced from her original family relationships and unconsciously projected onto the mother-in-law, the daughter-in-law can handle her much better and be far more content. There is obviously room in extended family relationships for very different kinds of psychological functioning: hierarchical relationships and responsibilities can be responded to and fulfilled in many different ways depending on the inner state of mind of the person. In effect, an inner autonomy develops through self-understanding, enabling the person to function well within the rich interdependencies of the extended family, rather than effecting any physical separation or leading to a more self-reliant, Western life style.

Even if the essential goals of psychoanalysis are consonant with functioning in an Indian milieu, other important objections have been raised over the supposed unsuitability of Indian patients for psychoanalytic therapy, as well as over the very nature of the psychoanalytic relationship and process for Indians. Some psychiatrists have asserted that a patient relates to the therapist as a family elder or guru, and therefore expects advice and guidance rather than self-exploration; that free-association—a sine qua non of psychoanalytic therapy—is impossible in certain cultures of India that restrain personal self-expression, particularly verbal expression. Further, the classical psychoanalytic relationship is viewed as being far too distant and uninvolved for an Indian, with patients put too much on their own, and with therapists relying too greatly on cognitive curative elements (such as interpretation) rather than ones using relationship (Pande 1968). They also assert that important secrets within the family relevant to a patient's state of disturbance are rarely communicated to outsiders because of the need to maintain family honor and reputation (Neki 1976b).

The psychoanalytic relationship in India is set up by the patient according to the psychosocial dimensions of extended family hierarchical relationships. Thus, the psychoanalyst is related to as the superior in the hierarchical relationship—which is usually modeled after a relationship with a parent or other extended family elder—in which patients initially expect their analyst to take care of them, solve their problems, tell them what to do and how to become a better person. In these hierarchical relationships there is an unspoken, subtle emotional exchange of dependency needs on the patient's part with narcissistic gratification in the analyst for fulfilling the ego-ideal of the superior who responsibly helps the subordinate. Although some actual giving of advice in the early phases of the therapy may sometimes be called for to establish a working alliance, since Indian patients are so accustomed to guidance, it is usually not difficult to get Indian patients to begin speaking rather freely. When the therapist conveys an attitude of genuine interest in what is on the patient's mind, of empathic receptivity to what is being conveyed, of emotional support to the patient, and of strict confidentiality, Indian patients, in my experience and Indian analysts', usually become quite open and expressive. Often there has been a precedent, some family member, more often a woman than a man, with whom the patient has been able to talk freely in the past. It is only when the Indian therapist responds as a typical elder in constantly giving advice and guidance that the patient will continue to ask for it.

Beneath the observance of an overt etiquette of deference, loyalty, and subordination, Indians keep a very private self that contains all kinds of feelings and fantasies that will not be revealed in the usual hierarchical relationship with an elder. In a psychoanalytic relationship, however, where the Indian patient feels that the therapist is empathic and receptive, and where strict confidentiality of communication is assured, the floodgates of feelings can open up widely. In effect, Indians are highly sensitive to the qualities of the superior in the psychoanalytic relationship as well as in other hierarchical ones. My distinct impression is that once one gets beyond the normal social reserve and etiquette of Indians, they tend to reveal their inner life more openly, and even to be more in touch with it, than most American patients I have worked with.

There are still other aspects to the relationship of Indian patients with their analyst as an extended family elder. Dr. Ramanujam (1980a) comments that Indian patients tend to come for therapy when all available family elders and mentors have let them down. They therefore expect the therapist to fulfill some of the responsibilities not attended to by the various parental figures. Ramanujam sees their view of the therapist not so much as a transference projection as a real part of the psychoanalytic relationship in India that must be given due weight. If these interpersonal needs of Indians are ignored, then little work can be accomplished on intrapsychic conflicts. This real dimension may well continue beyond the termination of the therapy, so that an analyst may be invited to a wedding, birth ceremony, or such.

In the case of Veena, the woman who had attained a high position as a professional and was now trying to arrange her own marriage, I wondered over a number of sessions why she was continuing to see me for therapy. She was making her arrangements in as sensible a way as possible, manifesting little in the way of either inner conflict or emotional deficit. It was only later that I realized that she had consulted me because her father was dead, her elder brothers were doing little to help her find a mate, and in any case they and her mother and other family elders were in a distant part of India. I was in effect a stand-in for the usual family elder at the time of arranging a marriage. More technically, I was an empathic selfobject that she could use as a sounding board to express her various efforts, not out of emotional deficit as is present with the patients Kohut presents (1971, 1977) but rather out of the need and expectation that a family elder of some kind be present to help her. As one Indian woman succinctly expressed it to me in a session in New York City, "We were not brought up to be independent." Thus, to whatever extent the analyst may be involved in Indian patients' transferences, the analyst also stands in for a real hierarchical superior, usually modeled after the extended family elders.

If one major aspect of the psychoanalytic relationship as related to hierarchical relationships is that of the responsible elder, another involves a central psychosocial dimension—what I have come to term the qualitative mode of the hierarchical relationship. The qualitative mode involves the close emotional involvement that Indians frequently expect in their hierarchical relationships—though these may vary considerably at different stages of the life cycle—with a warm, caring, and smiling supportiveness. This affective nature of Indian intimacy relationships is carried over to the analytic relationship with an expectation of much greater emotional connectedness than the typical American patient has, and correspondingly less emotional distance between patient and analyst. If the analyst does not respond appropriately to these patients' emotional intimacy needs, a working alliance cannot be established (Ramanujam 1980a). This closeness need not necessarily be verbalized, but can often be conveyed simply by a glance or smile—reflecting the strong nonverbal communication of emotion in Indian relationships (pers. com. Udayan Patel).

These expectations can be very strong. Veena, for example, complained to me in a session in India that when she was in the United States working on her doctorate, she called up her American woman therapist at 2:30 A.M., having just learned that her mother had cancer, and the therapist responded somewhat abruptly, asking her to call back after 7 A.M. Veena felt extremely hurt that her therapist would not spend time with her then when she was so intensely upset. Another patient whom I saw in New York City also complained that her therapist, a woman, was more preoccupied with her house upstate than with her. Upon investigation, I sensed that her real hurt was that the therapist was insufficiently involved and unresponsive to her in terms of her inner expectations. These are just two simple examples of what I sense to be very real differences in inner expectations of emotional involvement in the psychoanalytic relationship between Indian and American patients.

How consonant, then, is the psychoanalytic relationship in India, structured as it is by different facets of Indian hierarchical relationships, with the accepted principles of psychoanalysis as it has developed in the West? This question must be followed with another: is a Western-style, classical psychoanalytic relationship in which the analyst remains a relatively distant, neutral, and uninvolved figure fundamental to the psychoanalytic process? Many analysts would obviously firmly assent to this. On the other hand, it can and has been strongly argued that for psychoanalytic therapy to proceed, a working or therapeutic alliance must be developed (Greenson 1967), and that for this to happen, real aspects of the patient-analyst relationship must sometimes be taken into account and worked with by the analyst. As some have also asserted, a reparative experience is sometimes fundamental to the effective interpretation and resolution of certain deep-seated transferences and resistances (Alexander 1950; Menaker 1942; Roland 1967). More recently, Kohut's (1984) work on the self emphasizes the reparative experiences that occur when the analyst functions as a selfobject for certain kinds of idealization and as an empathic, responsive person for patients' needs for mirroring. Even the classical psychoanalytic relationship intrinsically calls for the psychoanalyst to be realistically reliable, empathic, concerned, and nonjudgmental in his or her way of relating to the patient—minimal aspects of the real relationship. It seems reasonable to argue, then, that once the real relationship and working alliance are taken as fundamental to the psychoanalytic process, it is possible to conceptualize variations of the psychoanalytic relationship in India and the West without seeing these variations as deviations, psychopathology, parameters, or even nonpsychoanalytic practices.

To understand how the psychoanalytic process occurs in India, it is essential to take into account how resistance, transference, and countertransference are influenced by social and cultural factors. Psychoanalysts have from the beginning recognized that patients enter treatment with strong resistances to self-exploration and the resolution of their problems, and that the therapeutic handling of these resistances is essential to psychoanalytic work. Some resistances are idiosyncratic to the unconscious defensive structure of a person, to his or her superego, and to particular internalized imagoes from familial relationships; other resistances are far more related to various cultural norms incorporated into the person's ego-ideal, as well as to predominant modes of relating in the prevailing social patterns. An American who comes from a northern European ethnic background that emphasizes a high degree of self-reliance, suppression of dependency needs, and noncommunication of feelings or problems with anyone, will initially manifest strong resistances even to coming for therapeutic assistance, not to mention to free-associating. These resistances, related to prevailing cultural norms, must be aired and analyzed for the therapy to proceed.

In the Indian milieu, patients' resistances related to sociocultural phenomena involve certain aspects of the familial self and familial hierarchical relationships. There is first the considerable circumspection in what one says in any hierarchical relationship, especially as the subordinate. Inner thoughts and feelings of a private self will only be revealed when there is some trust that the other will be receptive and empathic, and that confidentiality will be kept. I have found Indian patients to have far more secrets, and to keep major ones more easily, than American patients—constituting a potentially powerful resistance. One woman, Shakuntala, reported that her two most important inner struggles had been kept secret over a prolonged period of psychoanalystic therapy because she felt her analyst wouldn't be receptive (see Chapter Five). The same is true for the internalized cultural norm of not communicating any family secrets and disturbances to outsiders lest they damage family reputation and social standing. Once trust is reasonably established, especially around confidentiality, all kinds of family skeletons will be revealed. In Ashis's case, I strongly suspect that I was probably the only one he had ever told about his father's suicide. This separation between private and public self in familial functioning can also result in major resistances in family or couples therapy where crucial secrets and feelings will not be revealed in session (pers. com. Prakash Desai).

There are still other cultural norms around extended family social patterns that can become major resistances. A sticky one is a patient's assumption that the psychoanalyst, like any other person in an intimacy relationship developed outside of the extended family, will gradually become assimilated into the patient's extended family. Here, it must be tactfully explained to the patient that while the analysis is in process the therapist will not come home for tea or a meal, as that would interfere with the therapeutic process. In a different vein, the late Dr. Desa Dhairyam in Madras reported (pers. com.) that many traditional families would not let him treat their women in psychoanalytic therapy without having another family member present. This, of course, could prove highly inhibiting to a patient, and can only really be resolved if the therapist is female.

Still other family elders insist on seeing the therapist regularly, since the familial pattern is always to be involved with the younger person's life. In this situation, therapists generally refer the elders to another therapist, although occasionally they work with both the family and patient. There are, however, situations in which a patient deeply fears that the therapist is simply an extension of the family, trying to get the patient into line, especially if the patient is involved in some conflictual assertion of her or his wishes vis-à-vis family expectations. This can result in intense resistances. An example is a high government official who had many Westernized values and gave his daughter freedom to marry whomever she wanted. He and his wife would not, however, countenance her living with someone before she married, and when she tried to, they literally locked her up at home. Such serious fights erupted between daughter and parents that she was referred to a therapist, but the parents regularly wanted to see the therapist to ascertain what "changes" he had effected in their daughter. Needless to say, the daughter was less than cooperative in therapy and would probably continue to be as long as the family consulted her therapist.[6]

On the other hand, families are not infrequently counseled, since many

---

[6] This case was reported by a psychiatric resident in the psychiatry department of the All-India Institutes of Medical Science in New Delhi.

symptoms of children, adolescents, and young adults are unconscious reactions to the stresses and strains of ongoing extended family relationships.[7] Not infrequently, for example, a family is helped to identify its unconscious scapegoating of one child as the bad one, while the child is treated in individual therapy. In many of these situations, a skilled psychoanalytic therapist familiar with the family patterns and culture, as well as with the stage in the life cycle of the patient, immediately inquires into the stresses in the family, and then is gradually able to connect the patient's unconscious reactions and symptoms with the familial tensions she or he is reacting to (Hoch 1977; pers. com. C. Shamasunder).

There is still another important facet to working with resistances from a sociocultural standpoint. Therapists who work with patients from traditional cultural backgrounds, whether urban or rural, report that images from mythology or folklore can often be used effectively to deal with early resistances to psychotherapeutic work. Professor Narayanan of N.I.M.H.A.N.S. holds a men's therapy group in a room where there is a large picture of the famous battle scene in the *Bhagavad Gita* where Arjuna, a great warrior, throws down his bow in utter dejection, refusing to fight his kinsmen who have wronged him, and begs Krishna, his charioteer and an incarnation of Vishnu, to help him. When some of his male patients come with various symptoms but deny any psychological connections and simply want guidance, Professor Narayanan confronts them with the image of the heroic Arjuna suffering from severe depression and asking for help. More often than not, this allows these patients to own up to their own unhappy feelings and to begin exploring what is really bothering them.

V. K. Alexander (1979) of Alwaye, Kerala, successfully introduces illiterate, rural persons to psychoanalytic therapy by calling up an image of bubbles rising to the surface of a pond: the stream of bubbles cannot be stopped just by bursting the ones at the top. The depths of the pond must be explored to see what is causing them, just as the deeper layers of the mind must be investigated, which may cause some difficulties and pain. With more educated persons, like Professor Narayanan he cites the *Bhagavad Gita*. The patient is to tell everything that comes to his mind, and the therapist will help him understand its meaning in relation to his life.

[7]Drs. Illana Cariapa and B. K. Ramanujam, both of whom are child and adolescent psychiatrists who have also worked extensively with families, have reported this (pers. com.).

Although many countertransference reactions of Indian psychoanalysts obviously derive from personal sources within the therapist, other such reactions are also influenced by social and cultural factors that are internalized—as they are in the West as well, although they are generally unacknowledged. In India, for example, psychoanalysts may give the advice and guidance that is expected of them in their roles as family elders. On a more subtle level, when a patient comes to sessions anxious or distraught, the immediate reaction of an Indian therapist is to react as would a member of the extended family, by doing everything possible to relieve the patient's stress (pers. com. Udayan Patel). In either case, the analyst's reaction can circumvent the necessary exploration of what is actually causing the patient's problems, and must be controlled.

Social and cultural influences in both patients' resistances and psychoanalysts' countertransference reactions in psychoanalytic therapy have as yet been insufficiently explored. These factors are frequently as profoundly internalized in both patient and analyst as other ones from their more idiosyncratic family relationships and experiences. Cultural and social patterns are not simply "out there."

With regard to transference, I was obviously not involved in doing psychoanalytic therapy for a long enough period of time to comment extensively on social and cultural influences. There are, however, two aspects of transference that are distinctly different within an Indian psychoanalytic relationship from those in a Western one. It is extremely difficult for an Indian to express anger openly and directly to a hierarchical superior, and this is carried over into the psychoanalytic relationship. Thus an Indian patient will almost never express anger or other ambivalent feelings directly to his or her therapist, although blisteringly angry feelings may be expressed toward another hierarchical figure. Ambivalence and dissatisfaction with the therapist come out only indirectly: the patient wants to terminate therapy, does not come to sessions, fails at what he or she is doing, unconsciously displaces anger from the therapist to someone else, and so forth (pers. com. B. K. Ramanujam). The Indian therapist becomes highly sensitive to these indirect expressions of anger.

Another aspect of transference relates to termination. It is generally expected in Western psychoanalytic circles that through the resolution of the transference by the termination of analysis, the patient will become independent of the analyst, and will have little to do with the latter. In India, on the other hand, B. K. Ramanujam (1980a) writes that with the profound cultural emphasis on idealizations of and identifications with respected persons, at the conclusion of therapy the analyst still frequently remains an idealized hierarchical figure to be closely identified with, in a relationship like other important hierarchical relationships where respect predominates over deference. It is not that this process of postanalytic idealization is entirely absent in American analytic relationships, but there it seems to go on much more covertly because of the American emphasis on relative autonomous and egalitarian relationships as the ideal.

I have taken some time here to delineate carefully the adaptation of psychoanalysis, a Western import, within the Indian milieu. By delving into the essential nature of the goals of psychoanalysis, and of the psychoanalytic relationship and process, it should be clearer how psychoanalysis is actually adopted and adapted within a completely different social and cultural setting from the one in which it originated. The Indian psychoanalytic therapist naturally takes into account these social and cultural influences. Simultaneously, by making explicit various facets of the psychoanalytic relationship and the psychoanalytic process in India, a Western analyst can throw further light on the psychosocial dimensions of hierarchical relationships and of intrapsychic functioning within these relationships. I strongly suspect that such an analysis of the psychoanalytic relationship and process in America would also throw light on the psychosocial dimensions of American-style individualism with its congruent intrapsychic makeup. This, however, would necessitate a cross-civilizational experience.

Psychoanalysis in Japan

George DeVos (1980) in an "Afterword" in David Reynold's book, *The Quiet Therapies*, raises some fundamental issues as to why psychoanalysis has not become as popular in Japan as it has in the West, concluding that psychoanalysis is emotionally unsuitable for the Japanese. His arguments are remarkably similar to those of major Indian psychiatrists I have cited earlier (Neki 1975; Surya and Jayaram 1964), who also view psychoanalysis as wholly inappropriate for Indians. DeVos's basic point is that psychoanalysis is intrinsically connected with Western individualism and is profoundly oriented toward the autonomy of the individual, who creates meaning in his or her own life and becomes free from the family. This contrasts and conflicts fundamentally with basic Japanese cultural values and social patterns, in which persons remain deeply embedded throughout life within family and group relationships, parental figures are greatly respected, and major and even minor life decisions are made through the guidance of the hierarchical superior. If Japanese should become aware of their intense negative feelings toward their mothers or other family members, as they would in psychoanalysis, DeVos argues, this would seriously disrupt family cohesion and become highly destructive. DeVos further intimates that cognitive and linguistic processes would also interfere with psychoanalysis in Japan, since Japanese are not oriented toward the analytic discursive reasoning and talk of Westerners. Rather, they express themselves in visual-spatial metaphorical language, and have a cultural ideal toward more verbal restraint than self-expression and the free association of psychoanalysis.

Is DeVos correct that psychoanalysis is unsuitable for Japan? Or is it more accurate to say that psychoanalysis is slowly growing and expanding in Japan, as it is in India, as a Western therapeutic paradigm that can be profoundly adapted, transformed, and incorporated within Japanese society? And as it becomes harmonious with Japanese social, cultural, and psychological patterns, psychoanalysis simultaneously introduces a greater degree of individualization.

In Japan, as in India, psychoanalysis is clearly a Western import ushering in heterogenetic change.[8] But psychoanalysis can also be seen as a case study of the Japanese assimilation of a Western sociocultural product and process. To see how psychoanalysis has become assimilated in Japan, I shall first briefly delineate Japanese hierarchical group structures to provide a framework for comprehending the development of psychoanalysis and its current institutionalization in Japan. I shall focus on the psychosocial dimensions of family and group hierarchical relationships so as to understand the nature of the psychoanalytic relationship in Japan, and culturally related resistances.

Japanese society is oriented around specific group or institutional units—household, corporation, bureaucracy, business, educational or social institution, or village—rather than around occupational skills. These groups have very firm, clear-cut boundaries and are structured within each unit in a well-defined, pyramidal vertical hierarchy (Nakane 1970). Japanese usually become deeply emotionally involved and loyal to one group only, and make long-term commitments to the purposes and unity of the group. For women it is most often the family or occupational household; for

[8] The concept of heterogenetic change was formulated by the social anthropologist Robert Redfield to denote social change in a civilization that is introduced by influences from outside rather than being generated from within (Singer 1972, 609).

rural persons, it has traditionally been the village or hamlet;[9] for students it is the class at school or in college, and a specific activity subgroup from the class; and for urban men, a work group, which might include in certain cases a household involved in a particular occupation or business. Apart from family and friends, group involvement becomes all-consuming and there is little opportunity or urge for middle-class men to form outside relationships.[10] Even after-hour socializing is usually with associates from work, which reinforces group cohesion. This is in contrast to Indians, who although also emotionally enmeshed in the extended family, community (caste), and other groups, are nevertheless far freer to become involved with others outside the family and community, bringing them into the extended family.

Japanese are profoundly identified with their group and its reputation. Middle-class men's sense of esteem is far more involved with the particular school, college, and work group (corporation, bureaucracy, profession, or business) they are associated with than in the amount of money they earn. The group they are in reflects first on the esteem of their own mothers and family—something of considerable importance to a Japanese son—and then on their wives.[11] Like Indian marriages, Japanese ones are not simply between individuals but also between families, so that the importance of an alliance with a family of suitable background and reputation is still central to a husband's and wife's esteem.

Within a particular work group, Japanese men—and women too if they are present—are intensely emotionally enmeshed with the group as a whole and with each other in a series of vertical hierarchical relationships based primarily on seniority in the group rather than age or accomplishment. There are also horizontal relationships with those who have entered the group at approximately the same time. The group assumes a pyramidal form with only one person at the very top of the hierarchy; everyone has a distinct position (*za*) within this hierarchy by seniority, the position gradually changing with increased seniority. A variety of tasks, however, may be performed according to the overall needs of the group. The flexibility of assuming different tasks regardless of one's position in the group is a distinctive hallmark of Japanese group

[9] In Japanese society today, rural persons frequently have considerable contact in urban areas, one or more family members commuting to work, so that the traditional village group is not nearly as circumscribed as previously.

[10] In the lower middle-class artisan and subcontracting groups, men are frequently involved in voluntary community service groups (Wagatsuma and Devos 1984, 28–29).

[11] Wives of salaried men in a corporation, for instance, will relate to each other hierarchically in terms of their husband's position.

functioning, as is the decision-making process wherein the group gradually comes to a consensus under the guidance of its leader (*nemawashii*).

Integral to the hierarchical relationships within the group are basic familial values of a strong emotional interdependence between senior and junior, and unquestioning loyalty, compliance, and dependence by the junior with full expectations for nurturance, protection, and responsibility by the senior. The latter also carefully consults his subordinates on a number of decisions, and may take a somewhat retiring stance to let his subordinates participate more fully. No step is taken by anyone without the approval of the immediate hierarchical superior, who in turn looks to his senior for guidance; the subordinate may also look to another superior as a mentor or benefactor. Even more than Indians, Japanese have brought the full range of familial mutual reciprocities, loyalties, and obligations to the work group (Hsu 1985, 41–44; DeVos 1985, 157–158)—which is part of the genius of successful Japanese group functioning.

This hierarchy by seniority is frequently in a dialectic with a subtle hierarchy by quality, in which the leader of the group will gradually get the sanction and cooperation of his followers to promote someone of unusual abilities to do more responsible tasks than he or she would ordinarily do according to seniority and position. But even here, the junior person thus promoted must observe the proper respect to those senior to him—regardless of who they are—who occupy a superior position in the group. Or conversely, a person more senior but lacking the requisite abilities will be honored for his position but be given less responsible tasks. And in some cases, a powerful figure who is not most senior may actually be running the group indirectly (pers. com. Moses Burg). Thus, the kind of influence a person has in the group will depend not only on position but on personal attributes that can expand or contract the nature of that position.

Within any given institution—whether corporation, bureaucracy, university, or profession—there is usually a variety of these pyramidal hierarchies or factions. Although there is extremely close group feeling within a particular faction, the relationship between factions is frequently one of competition if not conflict, even within the same company or institution.

Institutionally, Japanese psychoanalysis revolves around hierarchical, closely bonded groups led by important professors of psychiatry and psychology who are psychoanalytically trained. They, in turn, train members who come through their departments, or other professionals who come to them for training and become part of their group. The power and influence of these leaders is reflected in the size and significance of the following they have built up. Psychoanalysis in Japan has thus become completely assimilated to Japanese hierarchical social structure in contrast to Western and even Indian institutionalization, where there are specific working psychoanalytic societies that train new members. In Japan, there is no psychoanalytic training institute that cuts across these well-defined factions with their particular leaders. One remains part of a group throughout life, loyal to and dependent on the professor, who assumes responsibility in guiding the junior member to different positions in the field. No job can be switched or psychoanalytic training abroad pursued without the express approval and support of the leader or mentor. In turn, junior members in their hospital, clinic, or university position begin to build up a following, who in turn are dependent on them—the size and quality of the following depending on the personal attributes of this member.

These pyramidal hierarchies are generally passed down in a pattern similar to that of the traditional *ie* family structure—the main house and its branches—which is more or less institutionalized in Japanese work groups. It is remarkably easy to trace the different group hierarchies or factions within psychoanalysis in Japan, since there is such a clear-cut mentor-disciple continuity. I could easily see this process at work in the Hiroshima group of psychoanalytic therapists with whom I was associated for a month. This group of thirty to forty persons was under the leadership of Dr. Mikihachiro Tatara, then professor of clinical psychology in the graduate school of Hiroshima University. The others consisted of therapists with positions in universities, hospitals, and clinics in various cities around the Inland Sea, and of Dr. Tatara's present and past graduate students. Two of the more experienced therapists had their own followers.

The historical development of psychoanalysis in Japan must be set against the background of German psychiatry previously ensconced in Japan, with its emphasis on diagnosis and pharmacology rather than psychotherapy; and indigenous mental health healers, as well as specifically Japanese forms of psychotherapy, such as Morita Therapy (Reynolds 1976) developed by Professor Morita, a psychiatrist, and Naikan Therapy with its strong roots in Buddhism (Reynolds 1983). Psychoanalysis is a major departure from both Germanic psychiatry and indigenous Japanese ways of dealing with emotional problems and symptoms.

The main hierarchical progression started with Professor Marui of

Tohoku University in Sendai, who initiated a course in psychoanalytic psychiatry in 1918.[12] Of the students he then trained in Japan, the best known ones are Drs. M. Yamamura and H. Kosawa. The former is now head of psychiatry at Gifu University. The latter was trained in Vienna in the early 1930s and opened a psychoanalytic clinic in Tokyo; he became the dean of Japanese psychoanalysis and the first president of the Japanese Branch of the International Psychoanalytic Association (I.P.A.) when it was officially formed in 1954; even now, though he is deceased, he is accorded considerable deference in Japanese psychoanalysis. Dr. Kosawa trained a number of students, the most important and well-known ones being Drs. Takeo Doi, Masahisa Nishizono, Keigo Okonogi, and Shigeharu Maeda.[13] These four students of Dr. Kosawa, plus Dr. Yamamura, are currently the five official training analysts of the Japanese Branch of the I.P.A. To become a member of this branch, it is considered essential to train with one of these analysts, regardless of one's training abroad, and to become a member of his group.

However, the complexion of psychoanalysis in Japan is considerably more complicated than this direct line of descent from Professor Marui to Dr. Kosawa to their disciples, the current training analysts with their own groups. The other factions and their interrelationships in Japan reflect the political shape of psychoanalysis in the West, particularly in the United States—the Japanese being tremendously influenced since the Occupation by American ideas and institutions. In the United States two important groups of psychoanalysts have thus far been excluded from the I.P.A. by the American Psychoanalytic Association: psychoanalysts of neo-Freudian training and persuasion, who may be either psychiatrists or psychologists; and psychoanalysts who come from a variety of

[12] In the 1920s he went to Johns Hopkins University in Baltimore for five years training in psychiatry, becoming further exposed to psychoanalysis.

[13] Dr. Takeo Doi was originally at Tokyo University and then at International Christian University and St. Luke's International Hospital; currently, he is director of the National Institute of Mental Health. He was trained at the Menninger Foundation in the 1950s and later at the San Francisco Psychoanalytic Institute. Dr. Nishizono is dean of the Medical School and head of the department of psychiatry at Fukuoka University in Kyushu, and is considered a powerful and influential head of an important group of psychoanalytic psychiatrists. He has published a couple of papers in English (1969, 1980). Dr. Okonogi, a psychiatrist at Keio University in Tokyo, is an influential leader of another important group of psychiatrists and has done more than any other analyst in explaining psychoanalysis to the public. He also has published a few papers in English (1978a, 1978b, 1979). Dr. Maeda is a psychiatrist at Kyushu University in Fukuoka, and seems to be affiliated with Dr. Nishizono. I unfortunately know little about his following or work.

disciplines and do not have a medical degree, the vast majority of whom are Freudian in orientation.

For example, a Japanese psychologist, Dr. Ohtsuki, also went to Vienna for psychoanalytic training in the 1930s, and returned to form an interdisciplinary group of psychoanalytic therapists, including many schoolteachers. Although this group is no longer functioning, one of its important members, Professor Moses Burg, an American psychologist who stayed on after the Occupation, has his own group of psychoanalytic therapists who work mainly with schizophrenic patients at various mental hospitals.[14] Because of their nonmedical status as well as Burg's neo-Freudian training, neither Dr. Ohtsuki nor Professor Burg, not to mention any of their students, has been admitted to the Japanese Branch of the I.P.A.

Three other major psychoanalytic groups have been started by Japanese psychiatrists and psychologists who went to the United States after World War II for psychoanalytic training; because of a neo-Freudian or eclectic orientation, they and their students have also been excluded from the Japanese Branch of the I.P.A. The earliest was Dr. Akihisa Kondo (1975), a highly respected clinician of the same age and seniority as the main training analysts of the Japanese Branch of the I.P.A., who introduced Zen Buddhism to Karen Horney and Erich Fromm.[15] Dr. Mikihachiro Tatara (1974, 1982) also did not have a close relationship with the Freudian training analysts because of his neo-Freudian background until he spent two years in Freudian training at the Austen Riggs Foundation. The third, Dr. Kenzo Sorai, trained at the Postgraduate Center for Mental Health in New York City, and then started the Sanno Institute in Tokyo with a broad eclectic psychoanalytic orientation that includes Jungian perspectives.

In more recent years, in the 1970s and 1980s, younger persons have gone abroad to the United States and England for training in psychoanalysis and have generally joined one or another of the groups I have cited above. The particular group they join depends on whether their

[14]Professor Burg (1960, 1969, 1980) is professor of clinical psychology at Toyo University and is director of the Orient-Occident Mental Health Research Center there. This center was started by Dr. Harold Kelman of the Karen Horney Institute, with whom Burg had further psychoanalytic training.

[15]Dr. Kondo trained in the late 1940s and early 1950s at the Karen Horney Institute in New York City. He introduced Erich Fromm to D. T. Suzuki, a renowned teacher of Zen; the latter two collaborated on a book about psychoanalysis and Zen Buddhism (Fromm and Suzuki 1970).

psychoanalytic orientation is neo-Freudian or Freudian. There are now American-trained psychoanalytic therapists in the groups of Drs. Nishizono, Okonogi, and Tatara, as well as two British-trained ones in Dr. Okonogi's group. This gives these groups far more opportunity for direct communication in English with other psychoanalysts from the I.P.A. and the West, as well as the ability to report new developments in psychoanalysis. Four Japanese have gone abroad for psychoanalytic training and have remained abroad.[16]

There are currently two psychoanalytic societies in Japan. One is the Japanese Branch of the I.P.A., with some twenty-four members. The other is the Japanese Psychoanalytic Association, which now has over a thousand members, 80 percent of them psychiatrists, with others coming from a variety of disciplines. All of these latter are interested in psychoanalysis, but only a limited number have actual psychoanalytic training. Notably absent from both associations are such senior psychoanalysts as Dr. Kondo and Professor Burg.

It is striking that unlike Indian psychoanalysts, the Japanese have from the very beginning openly asserted the uniqueness of the Japanese psyche and tried to formulate relevant theories that depart significantly from Western psychoanalysis. Although Girindrasekhar Bose (1966), the father of Indian psychoanalysis, developed his own unique theory of repression and psychological functioning, like Freud and other Western analysts he posited it as universal, not as uniquely Indian. Japanese psychoanalysts, on the other hand, not being burdened by a colonial legacy with its denigration of indigenous culture, have found it much easier to assert their Japaneseness. Thus, Dr. Kosawa dismissed the Oedipus complex as not central to the Japanese psyche, and substituted the Ajase complex, taken from a Buddhist myth. Here the focus is not so much on the son-mother-father triangle, as in the Oedipus myth, but rather on the son-mother dyad, wherein the son rages over feelings of loss of his symbiotic tie with the mother, but later repents after realizing her great sacrifices for him. This is obviously of another order not only from

[16] The two who are fully certified psychoanalysts are Dr. Yasuhiko Taketomo (1982, 1983, 1984, 1985), who is equivalent to the senior training analysts in Japan, and is a member of the Association for Psychoanalytic Medicine at Columbia University and clinical associate professor of psychiatry at Albert Einstein Medical Center in New York City; and Mrs. Nobuko Meaders (1983), who is now a supervising psychoanalyst at the Postgraduate Center for Mental Health, also in New York City. The other two are Dr. Tetsuro Takahashi of the Menninger Foundation, and Dr. Nakakuki, who started training at the Colorado Psychoanalytic Institute.

the Oedipus complex, but also from the much more recent work on separation-individuation.[17]

Even more seminal in focusing on the uniqueness of the Japanese psyche is Takeo Doi's (1973) work on *amae*. Doi discards the whole Freudian theoretical framework as unworkable for understanding the Japanese psyche, and uses instead Japanese terms for a depth psychological exposition of Japanese dependency relationships. These he views as existing only in a very minor key in Western relationships, so that there is almost no Western vocabulary to describe them. As in Dr. Kosawa's work, there is an affirmation of Japanese values, patterns of relationship, and inner psychological makeup, with no sense of inferiority vis-à-vis the West. Other papers by Drs. Kondo, Nishizono, Okonogi,

[17] The Ajase myth is as follows: In the time of Buddha, there lived a king named Binbashara. His wife, Idaike, fearing the loss of her husband's love as her beauty faded, longed to have a son with which to secure the king's love for as long as she lived. Hearing of her intense wish, a sage told her that within three years a hermit living on a mountain would die a natural death and start his life afresh to become her son. However, the queen, who so deeply feared the loss of her husband's love, chose to kill the hermit before the three years had passed. She wanted to have her son as soon as possible. Soon, as the sage had said, she conceived and gave birth to a boy, Ajase. During her pregnancy, however, she had been beset with fears of being cursed by the hermit she had killed and at one time had even tried to induce a miscarriage.

Ajase grew up spending a happy youth with his parents' love centered upon him, knowing nothing of the secret of his conception. But one day after he had reached manhood, he was approached by Daibadatta, one of Buddha's enemies, who revealed to Ajase the secret of his birth. At first Ajase reacted against his father, feeling sympathy for his mother's agony and anger against his father who had so distressed his mother. He helped unseat his father and then had him imprisoned.

Ajase soon learned that his mother was feeding his imprisoned father honey which she had first rubbed onto her body. This honey saved his father from starvation. Ajase then became so angry with his mother that he tried to kill her with his sword, blaming her for the attempt to save his father, who was his enemy. He was dissuaded from slaying her by a minister who counseled that although there were some sons who tried to kill their father, there were none who attempted to kill their mother. At that moment, Ajase was attacked by severe guilt feelings and became afflicted by a terrible illness called *ruchu*—a severe skin disease charaterized by so offensive an odor that no one dared approach him. Only his mother stood by and cared for him.

Thanks to his mother's compassionate nursing, Ajase recovered from the illness and was forgiven by the mother he had intended to murder. As a result, he was awakened to a real love for his mother, discarding his grudge against her and realizing her great sacrifices for him. His mother, for her part, was able to develop a more natural maternal affection for her son beyond her original self-centered concerns for herself and attachment to him. (Much of this version of the Ajase myth can be found in Okonogi 1978b.) This depiction of the Ajase complex as the prototype of the early Japanese mother-child relationship is quite different from the description of this relationship in American society (Mahler et al. 1975).

Taketomo and Tatara all attempt to explicate Japanese psychological makeup as being significantly different from Western, but not in the least inferior. Doi has been the most influential on a number of social scientists and Japan specialists; Kondo's views have been incorporated in the recent work of Reynolds (1983).

Although solidly established in Japan, psychoanalysis remains a small but growing movement, still set against a predominant Germanic psychiatry and academic-behavior psychology on the one hand, and indigenous folkhealers and psychotherapies on the other. One can speculate both on the reasons why psychoanalysis has been accepted and on its still quite limited scope. In Japan, as in India, social and cultural communities have simply not come apart to anywhere near the extent they have in America (Rieff 1968) and France (Turkle 1978). Thus, a psychoanalytic world view that guides the person in a world of crumbling cultural and social supports is not at this point very appropriate to the Japanese.

From an historical perspective, it is evident that Japan's radical effort to modernize after the Meiji Restoration in 1868, to keep the Western powers from taking over, was accomplished through assimilating Western institutions and technology but continuing Japanese hierarchical social patterns and their associated values within these new institutional forms. It is only with the American Occupation, after the shattering defeat of World War II, that more radical changes occurred, influenced by a value system and its institutional implementation that departs at times drastically from indigenous Japanese social and cultural patterns. From the effects of the Occupation and the current influences of the media, there are two major factors that have greatly enhanced the growth of psychoanalysis in Japan.

The first is the Western ideal of individualism in terms of increased personal autonomy, independence, and individualized choices in a variety of situations, together with an ideology of equality that has been partially but increasingly incorporated by the younger generations. This is radically different from the traditional emotional enmeshment in family and group, and on the level of ideals creates a generation gap. Psychoanalysis is clearly congruent with this new thrust toward individualization.

The second factor involves a greater emphasis on the values of rationality and self-reflection in social situations. These values are manifested in psychoanalysis in its greater dependence on rational, interpretive explanations for psychological behavior than is present in indigenous psy-

80

chotherapies such as Morita and Naikan, which rely on more intuitive and meditative means, respectively (pers. com. Akihisa Kondo). With the introduction of foreign psychological ideals and paradigms of personal functioning into Japan, psychoanalysis is becoming established as a new therapeutic mode.

Economics significantly influence the practice of psychoanalysis in Japan. National Health Insurance pays a very small amount for psychoanalytic sessions, so that it is generally not feasible for the usual psychiatrist, or even psychologist, to live by earnings from a private practice. Psychiatrists who can see innumerable patients for a very short period in a hospital, prescribing and administering various drugs, make far more money there than they could in private practice. Another contributing factor is the economic homogeneity in Japanese society, where 90 percent of the people consider themselves to be middle-class and to be generally unable to afford to see a psychoanalytic therapist more than once a week. Many of these middle-class patients come to university psychotherapy clinics; it is only a much smaller upper-middle class that can come more frequently to an analyst in private practice.

The Psychoanalytic Relationship in Japan

As in my clinical psychoanalytic research in India, it gradually struck me that to understand the nature of the psychoanalytic relationship in Japan, the kinds of expectations patients bring to therapy, and crucial resistances that are usually present, one must take into account the major psychosocial dimensions of family and group hierarchical relationships (see Chapter Seven). As these psychosocial dimensions profoundly differ from those of Western individualism, so do various facets of psychoanalysis in Japan.

In the qualitative mode of hierarchical relationships, Japanese patient and therapist form a hierarchical "we" relationship with vaguely defined outer ego boundaries, especially on the patient's part. This contrasts with the individualistic "I" and "you" relationship of the Western egalitarian psychoanalytic relationship, where patient and therapist have rather well-defined, relatively self-contained outer ego boundaries. Japanese analysts report an unspoken expectation on the patient's part for a lifelong, warmly nurturing relationship, in which the therapist will completely take over and take care of the patient and solve all of his or her problems and symptoms. This can evoke a reciprocating tendency in the therapist to do this, as it is a normal part of hierarchical relationships, with their lifelong commitments between mentor and disciple. The patient comes to the therapist not for self-exploration to deal with his or her problems, as in American society where one is far more on one's own, but rather for what the relationship itself can provide (Tatara 1982). If the therapist does take over completely, without gradually delving into the hidden aspects of a patient's problems, then a stalemate usually occurs and the patient will leave (pers. com. Keigo Okonogi).

The strong feelings of dependency (*amae*) that are rarely expressed verbally are part of a highly subtle emotional exchange and flow in Japanese hierarchical relationships whereby patients or juniors, by their dependence on and idealization of the therapist or senior, gratify the latter's own esteem in exchange for being gratified in their dependency needs (*amayakasu*). In Japanese hierarchical intimacy relationships, as in Indian ones, dependence on the other subtly enhances the latter's feelings of esteem by according him or her a superior position as the one who can gratify and guide, and helps to create a relationship of intimacy between subordinate and superior.

Another facet of the qualitative mode of hierarchical relationships is the greatly heightened concerned sensitivity (*omoiyari*) to the other's feelings, moods, and needs (pers. com. Y. Taketomo). Japanese patients expect the hierarchical superior, the therapist, to sense and know their needs and feelings—in fact their whole inner being—with only a minimum of overt verbal communication or even nonverbal cues, for Japanese are extremely restrained in facial and hand gestures. In the long-term relationships of Japanese family and group life, it is assumed that the superior, in the paradigm of the mother, will always be sensitive and nurturing to the subordinate. It is equally assumed that the subordinate will sense the superior's wishes and expectations, so that the therapist expects the patient to pick up various attitudes and even understandings with only a minimum of verbal communication. Anything really important is rarely to be communicated verbally in Japanese relationships.[18] I was startled in the supervision of five cases to see clearly therapeutic progress that could be easily understood psychodynamically, even though there was a minimum of interpretation, investigation, or even empathic reflections on the therapists' parts (Roland 1983). This strong empathic sensing obviously begins in childhood. Japanese children are raised by their mothers to be extremely sensitive and concerned with others' feel-

---

[18] When I questioned a well-known Japanese scientist what led to his vocational choice, he related that when he was around sixteen, his father left out a book on great scientists of the world for him to read. He then assumed that his father expected him to become a scientist. There was no other communication on the subject.

ings and needs rather than with their own, which should never be expressed directly, but also to expect others, especially a hierarchical superior, to be highly sensitive to themselves. Often a person may only become aware of what he or she wants when the superior has incorrectly sensed and responded to it (pers. com. Yoshiko Idei). Needless to say, considerable anger may be generated when the hierarchical superior—mother or father or group leader or mentor—lacks sufficient empathic sensitivity, responsiveness, or responsibility.

I have so far emphasized diffuse outer ego boundaries, dependence and interdependence, and empathic sensitivity in hierarchical relationships as these aspects are manifested in the analytic relationship. There is still another crucial facet of the qualitative mode that enters into the psychoanalytic relationship, and particularly in the manifestation and analysis of resistances. In the intense emotional enmeshment of Japanese family and group hierarchical relationships, individuality is largely maintained by keeping a highly private self (pers. com. Akihisa Kondo). Patients feel tremendous vulnerability in a situation where their inner world may be revealed. Japanese patients only feel comfortable in a very small room, or sitting close to the therapist in a larger room, as symbolic of the need for emotional enmeshment. In both cases, patients usually try to have something between themselves and the therapist (such as a small table or footstool) as a symbolic barrier to protect their inner self from the therapist's intrusion (pers. com. Mikihachiro Tatara). This private self with its various feelings, thoughts, and ambivalences is kept quite secret, and is communicated only by indirection and innuendo verbally and by some very subtle nonverbal gestures. As patients sense that the therapist is sufficiently empathic to pick up these innuendos and clues, they will reveal somewhat more of their inner world; otherwise, whole areas will be kept secret in a way that I have not experienced with any American patients—though I have had similar experiences with my Indian ones.

I have found in both Japanese and Indians that a highly private self with a specially set inner ego boundary is intrinsic to functioning in strongly emotionally enmeshed family and group hierarchical relationships. But in the Japanese—whose outer ego boundaries seem to be more diffuse in their family and group hierarchical relationships, and whose innermost ego boundaries are less open to being aware of their own wishes, feelings, and fantasies than are those of Indians—the private self is kept even more secret and communicated more indirectly. Thus Japanese analysts must be extremely careful not to be too intrusive into this private self through investigation or interpretation. Otherwise they will

83

severely disrupt the warmly nurturing analytic "we" relationship, resulting in therapeutic failure. Japanese analysts who ask questions are considered stupid at best—they should sense the patient's inner world without asking—or insulting at worst for being so intrusive (pers. com. Mikihachiro Tatara).

On the other hand, Japanese therapists have also referred to many of their patients as being like onions: when you peel all the layers off, you get down to nothing (pers. com. Mikihachiro Tatara and Mishiko Fukazawa). What they mean is that many patients are brought up to be closely in touch with others' feelings, needs, and moods while being completely out of touch with their own. Simply to ask what they are feeling usually elicits no response. These therapists find it necessary to go into great detail over what happened in a particular relationship and situation to try to get at any inner experience of the patient. In this sense, therapy becomes a kind of education for the patient, to first begin to become aware of himself or herself and not adhere so strongly to what is essentially a false self. Needless to say, the existing inner psychological structure can comprise a major resistance to psychoanalytic therapy, as well as being the subject of considerable therapeutic work (see the case of Mrs. K, Chapter Five).

In addition to other resistances idiosyncratic to patients and their particular psychobiographies, there are two further social and cultural factors that significantly contribute to resistances in psychoanalytic therapy in Japan, one intrinsically related to hierarchical relationships, the other to specific Japanese cultural ideals and child rearing. In structural hierarchical relationships where reciprocal responsibilities and obligations of senior and junior are carefully observed, any direct expression of anger, particularly by the junior, is strictly forbidden, the prohibition being deeply internalized into the superego. Clinical psychoanalytic work in both Japan and India confirms the enormous anxiety attendant on any direct assertion of anger toward the hierarchical superior. Anger in the subordinate may thus be consciously contained, or unconsciously displaced toward those lower in the hierarchy or toward another group or faction; or it may be turned against oneself in the form of frequent somatic symptoms, temporary depressions, or failures in life. More particularly among the Japanese, strict superego prohibitions against anger or even grandiosity may be unconsciously projected onto others. In the analytic situation, the patient expects the analyst to be displeased with him. The patient then counters this possible interruption in their nurturing relationship by a typical social maneuver for gaining acceptance by a superior: being extremely apologetic and blaming oneself, thereby short-circuiting any investigation by the therapist (pers. com. Mikihachiro Tatara). In social situations, this superego projection can be a major factor in the not infrequent symptom of extreme social shyness and withdrawal or anthrophobia (Kitayama 1981).

In the psychoanalytic situation, the therapist must carefully assess whether anger at others or sudden failures may be unconscious deflections from ambivalences that cannot be directly expressed to the therapist. Or the patient may show anger toward the analyst by leaving and seeing a therapist from another group or, more frequently, a folk healer.[19] There is no question that anxiety over the expression—or at times even the awareness of—anger and ambivalences toward the superior is a major facet of the unconscious superego in Japanese, as it is in Indians, and completely belies the point of view (Kakar 1978, 135–137; Muensterberger 1969) that the superego is not internalized but instead relies on the constant response of others in these societies.

The other cultural factor related to resistances involves the strong Japanese ideal of a very high level of skill, competence, and performance in everyone in both human relationships and tasks, and for achievement and success in men. Japanese mothers in particular inculcate expectations for high levels of performance (DeVos 1973). As a result, Japanese have internalized structures of strongly idealized self-images and very high ego-ideals in the areas of work, with constant tension in men between their inner idealized self-images and their actual position and influence in the group. The ego-ideal is fueled in good part by the internalization of maternal expectations, with deep feelings of gratitude and obligation to a mother who has been overwhelmingly devoted and sacrificing to her children, and with profound feelings of guilt and shame when not fulfilling maternal values. The mother in turn derives much of her own sense of esteem from her children's performance and success. These idealized self-images are further enhanced or become conflictual through identification with parental idealized self-images—particularly images and expectations of a reticent father (Taketomo 1982), or each parent's idealization or denigration of the other (pers. com. Mikihachiro Tatara). One's inner narcissistic balance thus depends a great deal on the nature of one's inner idealized self-images and how they are implemented or not in life performance and position. In subtle ways, there is a considerable mirroring in family and group relationships to maintain

---

[19] The point that no therapist from the same group would take on such a patient because of the insult to the initial therapist emerged during a discussion in the Hiroshima group. In American psychoanalytic circles, if a patient leaves a therapist the patient may well see another therapist from the same institute.

inner feelings of high esteem associated with these strong self-idealizations: each expects the other to reflect positively on oneself, while maintaining a position of modesty and humility (Miyamoto 1983).[20]

Just the fact of coming for psychoanalytic therapy is an admission of failure and a blow to one's self-idealizations, and immediately arouses resistance in many patients. Any questioning or interpretation by the therapist is usually experienced by the patient as a kind of criticism, and therefore interferes with the necessary nurturing atmosphere of the psychoanalytic relationship in Japan. In turn, Japanese psychoanalysts are also extremely vulnerable to criticism, and thus may sometimes not risk investigating or interpreting if they sense the patient will be critical of them.

Japanese psychoanalysts use a variety of methods to carry on the analytic process in the context of these culturally related resistances. I am most familiar with the therapeutic approaches to resistance-analysis of Dr. Tatara and his Hiroshima group of psychoanalytic therapists, as I worked most closely with them. They use several tactics to minimize their patients' vulnerability to intrusion and criticism, some not unfamiliar to a Western psychoanalyst. One approach is to assume the subordinate or inferior position with the patient when questioning or interpreting, conveying an attitude of ingenuousness or even naiveté. Or the exact opposite may sometimes be effective: taking the superior hierarchical position of the person who knows exactly what he is doing, so the patient feels a greater sense of esteem by being associated with a powerful, knowledgeable superior. Humor is still another approach, as is verbally reflecting or mirroring what the therapist senses the patient is feeling or thinking, enabling the latter to confirm or correct the therapist without feeling threatened.

At times a more direct approach is called for, and it is in this area of the occasional need for confronting a patient on a resistance that Japanese psychoanalysts seem to experience the most difficulty. Japanese psychoanalysts have confirmed their own difficulties in working with certain American patients who require a much more confrontive approach (pers. com. Akihisa Kondo and Mikihachiro Tatara). In general, however, psychoanalytic therapy in Japan works to a much greater extent by therapist and patient sensing each other's mind with a minimum of overt verbal or nonverbal communication. For example, nuances in verbal communication may be picked up in the form of subtly skewed

---

[20] Status anxiety can be intense in Japan. However, to balance these strivings for success, there are other cultural values for self-cultivation that transcend these strivings, and in fact view them somewhat pejoratively (pers. com. Yasuhiko Taketomo).

expressions in the respect language in various hierarchical relationships, these skewed expressions implying underlying unconscious conflicts (pers. com. Mikihachiro Tatara).

There is a still further dimension to the nature of the therapeutic relationship in Japan. In recent decades, important concepts of the therapeutic relationship have been introduced by psychoanalysts such as Winnicott (1965), Bion (1977), and Kohut (1971), such as the holding environment, the container, and the selfobject, respectively—all to convey certain therapeutic aspects of the analytic relationship as well as, at times, transference. My impression of the Japanese psychoanalytic relationship is that it is, in a sense, "free parking," to borrow an image from the game of Monopoly. In this game, as the players build houses and hotels on different properties, it is often a great relief to land on "free parking," where you will be beholden for the moment to no one. In Japanese family and group hierarchical relationships, where the person is intricately emotionally enmeshed with others, where the etiquette of hierarchical rank and obligation is meticulously observed (*giri*), and where one must be constantly sensitive to others' needs and feelings for the well-being of the group, I sense that Japanese patients can breathe a great sigh of relief to be able to explore themselves in the presence of an empathic, understanding therapist. Although all kinds of resistances and transferences emerge in psychoanalytic therapy, there is still the reality factor that the therapy relationship is a time out or free parking from strictly observed social etiquette in one's relationships.

We can now reconsider more directly DeVos's major arguments on the unsuitability of psychoanalysis for the Japanese. Psychoanalysis's emphasis in Western societies on individual autonomy and freedom from the family is not intrinsic to it. In Japan as well as in India, since the essentials of psychoanalytic therapy are to resolve inner emotional conflicts and/or deficits from the past—a kind of rearranging and reconstruction of the internal furniture—a person can be enabled through analysis to function much better within the closely emotionally enmeshed family and group hierarchical relationships.

What DeVos overlooks is that Japanese, like Indians, maintain a highly private self even when closely interconnected with others in the family and/or group; that the social self geared toward hierarchical intimacy relationships does not in the least completely define the person. When this private self is greatly conflicted from early familial relationships, the person becomes vulnerable to the inevitable frustrations, disappointed expectations, and demanding attitudes of a superior. On the other hand, when the person resolves his or her inner conflicts and developmental deficits through the therapy relationship, he or she can function with much greater equanimity in these hierarchical relationships. Intense anger toward family members and parents may indeed surface within the psychoanalytic relationship, as it did in the case of Mrs. K (Chapter Five); but this does not mean that the person is not able to contain this anger within the private self so that it does not spill over into the familial relationships.

As to DeVos's point that Japanese verbal constraint is unsuitable for psychoanalysis, both therapists and patients are able to communicate with a minimum of verbalization. Sensing is constantly being done in the family and group hierarchical relationships, different words, phrases, and gestures being consciously used to be congruent with what one senses to be the nature of the relationship in terms of hierarchical position and degree of intimacy. This socially traditional mode of nonverbal, empathic sensing and communication is simply carried over into the psychoanalytic relationship by both patient and analyst. How is this done? I suspect that it comes from the development of capacities for an extraordinary high degree of empathic sensing of the other in long-term relationships within a society and culture where there are shared cultural meanings that have remained remarkably homogeneous over many centuries. This enables its members to sense easily how another would feel or think in any number of particular situations and relationships. Thus in psychoanalytic sessions in Japan, free associations and interpretations don't always have to be verbalized. Much, much more is communicated by innuendo.

The Familial Self, Individualization, and the Modernization Process

The Indian Experience

As we move from the churning rapids of the Indian encounter with Western values and life styles as fostered and foisted upon India in the British colonial era into the quick-flowing but calmer waters of the Westernization/modernization process, different psychological processes and dynamics dominate the identity struggles described in the last two chapters. These psychological processes revolve around two fundamental issues: to what extent are the configurations of the traditional Indian familial self amenable to adaptation, even contributing to Westernizing/modernizing changes; and to what extent can the Indian self psychologically expand to incorporate a greater degree of individualization and individuation congruent with these changes? Distinctions must be made between the psychological encounter with civilizationally different values and ways of life—especially when these are asserted to be superior to indigenous ones—where identity dynamics prevail and the assimilation of foreign innovations, whether technological, ideological, or institutional. That the line may sometimes be blurred does not negate this differential analysis.

A clear perspective of the psychological processes involved in the modernization process necessitates a closer examination of the prevailing maps of modernization, for the particular modernization models from which we view our psychological data will strongly color our understanding. I shall therefore present the changing models of modernization before mapping out two broad psychological processes involved in modernization. Illustrative case material from India will reemphasize that these two major psychological processes, along with the psychological dynamic of identity, can sometimes occur within the psyche of the same person. That conflicts are potentially inherent in all of these processes goes without saying; but this does not negate the adaptive function of these processes in the expansion of the Indian (and Japanese) selves. Material bearing on the Japanese experience will appear at the end of this chapter.

Perspectives on Modernization

Until very recently Western social scientists have generally viewed traditional Hindu culture and society as being in intrinsic opposition to modernization—reflecting a bias of nineteenth- and early twentieth-century social science theory, which assumed that traditional (non-Western) and modern (Western) societies are essentially opposed types (Singer 1972).[1] Modernization in India has thus been viewed as a problem in transforming traditional institutions, culture, social patterns, and personality into a modern type. A seldom-examined basic assumption is that the Western model of modernization is universal, and that Western social institutions, culture, and personality are both ideal and necessary for modernization (Joshi 1977). Thus, a Western social ethic, nuclear family, and competitive individualism, among other factors, are all assumed to be necessary ingredients for modernization to occur. It follows from this theoretical position that when modernization does occur, it will ultimately secularize Hindu cultural traditions and social institutions, transform the joint family into a nuclear one, caste into class, and the person into a competitive individualist.

The psychological corollary of this viewpoint (from the perspectives of psychoanalytically oriented social scientists and social scientifically oriented psychoanalysts) is that the personality created by collectively organized societies and families is incomplete, underdeveloped, imma-

[1] Most influential of all has been the work of Max Weber (1958), who posited from his textual studies of Hinduism that traditional beliefs and institutions are inherently incompatible with modernity, and would therefore necessarily obstruct progress toward modernization—a position adhered to in the more recent analysis of Gunnar Myrdal (1968).

ture, passive, and dependent (Rudolphs 1976)—in contrast to the Western individual.[2] The implicit assumption generated from this point of view is that the traditional familial self is incapable of incorporating modernizing changes, and must somehow metamorphize itself into a Western-style individualized self to enter the modern era.

A more recent perspective has challenged the basic assumption of an intrinsic opposition of tradition to modernity, and calls for a rethinking of the whole process of social and cultural change in India as the indigenous culture incorporates various foreign innovations (Rudolphs 1967; Singer 1972; Srinivas 1966). In this approach, traditional Indian society is viewed as far more open to change than was originally thought, utilizing foreign contributions while preserving its own essential continuity.[3] Singer (1972) in particular investigated how Indian society and culture modernize and industrialize by traditionalizing various foreign innovations through a variety of adaptive strategies. Similarly, Srinivas (1966), Dumont (1971), and the Rudolphs (1967) have noted that with increased urbanization and industrialization, and with Western democratic political institutions since Independence, the caste system has by no means disintegrated into a Western-style class society. Classes have, certainly, formed, but they do not predominate over caste in the social structure. Rather, large, horizontal caste associations have been formed in the cities to provide assistance for jobs, marriages, loans, and such; and castes have participated in the political process in the guise of caste block voting for greater allocations of resources and higher social status. Even the literate upper castes, who have Westernized their life style more than the middle and lower castes, have usually maintained cultural continuity by simultaneously become Sanskritized to a greater degree than before.[4] I shall later examine through case material to what extent the same process of integration occurs psychologically.

Some of these same assumptions pitting modernity against tradition are also introduced into the study of modernization and the Indian extended family. Since changes in the family and in socialization processes

[2]V. S. Naipaul (1977, 107–108) cites the psychoanalyst Sudhir Kakar as taking this position.

[3]An example of this is technological modernization in the service of traditional values, where modern transportation is used for pilgrimage; modern concert halls using contemporary accoustical equipment play host to a great revival of indigenous cultural performances of music and dance traditionally given in the temple or home; and printing has spread the scriptures.

[4]Sanskritization refers to the upward mobility of castes in attaining greater economic and political means, while simultaneously incorporating social and ritual practices of the upper castes (Srinivas 1966).

have significant effects on the self, it is appropriate to discuss the effects of modernization on the urban upper-caste, middle and upper-class extended families from which my patients came. One Western theoretical lens focuses on industrialization and urbanization as invariably breaking up large, institutional families into nuclear ones. New relationships gain importance: romantic love and conjugal relationships, separate age groups among an emancipated youth, extra-familial ties in relationships that are primarily egalitarian and contractual rather than hierarchical, and a social mobility that overshadows traditional patterns of stability (Ross 1961).

This type of structural analysis does not, however, take into account the basic nature of the Indian extended family, and thus creates a false dichotomy between joint and nuclear households. The Indian family always remains an extended one, which it maintains through strong family ties and the traditional culture and social patterns of the family, whether the household is joint or unitary. The extended family frequently gets together on life-cycle rites, holidays, and vacations; may make mutual decisions on important family matters and sometimes maintains joint ownership of property; and remains the major social circle for the growing child, with neighborhood and school friends tending to be absorbed into the extended family. Thus any change would occur within the extended family, rather than leading in a unilinear progression to some Western-style nuclear family and social pattern; and any analysis of such change would have to take into account variations in major cities as different as Bombay, Bangalore, Madras, Calcutta, Delhi, and Ahmedabad—for which there is relatively little data at present.

Still another perspective on the modernization process relates to the self-conscious choice India has made since Independence between two basic orientations, one represented by Gandhi, the other by Nehru (Srinivas 1977). Although the Gandhian orientation has never been fully spelled out, in general it favors rural development and decentralization; some 80 percent of India's current population of well over 700,000,000 still live in villages, with an amazingly rich complexity of varied cultural and social traditions, but not infrequently in increasingly impoverished conditions. The Gandhian approach is concerned with providing fuller employment and therefore economic betterment for the rural poor through a variety of means, including land reform, the upgrading of agricultural technology; the continued revival of village crafts; better management of agriculture and forest lands and of water supplies; public health measures; and political decentralization that would give far more power to local districts and blocks. Nehru, on the other hand, stressed the need for industrialization, centralization, and the training of large numbers of Indians in modern science and technology, and thus looked to Western models and to a lesser extent to the Soviet Union and Japan.

Although these two orientations are by no means mutually exclusive, India in large part opted for the Nehru model. This is in good part because there has been an important social realignment in India accompanying the enormous growth of politically and economically powerful middle castes and classes, who have attained equality with the uppermost castes and classes (Kothari et al. 1981). These middle and upper castes and the very top layer of the lower castes, multilingual and educated in English, supply the various administrators, specialists, scientists, engineers, and professionals who play the central roles of running the Indian government and bureaucracy and the more modernized sector of Indian society (Srinivas 1977).[5] This group looks to the West for an ideology of modernization, are at times extremely ambivalent toward indigenous culture and institutions, or are frequently deculturated to varying degrees. Most importantly, they are almost completely out of touch with rural, traditional India (Joshi 1977). It is from these groups that all of my patients came, as well as the therapists with whom I worked.

Since the key to employment among the urban middle and upper-middle classes, as elsewhere, is now education, a new structural element of competition is introduced—something originally foreign to the Indian conscience which so stresses accommodation and cooperation. Moreover, in the English-language educational institutions to which many urban Indians now gravitate for a better secular education, the entire intellectual development is divorced from the childhood emotional absorption through familial relationships of the mythological and other aspects of Hindu culture and religion. There frequently occurs a layering in the Indian self wherein indigenous culture is integrated on an earlier emotional level, and Western culture predominates on a later cognitive one.

Relevant to contemporary Indian identity is another result of post-Independence modernization: a polarity and conflict between those who

---

[5] India now ranks tenth in the world in gross national production and third in scientific and technological personnel. There are as many doctors trained in modern (allopathic) medicine per capita in Indian cities as in any city in the West—although almost none are in rural areas. Since so many scientists and professors head west—80 percent of all graduates of the Indian Institutes of Technology by report—Sudhir Kakar (pers. com.) reported that some Indian social scientists have ironically asserted that India provides more aid to Western countries through their college-educated emigrants than the West does to India.

hold to Western ideology, values, and models for modernization and others who wish to defend and preserve traditional Hindu India (Joshi 1977). Often this conflict takes on an urban-rural cast, where villagers are on the more traditional side, and are frequently denigrated by modern educated urbanites (Srinivas 1977). Contributing to this polarity and conflict has been English-language education, which increasingly deculturates the educated urbanites who receive little intellectual content related to Hindu and other aspects of Indian culture.[6] Only in very recent years are there any new formulations for development that take into account unique Indian social and cultural realities—such as the *Agenda for India* (Kothari et al. 1981). It is toward this last orientation to modernization that Ashis so strongly gravitates, and in the past he was able to work under two major benefactors similarly inclined; in the present, he finds himself in an uncomfortable minority position. Thus, the models of modernization to which contemporary Indians now subscribe can become an important element in their identity.

Contextualization

Milton Singer, as cited above, stressed how Indian culture modernizes through traditionalizing various foreign innovations. This is accomplished through a series of adaptive strategies: a typology and enclavement of various foreign elements are first instituted; this is followed by a ritual neutralization of elements of the work sphere that are eventually to be incorporated; simultaneously, there is a change in typology of these innovations from "foreign" to "modern." This is followed by "compartmentalization": Singer hypothesizes that there occurs a culturally cognitive separation of various activities whose physical separation (such as workplace and home) is symbolic of a cultural difference—usually between modern and traditional life styles. Thus, a man at work might dress in Western clothes, disregard intercaste rules of association, especially in eating, and disregard other pollution rules and rituals, while strictly observing all of these codes and dressing traditionally at home, without any conflict. Changes then occur in the indigenous culture to incorporate these new elements through vicarious ritualization and a turning away from ritual to devotional religious observance (*bhakti*) to cope with the exingencies of urban life.[7] The foreign elements are then

[6] This point was incisively and perceptively discussed in a book review, "Search for Roots," of Krishan Sondhi's *Uprooted,* by Kapila Vatsyayan (1979).

[7] Singer (1972) discusses vicarious ritualization as occurring when upper-caste men are

deemed "traditional," being legitimatized once they are seen as traditional and no longer modern. Thus, the maintenance of tradition and cultural continuity is a strong factor in modernization.

Singer's observations have important psychological corollaries. That an Indian may say one thing to one person and something completely different on the same topic to another without any conflict is related psychologically to Singer's observation of Indians living simultaneously without conflict in traditional and modern life styles. These culturally compartmentalized activities would seem to a Westerner at such odds with each other as to cause considerable cognitive dissonance and conflict. Such dissonances go against the grain of a Western conscience, which is oriented toward universalistic principles of behavior—at least in men—and are generally felt to be in the realm of the unprincipled, hypocritical, or opportunistic. From the perspective of the Indian conscience, the suitable psychological term for the acculturation process of compartmentalization is *contextualization*.[8]

Specific contextualization of relationships and situations is essential to the functioning of the Indian conscience, as it is to Indian cognition (Ramanujan 1980). This process is simply and naturally extended to the modernization process. Contextualization is a more psychologically apt term for the process than compartmentalization, as the latter implicitly connotes conflict and anxiety in keeping different situations separate, rather than a normal cognitive-emotional mode of functioning. All of the culturally adaptive strategies Singer has cited are psychologically oriented toward contextualizing a new situation, thus making it livable and workable within the mode of the Indian familial self, particularly the socially contextual ego-ideal.

These men are able to function with minimal conflict in both traditional and modern life styles, in the family and work spheres, respectively—assuming there is no denigration of one by the other. This is profoundly related to their having a similar internal emotional-cognitive structure and conscience in both of these situations. They carry with

---

too involved in the work sphere to have time for the traditional rituals of their *jati*. They then subsidize others, including the women of the household, to keep performing the appropriate rituals that the men can then participate in vicariously. *Bhakti* has been one major way to cope with a decline in ritual involvement. Another is the inclination toward certain urban gurus who are more intellectual and rational in approach, such as Chinmayananda and J. Krishnamurti.

[8] This is different from the anthropological concept of contexturalization, which involves taking into account the widest, most inclusive setting. Contexturalization assimilates contexts, rather than separating them.

them into both groups an internalized ego-ideal that is oriented toward identifying with the group's norms, customs, and attitudes, with a strong deference and respect for hierarchical authority. No conflict is experienced because their ego-ideal functions on the basis of having harmonious group relationships, where consideration for others and the group norms are profoundly respected, and the reciprocal responsibilities and the deferences of hierarchical relationships are observed so as to minimize conflict and hurtful feelings. Even in the most modern institutions, this mode of hierarchical relationship strongly predominates. In a sense, no real psychologically dynamic compartmentalization takes place because as long as a given situation is properly contextualized with its own acceptable norms, these men, and increasingly urban women too, would be acting perfectly appropriately according to their inner conscience.

It is evident, then, that contextualization as a major aspect of the Indian familial self is an important psychological process in Indian encounters with social change. In fact, Ramanujan (1980) views the modernization process as a constant tension between assimilating Western innovations that are context-free (such as constitutional political institutions, universal education, linear time, modern science, and business and technology) and the Indian pull toward contextualizing everything. It is further evident that this process has not been sufficiently appreciated in psychological studies of the modernization process, where attitudinal change, achievement motivation, and acculturation stress have mainly been emphasized (Berry 1980).

It is also apparent that the Hindu mythic orientation plays a major psychological role in contextualization. Every relationship and encounter is consciously or preconsciously referred back to mythic images, folklore, and traditional conceptions, and encounters with the West and with modern innovations are no exception. Gandhi, for example, exhorted Indian women to resist the British as Sita resisted Ravanna; he literally labeled the British colonial power a Ravanna-raj.[9] Alternatively, some Indians viewed the British rulers as a variety of Kshatriyas, albeit a particularly difficult kind to cope with (pers. com. Ashis Nandy). The enormous assimilative tendencies with which Indian culture is usually credited is to a great extent based on the power of this contextualizing process. By drawing upon past images and mythology, an Indian will continuously invest the current and the new with familiar meaning, thus

[9] Ravanna is the ten-headed demon king of the Indian epic, the *Ramayana*, who abducts Sita, the wife of Rama (the incarnation of the god, Vishnu). Ravanna is usually viewed as the epitome of arrogant and evil power.

ensuring continuity within change.[10] Problems mainly arise in certain urban spheres where it becomes difficult for Indians to contextualize situations within reasonably traditional values—in part because change has occurred too rapidly for the situation to be contextualized, or because innovations are too far outside prevailing images and categories (Kakar 1978, 182–188; pers. com. B. K. Ramanujam), or when there is a high degree of deculturation through a highly Westernized, secular education.

Achievement Motivation

One strong psychological element that urges on individuals in the process of modernization is motivation for achievement. In an influential study, Edward Shils (1961) claimed that Indian intellectuals and scientists are not very achievement oriented, and concluded by positing an inherent opposition between Western individualism, high achievement motivation, and modernity on the one hand, and Indian self-transcendence and lack of achievement motivation on the other. These views pervade a certain segment of the social science literature on modernization in India (Kuppuswamy 1977). Much of this widely held perspective comes from David McClelland's (1961) major work, in which he demonstrates through an American sample that a high degree of achievement motivation is related to American-style independence and self-reliance, and urges toward self-realization; and to aspects of American child rearing that emphasize mastery and early achievement. These personality and child-rearing factors in high achievement motivation had been considered universal until the work of George DeVos (1973) in Japan, where he found quite different motivational factors to be present in the high achievement motivation in the Japanese: much more emphasis on affiliation motives around family and group obligations and family continuity, as well as the internalization of strong maternal expectations for achievement.

It is doubtful whether Indian intellectuals and scientists are as lacking in achievement motivation as Shils made them out to be, though the psychological dynamics may be different from those familiar in the West. In the social sciences alone, major contributions have been made in the

[10] Ashis Nandy (1980) also evaluates traditional Indian attitudes toward biography and history as profoundly oriented toward transforming each social reality into a psychologically and culturally significant myth, thus ensuring continuity.

last two decades. In my clinical work, I have come upon a very high degree of achievement motivation in certain patients, as well as considerable creativity and a high level of accomplishment in a few. In Indian psychological functioning, I find high achievement motivation to be strongly related to high we-self regard. That is, the person strives to achieve to reflect well on family and paternal reputation, enhancing their self-regard, as well as to gain the respect and approbation of family elders. This is, of course, different from striving for individual fulfillment or competitive success, though obviously these motives may also be present to varying extents. It is not that this dimension of we-ness is totally absent in American achievement strivings, but it is a chord far more softly played than in the Indian psyche.

Individualization and Individuation

Individualization and individuation are certainly occurring with modernization, especially in urban areas but apparently to varying degrees in rural ones as well.[11] This is happening within the framework of changing extended family hierarchical relationships. These relationships stretch to allow for increasing consideration of the child's, and particularly the adolescent's, specific wishes, abilities, and inclinations in the social, educational, occupational, and marital sphere, with a greater recognition that a person may function in a somewhat more independent way. It also usually means according to persons subordinate in hierarchical relationships, whether in the family or other institutions, a greater recognition of what is important to them, and what they have to say and contribute. With greater individualization, the personal identities of various family members are responded to much more than in the past, when persons were predominantly viewed in their hierarchical kinship positions and were usually referred to by the appropriate kinship term rather than their given name (Ramanujam 1977).

Since living space is so expensive in large cities such as Bombay, most families tend to live in unitary households, though they often cluster near each other, and only the well-to-do live in joint households.[12] In

[11] Drs. Illana Cariapa and C. Shamasunder, psychoanalytically oriented psychiatrists at N.I.M.H.A.N.S. in Bangalore, both of whom have worked extensively with rural patients, report significant changes in individualization in rural families.

[12] Joint households have traditionally, in fact, only existed where there has been sufficient economic means, and unitary households have probably always predominated—at least at certain phases of the life cycle.

these urban unitary households, there are greatly increased opportunities as well as pressures for the husband and wife to make decisions by themselves and be more self-reliant in daily matters than if they were living in a joint household, though more important decisions are still generally made in consultation with the extended family elders. This leads to a closer, more companionate husband-wife relationship than in the traditional joint household, where affection and closeness cannot be openly displayed because it is viewed as too exclusive and divisive a relationship in the context of the overall family (Gore 1978; Ramanujam 1977; Ross 1961). The father's relationship with sons and daughters is also somewhat closer than in the joint household, where the father is the overtly distant disciplinarian who cannot show too great involvement with his own children, since he is supposed to care equally for all. In child rearing, somewhat greater freedom is accorded the child and more consistent discipline tends to be instituted in early childhood, resulting in the formation of inner controls.

Although marriages are still almost universally arranged, there are varying degrees of liberalization regarding the number of opportunities granted for the boy and girl to meet each other and the extent of veto power either has over familial choices—*jati* norms and family culture determining the variations. Boys usually have much greater veto power, but in some educated urban families, the girls may be granted full veto power and varying amounts of choice in the selection of a mate. One interesting example of the latter was a south Indian Brahmin girl with a postdoctoral degree from an excellent university and strong career interests, who more or less dictated the requisites of her future husband, which her family eventually came up with. Family culture even may rarely impose upon the children the necessity to arrange their own marriage, that is, Western values may be thrust upon the children through Indian-style family functioning. One young woman from an upper-class, highly Westernized family consulted me, lamenting that her family was completely unwilling to arrange her marriage—in her family everyone must arrange her or his own, which she found extremely difficult to do. Love marriages have been slowly growing—some estimate them as high as 10 percent in the cities—but they are looked upon askance in most circles unless they receive familial approval, and, indeed, without family approval the marriage may be fraught with difficulties (pers. com. Shib Mitra).

Although parents and elders still usually determine educational and vocational choices for the boy, they now tend to take his abilities and wishes more into account than they did before. Sons often do not follow their father's occupation, but younger sons are given much more latti-tude than older ones, who are steered toward more conservative, safer occupations such as the civil service or family business, thus insuring family stability while encouraging growth and a possibly greater pros-perity (pers. com. Ashis Nandy). All of these modernizing familial changes are contained within the essential structures of the extended family, but tend to generate significantly increased individualization.[13]

To assess these psychological changes, a crucial question must be posed: is the familial self easily open to individualizing changes, or is it a pro-foundly unchanging organization of the psyche? The answer is both "yes" and "no," or more accurately "both"; and upon the elaboration of this answer depends a large part of our understanding of the expand-ing self and psychological correlates of social change in post-Indepen-dence, urban India. My strong impression is that with the changes in urban extended family functioning, profound inner emotional-cognitive structures of the familial self still predominate, but simultaneously there is a certain elasticity in developing more individualized modes of social relatedness and psychological functioning.[14]

To understand the incorporation of these individualizing tendencies within the Indian psyche, it is crucial to see how individuation develops within the Indian familial self, in contrast to the development of the individualized self of Americans. In contemporary psychoanalysis in America, it is assumed that individuation goes hand in hand with grad-ual psychological separation from the maternal figure, with the attain-ment of firm ego boundaries and of a sharp differentiation between inner images of self and other, and with increasing autonomy and ini-tiative. These developmental lines in American children are viewed as so intrinsically interrelated that Mahler has hyphenated this process as separation-individuation, and of course has assumed it to be universal (Mahler et al. 1975). In this early development, especially from one to two and a half years of age, but later as well, the mother's optimal role is seen as lending strong emotional support and presence to the gradual psychological separation and individuation of the child; both "overpro-

---

[13] This point on continuity within change is basically similar to the one Milton Singer (1972) made in his studies on industrialization in Madras.

[14] These impressions are in partial agreement with the work of Inkeles and Smith (1974) on attitude and behavioral changes in modernization. They see the development of greater ego skills and competence primarily through education and secondarily through work in the factory. A broadened awareness and outlook are associated with increased autonomy and freedom from tradition, but remain within the ongoing affective and interpersonal contexts of a given culture.

tective" and "emotionally unavailable" mothers interfere with the separation and individuation processes (Mahler 1972).

This fostering of separation and individuation in the early years is further played out in American adolescence in the increasing psychological and physical separation of the adolescent from the family through strong peer group affiliations, and through a culturally fostered autonomy. The adolescent has to make innumerable choices among a variety of social options, and live with the ensuing commitments. Both early childhood and adolescence in America result in the central impetus toward self-creation of one's identity, a trait fundamental to the American individualized self and to functioning in American-style individualism. Hierarchical relationships are also, of course, obviously present in American institutional relationships, but they are of an essentially different nature from those in India. In America, it is assumed that superior and subordinate are basically equal, that they are of essentially the same nature, and that both have rights as well as responsibilities that are spelled out in contractual terms. Indians, on the other hand, always perceive in any relationship a hierarchical order, wherein the superior and the subordinate will be much more connected emotionally and in terms of reciprocal responsibilities and expectations.[15]

No intrinsic connection between individuation and separation seems to be present in the development, inner structuralization, and functioning of the Indian familial self, although there is a profound relationship between individuation and separation in the realization of the spiritual self (see Chapter Nine). In urban Indians today, greatly increasing social individuation and developing ego skills are being fostered by the extended family through education as the middle and upper-middle classes exert tremendous efforts to get training in scientific, professional, and business skills in their scramble for a limited number of jobs. This greatly enhanced individuation still goes hand in hand with the intense emotional bonding and interdependencies of family hierarchical relationships, rather than with any Western-style autonomy or individualism. There is therefore a significantly different psychoanalytic developmental model for the Indian familial self, where greater individuation can occur but still within these dominant suborganizations of the familial self. It

---

[15] In a cross-cultural study of American and Indian college students, Professor Jai Sinha of the Sinha Research Institute in Patna found that on a collaborative task American students would cooperate but resist what they considered undue influence by the other; whereas Indian students would immediately form a hierarchical relationship, the subordinate being completely open and receptive to influence from the perceived superior (pers. com.).

is thus evident that individuation is not intrinsically linked to psychological processes of separation, differentiation, autonomy, and identity integration, as currently theorized by American psychoanalysts. (This point is further confirmed by Japanese psychological development and functioning, to be discussed later in this chapter.)

Important institutional innovations occasionally occur that incorporate this greater individualization and individuation, relying to a significant extent on certain aspects of the familial self to effect this new integration. I have encountered several small but important and innovative institutions in education, scientific research, and mental health, where the pattern is remarkably similar. All of these institutions have changed their system of authority from the usual structural hierarchy of unquestioned subordination and loyalty to the superior to one in which there is a benevolent leader in a hierarchy by quality, and in which the subordinates deeply respect him and profoundly need the reciprocal relationship to function well. In turn, the leader encourages maximum individual participation and initiative, with a minimum of structural hierarchy. The persons involved all form the extremely close emotional bonding of extended family relationships and spend a great deal of time together, not only freely exchanging ideas but also socializing together in after-hours—something that rarely occurs in the usual Indian work situation. Each person's contributions are warmly supported and encouraged by other members of the group, which include women as well as men, though the latter tend to predominate. Thus, individualization and individuation are fostered within these institutions through varied aspects of the familial self, involving an important hierarchical relationship by quality with the leader, with its attendant respect, idealization, and reciprocal mirroring; and the affectional intimacy relationships of the extended family and familial self in the group members' relationships with each other. Even in institutions essentially structured in a traditional hierarchical manner, I have seen an unusual top manager run the institution in this way.

Such profound social and psychological changes inevitably bring conflicts as well. I will touch briefly on three important problem areas: the impact of greater autonomy and independent decision making, changes in child rearing, and institutional structures.[16]

The greater autonomy that urban middle and upper middle-class men

---

[16] The changing role of women and the marital relationship I shall delve into more deeply in the following chapter.

have in shouldering the responsibilities and decisions of the unitary family is not always easy or welcome, and from reports of clinicians it can be disastrous in some cases. Brought up to be finely attuned to the reciprocal responsibilities and complex interdependencies of hierarchical relationships and to mutual consultations with extended family elders, rather than toward any autonomous initiative and decision making, these adult urban men experience increasing strain and anxiety if they are thrown too much on their own. Some Bombay psychoanalysts report that men not infrequently come for therapy half paralyzed in their functioning just after the death of a parent on whom they had depended for decisions. My impression is that only when there has been gradual individualization can these men function well in an increasingly autonomous situation. In other cases I have known, men function well when they have achieved a high degree of inner equanimity from one of the spiritual disciplines associated with the realization of the spiritual self.

In still other cases, problems are emerging in younger sons, who are now being accorded more individualized expectations for education and career than older brothers. Although some younger sons fruitfully take advantage of the greater leeway afforded,[17] others experience considerable emotional stress under pressure to show initiative and enterprise in career choice and implementation, which sometimes results in psychic paralysis or an inability to function (pers. com. Meena Alexander). Hitherto, emotional problems have mainly been manifested in older sons, the result of their incorporating familial expectations of bearing the burden of responsibility for all other family members.

In the area of child rearing, conflict can be engendered by parents who give ambivalent and often conflicting signals to their children for greater freedom and autonomy on the one hand, while expecting them to be highly deferent and obedient on the other. Or parents subtly side with their children's greater individualization in the areas of dress and behavior, or in their mixing with the opposite sex as college students, to the consternation of more traditional grandparents who feel deeply hurt that their authority in the family is being undermined (pers. com. B. K. Ramanujam).

In one of the Indian Institutes of Technology, I was told that almost

---

[17] An example is a psychoanalytic colleague, the youngest of four brothers and two sisters, who had been given tremendous freedom by his father, a physician, in contrast to his older siblings. The others all became physicians and put considerable pressure on him to enter a conservative profession from his early teens when his father died. However, the individualization process had progressed too far, and after considerable inner struggles after becoming a lawyer, he threw over the traces to become a psychoanalyst, which he had always wanted to be.

25 percent of the students had failed some of their courses and had to take them over, even though these students were the top science and engineering students in India and obviously had more than adequate intelligence and skills to pass all of their courses. Student difficulties seemed mainly evoked by an institutional structure that put these sixteen- and seventeen-year-olds too much on their own, and required a degree of autonomous, individualized functioning perhaps even greater than an American adolescent is used to.[18] On the one hand, institutional attitudes assumed these students would still get their primary emotional and social support from the extended family, in spite of the fact that living at the college often greatly reduced family contacts for long periods at a time; on the other hand, the administration made no effort to build infrastructures of extrafamilial, college supports of organized activities and groups, as well as a counseling system, such as are integral parts of an American college. Most students apparently try to handle their intense anxieties by completely suppressing all emotions (pers. com. Udayan Patel); a sizable percentage at least partly fail. Thus, this Indian Institute of Technology, completely oriented toward imparting a very high degree of scientific ego skills, partly undermines its own efforts because it so ignores the needs of a familial self.

Case Studies

Several different case studies will show the complexities of an expanding Indian self that uses certain aspects of the familial self in the modernization process, while also incorporating increased individualization and individuation in its functioning. The appreciable inner conflict or stress that is frequently present will also be seen.

ASHIS

Returning to some of the case material involving Ashis, I would like to evaluate it very briefly in terms of the theoretical framework of this chapter. Ashis, through his engineering schooling and his graduate work in America, as well as his strivings to be a writer, achieved considerable individuation and a very individualized way of functioning that often

---

[18] My tentative conclusions derive from some interviews with faculty members of this Indian Institute of Technology, as well as from discussions with some Bombay psychoanalysts who had on occasion worked with these students or knew them personally.

put him at odds with traditional bureaucratic, hierarchical relationships. He simply could not stand work relationships in which his considerable initiative, self-expression, and creativity could not be recognized and utilized. On the other hand, it became clear that even given the freedom to function independently in his job, he was not able to do it without a hierarchical superior whom he deeply respected, and who would be highly involved and appreciative of Ashis—involving the we-self regard and emotional connectedness of the familial self. With this special kind of person—who had to have the qualities of a high level of creativity and organizational abilities as well as a spiritual presence—Ashis would experience himself as being within his orbit and be able to function in a highly creative and effective way himself.

I would suspect that Indians who are highly creative and who through advanced education have achieved an unusual degree of individuation and individualization must still have the emotional connectedness of a hierarchical relationship; but they can only function optimally in one where the hierarchical superior recognizes and appreciates their unusual abilities and gives them considerable latitude. This is in contrast to a Western-style mentor-disciple relationship, where inevitably the disciple rebels to achieve his optimal creativity (pers. com. Howard Gardner)—thus ultimately reflecting normal Western intergenerational conflict.

SUNIL

Although I did not actually see Sunil in psychoanalytic therapy, I heard his story from his father, a psychoanalytically oriented psychologist in Ahmedabad who was keenly aware of his son's inner makeup. Sunil, while in Ahmedabad, was a fair to middling student at best, and seemed to flounder around in a number of fields—a history not unlike his father's. The parents then acceded to Sunil's wish to have some postgraduate (graduate) school experience abroad, and at great financial sacrifice they sent him to Boston. He did so extraordinarily well in his first year there that he was then able to get into a highly competitive doctoral program. Simultaneously, because of the problem of being able to bring only very limited funds out of India, Sunil spent a couple of years living in utmost destitution and deprivation, having to fast sporadically and to spend occasional nights on park benches or in all-night movies because he couldn't afford a room.

How can we explain this extraordinary academic turnabout and resilience in this son of an upper middle-class, upper-caste professional family? On the one hand, the much more individualized college instruction and living experiences in the United States were undoubtedly important factors enabling this young man to do far better academically. But his high achievement motivation, academic success, and especially his supposed new-found ability to live so completely on his own while experiencing such deprivation had quite another source. Sunil asserted to his father that the only way he could surmount such deprivation and do so exceedingly well in graduate school was out of an inner feeling that he was doing everything for his father.

How are we to understand such a declaration, apparently sincerely meant? Certainly not out of any sense of appeasement. It was basically out of the strong, sometimes subterranean, emotional connectedness an Indian son has with his father, especially in his need to gain his father's respect and in turn to enhance his father's we-self regard and family reputation by fulfilling paternal expectations; in this case the expectation was to become a successful professional. This contrasts with a more American narcissistic gestalt of internalizing and living up to parental values around self-reliance and mastery, and of experiencing achievement and competency as fundamentally reflecting on one's identity and self-actualization. Thus, Sunil illustrates both a certain elasticity in the familial self as it becomes more individualized, and a fascinating expansion of narcissistic aspects of the familial self in coping with situations demanding far more independence and physical separation than Indians are ordinarily accustomed to.

AMAL

The third case, that of Amal, illustrates the potential conflicts engendered by increased individualization occurring within traditional hierarchical relationships. Amal, a very likable, mild-mannered twenty-seven-year-old man from an upper middle-class, traditional Muslim family, came to the Family Institute of N.I.M.H.A.N.S. in Bangalore because of hysterical fits, for which he had afterwards complete amnesia. His hysterical attacks may well be the only ones ever completely recorded due to his quick-witted wife, who immediately switched on their cassette recorder whenever he went into this state.

Amal was the fourth of seven children born to a mother who because of illness could have children but could take little care of them or the household. From the time Amal was about ten years old, when an older sister married and left, he was given increasing responsibility for directing the servants and running the household, including helping to take care of his three younger siblings; two older brothers were being trained in his father's thriving business.

At the same time, Amal had evidenced remarkable interest and talent in dealing with all kinds of electrical appliances around the house. When Amal later dropped out of his commercial course in college after doing moderately well, his father, the unquestioned patriarch of the family, fully acceded to Amal's wishes for a two-year traineeship in a major German-Indian electrical industry in Bangalore, rather than pressuring him to go into the family business. At age eighteen Amal was one of two hundred out of more than a thousand applicants who were accepted for training. Over the two-year period he showed such talent and ability that he was then chosen as one of forty out of the two hundred to go for advanced electrical training to the main factory in Germany. He was jubilant, as this was the fulfillment of all of his career dreams. He would get this advanced training, return to India as a highly skilled electrical technologist, and his career would be made.

Amal made plans for departure and joyously told his father the news. His father adamantly refused to let Amal go, asserting that he needed Amal to continue running the household and would miss him too much. This completely quashed Amal's dreams, but there was no question of his going against his father's wishes. Amal acceded to his father and opened an electrical repair shop in which he worked only half-heartedly, a not uncommon way of indirectly expressing anger against a hierarchical superior.

Five years later, when Amal's father went to the hospital for a major operation, Amal began having his hysterical attacks, which lasted from thirty minutes to a few hours, followed by total amnesia. In these attacks, Amal with almost superhuman strength and beyond anyone's control would tear apart the house, ripping up bedsheets and mattresses and breaking furniture. The caretaker of the house had thus become the destroyer. After the attacks, he returned to his usual mild-mannered personality, disbelieving the wreckage he had caused or anything he had uttered.

In my first session with Amal, he stated that when his father refused to let him go to Germany he took it in stride. I sensed, however, that he really felt enormous disappointment and hurt, which I pointed out to him. When he got more in touch with these feelings, I interpreted to him that he had never been able to experience or express the rage he felt over this intense disappointment, and that it had unconsciously surfaced in his hysterical attacks, brought about by the father's serious illness and the ambivalence that it aroused in Amal. In the following session, Amal seemed to be reconstituting himself and his earlier dream of an electrical career by announcing plans for a sizable electrical manufacturing business in a large space his father and older brothers were constructing—in good part through prior counseling with them by a social worker and psychiatrist.

The fact that his father encouraged Amal's wishes and talents for training in electrical work, rather than insisting that Amal go into the family business, is part of the modernizing process wherein younger sons are encouraged to follow their own individualized inclinations once older sons fulfill parental expectations. When his father abruptly frustrated this development, Amal's profound disappointment, hurt, and unconscious rage surfaced only later in hysterical attacks and amnesia. Since direct expressions of anger toward a superior are forbidden by the Indian conscience, outbursts will often be accompanied by total amnesia afterwards or else will occur as part of a group demonstration. In either case the person does not feel responsible for his or her expression of anger (pers. com. B. K. Ramanujam).

Since Amal's highly individualized inclinations and skills developed so completely within a traditional father-son hierarchical relationship, there was no question of any rebellion or assertion of autonomy on Amal's part by going to Germany on his own (which would have been financially feasible for him). An Indian boy, whether Hindu or Muslim, is so oriented toward a hierarchical emotional interdependence with his father and toward the need to gain his father's respect and recognition, as well as toward superego prohibitions against the expression of angry feelings, that only in the rarest of cases is there any open rebellion against paternal expectations. This contrasts sharply with the adolescent rebellion of American youth. While Amal is obviously an extreme example of the conflict between increased individualization and traditional hierarchical authority, I would suggest that lesser degrees of this conflict are frequently present.

JOAN

Joan was a twenty-five-year-old Maharastrian Catholic woman who came from a middle-class family. Although specific aspects of her case were certainly influenced by relatively strong Westernization/modernization values and life styles in her Christian community, essential elements of individualization and individuation would seem to hold for girls in other communities as well. She came for psychoanalytic therapy recently married, living in a joint family household with her husband, her mother-in-law, two sisters-in-laws, and two brothers-in-law. She worked as a counselor-administrator in one of the best English-language private schools in Bombay and was highly regarded there. When certain of her problems surfaced at school, an enlightened principal suggested she go into psychoanalytic therapy.

Joan came to see me initially on a highly tentative basis when her former therapist, after two years of psychoanalytic therapy with her, moved to another part of India. She said she would see me for a few sessions before deciding whether to stay. I said that this was fine and didn't investigate any resistances, as I might have with an American patient. During the third session Joan decided to continue therapy with me three times a week. I had a very distinct impression that she did things only if she really wanted to, and not if pressured or feeling obliged. Her initial reactions were in accord with a number of experiences I had in institutional settings in India in which subordinates would only do what they really wanted, although outwardly deferring to the superior.

I encouraged Joan in that first session to express any feelings she had about her former therapist leaving. She first conveyed some feelings of sadness, and then related that she had found it extremely difficult to speak to him for a long initial period of a year, after which she was then able to express a variety of feelings. As she did so, her frequent minor illnesses had gradually disappeared. Many Indian therapists have remarked to me about the frequency with which Indian women have to bottle up feelings, particularly negative ones, within extended family relationships, which often results in somatic symptoms. Such physical evidence of emotional strain in Indians goes infinitely beyond my experience with American patients, but is similarly present in Japanese, where ambivalent feelings also have to be contained in long-term familial and group hierarchical relationships.

The main problem Joan still expressed was feeling intense discomfort and guilt over being happily married when others around her were so unhappy. She felt this way whenever she and her husband went out together, leaving her widowed mother-in-law and unmarried older sister-in-law at home and unhappy. Her mother-in-law compounded Joan's guilt by conveying in a very considerate tone how much she missed them if they stayed with Joan's mother or just went out to a movie. Joan expressed these same feelings of discomfort over newly married friends who were having problems—such as a very recently married friend who didn't have good sex on her wedding night because of her husband's impotence. (I should mention in passing that I found the frank, open expression of sexual matters to be on the whole much easier with my

Indian women patients than with American ones; this implies a more ready acceptance of the erotic in Indian culture, although sexuality is socially more firmly bounded.) The second problem Joan brought up was that she simply could not tell other teachers or the administration about the excellent, creative work she was doing with the students she counseled; later she said that she was unable to tell her mother-in-law how much she did around the house.

In these early sessions, other intense feelings surfaced around jealousy and anger. She expressed deeply angry feelings about how her assistant principal had lied to her, talked behind her back, and then accused her of taking some school property. She felt he probably wanted to get rid of her as she was more articulate and assertive toward him than most of the other staff, and he may have been threatened by her competence. From a couple of visits I made to the school to talk with the school psychologist, I noticed that Joan was actually quite deferential to this assistant principal. As other experiences showed me as well, Indians are quite capable of observing the expected etiquette of hierarchical relationships while at the same time having intensely angry feelings toward the superior. Fortunately, Joan spoke to the principal, who straightened the whole matter out so that she felt vindicated.

In the following session, for the first time she related a dream: "I was supposed to meet my daddy (now deceased) in Goa. I went with two friends along railway tracks to an office, which was like a bank. It was near Bombay Central Station. To my surprise, my father was in the office. I then went to the hostel at the postgraduate institute I attended, bringing some clothes with me."

Her associations to the two friends were that they weren't married yet and were lonely, evoking guilt in Joan. She sometimes invited them over to cheer them up. To Goa, she associated family trips to her grand-parents in a village, which was fun if her whole family went, but not if her older brother and sister didn't come along. She further associated to her siblings that her mother and the nuns at school compared Joan unfavorably to this older sister, who was very good in schoolwork and behavior at the convent school they attended; in fact, Joan was compared unfavorably to all her siblings. In relation to her father, she brought up that one time when she was in college she went with him alone to Goa and cooked for him while he repaired the house, which she liked very much. She admired her father, who was much more even-minded than her mother, who was very emotional, but there had never been any close communication with him. He wouldn't let Joan live at the institute hostel because of the extra expense.

Previous interpretations by her former therapist that her strict conscience did not permit her to be happy apparently had little effect on
Joan's guilt feelings. I therefore assumed that his interpretation, though
quite sensible, was nevertheless incorrect. Associations of being compared unfavorably to her siblings gave me an important clue to the
psychodynamics of Joan's problems of intense guilt over being happy. I
interpreted to her that the unhappy other person was really an old,
unhappy self of her own. That is, that she became tremendously sensitive to any unhappiness in others because she unconsciously projectively
identified with them, and then was not able to be happy herself.

This struck home in a very powerful way for her. She began associating that indeed she was tremendously unhappy and lonely as a child
and adolescent, and in fact only began to change in the third year of
college, when teachers and others began responding to her in a far more
positive way than her mother had. This continued in her postgraduate
schooling, and then in her work. She was currently the happiest she had
ever been in her life, being very happily married. She closed the session
by relating how she had misplaced a gold necklace and almost lost a
ring the previous night, then of wearing wrinkled saris that didn't look
good. I further interpreted that this self-destructive behavior went along
with her self-image of being the black sheep of the family. The following
session she related that she felt much better, wasn't nearly as bothered
by the assistant principal as before, and began to tell of plans for eventually getting pregnant—thus strongly confirming the interpretation.

By the time I began working with Joan I had already observed at a
couple of case conferences that the patient who was presented would be
experiencing considerable psychological disturbance, while the siblings
were reported to be quite normal and happy—quite different from my
American experience, where the siblings of my patients are always as
much or more disturbed.[19] It began to dawn on me that in the Indian
extended family where there are a large number of children, one or both
of the parents and other elders might unconsciously dump all of their
ambivalences and tensions on one child to preserve the equilibrium of
the family. Child and adolescent psychiatrists, Dr. B. K. Ramanujam in
Ahmedabad and Dr. Illana Caraiapa in Bangalore, later elaborated on
this theme, commenting that one child can become the "bad one" in the
family to maintain family equilibrium; all family members uncon-

[19]I work psychoanalytically with patients who are not schizophrenic. In the schizophrenic population in the United States, the patient may be the one upon whom various
family tensions are unconsciously displaced, the siblings often emerging considerably less
disturbed.

sciously comply with this, including the child who unconsciously accepts this designation of the bad child. This observation from their experience is quite generalizable, they said, to a variety of castes, classes, and religious groups, urban and rural, and in north and south India.

In Joan's case, her mother saw her older brothers and sister and her two younger sisters as much brighter and more devout—the latter value, especially, being highly important to the mother. Indeed, all of these siblings later went into religious orders. Her mother did not particularly appreciate Joan's intuitive gifts and lively personality, not to mention her very solid intelligence—for Joan actually went through the foremost postgraduate program in its field in India. Fortunately for Joan, her father, although not overtly close to the children, seemed far more emotionally stable than her mother, was fair-minded and even-handed with all of his children, and served as an important model of competency and intelligence for Joan.

From a sociohistorical perspective, modernizing educational opportunities that had recently opened up for urban Indian girls were on hand to help Joan work out of this miserable earlier self. Her particular Christian community encouraged girls to go to college, and to get training in some field that would be of practical value in the job market because of the need in much of the Bombay middle class—whether Hindu, Muslim, Christian, Parsee, or Jewish—to have wives work to contribute to family finances. She was thus in the first generation of girls in her family and community to go on for higher education, although others typically did not go for postgraduate education. In spite of an unhappy, denigrated self-image, she was able to draw upon the strength of her relationship, identification with, and encouragement by her father to take advantage of these new educational opportunities and to develop a more individualized and individuated self with considerable skills. Without these modernizing opportunities for college and a career, it is questionable how much Joan would have been able to develop a different self from her original unhappy one in the family. A similar pattern of development is, at times, rather typical for American women.

Joan took advantage of another important pattern of change in her Christian middle-class community, with its greater amalgam of Indian and Western values than is usually the case. Approximately half of the young adults in that community arrange their own marriage with parental approval, while the other half have their marriages arranged by their parents but with the children's approval. Joan took advantage of the first option, and not only married someone very congenial and suitable for her, but equally important, all of her in-laws were very receptive and friendly to her. This is by no means always the case when the bride goes to her husband's house; the mother-in-law may become rather competitive and hostile toward her. Moreover, in the rare cases of conflict between Joan and her mother-in-law, Joan's husband, who is the oldest son, openly sided with her—also rather atypical in a traditional Indian family. The very fact that Joan and her husband went out frequently and spent much time together apart from the family showed very strong, individualized values quite in contrast to more traditional family patterns.

But even with a career and a more conjugally oriented marriage, Joan's inner emotional makeup and ways of relating are not very different from the Indian familial self that is hierarchically oriented. Her tremendous sensitivity, subtlety, and tact in handling the varied complicated extended family relationships of husband, mother-in-law, sisters-in-law, and brothers-in-law in a joint household are typical assets of the traditional familial self. Witness an association of hers in an early session: "I was extremely anxious before I married as to how my marriage would work out. But now I get along beautifully with my mother-in-law and sisters-in-law." This is an association I have never heard from any American patient, nor would I ever expect to. Marriage as constituting highly involved extended family intimacy relationships, with the bride using all of her emotional resources to work out relationships with her female in-laws as well as with her husband, are basic aspects of extended family living and the familial self.

As the projective identifications of Joan's unhappy self were therapeutically worked through and Joan became more openly and self-assuredly happy, intensely angry feelings began to come to the fore both in her work and family relationships, signifying a significant shift in the transference in these relationships. Her anger, however, was not expressed toward me in the transference. I seemed to be kept by Joan as the even-minded father. Joan once again became extremely angry at the assistant principal, who had become unjustifiably nasty to her again. She responded by cutting off all feelings of sensitivity, concern, and sympathy for him. "I have no feelings (caring) for him!" is something I have never heard an American patient express toward her or his boss. On a more personal level, Joan's angry response was a transference displacement of how she would handle her anger toward her mother. But on a sociocultural level, it emphatically implied that a cornerstone of Indian hierarchical relationships is to have feelings of consideration and care for the superior—as, likewise, a similar reciprocation is expected. A not infrequent expression of anger in India is to cut off communication. But the more ultimate manifestation is to cut off any feelings for the other, since feelings are generally profoundly assumed to persist even when communication is temporarily cut off.

A further amplification of anger in hierarchical relationships occurred when Joan related two dreams. *Dream 1:* "My parents, my in-laws, and I are preparing a huge meal for the children at the X School [a school she consults at once a week in her after-hours]. I was very anxious if it would be enough food and if the administration would let the children come to my house to eat it." *Dream 2:* "I was going to the X School to buy vegetables outside the grounds for my family—they are cheaper there than in the neighborhood."

Among her associations to these dreams was a very recent dramatic incident regarding a school administrator who shouted needlessly and punitively at one of the boys and his mother to scapegoat them. The other teachers there were shocked, but stood around doing nothing. "I went over and simply looked at him till he toned down," said Joan. She gradually associated from this administrator to her mother, who would often shout at her when she was growing up.

Again, one must look at this material from both personal and socio-cultural levels. On the personal side, this is again the transference displacement of feelings of rage toward a mother who unfairly scapegoated her. On a more sociocultural level, her way of handling this school administrator bespeaks the pervasive nonverbal communication of emotions in Indian relationships through facial expressions and gestures, in this particular case both anger and an effective shaming reaction.

The pot continued to boil around Joan's intense anger and jealousy over her position in her original family. She angrily related, for instance, that the assistant principal did not crack down on some of the teachers who came in late and shirked their responsibilities, in contrast to her own diligence—evoking the old intense feelings of her mother favoring Joan's other siblings by giving them special privileges. She was upset that her mother-in-law complained to her husband about their going out a lot and about Joan not helping much around the house: "I do a lot of things, it's just that I never tell her." This feeling was compounded by anger at one of her students who did not really listen to her.

Interpretations around her feelings that others were being favored and she herself was not being appreciated and listened to, repeating a pattern at home, only resulted in the following session in increasing disturbance over not sleeping well and being in a nasty mood. She felt irritated that other girls had nicer saris and jewelry than she had—even though she reflected that this was not really true. She then told of identifying with her older sister-in-law, who was ill-treated by her mother-in-law. But she also related that she felt good about doing a lot of housework over a recent holiday, thus reestablishing herself in her mother-in-law's good graces. She also conveyed indirectly that she was an effective mediating and remedial presence within her in-laws' family.

The continuation of her transferential theme of unconsciously displacing intense anger and jealousy from her original family to that of her in-laws is an obvious one. Less obvious are the sociocultural implications. First, of course, there is the fact that her mother and mother-in-law unconsciously dumped all of their ambivalences onto one child, further confirming the scapegoating of one child that can occur in Indian families. Second, there is the important issue discussed in previous work on India (Kakar 1978, 73–76), showing that the daughter-in-law has a difficult time in her in-laws' household because her mother-in-law has such an intense tie to her son and becomes jealous and competitive with her daughter-in-law. While I do not in the least negate this level of psychosocial analysis, it is evident from Joan's case (as well as Saida's in the following chapter) that the wife carries over to her mother-in-law and other in-laws a variety of reactions from her own family that may make the adjustment considerably more difficult.

Transference displacements to the mother-in-law usually result from strong unresolved ambivalent feelings toward the mother, which in Indian women tend to be much more suppressed if not repressed than in American women. This occurs because of the cultural ideals of reverence for the mother, which are internalized into the conscience. As a result, the daughter-in-law may become highly vulnerable to a hostile mother-in-law (pers. com. Freny Mehta).

Joan characteristically carried over other kinds of transferences besides the negative ones. She went out of her way to please her mother-in-law and became quite upset if she could not—for example, if one of the sisters-in-law made tea for her mother-in-law before Joan could. From counseling sessions with groups of female college students, I have the general impression that this strong effort to please the mother-in-law is a carry-over from the efforts Indian girls generally make to please their own mothers by doing work around the house, and especially in the kitchen, as a way of maintaining the close emotional bondedness. In Joan's case, this effort to effect a new emotional bonding with her mother-in-law was complicated by her inability to tell her all the good things she actually did around the house. In one of our last sessions over a four-month period of psychoanalytic therapy, this problem finally came into focus.

Joan first associated to shopping for vegetables, but not telling her mother-in-law all the good buys she made. She felt that her mother-in-law and others should notice all the good things she did, and that they were in fact noticing somewhat more than in the past. It gradually became apparent that if she told the other what she did and the other was not appreciative—as her mother was not—Joan experienced deep feelings of hurt. I interpreted that she hid her light under a basket so as not to be vulnerable to being hurt. And this happened not only in what she did, but how she dressed. She agreed, but said that recently she had been dressing up somewhat more.

A third sociocultural implication relates to Joan as mediator of the relationships among her in-laws by her considerable sensitivity and tact. This confirms a point made by a number of anthropologists that in both social fact and cultural theory an Indian wife becomes a much more integral part of her in-laws' family than do wives in America (Das 1976a; Inden and Nichols 1977), and then attains status by having children. In Joan's case, it was apparent that she not only felt herself to be an integral member of her husband's family, but as the oldest son's wife also played an important role in mediating family tensions and relationships. Thus even without a child, she was subtly accorded a major place within this family.

The more Joan became aware of her intensely angry feelings and their familial sources, the more nervous and jittery she became, sometimes experiencing her emotions as going out of control. I then interpreted to her that she was experiencing a backlash response from a very strict conscience: she was being made to pay for feeling more overtly angry by becoming nervous and easily upset. She agreed that she had a very strict conscience, that even when she observed proper hours at school, she still expected her principal to criticize her.

My interpretation was confirmed when in the following session Joan was in a much better mood than she had been for some time, feeling far more content at school and home. She associated to kidding around and teasing her younger brother-in-law. Joan's intense reactions were in accord with my impression that internalized prohibitions against anger in all family and group hierarchical relationships are much stronger in Indians than they generally are in Americans, even in women (though they are similar in Japanese). Joan's extremely strict conscience might have been even stronger by virtue of her membership in this particular Christian community, as certain Hindu communities do allow women to be openly angry in particular contexts (pers. com. Manisha Roy).

It is one of the truisms in psychoanalytic work that intense reactions are not put to rest by one or two interpretations, but need repeated working through. There were other episodes with her in-laws in which Joan unconsciously displaced feelings from her original family, such as not joining her husband and mother at tea, then feeling left out and resentful, as she originally had when two of her sisters had secrets together and excluded her. But it is another truism that as one set of conflicts is gradually worked out, new ones emerge, often in a surprising way, in the dramatic unfolding characteristic of psychoanalytic therapy.

A dream heralded a new transference. The dream simply involved one of the boys at school who was obviously attracted to Joan. And shortly afterwards she mentioned that she was now trying to get pregnant. In the following session, the wish to be pregnant was expressed more strongly, but at the same time she conveyed new feelings of uneasiness, including a fear of the evil eye. I interpreted her upset as perhaps unconsciously related to inner attacks from her critical mother. What I did not fully appreciate until much later, in discussions with Dr. B. K. Ramanujam, was that women's fear of the evil eye is very much related to their fear of other women's envy over their children, particularly the other women in the extended family. Since having a child accords a significant increase in status and position within the family—especially having the first child and especially a boy—there is reason to expect ambivalent, envious reactions on the part of the other women of the extended family.

Joan felt much better by the next session. In the one following, for the first time she told of a very close attachment in her college and postgraduate school days to a German priest, who used to come frequently to her house for discussions, and who greatly appreciated her. She said that her relationship with me seemed more similar to the one she had with him than to the relationship with her father, so that if I did not say much in session, she became upset. I had realized for some time that Joan had turned to her father, husband, former therapist, and now me to gain a kind of appreciation she had never received from her mother; but I had no idea until this session how the transference relationship with me was a mirroring one related to this German priest.

In the following session, however, it became apparent that the attachment to all of us men involved more than a mirroring compensation. When she told of a fantasy of her husband going out with another girl, then having dreams about this and becoming quite tense, I interpreted that in her attachment to us there must be some deep fantasy of winning out over other women and fearing retaliation. This theme continued the next day in session when she expressed feeling sad and defeated when some of the mothers removed their children from a special workshop Joan had started; in this case the mother won out. I thus began to interpret an unconscious incestuous attachment and a punitive superego reaction—the hallmark of classical psychoanalysis. The cases of both Joan and Shakuntala (see Chapter Five) confirm cross-culturally that incestuous fantasies and fears of retaliation are fully present in Indian women.[20]

I was at this point about to leave Bombay in three weeks, not to return until six months later. Joan became upset by this impending separation, and in response to this and/or to the incestuous material now arising, she initially regressed to issues around her siblings and herself, but then recovered and felt much better. She consulted a palmist who told her good things would happen—evidencing that Indian Christians are as inclined as Hindus toward a magic-cosmic reality.

We then dealt with her fear of injury to her self-esteem when she revealed the good things she was doing. In the next to last session she reported a fantasy of winning a lottery, getting a lot of rupees and giving them away, but then retracting them and buying some gold bangles and special saris, which she would not wear until her old saris wore out. She also reported feeling quite tense, tension obviously related to this fantasy. I interpreted to her that she was raised with a strict Christian religious conscience to shun anything worldly, and that when she wished for attractive saris and jewelry her conscience caused her considerable tension. Joan responded that her mother was intensely religious, expecting the same kind of semi-ascetic ways as she followed herself. Although Joan did not pursue her original intention to go into a religious order, as all her siblings did, she nevertheless unconsciously identified with her mother's strict Catholic values. My interpretation seemed to be accurate, as Joan came to the last session in a far better mood, began to dress better, and reported clowning around at a recent wedding reception. She felt much happier in her life now with her in-laws, and was most appreciative of the help I gave her.

As Joan was freeing herself of a strict Christian religious conscience derived from her mother, she still remained a deeply religious person, though she seldom talked about it. To what extent this problem of having to suppress all desires for the material goods of life was idiosyncratic to this mother, or was part of some Westernized Christian values that

[20] This is an additional piece of evidence to support the universality of the Oedipus complex—though the Oedipus complex, itself, occurs differently in women and in men, even in the West.

had been taken over by her community, I am not certain. My impression of Hindu women patients is that they have in general a more comfortable feeling of desiring material goods while still being intensely involved in religious practices.

Six months later I saw Joan for a few sessions. She was indeed almost six months pregnant and doing well, but related some anxiety dreams. *Dream 1:* "A servant opens the front door to our house without looking through the peep hole and lets in a Sardarji boy.[21] Contrary to most Sardarjis, he is not very threatening." *Dream 2:* "Someone stole some of our bedsheets and towels, and I pursue him and get him. He seems to be no threat." *Dream 3:* "I had an earlier dream of someone stealing bangles." She associated to this third dream that it was similar to a dream of a friend of hers who had a spontaneous abortion. I then interpreted that she had some feelings of unconscious guilt that her wish for a child was being fulfilled.

In the following session, she conveyed that she was feeling quite happy. Since in most Indian families the girl goes home for the last few months of pregnancy to have her child, particularly the first one, so that her parents take care of her and pay for the birth, Joan and her husband were now living with her mother. She mentioned that she was now able to assert herself and get angry if necessary with her mother in a way she had never been able to do before; but she could also be more considerate toward her than previously. She had apparently worked out a great deal of her childhood conflicts around her mother through psychoanalytic therapy, so that her mother had now become much less threatening. In turn, her mother was now more responsive since attending Holy Spirit meetings for the previous six months.[22] Joan, however, still experienced considerable tension in buying clothes and jewelry; her conflict with her strict conscience was heightened by the fact that she and her husband were reasonably well off with their dual salaries, and were able to afford more purchases.

Two years later, in August 1980, I spent a month in Bombay and saw Joan for eight more sessions. One of the more profound insights of psychoanalysis is that the same problem may have multiple sources of motivation, and that one or another facet of this overdetermined motivation will surface at different points in the analysis. Joan now had a

---

[21] Every society has its negative images as to who is dangerous. In certain Indian communities, they consider the Sardarji, or Sikh, as the threatening one.

[22] These are Christian meetings that seem to have incorporated some of the Hindu *bhakti* singing and dancing.

son. She was again outspoken and bothered that the teachers at school were getting away with being late and being favored. She then associated to going through a period where she was constantly comparing her son with other infants and feeling he was the best. It gradually emerged that once she had a child, Joan became far more critical, aggressive, and even bossy, like her mother, unconsciously identifying with traits of her mother she didn't particularly like—a not unusual happening when one becomes a parent. The criticism of the teachers for shirking their responsibilities stemmed from Joan's identification with her mother's conscience as much as it came from her anger that her siblings were favored. In the next session she let me know that she didn't like my interpretation that she was like her mother because she felt she compared and criticized others much more gracefully and less hurtfully.

As the sessions progressed, still another major unconscious motivation underlying her reactions to the teachers emerged. It started with her assertion that she could not take praise for her competence from people she didn't respect, particularly Sashi, a teacher from the school where Joan consulted, whom Joan knew has been in therapy with me. Joan also mentioned that she was now leader of a group of teachers at her school to tighten discipline.

In the following session, Joan told a dream she had had a month before: "I was at college for the first day in a lecture taking notes. Some boys told me not to, they were not cooperating with the instructor. The principal of my school, whom I like and respect a lot, was there and he criticized the boys for not cooperating and creating a disturbance. When I continued taking notes, these boys took me to a police station where I explained it was my first day at the school and I didn't know I wasn't supposed to take notes. They let me continue college and I laughed to myself in relief after feeling so afraid. My husband was there and I was angry at him for not chastising the students." She associated to her school, where the teachers were very warm to the students, but where some of the older students had complained to her that some teachers were favoring some students over others. She was fearful if she sided openly with these students, they would tell the teachers and she would then be in trouble.

I interpreted that Joan is invariably outspoken on the side of good, law, and order, but that the dream conveyed forbidden feelings of rebellion. These are displaced onto the boys, as rebellious feelings are more forbidden to Indian girls than to boys, probably even more so than for American girls. She first associated to being preoccupied with unfairness. However, when she suggested that it was excusable for her mother to favor her older brother because he was such an excellent student and obedient son, it became clear that the rebellious feelings were still buried.

In the following sessions, however, she must have felt my permission from the past session to utter forbidden feelings, as she conveyed a central new transference dimension to her diligence and competence. She felt that I favored her over Sashi because she was much more disciplined and worked harder, thus expressing tremendous sibling rivalry in the transference with me. This sibling rivalry and competitiveness spread to many other of Joan's relationships, where she related that she constantly compared herself with others, felt she is doing well, and then extended the same comparisons in relation to her son. We did not have enough sessions to resolve fully this intense competitive transference, nor to ascertain fully to what extent her transference was for my approval as the strict mother, or in competition with her sisters for her father's love. There is also the possibility that her feelings of diligence and superiority were a profound identification with her mother's striving for her children to do extremely well so as to be the best family in their community. I should again emphasize that the striving for a good family reputation and to attain as good a position as possible in one's community or caste is a central psychosocial dynamic in Indian families, profoundly internalized in the family members' ego-ideals.

We finished our sessions with Joan feeling that she was functioning very well in a number of situations, was feeling very much improved, and feeling that she has no great need to see another therapist. She still was vulnerable at times to others' criticisms, but felt she could manage them.

Psychoanalysts are connoiseurs of inner conflicts, alert to how, in disguise, they poke their heads into everyday relationships. Analysts can become so caught up in this consuming task that they often overlook the broader picture of how their patient's conflicts reflect important issues of social change or the psyche of other members of their culture. Short-term psychoanalytic therapy with Joan revealed a punitive conscience that aroused considerable conflict over a few issues: intense anger toward her mother and other authority figures who treated her unfairly, intense sibling rivalry, incestuous fantasies and fear of retaliation, and inhibitions over purchasing and wearing good clothes and jewelry. Her ego-ideal for diligence, hard work, and competence, while strongly involved in inner conflict at times, nevertheless enabled her to do very well in college, in an excellent postgraduate school program, and then in her job at school.

What I would now like to explore is to what extent various aspects of Joan's ego-ideal and superego are generalizable to other Indian women, and to what extent they are more limited to her particular Christian community, or are simply idiosyncratic to her and her unique family background. These are crucial questions to be asked in cross-cultural psychoanalytic work, even though the answers may only be tentative. Nevertheless, it is only through clinical psychoanalytic work that an investigation of the conscience can fruitfully be made, since much of the superego and ego-ideal operates on an unconscious or preconscious level that is relatively unavailable to ethnographic observations.

My immediate impression in comparing Joan with other Indian women I have worked with, mainly Hindus and Muslims, is that all have a strong internalized conscience—though Joan's seems particularly rigid and strict. This contradicts both Kakar's (1978, 135–137) formulation that the Indian conscience is not internalized and Freud's (1925) view that women have a looser, less powerful superego than men; my observations of Indian women's conscience is more in accord with recent psychoanalytic work on women's superego (Bernstein 1983). To ascertain whether Joan's overly strict conscience was primarily reflective of her community or was idiosyncratically related to her mother would necessitate discussions with Indian psychoanalytic therapists who have worked with this community of Christians.

What seems further generalizable to Indian women from a number of communities is Joan's ego-ideal of sensitivity, tact, warmth, and consideration in both familial and work relationships. Although her degree of empathy and social facility may actually be on the high side, there is little question that other Indian women have this ideal and the capabilities to manage complex relationships and tensions within the extended family.

Still another generalizable part of her conscience involves the punitive superego reactions to becoming aware of her considerable anger toward her mother through our psychoanalytic work together. My strong impression is that both women and men have a powerful superego that arouses considerable anxiety and/or punitive reactions when anger is too strongly experienced or is at all directly expressed toward any hierarchical superior within the family or outside group. A related part of the conscience, which also seems generalizable, is that one should not have angry or competitive feelings toward one's siblings. This ego-ideal, which is frequently contradicted by the actualities of normal sibling rivalry, can also generate inner tensions.

More ambiguous are other aspects of Joan's conscience. It is difficult to say, for instance, whether her punitive conscience over her incestuous fantasies involving her father—unconsciously displaced to the priest and myself—are idiosyncratic to her particular family situation, or whether these fantasies are present in other Indian women in more muted form. That competitive incestuous fantasies with fear of retaliation are present in Indian women is obvious from this case, as well as from that of Shakuntala, a Hindu woman, in the following chapter.

Also ambiguous is Joan's ego-ideal of being highly competent, diligent, and punctual in her work and family habits. It is evident from both psychoanalytic and anthropological data that Indian women are raised to be highly competent and capable around the house. However, my tentative impression is that Joan's ego-ideal for diligence at work is unusually strong, and is related in part to her mother's strict expectations and to her image of her father, whom she idealized. But there is another major aspect to this ego-ideal: when Joan constantly came out on top in comparing herself to others, she activited a structure quite similar to that of other Indian women. Gossiping and constant comparison with other women have been cited (Anandalakshmi 1978; Das 1976a), and have turned up in my case data on college students in the following chapter. My impression from Joan's case and from these college students is that there is a profound internalization of certain strictures and ideals of behavior, mainly from the mother and other women of the family, with the negative images of what one is not supposed to be unconsciously projected onto other women—in Joan's case slackness and shirking one's responsibilities. Gossip and constant comparison then reinforce the woman's feeling that she is living up to her inner ego-ideal; the bad images, of course, are always perceived as being in the other.

Joan's punitive conscience over buying and wearing nice saris and jewelry seem more related to her own Christian community, and perhaps even more to her mother's personal, ascetic Christian values. Her mother's values are probably on the extreme end for this particular Christian community in Bombay. My strong impression is that, in contrast, urban Hindu women of the middle class in the householder stage of life spend a great deal of time dressing up—much more than American women do—so that they will reflect well on their family.

To return to the theme of an expanding self, through the Westernizing/modernizing influences of advanced education, a meaningful career, and a more conjugally oriented marriage in her Christian community,

Joan has developed a far more individualized and individuated self than that of her mother and the women in her community of her mother's generation. At the same time, she not only still functions primarily with the subtle sensitivity of the familial self in the complex relationships of a joint household, but also evidences none of the intense identity conflicts suffered by most American women who combine serious career involvements with a family. For Joan and other Indian women, her career is experienced as being as much a part of familial endeavors in their ego-ideal as having children.

RUSTUM

Rustum, an engineer in his middle twenties from the Parsee community in Bombay, sought psychoanalytic therapy for two problems. He was educated in the United States, and had worked in the West for a few years. However, he so frittered away his excellent salary that he was unable to repay a sister and brother-in-law the money they had loaned him to finance his education abroad; nor was he able to send anything home to support his parents, his father being a retired colonel in the Indian army. Although this particular problem was uppermost in his mind—and in his family's too—he told me of another problem that bothered him: that of a strong propensity to put himself in an unusually favorable light with others by telling tall tales—such as that his father was a famous general who had masterminded many a campaign.

The twice-a-week psychoanalytic therapy lasted a couple of months until I had to leave Bombay. Through the predominant modernizing values of the Parsee community, who under the British played a major role in the industrialization and modernization of Bombay, not only was Rustum directed to go to college and to have technical training as an engineer, but his parents also respected his more individualized wishes for the specific field of engineering he wanted to go into—one akin to his father's work in the army. The decision to send Rustum to the United States for his engineering education rather than to an equally good program in India was dictated by a noted astrologer whom his mother regularly consulted on all decisions, rather than through any Westernized values, as one might suppose. This, of course, is a typically Indian manifestation of the magic-cosmic self and its concern for personal and familial destiny, and further reflects Singer's (1972) and the Rudolph's (1967) thesis that many aspects of tradition lend themselves to modernization. The astrological decision destined Rustum to develop through his education in America greater individualization, with stronger components of more autonomous functioning than is typical for urban-educated Indian men. It also destined him to experience greater conflicts with hierarchical authority, like many other Indians who have been educated abroad, although in his case it was probably more extreme.

In the first phase of therapy, Rustum began expressing considerable anger and resentment at his father for constantly "bottling" him, or lecturing and belittling him. He brought up such incidents as his father denigrating Rustum's analysis of what was wrong with the broken elevator in their building, though Rustum himself felt that as an engineer he knew a lot more about it than his father. Rustum's father was treating him like a subordinate in the army, his father's attitudes being an amalgamation of traditional Indian male hierarchical attitudes and British military authoritarianism. This profoundly clashed with Rustum's far more individualized, autonomous self developed while in college in America and in his work experience in the West. Thus, attitudes of male authority that might have been partially accepted by Rustum at one time were now completely rejected, generating considerable anger.

In spite of Rustum's greater independence developed in America, he still expressed his anger indirectly because of the powerful superego that prohibits direct expressions of anger in male hierarchical relationships. I thus suggested to Rustum that his frittering away of his considerable salary was primarily an unconscious rebellious reaction to his father's denigration, as well as an unconscious masochistic incorporation of his father's negative expectations.

As Rustum became increasingly in touch through these interpretations with just how angry and resentful he felt toward his father, more positive feelings paradoxically began to surface. Rustum actually held his father in awe as an army officer with a very high rank, and very clearly identified closely with him in that strong idealization that is typical of Indian father-son relationships. In fact, Rustum's whole manner, attitudes, and bearing are those of the British aristocratic officer—an identification with his father, who himself had closely identified with the British model before Indian Independence; this pattern was quite congruent with the close historical association of the Parsees with the British.[23] Thus, nineteenth- and early twentieth-century British aristocratic manners are richly preserved in this father and son, perhaps even more than they currently are in England. Like Ashis and his father, the values and life style are extremely Westernized, whereas the father-son

[23] In part because of the British policy of fostering loyalty through favoring minority groups, the Parsees became perhaps the most Westernized of any group in India.

125

hierarchical relationship is Indian to the core. The incongruity of Rustum's identification with the British through his father surfaced at college in the United States, where Rustum was eventually dismissed from leading the school band because he insisted that the band conform in style and bearing with the grand old British tradition. On the other hand, he was often much in demand on social occasions with visiting notables at the college because of his fine manners and social poise.

Rustum's identification with his father had other components of the familial self, as well, but ones that sometimes intensely conflicted with his more individualized way of life. Rustum very much liked to share in his father's and family's reputation and power, that is, in the considerable influence his father had through having the right connections to get things done. But since Rustum had been so much on his own in America, he could not now stomach being constantly advised what to do. Nevertheless, he recognized that in the Indian setting sharing in his father's power went with these Indian modes of hierarchical authority.

This conflict of hierarchical authority with Rustum's more individualized self came not only from his relationship with his father. In the second phase of the therapy, it surprisingly emerged that many of his father's criticisms of Rustum were made in an effort to prevent him from upsetting his mother. His mother would apparently get very anxious, unduly suspicious, and all too easily upset in any number of situations. She would then pressure Rustum through her husband, daughters, and sons-in-law. Rustum would find it difficult to assert himself against the whole family. He well realized that, as is so often true in many Parsee families, his mother was clearly the more dominant of the couple, and her husband, though used to high positions of authority, was constantly subservient to her. Thus many of the father-son battles were covertly around Rustum's relationship with his mother.

As we delved more into the mother-son relationship, it became essential to differentiate what was within the normal range from what was more idiosyncratic and psychopathological. On the former level, this relationship was very like a traditional Indian mother-son relationship, with considerable ongoing closeness, in this case greatly enhanced by Rustum being the only son, and with his mother feeling very free to guide her son's life. On the latter level, however, Rustum's mother became unduly anxious over whatever Rustum did, and constantly tried to control him to alleviate her anxieties, either through others or by asserting that he was badly upsetting her.

Through increasing awareness of the nature of this relationship, Rustum was at times able to assert himself more with her: when she blamed him for losing some rupees, for example, he insisted that she look carefully in a cabinet where she put them herself, until she found them—which she eventually did. However, he still felt basically powerless with her, and felt that the only solution was to leave her and live once again in the West. I suggested that his inability to assert himself with her—he had recently given in to her on an important application—basically stemmed from the feeling she evoked in him that his independence would hurt and damage her, and that it pained him too much to see her suffer. Thus, he felt his only solution was to clear out. From a therapeutic standpoint, the problem as presented was worked through in terms of his rebellious actions toward his father and family, but as is so often the case in psychoanalytic therapy, this served as a mask for more profound problems that only emerged as the initial ones were worked out. It was our last session by then, and I strongly urged that he should stay in Bombay to try to work out this problem with one of the psychoanalysts there.

To put Rustum's case in the perspective of an expanding self in the modernization process, there was a great deal in his family to foster a more individualized life style with greater individuation: expectations for his receiving higher technical education of his choice, and even the decision to go to the United States for it, based on an astrological prediction. Nor was he beset as Ashis was by any of the identity conflicts between Indian and Western cultural and religious values. His efforts to integrate greater individualization within a familial self, however, were tragically complicated by idiosyncratic, skewed relationships with both parents. He was partly stymied by his father, who had incorporated too much British military authoritarianism and was too subservient to his wife to tolerate well his son's growing autonomy and independence. Their conflict was far greater than might have occurred in a more normal Indian father-son hierarchical relationship after the son had gone to college abroad, where there is usually greater accommodation. Rustum was even more stymied by his mother, who to alleviate deep-seated paranoid anxieties went far beyond normally close Indian mothering to control her son's every move. It was primarily this conflict that prevented a more salutary resolution and integration of Rustum's expanding self, as occurs with other Indians educated abroad. Rustum could only run.

Modernization and Japanese Identity

To discuss the psychological concommitants of social change in Japan we must assess the relevant influences unleashed first by the Meiji Restoration (1868) and then by the American Occupation (1945–1952). After Commodore Perry forceably opened Japan to the West in 1853, a group of anti-Western samurai instituted the Meiji Restoration, abolishing feudalism and the samurai class of warrior-administrators and replacing it by political centralization and Shinto-supported worship of the emperor and nation. Their goal was to prevent Japan from falling victim to Western colonial encroachment. But it was actually other educated samurai leaders, who greatly respected and admired the West, albeit with little affection, who were largely instrumental in the remarkable reconstruction and modernization of Japan (Bennett, Passin, and McKnight 1958, 10).

This admiration for the achievements of the West, with a wish to imbibe not only institutions, education, and technology but also Western cultural values, popular culture, and ideology (such as individualism, egalitarianism, and later Marxism) led to self-criticism and even depreciation of Japanese customs and culture. The pendulum of opinion then oscillated sharply between this receptivity to the West and phases of consolidation, a return to traditional values, and outright rejection of Western culture (Bennett, Passin, and McKnight 1958, 12). From 1868 to 1885, there was a great openness to the West, especially America, followed by a period of consolidation until around 1912; then significant liberalization in the 1920s, with a flowering of mass popular culture followed by ultranationalism, imperialistic expansion, and rejection of the West in the 1930s. But even when Western ways were most rejected, Japan still felt superior to and nonidentified with such Asian countries as China and India, which had not modernized and had fallen prey to the West (*Japan Interpreter* 1973, 57–58).

Before the American Occupation, there existed identity conflicts in educated Japanese men related to these sharp swings of the pendulum. However, these were minimal compared to those of the Indian intelligentsia, which were generated by a colonial presence that continuously denigrated Indian culture and with which these Indians had become partly identified.

From the very beginning of Japan's impressive modernization, the newly assimilated Western institutions—which came from various European countries as well as the United States—were subordinate to Japanese national goals; but even more important, the Japanese retained traditional patterns of familial hierarchical relationships with their associated values of emotional interdependence, reciprocal loyalties and obligations, and high levels of performance. Moreover, even the industrialization and urbanization of Japan was accomplished within traditional Japanese patterns. The rural *ie* family initially arranged jobs through its urban organizational contacts for its younger, noninheriting sons, who had to leave the main house in any case. The urban firms greatly preferred these kinds of workers to insure loyalty and commitment through family relationships. Marriages were also arranged from the rural main house for these sons. Thus, the *ie* was in total control of urban migration as Japan industrialized. As these sons became ensconced in urban positions, their loyalty and commitment gradually shifted to the firm or institution from the rural *ie* main house. School and university contacts with cliques then replaced the *ie* for jobs (Vogel 1967). Thus there was little need to culturally compartmentalize Western-oriented work situations in government, industry, or education from those at home, as Indians have done in gradually traditionalizing the former. The Japanese genius in modernization has been to incorporate the Western form, while ensuring full continuity of Japanese social patterns and cultural codes.

The swing of the pendulum became much stronger with the shattering defeat of World War II. A profound disillusionment with Japanese nationalism and imperial values set in, accompanied by a loss of confidence and sharp criticism if not cynicism over Japanese hierarchical structures and culture. This resulted in an agonizing reappraisal of being Japanese, and a tremendous reaching out for American values and culture. Meanwhile, the Occupation forces were deliberately fostering important institutional, social, educational, and ideological changes, including a new constitution and civil code that demilitarized and democratized Japan in fundamental ways. The Emperor system was abolished, the vast military apparatus was dismantled, a new, more democratic constitution was introduced, guaranteeing rights for the individual; the parliamentary system was strengthened; land tenancy was greatly reduced; and labor unions were encouraged. Male authority was systematically diminished with the abolition of the Emperor system, of male authority in the main house of the *ie* family over its branches, and of the male family head over his adult children. Simultaneously, through a new civil code, the social status and political power of women were significantly enhanced through voting rights, equal inheritance, rights for divorce, and free choice of a spouse. For the first time in Japan's history, a foreign power had instituted far-reaching institutional and ideological changes from above.

New cultural ideals were fostered through revised educational curricula and the media, which promoted democracy and equality, freedom and the rights of the individual, autonomy and self-determination of decisions, and rationality in the social sphere. These new cultural imports introduced a sharp and sudden departure from traditional Japanese social norms involving emotional interdependence and the social etiquette and reciprocal obligations of *on* and *giri* in a very tight-knit *ie* family structure; these changes were not nearly as easily assimilable into an older, traditional ego-ideal as previous Western imports. The new cultural paradigms with their institutional implementation intensified the old identity struggle between being Japanese and Western to a magnitude previously unknown, and has led to a constant self-examination of what it means to be Japanese (*nihonjin-ron*) that goes on to this day.

At a presentation I gave to the National Institute of Mental Health in 1969, a social worker asked: "Dr. Roland, we are continually beset by conflicts between the older Japanese values and the newer ones. What norms of mental health should we follow?" She was obviously voicing a conflict between the older ideals of normal functioning within Japanese family and group hierarchical relationships and those newer ones associated with Western individualism.

The Familial Self and Modernization

From a psychological standpoint, until the American Occupation Japan's modernization was accomplished completely through various facets of the familial-group self. There was little pitting of tradition against modernity as the Japanese easily moved into the newer governmental, industrial, and educational structures that were gradually assimilated from the West. Concomitantly, while there was a growing individuation in terms of new skills and greater education, there was little appreciable individualization. The Japanese remained totally enmeshed within traditional family and group hierarchical structures in a kind of familialistic communitarianism wedded to modern institutions and technology (Lebra 1984).

Facets of a traditional Japanese familial-group self—encompassing more permeable outer ego boundaries with considerable emotional enmeshment in the group, a we-self strongly identified with the group, and a high level of interpersonal sensitivity together with the mutual mirroring and idealization that support strong inner self-esteem—all lent themselves to the interdependencies of work-group functioning; whereas a socially situational ego-ideal oriented around the reciprocities and mutual obligations of varied hierarchical relationships according to internalized neo-Confucian codes were fully in accord with the hierarchical relationships of the group. In effect, these many modalities of the Japanese familial self were fully congruent with functioning in modernizing work groups, which in turn carried over many aspects of the *ie* family as occupational household.

Another central dimension of the traditional Japanese ego-ideal crucial to the modernization process has been internalized cultural values for a high level of skill and craftsmanship as a mode of self-cultivation, attainment of aesthetic ideals of perfectionism (pers. com. Yasuhiko Taketomo), and total involvement and dedication to a task—all of which contribute to the good of the group. A concommitant value is innovation in whatever task is at hand (pers. com. Sumita Iwao). Also deeply internalized into the ego-ideal are cultural attitudes involving the cultivation of will and persistance for overcoming obstacles and accomplishing difficult work, developing endurance in the face of adversity and hardship whether physical or interpersonal, and reflecting on one's weaknesses to correct them (White 1987, 27–32). These internalized cultural traditions have all contributed to tremendous task accomplishment in the modernization process.

There is a powerful achievement motivation that is deeply anchored in the Japanese familial-group self: the drive to task accomplishments. As with the Indian familial-communal self, one major dimension of Japanese self-esteem relates to reflecting well on the family and work group through high performance, thus gaining their respect, as a way of enhancing we-self regard. But another dimension is uniquely Japanese: internalizing and fulfilling maternal expectations for high levels of functioning interpersonally and in skills, and now for men in competitive achievement. This is supported by cultural attitudes that expect gratitude to be expressed to the wholly devoted mother, repaying a debt or obligation to her through fulfilling her expectations. Failure or rebellion incurs considerable guilt over hurting the mother who has sacrificed so much (DeVos 1973). Bolstering these high maternal expectations are later childhood identifications with idealized self-images of each parent and frequently, idealized images each may have of the other (pers. com. Mikihachiro Tatara), and wishes to fulfil the expectations of a reticent father (Taketomo 1982). Without doubt, this intense achievement motivation, coming from rather different sources from those of the Western

individualized self, has been a mainspring to the successful modernization of Japan and its current economic success.

Integral to the modernization program of the Meiji Restoration was an
educational system that developed and gradually became open at all
levels to various classes over the succeeding decades. On the one hand,
this resulted in increasingly greater individuation in terms of newer ego
skills that could be easily integrated into the familial-group self, leading
to an expansion of this self. On the other hand, competitive achievement
in the educational system introduced a new structural element that conflicted with older Confucian ideals of group harmony and cooperation.

At first, this system was used to advantage by the old samurai class
(now abolished as feudal leaders), who attained a disproportionate number
of important positions in the bureaucracy and corporations; by the beginning of the twentieth century, however, opportunities for higher education and good positions began filtering down to the other social classes.
By going to college, and particularly to the prestigious national universities such as Tokyo University, someone from a lower social class or
from one of the poorer samurai families could move into important
corporation or bureaucratic positions. Japanese society was gradually
transformed from one based on social class to one based on education
and competitive achievement. And as this educational and job mobility
increased for all, the competition to get into good schools and then
colleges, and with this to gain a good position, became increasingly
intensified, until at present it is at its fiercest.

The Meiji Restoration set in motion a new cultural ideal for men of
competitive achievement, which gained increasing momentum over the
years. This was fostered by families who wished to attain higher social
position with their son's educational and occupational achievements,
and was subsumed within the national goals of modernization and
service to the emperor. On the psychological level, the integration of
this new cultural ideal with the older ideals of maintaining group harmony and of a strong work ethic has fostered an expanding self that
has contributed significantly to the modernization process. Ambitious-
ness is fulfilled through advancing the interests of the group in which
one is a member. On the other hand, according to reports of senior
Japanese psychoanalysts, the historically newer ideal of competitive
achievement in education and work at times clashes with the older ideal
of maintaining group harmony. This has introduced significant inner
psychological conflicts in Japanese men, sometimes fostering unique Jap-

anese kinds of psychopathology (Doi 1985; Kondo 1975; Nishizono 1969).

These psychoanalysts assert that the *shinkeishitsu* personality—first described in detail by Professor Morita around the turn of the century, and for which he developed a special kind of psychotherapy (Kondo 1975; Reynolds 1976)—grew out of a clash of ego-ideals first fostered during the Meiji Restoration. This kind of personality and psychopathology is characterized by powerful perfectionistic ideals, various compulsive rituals, and considerable social shyness and fear of others, with a strong tendency toward withdrawal. The inner psychodynamics in these patients, according to Drs. Doi, Kondo, and Nishizono, derive from the incorporation of unusually strong familial and maternal expectations to be highly competitively successful and responsible. These men then unconsciously project an inner ego-ideal of being harmonious and cooperative onto other persons, who are then unconsciously experienced as being critical toward these patients' competitive aggressiveness, grandiosity, and anger. In other words, the person with a *shinkeishitsu* personality unconsciously fears that the other will sense and strongly disapprove of his intense inner competitiveness, as he unconsciously does himself from that other part of his ego-ideal that so emphasizes sensitivity and harmony with others. The person then feels intensely ashamed of himself and withdraws socially. These analysts also note that the majority of patients with a *shinkeishitsu* syndrome have been either the inheriting oldest sons or only sons, for whom family expectations for responsibility and achievement are the strongest.

In more recent times, another form of psychopathology idiosyncratic to the Japanese has emerged: parent abuse, particularly involving teenage boys who beat up their mothers. These boys are reported to have been initially successful in school, but to have reached a point where they did not do so well. Highly dependent on their mothers, while profoundly incorporating her expectations for a high level of competitive achievement, they are in a rage over their failure and entrapment in a relationship where they cannot realize their internalized ideals. They therefore turn on their mother, either through failing in school or beating her up, or both (Ogura 1978; Tatara 1981).

Individualization and Westernization

Although Western theories and ideals of individualism and egalitarianism were introduced long before the American Occupation, it was only with the Occupation that these ideals have had profound psychological impact, coming as they did with demilitarization, democratization, universal suffrage, a legal undermining of the male hierarchy, and profound changes in the family system. Since various facets of a traditional familial-group self still contribute heavily to Japan's economic success, it is evident that significant individualization has only taken place through changes brought about by the Occupation and Japan's greatly increased exposure to Western culture over the past four decades.

One of the more profound institutional changes the Occupation introduced was the breakup of the *ie* stem family. To understand the implications of these changes for individualization, we must first describe the *ie* structure. Current primarily in the upper classes until the Meiji Restoration, the *ie* with its male-oriented authority was then fostered by the new government for farmers, merchants, and artisans. The *ie* was actually a unique combination of kinship lineage and occupational specialization, organized into a corporate household. From the standpoint of lineage, the *ie* stem family maintained continuity by having the oldest or only son inherit, while the younger sons often had to move out of the main house to form branch houses, which were under the male authority of the main house. In turn, a branch house could eventually become a main house and form its own *ie,* with its younger sons forming new branch houses. Marriages were arranged for all sons and daughters by the elders of the main house, with the wife of the oldest son coming to the main house in an apprenticeship to her mother-in-law, and the wives of the younger sons in a subordinate relationship to the wife of the senior son and mother-in-law.

But the *ie* has been much more than simply a kinship organization. It is also characterized by occupational specialization, controlling property and capital in which unrelated members could also play a major role. When there were no sons, the main house chose a young man or son-in-law suitable for its occupation, adopted him for family continuity,[24] and trained him through a mentorship relationship. Even a branch head sometimes was established through adoption of a son or son-in-law, or entrusted to a valued servant or employee. Servants and household employees became integral members of a given *ie* occupational group. In addition, the main and branch houses sometimes formed an occupational corporation; or one *ie* could form a broader occupational organization with another through intermarriage. The occupational unit fre-

---

[24] Although the *ie* as a multi-generational family no longer legally exists, it is still not uncommon for this kind of adoption to take place to maintain family continuity through the male line.

quently became more important than literal kinship links, with non-kin simulating kinship roles. Kin and non-kin alike contributed to the over-all needs and purposes of the *ie* in interdependent relationships, with women subordinate to men (Lebra 1984, 20–23; Morioka 1986, 202–204; Nakane 1970, 4–8).

The Occupation deliberately sought to break up the *ie* by legally abol-ishing the status of the head of the household; by eliminating any au-thority of the main house over its branches; by having all children in-herit equally—a law which is not necessarily followed; by revising the house register law, which now prescribes one register unit for one cou-ple and their unmarried children rather than lineal continuity; by guar-anteeing the right for marital choice; and by emphasizing actual kinship rather than kin and non-kin alike in an occupational structure. Further contributing to the decline of the *ie* in the post-Occupation period has been the large growth of corporations with salaried employees. Ideolog-ically, the *ie* values for corporate unity, hierarchical interdependence, and trans-generational perpetuity have been replaced by personal choice of a marital partner, by an equalizing dyadic conjugal bond, by defini-tion of the family as a collection of equal individuals, and by the restruc-turing of the family as basically nuclear rather than extended and hier-archical (Lebra 1984, 23–24; Morioka 1986, 203–205).[25]

It is in this area of familial change that individualization has most progressed. In marital choice, significant individualization has been in-tegrated with more traditional familial hierarchical concerns. The ar-ranged marriage with traditional go-betweens still occurs, although it is often depreciated as inferior to a love marriage. However, even when a marriage is arranged the couple goes out with each other at least a few times and decides on their own whether or not to marry. Even in the love marriage, where the couple has met each other without a go-be-tween, the two have already taken into account parental expectations for a mate from a family of similar background and social rank, edu-cation, income, and reputation, and almost inevitably seek parental ap-proval (Tanaka 1986, 231). Marriage is still considered as being be-tween families as well as individuals.

Another significant area of individualization involves middle-class youth, particularly in their college years, when they have a moratorium be-tween the grueling examination stress of high school and the tight-knit

---

[25] A further change has been noted in Buddhist practices of ancestor worship with the breakup of the *ie*. Instead of worshiping the deceased founding couple of the *ie*, which gave legitimacy to the living heads of the *ie*, a variety of ancestors with whom there have been emotional bonds are now being worshiped.

work-group responsibilities and reciprocities after graduating. Exposed to media influence and the latest intellectual trends and student movements, they are much taken with the ideals of greater personal autonomy and self-determination, with considerably less strict adherence to the social etiquette of formal hierarchical relationships—the latter sometimes being met with subtle, vicarious encouragement by parents. It is thus in the college years that Japanese youth most imbibe the individualizing ideals of Western culture, resulting in something of a generation gap. But this builds on individualizing trends that emerge even earlier in their lives, when a boy's particular wish for a field of study and career is taken into account.

Nevertheless, there is frequently a two-layer psychological structure in the personality of these younger persons. The striving for autonomy and independence is on an upper, more superficial level, while more basic issues of dependency, achievement, and fear of failure are much more deeply rooted as in traditional Japanese psychological makeup (Nishizono, unpublished). These younger persons, according to Drs. Okonogi and Wong (pers. com.), need considerably more direct verbal interaction in psychoanalytic therapy than do more traditional Japanese, who tend to communicate nonverbally and by innuendo.

Another area of conflict between traditional and individualized modes of functioning involves differences between rural and urban-based families, as clearly emerged in Mrs. K's case (see Chapter Five). Still another way these issues have surfaced is in the experiences of Japanese psychoanalysts themselves, who have trained abroad in America or England, partially assimilating much more individualized modes of functioning and then readapting to Japanese group hierarchical relationships, which has by no means always been easy for them.

Further individualization occurs in the middle and upper middle-class nuclear families that have proliferated in the urban areas with the formal break-up of the *ie* stem family.[26] Although obligations to the elderly still continue, with a not infrequent three-generational household for better care of them, such an arrangement is more seen today as two nuclear families living together, rather than as a hierarchically bound unit. Husbands and particularly wives make more decisions on their own now, with far less direction from family elders.

However much the salaried man is now freer of these familial hierarchical restraints, he has become tremendously immersed in group hier-

[26] In the lower middle classes involved in subcontracting work in the inner cities, an *ie* type of household occupational unit with employees in hierarchical reciprocities and emotional interdependence tends to persist (Wagatsuma and DeVos 1984, 12–14).

archical relationships at work. Dr. Kondo, who had initially expected upon his return to Japan in the early 1950s that with increasing affluence there would be much greater individualization among the Japanese, has found over the years no correlation whatsoever. Men, instead, have become even more involved in close group functioning for much longer hours. His experience is that as various Japanese patients, including a good number of corporation presidents, have become involved in even once-a-week psychoanalytic therapy, they gradually evolve a more individualized self while still functioning as well if not better in their family and group relationships. What he is suggesting is that the psychological dimension of greater individualization—central to the expanding self of Japanese as well as Indians—is not a result of greater affluence, material goods, and leisure, but rather is much more tied to cultural and psychological change introduced from Westernizing influences.

An integration of these divergent Japanese and Western value systems has been worked out by Dr. Tatara in his mode of teaching his graduate students in clinical psychology—a solution similar to ones by innovative Indian institutions cited above. This integration uses the position of the respected hierarchical superior—in this case the professor to whom students completely defer—to institute a mode of learning in which the students are encouraged and cajoled into thinking for themselves and questioning and challenging the professor. This initially stirs up considerable conflict, as students are accustomed to imbibe their teacher's words without questioning. But since these new values of greater participation and independent thinking are fostered within the traditional hierarchical relationship, Dr. Tatara's students gradually function in this manner, and in all probability will eventually pass this on to their own students. Thus a traditional professor-student mentorship inculcates greater individualization, originality, and creativity.

Case Studies

KIYOSHI

Pressures on teen-age high school boys are particularly fierce today in Japan, as the college a boy is able to get into almost completely determines his future opportunities in business or the bureaucracy. Since so much status and esteem are tied to the group one is part of, the high school a boy is in and how well he does there and in his examinations for college carry tremendous weight. It is not that these pressures are unknown in other industrialized countries, including urban India, but they are much greater in Japan, where extremely high standards of performance and group status are central to the culture. Should a boy perform poorly in school or drop out, it is a source of considerable anxiety for his parents.

Kiyoshi was a seventeen-year-old boy, whose case Dr. Totoro Ichimaru presented in a supervisory group in Hiroshima after seeing him weekly for thirty-two sessions. Kiyoshi came for therapy not only because he was at the bottom of his class in his third year in high school, but also because he had a vocal tic of compulsively crying out periodically, and another tic of smacking his lips. He became so preoccupied with these tics that he found it extremely difficult to concentrate and do his schoolwork. He also seriously bit the fingernails on his right hand. He felt passive and hopeless about getting into a decent college, and having relationships with girls and friendships with boys.

Kiyoshi came from a family that had to move every few years because his father's promotions in his company depended on his moving. Thus Kiyoshi changed cities when he was four, six, eight, and ten, only coming to Hiroshima at age fifteen. Although this is unusual in Japan, the father's consuming involvement with his corporation is not. Men work extended hours, and frequently commute long distances, and are often only weekend or Sunday fathers at best. Corporations count on the wives to handle everything at home (Lebra 1984). Kiyoshi had a brother five years older, who was quite wild when he was younger. There were no sisters, although his mother miscarried a girl between the sons' births. Kiyoshi had endeavored to get into a good private high school in Hiroshima, but he did not do well enough on the examination. He therefore went to a public high school, where he was afraid of some of the tougher boys.

Most revealing in the therapy sessions was the way Kiyoshi related to Dr. Ichimaru. He sat very close to Dr. Ichimaru, so that the latter felt a suffocating closeness and discomfort at the lack of boundaries between himself and the patient. This closeness was further engendered by Kiyoshi, who entertained Dr. Ichimaru by telling him jokes all the time, thus drawing Dr. Ichimaru even closer. But on another level, Dr. Ichimaru felt he was being given absolutely no opportunity to express himself, that he was being totally disregarded, and then pushed away by the patient who intermittently cried out.

In an American patient, this kind of transference would be regarded as the severe psychopathology of a borderline patient, whose lack of outer ego boundaries are usually the sign of a pathological symbiotic tie to a mother who is not able to let her child separate, but who deep down has little regard for her child's inner world. When I brought this up to the group of psychoanalytic therapists during our supervisory sessions, they asserted that in the Japanese therapy relationship, Kiyoshi's way of relating is more on the neurotic side, since the mother-child relationship is relatively boundaryless, and such behavior is thus considered far less severe psychopathology than in America.

Unlike an American therapist, Dr. Ichimaru did not deal at all with Kiyoshi's way of relating to him. He remained a steady listening and empathic person to Kiyoshi, rarely interpreting—in fact, rarely was he given the opportunity to say anything for some time. A picture gradually emerged of an overly close mother-son relationship, even for the Japanese, where the father was too busy at work and too unassertive to be able to come between them. Kiyoshi, in fact, slept between his parents until he was thirteen, which is on the late side even for Japanese, who rarely sleep alone (Caudhill and Plath 1974). Kiyoshi's mother treated him as a girl when he was a child, giving him dolls and such to play with—possibly to replace the girl she had miscarried; and now was directing him in everything he did, which he greatly resented.

The significance of these family relationships is that Kiyoshi's mother had bent the normally symbiotic Japanese mother-son relationship out of shape by using her son too much in terms of her own needs while disregarding his; Kiyoshi's father was pushed out of the picture, as was his older brother. Kiyoshi could, in effect, only assert a fragile self by not doing well in school; his symptom of crying out was possibly an unconscious accusation against his mother. His hopelessness and powerlessness at the beginning of therapy only generated other feelings of demand and entitlement that mother and therapist take total care of him.

Dr. Ichimaru established in the beginning that he would work with Kiyoshi only, referring the mother and father, against her pleading, to see another therapist. As Dr. Ichimaru cut into this mother-son symbiosis and remained steadfastly empathic, Kiyoshi gradually became considerably more assertive with his parents and others, and began talking in sessions about things that bothered him rather than constantly entertaining the therapist. He tried harder at school and revived hopes of getting into a decent college. As he became more assertive and hopeful, his demandings and feelings of entitlement diminished. At the same time, his mother was desperately trying to reassert their old symbiotic tie by insisting that he go shopping with her at the time of sessions.

Kiyoshi brought up two major, interrelated areas of difficulty in his sessions. The first was his intense feelings of loneliness, and the difficulty of making and hanging onto friends because of the frequent moves his family made. Kiyoshi felt deeply resentful of his father, with whom he had little relationship since his father not only worked long hours but either played golf or retired to his study when he was at home. The second problem area was with girls, with whom he felt completely inadequate. He gradually tried to establish relationships, but at first could only do it passively and indirectly, approaching one girl through another.

Later in therapy, Kiyoshi became considerably more assertive, talking to a girl he was not interested in and to boys at school in the Hiroshima dialect, which is more aggressive than standard Japanese. But with the girl he was really interested in, he talked in standard Japanese. It was even more significant that his diary was written in a more feminine manner of expression, showing disturbances in gender identity rooted in his mother's treatment of him as a girl. This observation during the supervisory group (by Yoshiko Idei) was based on the premise that the more authentic, private self of Japanese is expressed in the diaries they frequently keep, revealing their innermost thoughts and feelings that are rarely if ever expressed openly. The therapists were thus highly sensitive to the different modes of communication Kiyoshi used: the Hiroshima dialect when he endeavored to appear strong and assertive; standard Japanese when with a girl he was interested in but with whom he felt inhibited; and a more feminine mode of expression in his diary, which revealed his more inner self and indicated problems in gender identity.

HIROSHI

Hiroshi was a sixteen-year-old high school student whom Professor Najima presented in a supervision group in Kumamoto after seeing him for twenty-three sessions of weekly psychoanalytic therapy. Hiroshi's problems ostensibly started after he was six months into the ninth grade in October 1981, when he stayed home from school with a headache and stomach ache, and then refused to attend school after that. Instead, he watched television, listened to music, and on the weekends shopped for records. Both of his parents were deeply distressed and ashamed of his nonattendance, and reluctantly let him go to a psychotherapist when they were so advised.

Hiroshi's father, a junior high school principal, like fathers of many Japanese children today is completely absorbed in his demanding position and has little relationship with Hiroshi. The mother is far more assertive than the father, and Hiroshi is thus totally involved in an intense mother-son symbiosis. A sister ten years older is more like the mother, but is uninvolved with Hiroshi. He was actually raised partially by a grandmother until he attended elementary school, at which point his mother gave up her position as a schoolteacher to take complete charge of Hiroshi.

The main issue that emerged in sessions was a longstanding struggle of Hiroshi with an aggressive and controlling mother, who was constantly telling him what to do. He always felt defeated by her no matter how he struggled. When she was around, he gave an appearance of conforming to her demands, but passively resisted what she wanted the moment she was absent. He felt desperate, with little sense of knowing what he wanted or of his own will. Hiroshi voiced some wish to be independent, but felt he was so totally dependent on his mother, with little if any relationship with his father, that he was unable to separate at all from her. This same passive, unexpressive manner was how he related to Professor Najima.

As in the case of Mrs. K (see Chapter Five), in the beginning of therapy Hiroshi demonstrated the onionlike nature of some Japanese who are totally out of touch with their own wishes and will, and who have very little sense of an inner self. It is apparent that this derives from a mother-child symbiotic relationship in which the mother is unempathic with the child's inner world. Hiroshi's overbearing mother hardly took into account Hiroshi's inner needs and wishes, instead contantly directing him according to her own. Like Kiyoshi, Hiroshi passively asserted himself to preserve a highly fragile sense of self in one of the few areas under his control: attending or doing well in school.

Professor Najima, like Drs. Idei and Ichimaru, related to Hiroshi in an empathic manner with little investigation, reflection, or interpretation. As a result, Hiroshi could use this therapeutic relationship as "free parking" apart from the pressures of his mother and school. He gradually became able to express a great deal about his subterranean struggle with his mother over his schooling. She had ruled out a private school he wanted to go to with his friends, as the public school had higher standards. This need for excellence and her practice of deriving her esteem from her son's placement in a school is characteristic of many Japanese mothers. He attended public school for several months until he was unable to play soccer, his favorite sport, because of a sprained ankle. Once he was cut off from the one activity that was his and not his mother's, he suddenly stopped going to school.

His mother then promised Hiroshi to transfer him to the private school if he attended public school for a week. In the early weeks of therapy he refused to trust her word, but feeling more of a sense of self after three months of therapy he went to classes for a week. His mother then renegged on her word, and his father passively went along with her. Hiroshi reacted by dropping out of school once again. This time he openly said that since she went back on her promise, he no longer cared how he reflected on his parents, and began to dress and wear his hair in a more delinquent style.

His commentary serves to illustrate that a major motive in Japanese performance is how one reflects on others of the family and group by doing well, and thus enhancing their esteem. Inner esteem is always connected to a we-self in both hierarchical relationships—in this case parent-child—and relationships with the family or group as a whole. Obviously, by not attending school and even dressing in a delinquent style, Hiroshi could hurt the esteem of his parents.

The issue of we-self esteem becomes further illuminated from a completely different standpoint. After some four months of therapy, a teacher from the school contacted Hiroshi and urged him to come back. Hiroshi actually did begin to attend school, but much more in activities such as the brass-band club than in his classes. It therefore emerged that Hiroshi was also staying out of school out of a fear of rejection by the school and his classmates. He was evidently greatly dependent on how they viewed him. Once he felt accepted by this teacher, it became much easier for him to attend.

Since his mother put complete stock in his attending classes and did not care about his activities, Hiroshi was still asserting his will indirectly by going only occasionally to classes. In later sessions, however, he was able to assert that he now knew much better what he wanted—such as a license for a motor bike. In the current phase of therapy, he continued to come regularly, but was frequently late and was often silent. He seemed to be testing the therapist as to whether the latter would put some kind of pressure on him to do things, as his mother did. The therapist was keenly aware of this and continued to remain silently empathic on the whole. Obviously, the psychoanalytic therapy still had some way to go.

What do these two teen-age cases contribute to our understanding of school pressures and problems, and Japanese psychological functioning? On a social level, both cases confirm social science observations that as Japan has successfully modernized, men are so caught up in their work group that they often have relatively little relationship with family members. As a result, their wives assume even more responsibility for their sons' education, leading to the popular phrase today, "education mama."

And as the pressures to get into a good school and college escalate, mothers' involvement with their sons' schoolwork correspondingly increases.

On a more psychological level, it is apparent that a normal mother-son symbiotic tie becomes greatly intensified by the father's absence. The boy becomes more totally dependent on his mother and on fulfilling her high expectations, as she is on him. Integral to his doing well is the wish to enhance her esteem by reflecting well on her and the family; and in turn, much of the mother's esteem derives from how well her son is doing. In a corporate situation, a given wife may thus be lower in the hierarchy than other wives whose husbands have higher positions, but if her son is doing better than their sons at school, then she will have attained a special status as well as becoming the object of their jealousy.

In both Kiyoshi's and Hiroshi's cases, their mothers were highly involved with directing their sons' lives, but were out of touch with their boys' inner world and wishes. This manifested itself somewhat differently in each case, but in both the lack of maternal empathy was central. Both boys were so dependent on their mothers that they could not assert themselves in any direct way to preserve a sense of self. Rather they had to do poorly or drop out of school to attain any measure of an inner independent self; at the same time, they felt entitled to be taken care of. In more extreme cases, teen-age boys who are doing poorly will sometimes physically assault their mothers in an outburst of rage. Kiyoshi, however, contained his rage through compulsive tic symptoms, while Hiroshi simply refused to attend school. Nevertheless, both boys were able to respond very positively to a steady, silently empathic male therapist who cut into the mother-child tie and enabled their selves to begin to be accepted and understood.

Westernization/Modernization and the Expanding Self in India and Japan

Without question, the Japanese familial-group self has excelled to a greater extent than the Indian one in the kinds of functioning required in the modernization process. Internalized standards in the ego-ideal for very high levels of performance and engagement in relationships and tasks, high achievement motivation, and the ability to work harmoniously and co-operatively in a well-functioning group are perhaps the most crucial psychological factors in Japan's successful modernization. Personal ambitions are fulfilled through furthering the goals of the group. In short, the Japanese experience clearly disclaims any necessity for the development of a predominantly individualized Western kind of self for implementing the modernization process. In India too, substantial modernization has been accomplished in part through the Indian familial self.

Although there is perhaps an even greater clash of Western cultural values and social patterns with indigenous ones in Japan than in India, neverthless the Japanese have not experienced the intensity of identity conflicts that Indians have. The reasons for this are easily evident. Until their defeat in World War II, the Japanese had voluntarily assimilated various Western institutions, technology, education, and even ideologies, but had essentially preserved and valued their own social patterns and cultural codes.[27] Even when the American Occupation took advantage of the crushing disillusionment with the imperial system to foment far-reaching changes, a great deal of traditional culture and society was still respected. It was primarily the male power structure with its "feudalistic" values that was denigrated and partially dissolved.

This is not to negate the presence of identity conflicts in contemporary Japanese over the clash of highly differing cultural ideals for personal functioning, especially between close-knit family and group hierarchical patterns with those of egalitarianism and individualism. Japanese psychoanalysts, for instance, trained in both England and the United States, have self-reflectedly reported much more of an intense identity struggle upon returning home over contrasting Western and Japanese values and modes of relating than have Indian analysts, but have much less of an inner identity struggle over the subtle emotional issues of superiority-inferiority and self-esteem between Western and indigenous culture. Both groups of analysts, though, have conveyed their own particular resolutions and integrations of these issues within themselves in what I strongly sense to be an expanding self. That is, they have effected workable integrations—sometimes not without problems—of both indigenous and foreign values and modes of being and relating that go beyond either the traditional or the Western.

Indians, on the other hand, were exposed to a prolonged, accelerating denigration of their own culture and social patterns by a colonial presence that not only generated far more intense identity conflicts over internalized values of indigenous and Western culture than experienced by Japanese, but also resulted in major social movements for reasserting and reforming Indian traditions. Since British colonialism lasted over a century and a half, and the American Occupation but six years, Indians

---

[27] This is consonant with Japan's past assimilation of Chinese culture.

have more extensively internalized various aspects of Western culture than have Japanese; that is, the West is now a more integral part of the urban Indian self than it is of the Japanese.

Strongly related to these identity issues, especially for the Japanese, is the other major psychological process related to Westernization-modernization: that of individualization. It is my distinct impression that paradoxically, although Japan has modernized far more successfully than India in terms of economic and industrial development, the integration of more individualized functioning into an expanding familial self is much more filled with inner conflict than in India, and will take many more decades to accomplish. Starting from a more overtly individualistic culture, Indians, with all of the problems that British colonialism generated, nevertheless have had a much longer period of time to assimilate Western values and modes of functioning that are far more individualized. Moreover, this individualized functioning has gradually been incorporated into the Indian extended family which, as the psychological locus of Indians, has flexibly given greater scope to adolescents. As a result, adolescents and adults can function in a more individualized way than before within the broad context of their familial self; though this process is not without conflict, as I have amply documented from case material.

In contrast, the Japanese—starting from a more homogeneous cultural base and a more covertly individualistic mode, where essentially to this day one is still completely either in or outside of Japanese society with its closely enmeshed group functioning—have been much more recently directly exposed to a set of values around Western individualism and egalitarianism through the American Occupation that are even more foreign to them. Although Japanese middle-class youth have greater latitude than before in terms of educational and vocational choices, and are given even greater freedom in their college days, nevertheless this is sandwiched between the examination stress of high school and the tightly knit functioning of the adult work group, both of which are largely antithetical to more individualized functioning. And even with some lessening of the social etiquette of formal hierarchical relationships, the freer choice of a marital partner, and the ability of women to assert themselves somewhat more, my strong impression is that individualization will take longer to assimilate into a Japanese expanding self, while tending to generate more inner conflict than in urban Indians.

The Dynamics of Change in Urban Indian and Japanese Women

Sociohistorical Perspective on Indian Women

If social change is the theme of the modern era, East and West, perhaps no more profound social psychological changes have occurred than in the women's sphere. The underlying dynamics of women's change in India and America are, however, of a different order, reflecting the profound civilizational differences between the two countries. The women's movement in America is oriented toward women striving for a more individualized, autonomous self, to have an identity of their own in their work and familial relationships—the predominant mode of American psychological functioning previously reserved overwhelmingly for men. In contrast, sweeping changes in marital mores, education, and work in the urban Indian women's sphere are better understood within the paradigms of the previous chapter: various aspects of the familial self become readily available for modernizing changes, while simultaneously, through these changes, there is a markedly increasing individualization and individuation.

In contrast to the identity struggles of many urban-educated Indian men exposed to strong Westernizing influences and British colonial denigration, urban Indian women have experienced far less conflict over their Indianness, remaining considerably more anchored in the traditional culture and less seriously beset by the currents of Westernization. They continue to spread a web of meaning over modernizing changes and processes through utilizing the cultural framework of folklore (pers. com. A. K. Ramanujan) and mythology, supporting a spiritual reality and self in its continuity with everyday relationships and events.

Even to begin to assess these psychological processes of change in urban Indian women it is essential to provide a backdrop of historical perspectives. Undoubtedly, the strongest initial push for change involving Indian women was precipitated by nineteenth-century British colonial criticism and efforts at reform. The overwhelming impetus for the nineteenth-century Indian reformers to improve the lot of upper-caste urban women came completely from upper-caste, partially Westernized Hindu men in their identity struggle to reassert a measure of self-respect vis-à-vis the British,[1] as well as to insure meaningful continuity of Hindu familial and caste traditions (Sakala 1980, 3–13). Beleagured by criticisms from British educators, administrators, and missionaries to the effect that the place of women in a society determines its civilizational status (Leonard 1976; Mazumdar 1976; Nandy 1980b, 1–31), influenced by the introduction of liberal humanitarianism and rationalism, and beset by problems within their own communities, many of these upper-caste male leaders strove for a variety of reforms, including widow remarriage and the education of girls (Mazumdar 1976), the abolition of *sati* (Nandy 1980b), child marriage (Das 1975), and polygamy. The lot of upper-caste urban woman gradually improved through the efforts of both British and Hindu reformers, but these reforms were restricted to a very small, elite segment of the society.

To give indigenous authority to these changes, the reformers generally fell back upon those aspects of Hindu culture and history that were highest in traditional status or were most overtly supportive of women's position in society.[2] It is important to note that just as there are structural antitheses within Hindu culture between the hierarchy of caste and family and the context-free condition of the renouncer, so has there also been an essential antithesis between major movements enhancing the public and religious status of women, such as Buddhism and Jainism in

[1] A number of leaders paradoxically attempted to reassert an Indian identity by relying on the female religious principle of *shakti* and the various mother goddesses standing for strength and power, indicative of the enormous power accorded the mother within the Hindu family and pantheon (Nandy 1980b, 32–40).

[2] Thus, for example, Dayananda in the Punjab relied on the sacred Vedic ideals of ancient India, when women were much less subordinate than in the later Brahminic structural hierarchy, as propounded in the writings attributed to Manu and Kautilya.

earlier periods and the *bhakti* movement in later ones, and many of the conceptions and practices of traditional Brahminic hierarchy (Thapar 1966). In both past and present, movements encouraging an enhanced position of women seem to be more urban-based.

In the nineteenth century, upper-caste urban women remained within the extended family and home, since in a primarily agricultural economy, enhanced social position has always meant that women do not have to labor outside the family—which is still generally true in rural India (Srinivas 1978). Nevertheless, by the 1880s women's associations were started by some of these urban women for social reform, and by 1905 they were taking political stands, including asking for the vote in 1917.

From 1918 on, however, greater numbers of women began to be involved in the National Movement, drawn by the charismatic influence of Gandhi. Large numbers of urban and rural women became involved in his Satyagraha campaigns from 1930 on, and the earlier women's associations grew enormously across India in the struggle for independence (Leonard 1976; Mazumdar 1976).[3] Inspired by Gandhi's emphasis on self-reliance, these women became involved in an enormous variety of reform and social uplift causes ranging from adult literacy to slum clearance to problems of malnutrition.

Gandhi viewed women's capacity for self-sacrifice, nonviolence and perserverance as being particularly apropos for his approach, and tried to further the enhancement of women's position in society in a number of ways: not only through all of the reforms previously advocated, but also through greater equality within the marital relationship, the political sphere, and in the inheritance of property. In a culture where sex segregation, especially in the public arena, is of particular importance, the involvement of large numbers of women in the National Movement was predicated upon a profound trust of Gandhi not only by the women but perhaps even more importantly by their husbands and fathers (Srinivas 1978). As they participated in large numbers, Indian women assumed public positions of importance and influence, not to be relinquished afterwards. The momentum of the National Movement carried women's rights into important legislation in post-Independence India, supported by Nehru's concern for economic equality and protection

---

[3] Most of the women who participated were unmarried or widows from urban families, the married ones generally coming only from reform-minded families; in rural areas, they were frequently agricultural laborers rather than those from the better-off landowning families. Thus, the typical Hindu married woman did not usually participate actively in the National Movement (pers. com. Geraldine Forbes).

(Mazumdar 1976). Many have commented that the easy acceptance of women in the public sphere in India also derives from women's inherent powers within the social and cultural spheres—that is, within extended family relationships and in the Hindu cosmology, the two being closely intertwined (Nandy 1980b, 32–46).[4]

This brings us to the modernization process for women in post-Independence urban India. Modernizing changes have been noted in several distinct areas, particularly for middle- and upper-class urban women in Hindu, Muslim, Christian, and Parsee communities. The marital age has gradually increased, so that most marriages are now arranged when the girl is at least in her late teens and often in her early twenties. Large numbers of these girls are at least school-educated, are frequently college graduates, and not infrequently go on to postgraduate education. Many of these girls, particularly in a city like Bombay, prepare for some type of work to help augment family income, while those with more advanced education are often strongly oriented toward a career.

It is essential to note that the age of marriage, the degree of a girl's influence on the arranged marriage, the amount of education, and the preparation for a job or a career are overwhelmingly influenced by family culture and *jati* norms, varying considerably between *jatis* and between families within a *jati* (Das 1976a; Leonard 1976; Mehta 1976; Srinivas 1978)—rather than by various facets of an individualized self, as with contemporary urban American women. This influence by family culture and community is equally true in the various Muslim, Christian, Parsee, and Jewish communities. That is, a particular family may emphasize higher education for all of the children, girls as well as boys, and will then try to arrange a suitable match in which the husband will be equally if not better educated, with a similar occupational rank (Leonard 1976), and in which the husband and his family will support his wife's career. Generally speaking, the amount of education a girl receives is also strongly determined by *jati* norms, so that she is not better educated than the boys in her *jati;* otherwise, her marriage becomes extremely difficult to arrange. The more educated she is, the larger her dowry generally must be because of the difficulty in finding a well-educated boy from a suitable family (Srinivas 1978). When she is married and works, her working status and earnings are usually subordi-

[4] Another perspective on the great surge in women's rights in the National Movement is the historical one that women's issues make their greatest strides during broader, more encompassing reform movements—such as the Abolitionist Movement in nineteenth-century America or during the American Vietnam protest and the Civil Rights Movement of the 1960s (Roland and Harris 1978: 179–180).

nated to the family structure and relationships, with her working status being viewed in comparison to her husband's in terms of prestige and monetary value (Das 1976a; Madan 1976; Mehta 1976).

In essence, a woman's education and work capacity are to enhance the reputation first of her original family in the marital arrangements, and then the position, honor, and material well-being of her in-laws, of which she feels and becomes an integral part. In the urban middle and lower-middle classes, her higher education is respected more in terms of the honor and earning capacity she brings to her in-laws than in appreciation of her knowledge per se (pers. com. Manisha Roy). With the support of her original family and then her husband and in-laws, career and family become easily managed; for child rearing she has help from her extended family and servants and can manage much more easily than in the contemporary American nuclear family, unless extended family members and/or servants are unavailable. In these latter cases it can become more difficult, since she is usually expected to handle household as well as work responsibilities. Without familial supports, especially of her husband and in-laws, a career becomes virtually impossible. Studies such as Rama Mehta's (1976) on the Oswal caste of Rajput and Karen Leonard's (1976) on the Kayasthas of Hyderabad clearly show how the modernization of the women in these castes in terms of much later marital ages, advanced education, and careers has been generated by the caste elders and has taken place within the traditional values and hierarchical relationships of the extended family and *jati* in response to broader socioeconomic changes.

The careers first open to women were primarily in the fields of education and medicine, which were eminently suited to separate sexual spheres, particularly since women usually went only to a female doctor and an all-girls school. This has now changed appreciably, with women going into careers and jobs in a number of fields. Like their Western counterparts, Indian women frequently encounter considerable discrimination, only rarely attaining the higher positions within a field, be it in media, science, or management. Even now, the percentage of girls in secondary schools and colleges is still approximately a quarter of the total enrollment, since family priorities for education are still centered on the boys.

Within the family itself, women's education was first furthered by the male reformers as fathers or husbands, who sometimes evoked conflict with the older, more orthodox women of the family—Justice Ranade, for example, educated his wife, who was then ostracized by the women of his family (Sakala 1981). However, as the total family, women included, have gradually recognized the advantages to the family for the girls to be well educated, the older uneducated or less educated women have been fully open and supportive of their daughters, granddaughters, and nieces in getting an increasing amount of schooling (pers. com. Veena Das; Leonard 1976; Mehta 1976). Expectations remain that as the girls attain higher education and positions of work, they will keep up traditional familial manners, attitudes, values, and responsibilities within the extended family hierarchical relationships (pers. com. Manisha Roy). In the present generation, most of the girls who are going to college still rely on guidance from their more educated fathers and older brothers, a situation that will obviously change in urban India in succeeding generations.

On a more psychological level, modernization in terms of later marriages, somewhat more say in the marital decision, higher education, and preparation for job or career all take place psychologically within the bounds of the familial self.

Individualization and the Extended Family

Consistent with some of the perspectives and paradigms elucidated in the last chapter, modernizing changes for women also result in significantly increased individualization and individuation; but these latter are primarily oriented toward familial functioning and the familial self rather than toward any Western-style individualism and the individualized self. This growing individualization is an essential element in the expanding self of Indian women, and is now resulting in important changes in women's central relationships with each other as well as within themselves; but individualization can also generate considerable conflict over traditional attitudes and values around women's position in the structural hierarchy.

Within the broad form of the arranged marriage there is an increased leaning toward a more companionate marriage, in which the wife's various emotional needs, including sexual ones, are taken more into account by the husband, and in which she is more recognized as a person (Gore 1978; Kapur 1974). This contrasts with a more traditional marital relationship in which women's intimacy needs are largely fulfilled through the other women of the family, the children, and younger brothers-in-law. This does not necessarily mean that the current Indian marriage is heading toward a Western-style highly individualistic and egalitarian, romantic love marriage—a conclusion that is sometimes erroneously drawn (Ross 1961). That the wife's increasing expectations for greater involvement and recognition by her husband are not always met by a husband who is himself rooted in older traditional attitudes of satisfying intimacy needs with the other men of the extended family and his mother is amply recorded (pers. com. R. Kakkar and B. K. Ramanujam; Kapur 1974). Sometimes these changing expectations seem to be unduly complicated by the Western literary romantic notions absorbed by women, who then became deeply frustrated by the vast gap between their romantic expectations and their actual experience in a marital relationship (Roy 1975).

As many of the highly educated urban women with jobs or careers have become increasingly individualized, they are sometimes faced with a delicate situation in their marriages. They are expected to observe the etiquette of female-male deferential behavior within the structural hierarchy of marriage, while indirectly maneuvering for what they want. But having now attained much more of an identity and mind of their own, they tend to become far more openly assertive in their opinions, sometimes challenging the authoritative façade of their husbands (pers. com. B. K. Ramanujam). This can upset the particular balance of the Indian husband-wife relationship, where the man is accorded a superior position in the structural hierarchy, but where the woman looms large in the male psyche. Her influence is so pervasive because she is accorded a variety of powers in enhancing the family, on the one hand; on the other, as mother she is experienced as unusually powerful due to the prolonged, intense mothering of children and the expectation of a lifelong close attachment to her.

Several women, quite psychologically sophisticated, have related to me that their husbands simply cannot tolerate too open assertiveness on their part because of unconsciously perceiving them as being so covertly powerful, like their mothers. These women often gave in to many of their husband's demands, some on rather important career issues, because to assert themselves would be to profoundly disturb the marital relationship—that is, the husband would begin to experience his wife as the powerful mother.

Further conflict in the husband-wife relationship is now occurring in certain urban families where the wife is working and there are insufficient members of the extended family or servants to take over child-rearing responsibilities and household chores. Husbands tend to look to their wives to fulfill their traditional roles of handling everything around the house, even after a full day's work, which can evoke considerable resentment on the wife's part (Kapur 1974)—a not unfamiliar problem in American circles as well.

Greater individualization is also affecting the traditional daughter-in-law/mother-in-law relationship. In the earlier times of child marriage, the girl would gradually spend more and more time in her husband's family—in south Indian cross-cousin marriages, it would be with her own relatives—being instructed and molded into the traditions of that family by the older women. Today, the urban upper-caste girl upon marriage is usually at least twenty, is generally college-educated, occasionally with postgraduate degrees, and is expected to do some work outside the family. She is thus far less malleable by her mother-in-law and the other female in-laws, though she is still highly attuned toward getting along well with them.

Older, uneducated women may make special efforts to adapt to their newly educated, career-oriented daughters-in-law, recognizing the necessity of their community to adapt to new socioeconomic exingencies (Mehta 1970, 1976). In a transition time such as this, however, there can also be intense clashes between a more traditional-minded mother-in-law and a daughter-in-law who has become far more educated and individualized. In another generation or two, as a greater number of these girls have gone to college and then become mothers-in-law themselves, a more flexible hierarchical relationship will undoubtedly develop; and in fact, this seems already to be occurring with educated mothers-in-law. Generational conflict among the women of the extended family will not disappear with increased education, but the developing individualization will be more easily assimilated.

In terms of education, girls are reported to be doing exceedingly well in school and college, often better than their male counterparts. This may well be related to the fact that girls are less gratified and indulged within their families than their brothers; they are raised to be highly competent and responsible—essential traits to function well in their in-law's family (Jain 1975). A girl is, however, expected to carry into the college situation various facets of a familial self such as being modest and self-effacing and not mixing with boys—the former traits being sometimes incongruent with participating fully in classroom discussion. It is patently clear from the popular Hindi movies that improper, sexually seductive, and overtly assertive behavior are now equated with Westernization; while the traditional values of the familial self, centered on modesty and shame, are associated with a traditional Indian girl and mother (Nandy 1979). Thus expressed in contemporary guise is the older cultural version of the two sides of a woman's sexuality: enhancing the

153

prosperity and continuity of the extended family, or bringing chaos and ruin through promiscuity (Vatsayayan 1975).

In summary, as urban women have successfully participated in the modernization process through various structures of the familial self, they have become far more individualized in their views and opinions, wishes, and sense of self than before. Although this can and sometimes does generate conflict in the husband-wife, male-female, and mother-in-law/daughter-in-law relationships, a gradual accommodation seems to be taking place nevertheless.

Case Studies

Underlying the observable waves of modernization are the deeper psychological currents within urban Indian women. By diving below the surface of behavioral observation through therapeutic exploration of the psychic depths, a more profound perspective emerges of the shifting currents in the female psyche as they interact with the more easily discernable social tides of change to effect an expanding self. A much richer, more complex inner world comes to light than one would ever suspect. The first woman I shall discuss, Shakuntala, serves to illustrate the highly complex nonlinear intertwining of traditional themes involving both the familial and spiritual selves with modernizing ones involving increasing individualization. The second woman, Saida, shows some of the more hidden psychological bases of the traditional daughter-in-law/mother-in-law relationship and the effects of modernization and individualization.

Shakuntala

Shakuntala, a woman in her late twenties, comes from an upper middle-class, upper-caste family from north India. She is an attractive, socially sophisticated, intelligent, and artistic woman, who is currently a college lecturer in the humanities in Bombay. Students gravitate to her for informal counseling. When she began getting in over her head with a couple of them, a psychologically sophisticated administrator suggested she see a psychoanalyst—which she did for over a year, and then stopped. The administrator, upon learning that I was in Bombay, suggested that Shakuntala see me.

In the initial session, Shakuntala hinted at highly ambivalent feelings concerning her former therapist. "I would have to lie down and he would sit silently most of the time. . . . At times I didn't come." She didn't like "must" situations; they reminded her too much of her relationship with her mother, who was always ill. I told her that coming to therapy was strictly up to her, which eased the situation appreciably. Like Joan, Shakuntala's attitudes showed that although there is deference in Indian hierarchical relationships, the person has definite feelings of what she may or may not want to do, and when the relationship is not a satisfactory one, she will cut it off in one way or another.

But what struck me much more was that she had been in psychoanalytic therapy twice a week for well over a year, and had been able to keep two of the most important areas of her life completely secret from the therapist. I have not yet encountered anything close to this with American patients. She felt the therapist would not be receptive to these two major concerns of hers, and so simply never brought them up. What impressed me was the radar sensitivity of Indians to how receptive the other would be to various aspects of one's inner life, and their ability to keep some secret, within the private self.

At the initial session, I asked her how she felt about seeing an American therapist. She replied that it would actually be easier in ways than seeing an Indian one, as Indian men have double standards. She intimated that I, as the liberal American, probably would not. She was not yet married—extremely unusual for an Indian woman in her late twenties—but felt intense pressure from her parents, particularly her mother, to have an arranged marriage. "I don't know if I can die in peace without your being married, I worry so," evoked considerable guilt in Shakuntala. She then revealed that she was tremendously attached to a close friend's husband, Kumar, a man some fifteen years older, and intimated that there might be a sexual relationship going on; but she was highly reluctant to talk about this.

This central conflict of her life, whether to give in to familial pressures, and particularly her mother's, to have an arranged marriage, or whether to continue a long-term affair with Kumar came to occupy the center stage of our work together, but had not been revealed at all to her former therapist because of her strong expectations of being criticized and judged by him. Although this seemed to be a realistic evaluation of the attitudes of an Indian urban man, I came to know of certain exceptions among the Bombay analysts. It eventually emerged that her fear of being judged by Indian men was also an unconscious projection of her own quite traditional, deeply internalized conscience, which condemned the affair. Coming to see me as the liberal American, the resistance to communication was far less intense.

By the end of the first session we agreed that she would come two or three times a week—three times if her teaching schedule permitted—for the four months I would be in Bombay. She spoke increasingly freely as confidentiality was firmly established and the issue of the double standard discussed. She seemed more than glad to pour forth her intense feelings around Kumar and his wife, Veena, as well as her conflicts over having her parents arrange a marriage. This is an important commentary on self-presentation and the inner private self in Indian hierarchical relationships, where women may be extremely circumspect in what they say in any number of social situations. But given a nonjudgmental, confidential, and receptive relationship, Shakuntala revealed a great range of feelings and fantasies from her private self. I have generally found that if it is possible to get beyond the outer barrier of social reserve, Indian patients tend to be in touch with a wider range of feelings and fantasies than most Americans. In effect, if the psychoanalytic relationship can be transformed from a structural hierarchical one in which the analyst is deferred to, to that of hierarchy by quality in which the analyst is related to as one of the more trusted, empathic members of the extended family or a respected mentor, then associations and emotions are freely expressed.

The sociohistorical context of Shakuntala's situation was highly pertinent to her inner struggles. Shakuntala's family—like other highly educated, middle- or upper middle-class urban elite families—have modified the arranged marriage first to allow their daughter to receive college and then postgraduate education, and then to have a veto over their choice. Her conflict would never have emerged in the form it did if it were not for the modernization that her family had undergone. In a more traditional family, or her own but a few decades before, Shakuntala would simply have had her marriage arranged—in past eras at an early age—and would not have been able to wriggle out of two or three arrangements at the last minute, as had already occurred. The affair itself could be managed far more easily in the modern, cosmopolitan atmosphere of Bombay—where a single woman can live on her own, as Shakuntala did, in a room in someone's flat with a certain degree of anonymity and privacy of relationships—than perhaps in any other Indian city.[5]

At the beginning of our work together, a particular drama was ensuing between Shakuntala, Kumar, and Veena. Shakuntala revealed that

---

[5] This is not at all to suggest that affairs do not go on elsewhere in India. It is only that they can be managed more easily by a single woman in certain circles in Bombay.

she has been a close friend of Veena and Kumar for the last ten years. They were all from the same community and easily socialized together. Veena doesn't really know that she and Kumar are having an affair, although Shakuntala senses that Veena is very uneasy about Shakuntala's relationship with Kumar. Shakuntala feels Veena is acting in a very subtle way to edge her out. In front of Kumar, Veena enthusiastically invites Shakuntala over, but she then conveys to Kumar privately that Shakuntala doesn't really want to visit, thus slowly manipulating matters to cut off the relationship. In the past, Veena had subtly alienated Kumar from his favorite niece because the latter tended to be too exclusively involved with Kumar. Shakuntala, on the other hand, goes out of her way to be a close friend of Veena. In fact, Shakuntala sees all of them as her second family, is very attached to Veena and the children as well as to Kumar, and so is both disturbed and angry over what she senses Veena is doing, though she realizes that Veena sees her as a rival.

This pattern of having an affair with a married man by remaining close friends with his wife and children is completely alien to anything I have seen in American life with my patients, or socially.[6] I was not quite sure what to make of it. Later conversations with Niti Seth, a psychologist, revealed that a few of her single women friends in Bombay who were involved with married men inevitably had close relationships with his wife and children. Our discussion pointed to the profound need of the Indian woman for a strong emotional enmeshment and connectedness within family relationships, which is then carried over into the affair with a married man and his family. Also characteristically Indian was Veena's subtle maneuvering to edge Shakuntala out. These subtleties are usually sensed rather than openly discussed, Indians being constantly attuned to underlying feelings and motives that are rarely communicated overtly.

By the sixth session, Shakuntala told of mending fences with Veena by confronting her about not inviting Shakuntala over when the two of them could be together. Then her associations suddenly went off in another direction. Shakuntala began speaking about her favorite aunt, who had wanted Shakuntala to marry her son, Shakuntala's first cousin. Shakuntala and the boy both wanted to marry, but Shakuntala's father evoked the norms of their north Indian community, which forbade first cousins to marry. When this aunt became widowed in her thirties, she turned to the religious life and became a holy woman, a recognized and

---

[6]Inevitable exceptions among American women have been reported to me by readers of this manuscript, and it has also been pointed out that this pattern is not infrequent in Western Europe.

respected guru with an appreciable following and an ashram at Simla. Shakuntala revealed that her aunt initiated her and told her she has very great spiritual potential and could stay in the ashram—or she could also get married. Recently, her aunt had written Shakuntala criticizing her for neither marrying nor coming to the ashram to advance herself spiritually. What emerged dramatically was that her inner conflict was not simply between continuing her affair with Kumar and having an arranged marriage, but equally between the affair and renouncing the world to go to her aunt's ashram—something her mother would also oppose.

Shakuntala had told none of this second conflict, nor any of her intense spiritual aspirations, practices, and experiences to her first therapist. She sensed he would simply not be in tune with the spiritual side of herself, and so she kept this major dimension of her inner world to herself. This was a further reason for not seeking out other Bombay psychoanalysts after leaving her first therapist. This fear actually had some grounding in reality, as many of the psychoanalysts I met in Bombay have made their main ideological investment in highly individualized, at times Western values, and are often extremely ambivalent if not negative toward Hindu religion and spiritual practices (N. Seth 1980). I encountered Shakuntala's attitude again and again, when people told me in a social context of their hesitation to communicate anything of a traditional spiritual nature to anyone unreceptive to it, and particularly to someone, whether Indian or Western, with Western-oriented, rational, positivistic values.

I should further note that Shakuntala's colleagues at the college, even ones who were reasonably close to her, seemed to have had no idea whatsoever of her intense involvement in spiritual pursuits. From conversations with them at a time when I was asked to lecture in a couple of their classes, I gathered that they saw her primarily as a lively, highly socially sophisticated woman, something of a social butterfly. Thus it is apparent in Shakuntala and other Indians I encountered that efforts to realize the spiritual self are often kept very private—in some contrast to Americans I know who are inclined in this direction.

In the ensuing several sessions, Shakuntala offered some commentary on the nature of marriage for an urban educated Hindu woman, as she struggled with her involvement with Kumar in contrast to an arranged marriage. She said that the lot of an unmarried woman, even in the modernized sector of urban Indian society, is highly insecure unless she is strongly career-oriented—which Shakuntala is not. Since an Indian woman's security is tied first to her father, and then to her husband and son(s), as Shakuntala got older and her parents would pass away, her insecurity would only become worse. She faced the further reality that Kumar would never leave his wife and children, as he felt responsible for them and devoted to the latter, and needed to preserve his highly successful position in society, which would be jeopardized if he left his wife. Even more painful was the realization that Shakuntala could never have a child by him, as this is totally unacceptable in even the most Westernized sectors of Indian urban society—in contrast to contemporary American urban society, where occasionally single women from the upper-middle classes plan to have children.

Nevertheless, her passionate involvement with Kumar and her feeling very special offset all of these reality considerations. In an arranged marriage, she felt there usually is much less sexual passion, at least for some years, and she would have to adjust completely to her husband; although she asserted that in the very process of giving over, an Indian wife slowly gains control. As Shakuntala confronted her dilemma in our sessions, she became deeply involved one day in prayer and meditation, and felt appreciably better.

Her associations turned to her parents, particularly her mother, who were to come to Bombay for an extended stay with Shakuntala's brother and sister-in-law. When she fervently expressed the wish to stay with her parents apart from her brother and sister-in-law, I interpreted that she would like to go back to old times. She responded by crying for some time, telling how greatly indulged and specially treated she had been as a child, and how hard it was living on her own—she just barely made ends meet in Bombay. She felt depressed at being separated from her parents and would have liked just to lie beside her mother again.

I have never heard an American woman patient express such a wish. The difference in normal dependency and interdependency relationships became clearer in the following session, when Shakuntala elaborated that in an Indian family, dependence on one's parents, especially the mother, is simply enormous, for a girl as well as a boy; that if a parent dies, it's as if part of you disappears. Conversely, she sensed that she meant so much to her mother that she was profoundly letting her down by not marrying, and therefore felt terribly guilty. The problem in Shakuntala's case was that the relationship with her mother did not work well.

In spite of being intensely involved in the Durga Puja, a major religious holiday, she came to the following session complaining a great deal about back pains, feeling she was being repaid for being mean to her mother by not agreeing to an arranged marriage. Her mother let her know that she would not have peace even after she died if Shakuntala did not marry—thereby using traditional beliefs about reincarnation to evoke guilt in Shakuntala. Shakuntala now wavered over proceeding with the arranged marriage for her mother's sake, gaining only security for herself. Nevertheless, she had begun to differentiate herself from her mother by seeing a back specialist, something her mother had never done. Shakuntala had always felt pressure to relieve her mother's suffering, but felt she never could. She closed the session by saying that I was the only one she could really open up to, indirectly conveying the sense that her intense dependency needs were being partially fulfilled through the therapeutic relationship.

On the surface, it appears that Shakuntala's love affair with Kumar was simply an expression of Westernizing/modernizing influences in highly cosmopolitan Bombay, where this couple had worked out a covert love relationship not uncommon in many Western countries—with an Indian familial variation. The affair was also clearly facilitated by her considerable individualized development, which included sophisticated social skills, living on her own, education encompassing an advanced degree, and a career. Nevertheless, new material brought out other dimensions to this relationship that were much more in accord with Hindu culture and disclosed a far more traditional psychological makeup.

For many years Kumar had voiced a strong desire to go on a pilgrimage to the temple of a highly revered, deceased holy man, of whom he was a fervent devotee, and now invited Shakuntala to undertake this pilgrimage with him and his family. More important for Shakuntala were the after-effects of the pilgrimage. Although she had never been a devotee of this holy man, Shakuntala experienced visions of him and his presence for at least two months after they returned to Bombay. Shakuntala was absolutely convinced that she and Kumar had been connected to each other in past lives through their relationship with this holy man, that she was simply living through her past attachments (*samskaras*) to Kumar, and that when these were eventually satisfied, the relationship would end (not necessarily in this life). That this intense attraction was based on past lives is a traditional theme of Indian folklore, in which a couple, whether married or not, is irresistably drawn to one another from their love in past lives. In this particular variation, the connection was experienced by Shakuntala as being through a particular holy man. Thus, the intense inner meanings given to this love relationship and how she experienced it were fully in accord with certain themes of Hindu culture, however much it was aided and abetted by modernizing influences and greater individualization.

After this pilgrimage, Shakuntala became more inwardly convinced of the validity of their love relationship, and more willing to dispense with the securities of an arranged marriage for the specialness Kumar afforded her. Although I had previously tried to delve into the resistances against discussing her sexual relationship, it wasn't until this point that Shakuntala revealed the intense emotional and sexual passion. Certain superego pressures were apparently relieved by her inner experiences.

She then began discussing with me sexuality as related to spiritual powers. She mentioned that only the most spiritually advanced persons have transcended their sexuality. Even those who have renounced the world often have strong sexual urges, recounting one or two stories she had heard from her aunt about some notable swamis. She talked more about the *Kundalini,* how it is related to sexuality and to various spiritual powers when it is cultivated and aroused. At one point, she associated quite informally about reincarnation, mentioning that her aunt knew who she was in her previous three births.

Shakuntala then brought in her first two dreams. "In the first dream, my aunt dies. In the dream she is very small like a child, she is on a raised platform. There are certain decorations around this platform that remind me of a *puja.*" Shakuntala's association to this dream was that it might well be prophetic, as her aunt was apparently ailing. This reflected what I found to be the response of many Indians to their dreams: a constant serveillance for the clairvoyant, telepathic, or the prophetic—part of the profound Indian concern with destiny. The second dream was much more complex. "The first part is vague, seemingly with Kumar and possibly Veena, who seems to have turned into my mother at some point. Then, their four children are going into a cart, the cart swaying from side to side like a see-saw, the children going in and out of some square structures. Kumar's oldest daughter (the second oldest child) falls out of the cart and is run over by a truck. I see it and cry out, then I come running over crying out Uma, Uma (the name of her deity) and I pick up the bloody child. Kumar suddenly turns into her uncle, and her mother (originally Veena in the dream) has to go to the toilet. Someone offers her some cool melon juice. Others there seem rather unconcerned about the child, who is taken to the hospital, where an aunt (the uncle's wife) pulls on the tongue of the child and says she will live. The girl is all right."

In her associations, the uncle is someone who likes Shakuntala a great deal and feels she is very spiritually advanced and above this world. Shakuntala feels she definitely isn't above this world, though she has had some intense spiritual experiences. Her associations to the daughter who was run over are that she is a sickly girl whom Kumar is concerned about, and she is not an overly good-looking girl as yet. Shakuntala feels that this daughter is overly in love with Kumar, and has many compulsive, cleaning rituals around the house, which Shakuntala feels might be due to guilt.

There was no time to get further associations. However, it appeared that Shakuntala was still struggling with her own intense love for Kumar, which the dream strongly implied had unconscious incestuous roots—the daughter-father relationship probably standing for Shakuntala's with her own father, with Veena and Shakuntala's mother being interchangeable. I did not interpret this at this point in the therapy.

At the same time, Shakuntala decided to burn one of her bridges. She had an ardent Christian suitor with an excellent position, whose marriage offer she now rejected. Both of her parents were against this marriage because he came from another community and religion with very different traditions. What is highly revealing is her own internalized attitude of a profound obligation to preserve and pass on the traditions and customs of her own community through marriage and children—thus fulfilling a basic thrust of Indian society and culture—and not to hurt her parents by having a love marriage with a person from a different community. Thus, the familial self in a sophisticated urban woman still tends to remain extremely powerful, even in persons like Shakuntala who are fully exposed to many modernizing influences and are increasingly individualized.

As Shakuntala broke off the relationship with her Christian suitor, the conflict between her relationship with Kumar and an arranged marriage became much more intense. On one hand, she became more intensely involved with Kumar when Veena and the children visited Veena's family. Even then Kumar had to be extremely circumspect. Little is truly secret in India, especially in households, because of the ever-present eye of the servants (pers. com. Ashis Nandy). On the other hand, Shakuntala felt more constrained to proceed with the arranged marriage, as her parents were very upset when their son and daughter-in-law did not show them proper respect—their son asking for a set sum for expenses each month during the visit (traditionally, the son either foots the bill or the father volunteers to help out with expenses). Undoubtedly compounding Shakuntala's guilt over hurting her mother were her unconscious incestuous fantasies.

Shakuntala then revealed that six years previously an excellent marriage had been arranged for her. The wedding date had been set after consultation with the family priest and everyone was invited. Somehow, two days before the wedding Shakuntala managed to wriggle out of the arrangements. The priest, however, judged it was important that she be married then, as it was an extremely auspicious time. Two days later she went through the full marriage ceremony, circling the sacred fire seven times, and was married to one of the most important gods in the Hindu pantheon.

Up to this point I have sketched in with various hues and shades the kinds of conflicts Shakuntala was involved in in her life. But a psychoanalyst is always listening for another level of psychic reality behind a person's overt conflicts, covertly asserting a significant role in them. Where is the play of the personal idiosyncratic? Where do normal social relationships become leaned against and pushed out of kilter by particular actors in the person's life drama? This becomes even more difficult for a foreign analyst, who is not sensitively attuned to the familiar in a society so different from his own, to assess.

For over three months I listened empathically to Shakuntala, trying to relate to her material on her own grounds and within the framework of her own cultural meanings; simultaneously, I was trying to assess the presence of any unconscious motivation that was covertly influencing her present struggles. One entrée turned out to be her back pains, which considerably worsened when Veena returned with the children after Shakuntala and Kumar had spent a great deal of time together.

The next session she told the following dream: "A man is standing in water, a vast sea or ocean." When I asked her to describe the man, he turned out to be a composite of Kumar, her father, and her brother. My way of working with dreams is always to interconnect them to a relevant context in the person's life and/or therapy relationship (Roland 1971). Taking the sea or ocean as a symbol of the mother, I interpreted to Shakuntala that her current relationship with Kumar, as previously with her father and her brother, rescued her from the relationship with her depressed mother, while simultaneously restoring a childhood sense of being highly special. However, when she lost the closeness to Kumar, as when Veena returned and her access to Kumar was greatly restricted, she unconsciously regressed into the childhood relationship with her mother, became strongly unconsciously identified with her, and therefore had her back problems increase.

This touched off a number of associations about her family, including a slip of the tongue that confirmed my interpretation of her unconscious identification with her mother. Shakuntala related a tragic tale that had wound itself through her life from birth and was still entwining itself around her fate. Some years before Shakuntala was born, an older and only brother, age two, fell out of a second story window when he was waving goodbye to someone, and died. One need not be born in India to assess its effect on Shakuntala's mother. The depressed woman eventually gave birth to Shakuntala. The whole family lavished its attention on the new infant, going beyond even the enormous gratification normally accorded an infant in an Indian family. One and a half years later, a baby brother was born, and her mother's and the others' attention characteristically shifted to the boy.

Shakuntala then seemed to have displaced a major part of her emotional involvement to her father, who was someone she could talk with easily and be close to. He came from a much more sophisticated and educated urban family than her mother, and was more socially and aesthetically oriented. Thus, on one level Shakuntala identified with his sophisticated, urbane personality, forming an important identification that enabled her later to move into a more modern life style.[7]

Her mother, on the other hand, was from a rural, landowning family, where her mother (Shakuntala's grandmother) was considered to be a holy woman or saint, a woman who had realized God and was still worshiped by many. Shakuntala's mother was much more religious than her father—not unusual in many Indian families—and her mother's sister was, of course, the aunt who was Shakuntala's guru. Thus, in the religious dimension, Shakuntala clearly identified with her mother's side of the family. This side of the family was also psychic. They apparently have had experiences of a twitching in one eye, which always presaged a death in the extended family. Shakuntala reported having occasional clairvoyant dreams, such as a dream of a building collapsing with her father in it, which actually occurred two weeks after the dream. Her father had just one psychic dream in his life: the night before he was taking a major civil service examination that would determine his career, he dreamt of an exam with all of the questions and answers. He did exceedingly well the next day.

Another dream in the following session enabled me to continue my interpretive work. "I am with my brother in bed. There is something sexual going on, but it's vague. Then I am outside and a man wearing a flesh-colored shirt comes up to me and is being sexually offensive. Kumar is there as are other women. This man goes out and badly beats Kumar up. He then gets away in a car with a license plate number IJQQ."

---

[7] This identification with a sophisticated, educated father seems to be true of many women reform leaders (pers. com. Geraldine Forbes).

As she associated to the man and his flesh-colored shirt, similar in color to one of her own saris, she realized that the man beating Kumar up was actually part of herself. I then interpreted that her intermittent rages at Kumar, which occurred when he had to withdraw after they were very close together, were an unconscious displacement of infantile rage when as an infant she was at the center of everyone's attention and then was suddenly displaced by her brother. Kumar was becoming the image of her mother in the early childhood relationship. Further, her guilt over hurting her mother by not getting married was greatly intensified by her more unconscious guilt over rage at her mother for favoring her brother. Shakuntala responded that she had only recently recognized that she always felt inferior to her brother when he was around. I related this to a poor self-image around him because of her mother's favoritism. A few sessions later, she mentioned that for the first time she felt much more comfortable and less inferior around her brother—thus confirming the interpretive work and resolving some of her feelings of inferiority around him.

In an Indian family, the ideal is harmony and good relations with one's siblings. Nevertheless, it is amply clear from Shakuntala's case and others that there may be seething feelings around siblings that unconsciously play a major role in adult relationships.

In the last sessions before I left Bombay, I interpreted further unconscious determinants in her relationship with Kumar: the specialness of the relationship evoked her own early childhood feelings of specialness; and the separations from Kumar, and now the impending one from me, touched upon the anxieties and rages of being displaced by her younger brother. Shakuntala was fully receptive to these interpretations, while also asserting that she still felt closely connected to Kumar through the deceased holy man, whose presence she had recently experienced quite strongly.

In one of these last sessions, Shakuntala associated to her horoscope. Since both Jupiter and Mars are very strong influences on her—the former being favorable to marriage, the latter not—the prediction had always been that she would have an extremely difficult time getting married, and further, that she would almost go crazy. Moreover, she is a *mangal*—someone born under the dominant sign of Mars—and is thus regarded as being possibly disruptive and a risk to a marriage unless married to another *mangal*. Her family paid considerable attention to these astrological predictions, keeping the chart highly secret. If word had leaked out, her chances for a good marriage could be greatly jeopardized. The family's attitudes showed the tremendous involvement of

Indians in the magic-cosmic world in trying to gauge and cope with their personal destiny in the major relationships of the life cycle.

I next saw Shakuntala six months later, for twelve sessions. Frequently, after a psychoanalyst has had a hiatus in the analytic work—more often than not during a vacation period—the patient strikes the analyst in a fresh way so that subtle, assumed aspects of the patient and the relationship become objectified. Shakuntala struck me as a very lively, highly emotional and sensuous woman, mildly seductive, who subtly evoked feelings of being special, to the extent of sometimes introducing exceptions to the formalities or structures of the analytic situation. Her considerable sensuality seemed in accord with my other Indian patients, colleagues, and friends, both female and male, and decidedly greater than among most American patients and friends. While the sensuousness in Indian sculpture and poetry has been repeatedly commented upon, it is obviously a personal quality as well, though varying widely from person to person.

Shakuntala had felt quite disturbed when I had left Bombay, as she had no one to express her feelings and thoughts to about Kumar and the arranged marriage. From her associations, I interpreted that she experienced my going away as an abandonment. As we got past these feelings, Shakuntala related that her aunt had recently written to her that she was wasting her spiritual talents, that she was one of the very few who has the potential to reach the highest spiritual realization, and so she should come and eventually be the spiritual head of the ashram. Shakuntala was visibly upset by the letter. She then related an incident when, many years before, the then co-director, a swami, fell at her feet worshiping her and calling her Ram, a major incarnation of Vishnu.

She mentioned in passing that her mantra and deity are different from both her aunt's and mother's. I was curious as to how she arrived at that and so asked her. She related that when she was sixteen, she went on a pilgrimage with her family to the shrine of a goddess. Upon reaching it in an ecstatic state, she had a profoundly moving experience of the statue of the goddess coming alive. At that point they knew this was her chosen deity. Later, she had another intense spiritual experience when visiting another important shrine of this major goddess in the Himalayas. Shakuntala's choice of this deity, different from those of her mother and aunt, demonstrates the catholicity of religious objects, the freedom of choice, and the profound individuation in Hindu spiritual practices.

Shakuntala experienced considerable problems in developing her spiritual potentials, as she simply lacked discipline in everything. What I had begun to observe as her tendency to dismiss the structures of the psychoanalytic situation, such as the time and duration of sessions, manifested itself in a number of areas. She pursued painting and poetry passionately for a while, and in spite of being talented then gave them up. Even her meditation was not done systematically, which interfered with her spiritual progress. However, over the intervening months she had formed a small weekly meditation group.

After our initial sessions, she felt less disturbed and reported being able to meditate better. Since the old conflicts around pressures for the arranged marriage and her love relationship with Kumar continued, I decided to delve more deeply into the relationship with her mother. Shakuntala expressed being extremely vulnerable to her mother's unhappy, depressed moods, and feeling even worse when her mother told her that her whole well-being depended on Shakuntala getting married. Her mother's depression had bent the normally close Indian mother-daughter relationship out of shape. I then stressed that her mother would be depressed whether or not Shakuntala married, and by so tying Shakuntala to her whole state of well-being, she was having a destructive effect on Shakuntala as well as on their relationship. When Shakuntala later told her mother what I said, she replied, "Tell Dr. Roland I am a mad (crazy) woman."

One of the surprises in psychoanalytic work is that one never knows how a patient will respond to an interpretation, especially a meaningful one. Shakuntala came in the next session and for the first time in our work together began seriously to consider developing her career. She related that she had rarely followed anything through, that her position at the college was the first thing she had stuck with, but although enjoying it, she never actually took it very seriously. She now imagined going abroad for a doctorate to develop a career as a college professor; or perhaps she would pursue a career as a film director, like a friend who had left an unhappy marriage. She realized from our sessions together and from talking with an accomplished woman professor at the college that an arranged marriage at this time in her life and development would mean being tied down and suffocated. I nevertheless wondered aloud to her if her image of an arranged marriage wasn't that she would become like her depressed mother. She responded that she had always wanted to be different from her.

I assessed Shakuntala's moves to develop her career and abandon the idea of an arranged marriage as important steps toward true psychological differentiation from her mother. In an Indian family, the sense of self always includes the other to a much more significant extent than in most American ones, and there is far less separation; but in Shakuntala's family, her mother's depression gave Shakuntala almost no room to breathe without enormous guilt over hurting her.

In psychoanalytic therapy there is a dramatic unfolding and movement that cannot usually be predicted, but makes total sense in hindsight. Shakuntala came in the following session once more talking about the usual ups and downs in her relationship with Kumar. But for the first time I sensed intense feelings of sadness that did not seem related to him. After we discussed further how Shakuntala's mother made her totally responsible for her mother's happiness, I interpreted that her intense sadness—which she acknowledged—resulted from an inner feeling that she had to make a choice between Kumar and her mother, that she could not have them both. The sadness was in effect a further step in the process of differentiating herself from her mother.

She reported a dream in the following session. "Kumar drops off his youngest son at my flat and takes me in his car to a place with a large lawn and trees. We are about to kiss when a policeman comes over and insists we get out. I said, 'this is absurd, Kumar is simply my *maman* (maternal uncle),' but the policeman insists Kumar return tomorrow at 5 P.M. I am very uneasy." Her asssociations to the large lawn and trees were to her house where she grew up. The *maman* or maternal uncle represents a usual niece-uncle romantic attachment, but she never had such an involvement with her *mamans*. This was clearly a diversionary tactic in the dream. Five P.M. reminded her of the exact hours of our analytic sessions. To her uneasiness over time, she associated being worried about Veena because Kumar had recently spent a couple of unaccounted hours with Shakuntala.

I suggested to her the clear unconscious equation of Kumar with her father in the dream (the romantic involvment taking place where she grew up), that one important component of her relationship with Kumar is incestuous fantasies around her father, that the policeman (now equated with me) was her conscience, and her fear of her mother was now displaced onto Veena in the triangle. Shakuntala responded by recognizing the feeling of illicit love and its attraction. I felt at the time, but did not say out loud, that Shakuntala's recent efforts to get me to lecture at her college were in part motivated by wishing to have me as the helpful person—thus offsetting any unconscious images of a projected, punitive conscience.

In hindsight, one can see that as Shakuntala differentiated herself from her mother as a result of our therapeutic work together, incestuous themes around her father and a punitive, maternal superego came to the fore—a not unusual progression in psychoanalytic therapy with women. Earlier, Kumar had unconsciously represented the mother who treated her specially as an infant and then deserted her for her brother; then, he was unconsciously equated with the father and brother whom Shakuntala had used to separate somewhat from her highly depressed mother who was engulfing her; and now Kumar was unconsciously the father-image with whom Shakuntala had incestuous fantasies with the backlash of a punitive, maternal superego. This dream, together with the cases of Joan and Saida, give clear evidence of incestuous fantasies and a punitive maternal conscience in Indian women, thus supporting the universality of the Oedipus complex.

Shakuntala readily accepted my interpretation that the unconscious incestuous tie to her father partially motivated her involvement with Kumar. However, this did not in the least conflict with her view that her relationship with Kumar was also a carry-over from a past life related to the holy man. In the Hindu mode of metonymic thinking (Ramanujan 1980), attachments from past lives (*samskaras*), cosmic influences—and we can now easily add unconscious motivations and fantasies from childhood relationships—are all perceived as interrelated with present-day relationships. Psychoanalysis connects the last two—unconscious fantasies from childhood and present-day relationships, whereas Hindu psychology traditionally integrates the first two and the last—attachments from past lives, cosmic influences, and current relationships. Thus, the interpenetration of the past lives, the present biographical past (conscious and unconscious), the cosmic, and present-day relationships can all be readily assumed in Hindu cognition in a person like Shakuntala without the dissonances and clashes characteristic of the Western mind.

In the final sessions before I left Bombay, she continued the theme of sexuality and incest by first relating a visit with some students to the Rajneesh Ashram in Poona. Sexuality so abounded and the vibrations there made her so uncomfortable that she was unable to meditate. When she then associated to a college girl she was counseling who clearly had incestuous feelings toward her widowed father, I raised the question of Shakuntala's incestuous fantasies with her own father.

Unfortunately, our month's work had to stop abruptly. In our final session, she responded with considerable anger over my going away from Bombay once again, leaving her hanging. In a last brief meeting, she was feeling much better about our work together and was still trying to formulate plans to develop her career; but she remained highly reluctant to see any of the Bombay psychoanalysts because they might be out of touch with her most salient inner struggles.

Two years later, I returned to Bombay and met with Shakuntala for eight sessions over a period of approximately three weeks. She caught me up on her life. Although she still had some desire to take her career more seriously and felt she had grown in her teaching, she had not taken any real steps to further it over the two years I was away. Her parents had left Bombay because of a not unusual mother-in-law/daughter-in-law conflict but, more unusually, with the son siding with his wife. Her parents decided to sell their house in Lucknow and provide for Shakuntala's security by buying her a flat in Bombay. Her aunt, in the meanwhile, had died. Shakuntala had recently visited the ashram, very much wanting to stay, but had returned to Bombay for Kumar. In spite of the ups and downs of this relationship, Shakuntala now accepted its inevitability, and was living with and enjoying it. Although Kumar seemed to have lost a lot of his verve, she felt she had been able to evolve through the relationship—one without strings or conditions, which she had always wanted. (In one of her rare letters, she wrote, "All relationships are conditional. I only believe in God and myself.")

She then mentioned that both her father and the man she rented her room from had recently become more involved in astrology. She was apprehensive that if her father delved too deeply into her horoscope, he might figure out from the configurations that she was involved in an affair. This is still another example of the assumption of a very close correlation between the reading of the planets and everyday relationships.

Although colleagues saw her as a social butterfly, inside she felt highly traditional; in fact, she felt practically married to Kumar. But the one she really felt married to was the god. For the first time, Shakuntala elaborated that girls from her north Indian community are married to this god, or sometimes to trees or pots, as a ritual to offset bad planetary influences, in order to make it easier to get married. Intrinsic to Hindu astrology are ritual practices such as this to offset negative planetary influences or *karma* from past lives, conveying a far more active attempt to change destiny than Westerners frequently assume. Shakuntala had always taken the marriage to the god seriously and as inevitable, and was unwilling to discuss it in any detail.

In the following session she told a dream of her father turning into Kumar and vice versa. This continued the theme from two years previously of Kumar being closely associated in her unconscious with the father imago. She then associated for the first time that she could always charm and get around her father, as could her brother, too. She gradually described her father as being quite different from the usual stereotype of the overtly distant, disciplinarian Indian father. Instead, he was a man who was not only deeply and overtly attached to Shakuntala, but also set few limits on her. It is this tendency to ignore limits that emerged in our work together. She recognized that her own lack of self-discipline was profoundly related to his being so lenient with her. Although his leniency and overt attachment to Shakuntala were on the unusual side, there seem to be strong currents of father-daughter attachments underlying a more distant, authoritative façade in other cases.

Shakuntala associated that if she had more discipline, she would make much more progress spiritually by meditating for a fixed period every day, even when she did not feel like it. Instead, when she was in the mood, she went into deep meditation, sometimes at one of the temples in Bombay (which contains a statue of her goddess) where she went a few times a month at midnight or in the early hours of the morning. She felt strongly that she would also meditate more if she were in a daily meditation group with a number of people. When she did try to meditate and perform a *puja* in the evening in her flat, inevitably one of her friends dropped by, interrupting her—showing the informality of social life in India. These friends were far more interested in the movies, picnics, and parties than *pujas* and pilgrimages, and apparently knew little of Shakuntala's inner inclinations. The older couple from whom she was renting a room, who participated in her weekly meditation group, thought it unusual for someone as young as she to be so involved in meditation. Veena, interestingly enough, was one of the only persons Shakuntala could share some of her inner experiences with; sometimes they went together to a *bhajan*.

In another session, she told of being interviewed by someone conducting a study on psychoanalysis and religion. She was asked to draw different size circles for the two to connote their importance to her. Shakuntala felt strongly that to get the accurate relationship between the two, she must also draw circles of herself in relationship to each of the circles of religion and psychoanalysis. She saw the circle of herself as roughly equal to the circle of psychoanalysis, whereas her own circle was much smaller than that of religion, since her everyday self disappeared once she was in meditation.

In those last sessions, Shakuntala realized that when she was in therapy with me, all kinds of feelings and wishes arose intensely—such as wanting a child with Kumar; but then they were repressed when I left.

She felt on the whole in a better position in her life: she accepted the relationship and its limitations with Kumar, liked the college teaching, though still desiring to develop her career more, and was progressing in her meditation though still wanting a regular meditation group of like-minded persons. She seemed to have definitely rejected the option of an arranged marriage. She felt she was going too much by her real feelings now to assume the attitudes of most Indian wives, whose sense of duty and wish for closeness to their in-laws, and of devotion to their husbands, is so strong that they can become out of touch with their real feelings. Shakuntala dealt with my leaving by associating me with someone she knew who frequently visited India but didn't stay. We both come and go. Underneath, I sensed a deeply disturbed reaction. She continued, however, to be adamant against seeing any of the Bombay analysts. Her parting remark to me was, "Dr. Roland, meditation is better than psychoanalysis . . . but best of all is meditation and psychoanalysis!"

Clearly, the intertwinings of traditional and modern themes can be extremely complex and nonlinear in a person like Shakuntala. Just to take her love relationship with Kumar, one must take into account her modernized, semi-autonomous living circumstances in Bombay; aspects of the familial self, by which she was tremendously emotionally involved with Kumar's wife and children; cultural meanings whereby she was convinced they were involved from a past life, and astrological readings that predicted she might not ever marry; aspects of the spiritual self such that she experienced the connection with Kumar through a highly venerated, deceased holy man with whom she had had a number of profound spiritual experiences; and transferential issues, in which Kumar at various stages of the therapy unconsciously represented her mother, father, and brother. Even the way Shakuntala assimilated our psychoanalytic work together, by seeing it as quite congruent with astrological readings and other cultural meanings of living out attachments from past lives, indicate that traditional and modernizing influences can blend in Indian cognition as they do not tend to do in Westerners. Like other Indian women, but unlike Ashis, she had no identity struggles whatsoever over asserting a Hindu identity as against a Westernized one.

It is also evident from this case that one of the standard Freudian psychoanalytic positions is not supported. Beginning with Freud, most psychoanalysts have relegated the pursuit of the spiritual self to some kind of unconscious psychopathology or regressive motive. Although Shakuntala was indeed struggling with unconscious conflicts, it would be a gross misreading of this case to dismiss her spiritual experiences and strivings on the basis of these conflicts.

Further, unless the spiritual dimension were fully taken into account in this case and two others, psychoanalytic therapy could not proceed optimally, and might not proceed at all. To the extent that spiritual aspirations are genuine, psychoanalytic therapy will enable the person to become more involved, which occurred with Shakuntala as she partially resolved some of her unconscious conflicts. Further therapy would probably have helped her even more with her meditation by resolving her problems with self-discipline.

There is still another position that I would dispute: that the person who has realized the spiritual self is totally free of psychopathology, by definition.[8] A more accurate formulation based on this case—perhaps the first one of a seriously practicing religious mystic reported in the psychoanalytic literature—is that both the spiritual dimension and unconscious conflicts and/or developmental deficits can be present, each in their own right, each in varying degrees, and in a highly complex interrelationship. That is, a person can be quite spiritually advanced and still have unconscious conflicts; conversely, a person may be relatively free of psychopathology, but may not necessarily be spiritually aware. Shakuntala is the only patient I have ever had who was functioning on the whole quite well socially and in her work to say very simply one time, "I have experienced God."

Six months of psychoanalytic therapy is not nearly enough to resolve problems of the nature Shakuntala had, though my impression is that it helped her considerably. Where the psychoanalytic work would lead is something that one never can fully predict. She might well have developed her career further as she became more firmly differentiated from her mother. Where the resolution of the incestuous fantasies around her father would lead is very difficult to say. They obviously not only served in the classical psychoanalytic sense of a young girl's romantic attachment to her father, but also to help her to escape being enveloped by a depressed mother.

Can we generalize from Shakuntala's issues to those of other urban Indian women? The pull to a life devoted to spiritual pursuits, in conflict with various emotional attachments to relationships, is an ancient In-

---

[8] David Shainberg, a psychoanalyst in New York City who has been greatly involved with Zen Buddhism and with the Indian philosopher, Krishnamurti, voiced this viewpoint at a meeting sponsored by the National Psychological Association for Psychoanalysis in March 1978 on "Eastern Spiritual Diciplines, Psychoanalysis, and Cults."

dian theme. In Shakuntala's case, however, it assumes a very different guise from that of other Indian women of her age, who are almost all married or widowed. A life totally devoted to spiritual pursuits is sanctioned for only the rare few. Once a woman is married, it would only be sanctioned for those so inclined once their children were married, or they were widowed without children. Otherwise, such a woman could pursue spiritual disciplines at home, as Veena did, as time and duties permitted. Ironically, by spurning the arranged marriage for a love relationship with Kumar, Shakuntala kept open her options to go to the ashram at any time.

Still another twist is that Shakuntala was involved with a man who did share her spiritual interests. This can be a distinct problem in an arranged marriage, where the partners may have widely discrepant inclinations in this direction; and indeed this very issue did arise with another woman patient.

Much more relevant to other urban Indian women is the issue of individualization versus familial functioning. Although there is today greater familial sanction for individualization, it is also apparent that increased individualization can create a variety of conflicts. In Shakuntala's case, the high degree of individualization in her life and in the intense relationship with Kumar led her to reject an arranged marriage as too limited, thus putting her in conflict with her mother. In other cases, the conflict over individualization emerges between the woman and her in-laws and/or spouse.

What is most striking with Shakuntala, and I suspect highly relevant to other urban Indian women, is that whatever she was experiencing was given meaning within traditional cultural images. My sense is that most modernizing changes connected with education, work, relationships, and such will all be experienced sooner or later within indigenous cultural meanings.

SAIDA

The proverbial daughter-in-law/mother-in-law conflicts in Indian families are well attested in both folklore and social science analyses. The latter dwell more on how these conflicts are generated by the very structure of the Indian family, wherein potential rivalry is generated as the mother-in-law experiences the new bride as an intruder to her intense emotional relationship with her son, through whom she has gradually attained status with her own in-laws.[9] How a particular mother-in-law

[9] A question has been raised whether there is less strife in the mother-in-law/daughter-

and daughter-in-law actually get along varies enormously according to their personalities and the other family relationships; conflict is by no means inevitable.

Relatively little has been written from a psychodynamic perspective on the nature of this relationship and the conflicts engendered, or on how modernization has affected it. Perceptive observations by a social worker, Mr. Bhatti, and by a psychoanalyst, Mrs. Freny Mehta, shed important additional light on these conflicts. Mr. Bhatti has observed that the husband is frequently the key to battles between his wife and mother. Unless he maintains a harmonious relationship with both, giving each her due and fulfilling the needs of each, one of the women will feel the other is being favored, thus generating jealousy and conflict. Mrs. Mehta reflected that girls raised with deeply internalized cultural attitudes of venerating their mothers and inhibiting any angry or rebellious feelings unconsciously carry these reactions over to their mothers-in-law. They are therefore helpless to cope with them.

Saida was extremely unhappy with her mother-in-law over the two years of her marriage, and had had intermittent nightmares and hysterical outbursts of screaming at night. She depicted her mother-in-law as highly self-preoccupied, demanding, and critical of everyone around her. Saida tried to fulfill her traditional, familial ego-ideal of being the flexibly subordinate and dutiful daughter-in-law in this traditional, upper middle-class Ismaili Muslim family, but the more she did and the more she gave, the more she felt her mother-in-law demanded. She caught herself automatically siding with her mother-in-law's frequent caustic criticism of the servants, but then asserted her own judgment and disagreed the moment she was apart from her. In short, she was miserable. Fortunately, her husband secretly sided with her, but he dared not openly oppose his mother. In most other cases with which I was familiar, the husband remained completely neutral in these conflicts, standing aside to leave the two women to thrash it out, or openly sided with his mother.

These burning conflicts were fanned by the considerable modernizing influences in Saida's life. A considerably older brother had taken an active interest in her education and had sent her to English-language

---

in-law relationship in the south, since the two frequently know each other as aunt and neice or grandmother and granddaughter. From reports of some of the psychologists at N.I.M.H.A.N.S., this is apparently not so. When the aunt, for instance, becomes a mother-in-law, she then has a different set of expectations for her niece as daughter-in-law. The latter, on the other hand, may be expecting a continuation of the old kind of relationship, which can generate even more conflict.

schools in Bombay, unlike her other siblings. She then went on to a first-rate college, and from there to an excellent program in management, eventuating in a good position with considerable responsibilities, where she was well respected.

What might have been experienced by a traditional bride with far less individualization than Saida as unhappiness was felt by her as sheer misery and oppression. She sensed her very self being gravely threatened by her mother-in-law—a self slowly forged over the years of schooling and career. Thus, the modernizing influences in her case poured oil on the flames of her discontent. She could neither stand her mother-in-law nor do anything about her.

Interestingly enough, her mother-in-law was a religious intellectual in her Muslim community who respected Saida's career, as it brought considerable status and some income to this business family. Even here, conflicts inevitably sprang up, reflecting another clash between the traditional and the modern through differing expectations. One weekend Saida accompanied her mother-in-law on a pilgrimage to a nearby town—as she had often done previously—the original plans calling for them to return to Bombay by Sunday evening so that Saida could go into work Monday morning. But once they reached their destination, her mother-in-law decided she wanted to stay an extra day, fully expecting that Saida in her role of daughter-in-law would remain with her. Saida, with a more modern work consciousness, insisted she be back in Bombay in time for work on Monday morning. Strife ensued. Saida returned Sunday evening, and her mother-in-law remained angry at her for long afterwards. This resulted in further misery for Saida, as she simply could not handle her mother-in-law's anger.

Saida's mother-in-law truly seemed to be a difficult woman. But why was Saida so completely paralyzed by her and so totally unable to cope with her? I found three distinct causes. As these were analyzed on a three-times-a-week basis over four weeks in psychoanalytic therapy, she was gradually able to assert herself more and to feel less disturbed. My impression is that several more months of psychoanalytic therapy would have enabled her to handle her mother-in-law reasonably comfortably.

One of the basic causes of her reactions of impotence stemmed from her own profound identification with a rather weak mother. Her mother was subservient to everyone, including one of Saida's older sisters, who tormented Saida from intense jealousy over Saida being the parents' favorite. Thus, her mother-in-law was partly unconsciously experienced by Saida as the tormenting older sister who had to be placated, Saida deeply identifying with the subservience of her mother. Nor could she draw upon her work identity to help her out at home. It only made her more dissatisfied, as her relationship with her mother-in-law clashed with her experience at work.

As we discussed this whole picture and Saida felt somewhat better, a second cause emerged: intense jealousy and extreme hurt that her mother-in-law clearly favored her own daughters over Saida—a rather traditional form of favoritism. This took two forms. The mother-in-law gave all kinds of gifts to her daughters but few to Saida, even though Saida constantly gave gifts to her mother-in-law; and she encouraged her daughters to visit her frequently, while practically forbidding Saida to visit her own parents—though Saida occasionally did so on the sly. I interpreted that Saida wanted the same closeness and special relationship with her mother-in-law that she had with her own mother, that this was clearly an impossibility, and that the more she wanted it the more hurt she would feel. This interpretation helped Saida considerably. She began to back off from wanting so much from her mother-in-law and then feeling painfully disappointed. She even stopped herself from buying something for her mother-in-law one time, and then felt less hurt the next day when she learned her mother-in-law had given some gifts to her own daughters but not to Saida. Saida also began to visit her parents more frequently without first asking permission.

In the final week of the therapy, she said that although she was feeling appreciably better than before, she was still having a difficult time with her mother-in-law. "She wants me to dance to her tune." I countered with, "why do you have to?" She excitedly brought in two dreams the next session. I sensed they must be clearly related, and in effect answers to the question I posed to her the previous session. The dreams and associations were as follows.

Dream 1: "I am getting on a bus with Usha [a young married woman whom I had helped with psychoanalytic therapy, and who had referred Saida to me] and we sit down together. The driver collects some rupees from Usha, thinking we are together and not listening to my wanting to pay my own fare. I finally turn to Usha and say, 'let's settle it between us.' We do.

"In the next scene I am at my parent's flat, but the bedroom is similar to that at my in-laws. My brother's oldest child, a daughter who is fourteen, steals my chocolate from the shelf. I go to my mother to complain to my brother, my niece's father, but my mother says not to. My niece's younger brothers are constantly complaining to their father about her."

Saida said that actually her niece and nephews get along very well together. In the dream, the niece represented Saida's older sister, who tormented her. I sensed that the first part of the dream related more to the therapeutic alliance with me, and I focused on the second scene, interpreting that one reason she felt she had to dance to her mother-in-law's tune was that Saida's mother had taught her that it is all right for boys to complain but not for girls, making it impossible to cope with her older sister and therefore her mother-in-law.

Dream 2: "I am driving with my husband in a dead-end street. We go into a lock-up [police station]. There is a police inspector there with a lot of men on sleeping rolls, and some Parsee girls with babies who are dressed in a somewhat sexually loose way with all the men around. The inspector there is of no help. My husband and I go into another room with a man who has a beard and is taller. He gets rid of the people in the room and then tells us how to go off."

She described the inspector as short, squat, and dressed in a white longhi, similar to Muslim men at prayer, including her father, who wears one. To my inquiry, she responded that he was very hot-tempered, religious, and difficult to get along with. Saida was her father's favorite, and so would often ask for things for the other children in the family— a not infrequent occurrence for favorite children. Nevertheless, she was still extremely afraid of him as a child. It was her older brother, not her father, who gave her all the support and guidance.

This second dream was a further answer to why Saida felt she had to dance to her mother-in-law's tune. She unconsciously associated her mother-in-law with her very difficult and religious father and was deeply afraid of both of them. Following this interpretation, she conveyed that she was becoming more assertive with her mother-in-law, though she was still quite afraid of her. There is no question that further psychoanalytic work was needed on Saida's relationship and reactions to her father, including possible incestuous fantasies that seemed to surface in the second dream. Working this through would enable her to be much more comfortable and less afraid in asserting herself with her mother-in-law. I referred her to another analyst in Bombay.

Reflecting on this case, I recognized that unlike most American patients Saida and her husband were in no position to leave his family. With an American patient I might first work toward enabling her to separate from a masochistic relationship with difficult in-laws. It wasn't simply that it would be financially problematic for Saida and her husband to live on their own as, like other young husbands and wives, they do not earn very much; it was also that they had made a basic commitment when the marriage was arranged to live in a joint household. Thus, the basic Indian cultural pattern of familial interdependence versus the American ideal of individual autonomy had to be recognized. My supposition, however, which was borne out, was that if Saida could resolve inner conflicts engendered within her original family and now being unconsciously displaced and projected onto her mother-in-law, she could handle her mother-in-law much better and be happier. This is an important commentary that within extended family hierarchical relationships, there is usually enough room for maneuvering to cope with even difficult relationships, depending on one's inner emotional state of well-being.

This illustrates my fundamental thesis that while psychoanalysis may have different social values associated with highly varying cultural contexts, its basic orientation toward resolving unconscious conflicts and developmental deficits enables the person to function better regardless of the social pattern. Thus, the therapy with Saida did not in the least change her familial self with its orientation toward the fulfillment of reciprocal responsibilities in familial relationships. Rather it focused on certain idiosyncratic elements in her background that were interfering with her coping well in the Indian familial interdependencies of a young married woman with a difficult mother-in-law.

Female College Students

A newly ubiquitous phenomenon of modernization in the urban areas is the large number of girls going to college, most of whose marriages will not be fully arranged until they graduate—a radical departure in education and marital age for girls from the practice of only a few decades ago. I had the opportunity to co-counsel three groups of sixteen to seventeen-year-old girls from National, Ruya, and Jai Hind colleges. Coming from remarkably heterogeneous religious and regional backgrounds, they are the first-generation females in their families to go to college.

Mostly educated in all-girls English-language schools, these girls are for the first time in an educational milieu with boys, can dress as they wish rather than having to wear special school dresses, and in general are in a much more unstructured environment, where there is much more choice of courses and activities, which contributes to their increasing individualization. In many cases they are expected not to speak to or socialize with the boys at college.

Problems raised by two of these groups had a similar ring. In one college where a great deal of group cohesiveness had developed—the girls were from middle-class, traditional, largely Hindu families—they raised a problem that each of them had experienced, but none had ever shared with anyone else: as each came to college in the morning, she felt extremely uneasy and lacking in confidence with students she did not know. These girls experienced these other students as looking at them, and possibly reproaching them for the way they dressed, walked, behaved, and such. In contrast to this, they had none of these uneasy feelings with a friend who might actually be highly critical of their dress, behavior, and such because the friend was concerned for them. Some of this can probably be explained as a normal late adolescent girl's need for acceptance. But reactions from a somewhat more sophisticated upper middle-class group—though still traditional, in a college with somewhat more liberal social patterns—suggest deeper psychodynamic explanations.

These latter girls were quite vocal in complaining about anyone and everyone, including close friends, talking behind their backs, commenting critically on their dress, behavior, and talking with boys. Each acknowledged that she also became compulsively involved in talking critically about someone else, often a friend—even while hating this in others. What emerged is that in criticizing another, the girl was unwittingly critical of a forbidden side of herself, thus giving herself some feeling of moral superiority.

Interestingly enough, when questioned about parental attitudes toward dress, behavior, and being with boys, girls in the first group did not perceive their parents in their unitary families as being unduly critical or restrictive of them. In fact, they felt their parents to be loving and considerate. What did emerge, however, were pervasive parental attitudes, often conveyed by indirection, that a girl must be extremely careful of her dress, behavior, relationships with boys, and such in public because of what the neighbors, family elders, and strangers might say, what effect this would have on the girl's and the family's reputation, and how it would effect her and her sisters' marriageability. Examples would readily be given of neighbors' daughters and the effects of their misbehavior—girls these students readily identified themselves with. Thus, the neighbor or stranger, one who does not have the concern and consideration of a friend or family member, was seen as a potential menace.

In the modernizing process of going to college, these girls from traditional families were exposed to a far more unprotected, stimulating environment, including the presence of boys. Since sexuality tends to be more controlled than repressed in Indian personality, the stimuli of college started arousing sexual impulses that then evoked deeply internalized parental attitudes toward the stranger. The girl would then become extremely uneasy about her behavior. What she would do that might be improper and draw criticism, as happened with the neighbor's daughter, was constantly in the back of her mind in public. The other students thus became the feared stranger, and the girl became as circumspect as possible, except among friends.

In the second group, where there was a college atmosphere of somewhat greater freedom, these internalized parental attitudes resulted in unconscious projective identifications, where the other girl was perceived to have all of the forbidden tendencies within oneself, and where one unconsciously identified with the accusing stranger. Conversely, the image of the accusing stranger was easily projected onto the other girl; in this case, one felt oneself to be the object of secret criticism.

A further related problem that appeared in all three groups was marked shyness, which inhibited these girls from participating in classroom discussion. Although shyness and modesty are traditionally important virtues for an Indian girl to cultivate, on a deeper psychological level these girls so incorporated parental attitudes of behaving with the utmost circumspection in public to preserve family reputation that shyness became much more intensified in the college setting. Their going to college thus encouraged a more open, individualized expression, on the one hand, but a stimulating coeducational situation in public evoked profound inner responses of watching their step. These girls' shyness was circumvented in one group when the social worker used art materials such as collages to enable them to express their feelings and concerns much more openly than they were able to do in discussion.

Although these three groups of girls evidenced a somewhat greater degree of emotional disturbance on the personality inventory than their classmates, one can easily surmise that the kinds of conflicts that arose during these group counselling sessions are characteristic, to at least some extent, of most girl college students from their backgrounds.[10] These conflicts give evidence of the profound unconscious internalization of the conscience of the familial self in its identification with the reputation of the extended family. Although I have focused primarily on the conflicts, I should also emphasize the adaptive aspects of maintaining a continuity of traditional cultural values and social patterns while simultaneously incorporating and integrating the modernized val-

---

[10] An interesting question would be whether the girls who come from more professional and intellectual families which accord them a greater degree of individualization at home would respond in much the same way.

ues of increased education and individualization, and a much later marital age.

Sociohistorical Perspective on Japanese Women

Of essential importance for Japanese women today, especially for middle- and upper middle-class women, are the breakup of the *ie* corporate household and the rapid rise of a post-Occupation corporate economy, with greatly increased urbanization and industrialization. In the midst of these social changes, women's position has become transformed, as well as showing remarkable continuity.

In pre-Occupation Japan, daughters left their original families in arranged marriages, with very little if any participation in the decision, to be totally incorporated in their husband's and in-laws' *ie* household with its own set of customs, which frequently differed from those of the girl's original family. The marriage was arranged essentially on the social rank, occupation, and reputation of the two families, with the nature of the mother-in-law counting for more than that of the prospective husband (Lebra 1984, 141). The woman thus became totally emotionally enmeshed in her in-laws' household in an apprenticeship with her mother-in-law if she married the oldest or only son; or in a looser one with her mother-in-law or the senior son's wife if she married a younger son. What made this apprenticeship more grueling than that in an Indian family was the Japanese emphasis on subordinate members in a group holding to the opinions of the superior. The daughter-in-law had to give over her views and wishes completely to those of her mother-in-law and/ or sister-in-law, and had to comply completely with their expectations for work and proper etiquette. The endurance and sacrifice that is supposed to shape character in Japanese women usually took place in these female apprenticeship relationships.[11] Nevertheless, like the Indian daughter-in-law/mother-in-law or sister-in-law relationships, these hierarchical relationships within the extended *ie* family usually became ones of intimacy over the years, infused with feeling (*ninjo*) and dependency (*amae*), especially for the wives of younger sons.

Although the woman's main intimacy relationships were with her children—with whom she would be tremendously symbiotically in-

---

[11] It is pertinent to note that daughters of mothers who were married to men adopted into the mother's family, so that the mother had little to endure because she had no mother-in-law, had little respect for their mothers as a result (Lebra 1984, 35–36).

volved by Western standards, though not by Indian ones—her adult intimacy relationships would be much more with the other women of the *ie,* including servants, than with her husband or the other men of the *ie.* Women's and men's social spheres were quite separate, with cultural norms dictating that their natures and therefore kinds of work are different. There could be no overt displays of intimacy or affection between husband and wife, as the marital bond was considered to be subordinate to the demands of the household, although the relationship could become close over the years—all of this being quite similar to the Indian situation. Women in public were to be completely deferential and subordinate to men, were dependent on men (originally father, then husband, and finally sons) for their status, were under the authority of the male head of the *ie,* and had no franchise in the political sphere. Japan was one of the only highly modernized nations in which women had not been given the vote as late as 1945.

This structure of male authority was balanced, however, by the fact that women maintained a total matriarchy in managing the finances and running the household, in being responsible for the reputation of the *ie* in its obligations to others, by taking care of the older generation as well as their husbands,[12] and by raising the children. Sons in particular are closely tied to their mothers throughout life and beyond, worshiping her as an ancestress after death. Women's household position has thus been given tremendous respect and weight by the culture. As generalized caretakers within the *ie,* women would become increasingly involved in the affairs of the main and branch houses, of corporate alliances through marriage, and the community as their children got older, often reaching positions of leadership (Lebra 1984, 299–301). If these women did work at all, it was usually related to the *ie* household's occupation or business. Occasionally, women took on other respected occupations, particularly as schoolteachers or in health care, in which case the in-laws would help provide child care; lower-class women would generally have to work in low-level jobs, sometimes earning more in the large entertainment field.

In the post-Occupation period, women have become far more individualized and individuated than before, and have much greater legal and political power, but within a social system and roles that have maintained remarkable continuity. Like Indian women, almost all Japanese women marry. Whether they have an arranged marriage with go-betweens or a love marriage with parental assent, they now have the choice

[12] The amount of daily body care, sartorial assistance, and fulfillment of other needs that a Japanese wife traditionally gives to her husband means that many Japanese men are totally dependent on their wives for basic necessities.

of whom to marry, and the nature of the prospective husband and his occupational prospects are taken more into account than the nature of the future mother-in-law. Moreover, there is an ideological change toward free choice, so that a love marriage is considered more desireable and of higher status than the arranged marriage.

With the breakup of the *ie,* the newly married woman is not nearly as involved in strict hierarchical apprenticeships with a mother-in-law or senior son's wife and, by report, in all classes she is usually rather reluctant to contract for a marriage with a more traditional arrangement (Condon 1985, 38–42; Wagatsuma and DeVos 1984, 23). Having received far more education than her forebears, the middle-class woman is much less open to complete compliance in a female hierarchical relationship. She is thus much less under the authority of her in-laws, and relies instead on the media for advice in child rearing and homemaking. Obligations for taking care of the elderly, particularly an oldest or only son's parents, are still recognized; but the mother-in-law now becomes more dependent on the good will of her daughter-in-law than vice-versa.

For the middle-class wife of a salaried man or professional, this new-found freedom from the authority of the mother-in-law or senior son's wife cuts two ways. Although she is far freer of the constraints of her female in-laws, she often will not have the intimacy with them, or with other women of an *ie* household, that would have ordinarily developed. Moreover, the separation of the male and female spheres remains, with relatively little intimacy between husband and wife. Middle-class men are overwhelmingly socially and emotionally enmeshed in the *ie* mode of hierarchical relationships in their corporation, bureaucracy, business, profession, or other institution, from which they often return home late in the evening after long hours of work and after-hours socializing with associates. Male hierarchy, intimacy, and power that have been seriously eroded with the demise of the *ie* household have resurfaced in Japanese corporations and institutions, with men very much drawn to this extra-familial male life (pers. com. Masahisa Nishizono). Although many educated women are moving toward a more equalizing, companionate marriage, it is frustrated to a considerable extent by the fact that the salaried husband spends time at home only on Sundays. Thus, there is remarkable continuity in the pattern of men being totally involved in their work group, and in women taking full responsibility for all household matters and being totally emotionally immersed in the raising of their children.

The middle-class urban housewife looks to her children as her main source of intimacy at home.[13] Friendships with neighbors become problematic, as any relationship with them involves a new obligation network. Instead, she must rely on ties to old schoolmates, if she has not moved to another suburb or city; and as the children become older, she may slowly develop new friends by joining the Parent-Teachers Association, community service groups, or others involving some aesthetic or educational activity. In effect, with the break-up of the *ie* extended family, the greater individualization of the educated Japanese woman has come at the expense of intimacy relationships in the female sphere.

Although there are now well over a million Japanese women who have completed a four-year college, and although almost half of Japanese women work out of economic necessity, there are remarkably few women who have a career. And those who do are rarely married.[14] Unlike Indian women, where *jati* and family norms govern the possibility of higher education and combining career with a family, the Japanese cultural norm dictates that a person be totally immersed and dedicated to one group alone. For an educated woman to have a career thus means complete involvement in her work group. For those few who have the abilities and make this choice, there is little if any discrimination. They simply march up the ladder of accrued seniority in their positions in the group. But being involved in such a career is seen as seriously detracting from the equally valued career of housewife and mother, which also requires total immersion and dedication. And for those even fewer women who now combine the dual careers of work and family, they are usually married to men who are willing to have similar dual careers. Thus, what is referred to in America as a dual career couple in Japan is now a quadruple career couple.

These changes for women have not been without psychological problems. One is the considerable inner conflict and anxiety many women experience over just how assertive they can be while still observing proper behavior (pers. com. Moses Burg). Norms involving subordination and assertiveness have obviously greatly changed since the Occupation, but

[13] In turn, Japanese mothers become considerably influenced by their children, keeping up with them as the latter grow older and become exposed to the latest ideas and student movements.

[14] Middle-class women usually work in low-level jobs for a few years after high school or college before they marry (at ages 20 to 24), when they leave work to raise a family. They tend not to return to these jobs when their children are older unless there is economic necessity. Outside of the male corporation and bureaucratic world, respected careers for women are in teaching, the health-care professions, and some service businesses; women from the lower-middle class work in low-level office or factory jobs, but might gravitate to higher paying work in the entertainment field, for instance as a bar hostess.

where the lines are to be drawn is frequently ambiguous. This provokes anxiety in women in a society where the meticulous observance of social etiquette is still a major value and social pattern.

Case Study

Mrs. K

Mrs. K, a forty-one-year-old housewife married to a high school teacher and without children, came for therapy through a friend she greatly esteems, who spoke very highly of Dr. Yoshiko Idei because she herself had been helped through therapy by Dr. Idei.[15] Otherwise, Mrs. K would never have sought psychoanalytic therapy, as she comes from an old traditional rural family and community, and until marriage has been minimally influenced by Western values.

Mrs. K came with three main complaints. The first was a somatic one: her left eyelid hung down, which started after she helped take care of a sister-in-law's husband, who had had a brain operation and then died some time later. The second symptom was related to her first baby, who had died soon after birth some fourteen years previously. When her father-in-law said that it was because of a congenital defect, she became faint, and later felt being extremely unstable and vulnerable even to trivial everyday happenings. Her third complaint was that she felt no hope for her future life because she had no children of her own. She had visited more than eight departments of a university hospital to ask for help. For a baby to have died from a congenital defect is a blow to the esteem of a Japanese woman, but it is not nearly so great as being childless, since raising children is so fundamental to her life purpose.

Mrs. K was the younger of two daughters, her father being a retired high school teacher and now a calligraphy master. Mrs. K completed junior college for young ladies from respectable families in southern Osaka and married Mr. K from a middle-class household in northern Osaka. She had been married previously in an arranged marriage to a young physician who was not only alcoholic but who also couldn't give up a love affair he had been involved in—which resulted in her divorcing him after a year and a half. She reported having a difficult time

---

[15] This case was described in detail in supervision in Dr. Tatara's group by Dr. Idei, who had already seen Mrs. K once a week in psychoanalytic therapy for some eighty-two sessions, with thirty dreams and associations translated from the Japanese to English. I asked her to translate the therapy sessions so that the dreams could be understood within the context of the ongoing sessions.

adjusting to her current in-laws because they put more value on one's will and wishes than was approved in the traditional rural value system she was brought up with. Differences in value system and customs between the in-laws' family and the original family are not unusual, but it introduces strains for the daughter-in-law, as she is expected to adapt completely to her in-laws' ways of living. By age thirty-two, she had had two miscarriages and the child who died from congenital defects.

Dr. Idei described Mrs. K as a rather small, slim, well-dressed woman who sat stiffly and gave the impression of being fragile—eliciting a response of feeling protective toward her. In the initial sessions, Mrs. K conveyed feelings of being very distant from others, of great futility about her life, and of being highly passive and sad. She further communicated intense feelings of inferiority over her childlessness, and painful feelings around her miscarriages and the baby who died of congenital defects.

Mrs. K was extremely evasive about everything during the first year of therapy. She looked away from Dr. Idei when talking, was emotionally flat, and for a long time was extremely guarded. In the ninth session she told how she must hide any imperfection, and felt herself to be a kind of shell hiding from people. In sessions eighteen and nineteen, Mrs. K constantly denied that she wanted to say anything or had any feelings; she communicated only by innuendos. This degree of defensiveness resulted in Dr. Idei becoming sleepy, a not uncommon reaction of therapists when patients are unusually defensive. Then, by the twenty-ninth session, Mrs. K was gradually able to say that she talks only about minor points to avoid her main problems. Almost the only way Mrs. K was able to reveal her inner life was through frequent dreams with occasional spontaneous associations to one or another part of the dream.

Unlike many Western psychoanalysts, who would have openly and directly dealt with this extreme kind of resistance to communication, Dr. Idei responded by being extremely evasive and indirect herself, communicating only by innuendo. By the eleventh session, Dr. Idei sensed that Mrs. K was probably not having sex with her husband, and in the thirteenth session she further sensed that Mrs. K was afraid her husband might be having sex with his stepmother; but Dr. Idei said absolutely nothing about these matters. Nor did she ask for associations to different aspects of the dreams, although Dr. Idei is trained in psychoanalytic dream analysis, in which associations are considered central to understanding a dream. Instead, she worked in a highly intuitive manner with Mrs. K's dreams. Dr. Idei correctly sensed that had she dealt more directly with Mrs. K's strong resistances, Mrs. K would have experienced this as highly intrusive. That would have been so disruptive to their relationship that Mrs. K almost certainly would have terminated therapy.

What light does this mode of communication and interaction shed on the Japanese familial-group self and social change? Mrs. K apparently grew up with a mother who in normal Japanese style was highly caring, nurturing, and strongly emotionally involved with her daughter, in a relationship that would be considered highly symbiotic in American child rearing but quite normal in Japanese families. What was skewed from usual Japanese patterns was that her mother was overanxious and overcautious, on the one hand, and on the other, she was profoundly unempathic with Mrs. K's feelings and wishes, as she indeed was with her own—instead being driven by the perfectionistic "shoulds" of a strict conscience. Mrs. K grew up constantly being sensitive to and giving over to her mother's moods and expectations ("usually, I could anticipate mother's feelings and then always adjust myself to them."), which she later continued with her husband and in-laws, while being profoundly out of touch with her own wishes and feelings. The constant empathic sensing of the other is quite usual in Japanese development and functioning, as is the resulting "onion" nature of many Japanese patients, where there is frequently a development of a false self.[16]

Quotations from some of Mrs. K's later sessions as she was becoming more in touch with herself poignantly illustrate this. "So far I use mother's response as the major criteria to evaluate myself; therefore, unfortunately, I do not even know what kind of person I am" (session 62). "My motto used to be 'strict,' but recently I become loose when I deal with daily happenings" (session 63). "My mother does not have her own thoughts and feelings; instead she does what she should. . . . I am very similar to my mother and I am not flexible enough" (session 71). "In my original family we do not give much conscious consideration to our wishes" (session 77). And in a dream in session 71, she poignantly depicted her futility over fulfilling her own wishes. "It is a scene from the time I was staying with aunty and worked for a company. I am looking for shoes. Her neighbors kindly offer many shoes for me, but unfortunately I cannot find any of my size. Then one of them brought some popular shoes saying, 'This will fit you.' I try, but it's still big. So I put on clogs reluctantly." Associations: "Aunty puts on only clogs.

---

[16] The very cultivation of *omoiyari*, or concerned empathy for others, may well contribute to Japanese being somewhat out-of-touch with their own wishes and feelings, and thus sometimes cultivating a false self (pers. com. Yasuhiko Taketomo).

They may be her taste but not mine. Therefore, I just tried one pair and gave up. I guess there will not be any I like."

Mrs. K's evasiveness served in many respects to preserve a fragile inner self from her mother's overanxious intrusiveness, and to ward off any further wounds to her very low self-esteem derived from her mother's lack of empathy. Mrs. K could not risk further injury to her self-esteem by communicating relatively openly and then having someone not be empathically sensitive to her. Still another important dynamic behind her evasiveness emerged in session 27, after she had become aware during the previous session that she had always been so sensitively in touch first with her mother's and then her in-laws' feelings, and had always given over to them. She realized that if she really communicated with others, she would be in danger of merging with them, as she would be impelled to be completely empathic and considerate of others' feelings while ignoring her own. By her evasiveness she thus kept a protective distance from others.

Mrs. K's evasiveness and denial of feelings and wishes were on the extreme side, to be sure, but these same modes existed to varying degrees in everyday relationships, according to Japanese psychoanalysts. In general, the indirectness of communication is usually discussed in the social science literature as adaptive where no one is to stand out too much, where family and group needs and decision making are central, and where the too direct assertion of one's views becomes disruptive to family and group functioning. On a more personal psychological level, however, indirectness of communication preserves the individuality of a highly private self by preventing intrusion, and by also putting a brake on becoming too close to and merging with others; simultaneously it helps to preserve inner feelings of esteem by not risking too open assertion of one's feelings or needs that may not be correctly understood by the other.

To the extent that the other is in tune with one's inner world, as Dr. Idei was with Mrs. K, then the person will experience her individuality as being confirmed and will gradually become much less evasive, as Mrs. K eventually did. In effect, in Japanese intimacy relationships there is a constant sensitivity to the other's empathy and concern with oneself. In the analytic relationship, therapists actually progress through their empathy from being in an outsider relationship with the patient to an insider intimacy—Japanese always sharply differentiating between the two.

But the issue of evasiveness of communication and being out of touch with one's inner world is an important problem in the psychological

189

concommitants of social change, as well. There is an enormous difference between the culture of Mrs. K's traditional rural family and that of Mr. K's more urban one, the latter reflecting more modernizing trends over a period of decades. Mrs. K was deeply resentful that Mr. K and her in-laws could much more openly express their needs and do what they wanted, in contrast to her constantly having to be sensitive to the other and denying what she was feeling and wanting. Again her mode of functioning was on the extreme side and connoted psychopathology, but this kind of contrast between wife and husband also reflects changing modes of being in Japan. In effect, the husband and his family stand for a greater degree of individualization, of being more in touch with one's self, wishes, and feelings.

There is also no question that this change is not simply a rural-urban one, but is related to the gradual assimilation of more Western modes and values of individualistic functioning. To illustrate this, one of the colleagues in the therapy work group amusingly commented that he was surprised that Dr. Idei could be so indirect and evasive herself when necessary, as in this therapy relationship with Mrs. K. Her reputation is one of being much more articulate and assertive than Japanese women tend to be. She and other Japanese trained in the United States have reflected how they have all had some difficulties readjusting to the Japanese therapy relationship because they had tended to become far too forthright and assertive in their psychoanalytic approach. These values so prized by Americans are maladaptive in Japanese-style relationships, including the psychotherapeutic one. By drawing upon an older, indigenous side of herself, Dr. Idei was able to work therapeutically in a highly successful way with Mrs. K. Nevertheless, it should not be overlooked that Dr. Idei, along with other Japanese psychoanalysts trained abroad, are bringing to bear much more individualized values and ways of functioning than have been traditional in Japan, even though these may be considerably modified.

A further telling anecdote illustrates this individualization even more clearly. At one point after a Japanese psychologist had entered psychoanalytic training in New York City, he found himself walking down the street talking to himself. "Masao, what do *you* want? What is it *I* wish? Just what is it that *I* want?" He commented further, "This was the very first time I ever had those thoughts." On another occasion, he told me that upon returning home after three years in New York City, he, his wife, and daughter went to a restaurant. When they sat down, he asked his eight year-old daughter what she wanted to eat. She replied, "I don't know." This was so unusual that the father asked, "Is something wrong with you, are you not feeling well?" "No," the daughter answered, "I am just becoming Japanese again." What he was again illustrating was that the wishing, wanting, individualistic self is experienced by Japanese as being far more Western in its mode of being than Japanese. But to varying extents, especially since the American Occupation, it is being slowly assimilated into Japanese ways of functioning. Therapists, for instance, who have worked with patients more exposed to Westernization have reported that the latter can free associate more easily, are more in touch with their feelings and wishes, and are more open to investigation (pers. com. Keigi Okonogi, Yasuhiko Taketomo, and Normund Wong).

To follow the interaction between patient and therapist over a course of almost two years of psychoanalytic therapy is to come upon other subtleties of Japanese communication and psychological makeup. Mrs. K, for instance, in the very beginning of the therapy formed an idealizing transference with Dr. Idei, a not unusual occurrence with many American patients. But one of the ways she conveyed it was particularly Japanese: she perceived Dr. Idei to be older than she really is. The older Dr. Idei was, the greater the respect Mrs. K had for her by traditional Japanese attitudes toward age.

But most striking over the course of the therapy were the minimal interventions by Dr. Idei, whether they be interpretations, reflections of what Mrs. K was feeling or saying, or simply some kind of investigation. In psychoanalytic terms, Dr. Idei became a mirroring selfobject to Mrs. K, but one whose empathy was mainly conveyed nonverbally. During the first few months of therapy, Dr. Idei listened quietly as Mrs. K gradually and indirectly expressed her feelings about her low self-esteem related to being childless, and avoiding social occasions with other women who have children. Nevertheless, by the eleventh session Mrs. K expressed some sense of hope ("feeling better, might be able to change myself").

Then, when Mrs. K clearly expressed in session twenty through dream symbolism that she would like to have sex with her husband ("I want to open the safe deposit box, but I cannot."), even though Dr. Idei had sensed some sessions before that they were not having sex together, she said nothing. Nevertheless, in the very next session, Mrs. K openly admitted for the first time that she and her husband have not had a sexual relationship for some years. And in still another instance immediately following, Mrs. K began to grope with painful, mixed-up feelings over wanting a child and not having one—after suppressing these desires for some years—as well as whether ever to become dependent on anyone. Again, Dr. Idei said nothing, but Mrs. K became much more able to be with other women and was now much less depressed.

In one of Dr. Idei's few interventions, she expressed herself in a highly metaphorical manner. In the thirteenth session, Mrs. K voiced her great reluctance to go to her high school class reunion because of her childlessness, and reported a dream in which she made an omelette very different from others in a cooking lesson. Dr. Idei simply stated, "It's all right to make an omelette different from others," thereby conveying metaphorically that it's acceptable for a woman to be childless. It is evident that Mrs. K clearly understood, for in the fifteenth session she reported going to her high school reunion and feeling comfortable with her former classmates in spite of being childless. This is a simple example of the ease with which metaphorical communication is used by Japanese.

Only rarely did Dr. Idei deal with Mrs. K's extreme defensiveness. It was not until some six months of therapy, in session twenty-four, when Mrs. K said, "I don't say anything in the midst of trouble," that Dr. Idei commented, "even to the therapist." In session twenty-eight, Dr. Idei simply asked after realizing from an earlier dream that Mrs. K was very angry at her husband, "Is there anything new in your life, though it might not necessarily be feelings about a baby," implying that Mrs. K was covering up feelings about her husband. Mrs. K replied that she was aware that she was highly evasive about this problem—though neither of them specified what the problem was—and that she tended to divert attention to subsidiary problems.

Nevertheless, by this minimal investigation, Mrs. K became in touch with her rage at her husband in session thirty-four through a dream: "I am furious. I want to ask him [husband] why, but I can not say anything because a guest is there. For the first time in my life I express verbally inexpressable anguish and throw a saucepan at him." Without any interpretation by Dr. Idei, Mrs. K became much more assertive at her women's club and her eyelid symptom diminished, but she then had an intense reaction that there were critical eyes all around her. Her symptom was permanently relieved as she got in touch with her rage at her husband; but again it was without the kind of interpretation that would be characteristic with a Western patient.

It is apparent that the eyelid symptom was a hysterical identification with her husband, unconsciously serving to contain her tremendous anger at him. Hysterical symptoms are not uncommon in Japanese and Indians, as with Freud's Viennese patients; but they are very rare today among most New York City patients, except among certain ethnic groups such as Hispanics. As Mrs. K got more in touch with her rage at her husband, the symptom not only diminished, but she then had a powerful, unconscious superego reaction that all eyes were critically on her— a common reaction, deeply ingrained in Japanese (and Indian) women's conscience, that they will be judged severely if they become aware of their intense anger and assertiveness. And because of this powerful superego, these impulses are usually kept in check, either consciously contained or unconsciously displaced—somatic symptoms being extremely common in Japanese (and Indians) as a way of handling unacceptable emotions in the family and/or group situation. Preoccupation with the somatic symptoms themselves then diverted Mrs. K's attention from the more crucial issues of being childless and not having a sexual relationship with her husband, which she gradually became aware of after almost a year in psychoanalytic therapy.

But the actual direction that the rage at her husband took is also characteristically Japanese. Mrs. K realized in the forty-eighth session that she was furious at him for not showing kindness and consideration over her painful feelings of childlessness. Mrs. K felt strongly entitled that husband, therapist, and mother should all sense these painful feelings without her having to communicate them. This strong sense of entitlement, and blame and rage over not receiving consideration, support, and empathy is something I have sensed in case after case that was reported to me. I hope to clarify this particular constellation in Japanese psychological makeup that so differs from Indian and American cases in Chapter Eight.

It is at this dramatic point in the therapy that Dr. Idei made her main interpretation: "You are so indirect and evasive in communicating your feelings to your husband that it makes it extremely difficult for him to respond." It was after this intervention that Mrs. K began to deal much more directly with her relationship with her mother. In the following sessions, her mother emerged as tremendously emotionally involved with Mrs. K, but always in an overwhelmingly anxious way, with little empathy. Mrs. K became as a result completely out of touch with her own feelings and wishes, while being highly sensitive to and giving over to her mother's needs and expectations. Through these realizations, Mrs. K gradually became aware of her own wishes and goals, more interested and involved in everyday activities, more empathic with her husband, and was able to have sex with him for the first time in years. She was also able to see how she had unconsciously transferred her whole relationship with her mother onto her husband—expecting worry and care while doing little for herself, completely living up to his expectations with little sense of herself—and simultaneously realized that she was empathically out of touch with him. All of this occurred without further interventions by Dr. Idei.

It was from this case in particular that I was struck that the therapist had made hardly any interventions, and yet the patient had improved considerably in a way I could understand psychodynamically. When I expressed this startling observation to Dr. Tatara, he responded with a broad, knowing smile and asked, "And what do *you* make of this?" Dr. Totoro Ichimaru chimed in that when he had presented a case of a Japanese woman at the William Alanson White Institute in New York City, many of the audience had reacted the same way as myself: how did this patient improve so much with a minimum of intervention?

I gradually realized that the subtle sensing of each other's feelings and mind that is pervasive in normal Japanese social relationships is simply carried over to the therapeutic relationship, where so much is mutually sensed by both patient and therapist. I should add parenthetically that when Dr. Tatara later told me that clinical psychologists in Japan have for years been primarily involved with Carl Rogers's nondirective therapy, which is so empathically based,[17] I decided to ask him if the Japanese psychologist is constantly verbally reflecting back to the patient what he or she is feeling, as an American Rogerian would do. He responded, "of course not." In effect, the Japanese therapist, whether Rogerian or psychoanalytic, responds empathically mostly in a silent way or by innuendo.

[17] In the American occupation after World War II, Herbert Passin, now a Japan specialist in the East Asia Department of Columbia University, introduced Carl Rogers's work on nondirective psychotherapy to Japanese psychologists. Professor Passin related that he thought that of all the Western psychotherapies this would be most congenial to the Japanese because of its fundamental emphasis on empathy.

The Indian Self: Reflections in
the Mirror of the American Life Style

If you are traveling at night in a car with the inside light on and look through a side window, you simultaneously get a glimpse of the outside scenery and reflections in the window of yourself. Indians in the United States similarly catch glimpses of the emotional landscape of American social interactions, in profound contrast with Indian ones, while they simultaneously see aspects of their own Indian familial self face-to-face with a totally different life style from their own. And if as an Indian you travel this American road long enough, the outside landscape and the reflections in the window begin to come together into the unique integrations of an expanding self.[1] This metaphor, of course, is just as applicable to Westerners moving eastward, as anthropologists and others can testify.

In this chapter I recount the experiences of a small group of Indians who have been involved in American relationships and also, for at least some limited period, in psychoanalytic therapy—thereby gaining a greater degree of self-awareness in their observations.[2] My purpose is not sim-

[1] "After living in America for many years, I have finally managed to become a bicultural man" was the self-reflective comment of an Indian professor at the Annual Meeting of the New York State Sociological Association, October 1984, in New York City.

[2] My sample is a small one of eleven persons, eight women and three men, all but one of whom are highly educated, well-functioning professionals, mostly with doctorates in

ply to delineate major differences in the emotional patterning of relationships between Indian and American life styles, but more centrally to highlight intrapsychic aspects of the Indian self as these become reflected in the mirror of American relationships. Depending on the nature of the specific encounter with Americans, one or another facet of the Indian self comes into focus. And as the Indian self thus becomes illuminated in an American setting, I shall show how it integrates certain aspects of individualism into an expanding self. This, I may add, is no idle exercise, because the influence of the Indian community in the United States on urban Indians at home is not inconsiderable.

Indian Intimacy Relationships and Symbiosis-Reciprocity

The most striking differences in the emotional patterning of relationships between Indians and Americans are the configurations of intimacy, which reflect that dimension of the familial self I conceptualize as symbiosis-reciprocity. My Indian subjects, female and male, are in complete accord on these major contrasts. This is particularly impressive because the majority of my subjects are women, who commented on the differences in intimacy relationships between themselves and American women—who generally have a much greater intimacy network than American men.

What my subjects emphasized over and over again are the strong emotional connectedness between Indians, usually experienced on a nonverbal level; a more symbiotic mode of thinking of and being constantly sensitive to the other, with internalized expectations of full reciprocity; a tremendous (from an American's view) giving and taking or constant mutual indulgence of warmth and concern; and a sense of weness and partial merger. This is in contrast to the relative lack of close-

---

one or another field; two of them are also recognized artists. The one exception is a successful small businessman. This sample in good part reflects the surge of Indian immigration since the new Immigration Law of 1965 whereby professionals, engineers, and businessmen and their families have immigrated to America. I have seen four of the eleven persons in short-term psychoanalytic therapy and interviewed the others, usually for at least three hours. Since this sample is so slanted toward Indian women, I have supplemented it with occasional examples from the excellent article by Prakash Desai and George Coelho (1980, 363–386). I should further stress that my subjects related that their own observations are supplemented and confirmed by observations of Indian friends. Thus, while the sample is small, there seems a great deal of consensus.

ness, sensitivity, warmth, consideration, intimacy, and emotional exchange they experience in most American relationships. One Indian psychologist termed this a convenience-inconvenience continuum, with Americans much more oriented toward the convenience end of the continuum, and with Indians accepting the inconvenience in the constant giving and taking of intimacy relationships. She also commented on the much more frequent gift-giving of Indians, Americans tending to restrict gift-giving to the immediate family or friends who are well-defined as highly intimate. Or to take the observations of an Indian male psychiatric resident: "In the normal, superficial relationships with Americans it's O.K. The problem comes with more intimate friends, with both men and women. When it reaches a level of intimacy, I don't necessarily mean sexual either with women, I feel very pained because I expect more giving and taking, more reciprocity than what Americans are apparently used to. Even their need for privacy, and I am a very private person, disturbs me. I just can't drop in to see my friend at any time." Indians frequently find this intimacy gap to be quite painful.[3]

Indian expectations for emotional connectedness readily surface in the psychoanalytic relationship, where Indians assume a far greater closeness and dependency in the relationship than Americans characteristically do. I have mentioned that one Indian woman was deeply distressed that her American therapist would not talk with her at length at 2 A.M., when she had just learned that her mother was terminally ill with cancer in India. My American patients would be highly reluctant to call me at this hour, feeling they would be infringing upon my privacy, and would indeed wait until the following morning. Or to take an example from my own practice, when I was on vacation one summer and could not be reached because of a telephone strike, one Indian woman broke off treatment, telling me in the fall how utterly painful it was not to be able to call me. To be sure, this break in communication might have been even more painful to her because of an extraordinarily close tie to her mother that had become revived in the transference, and was something that other Indian patients would probably not have done even though they felt very upset. For an American patient to have terminated therapy in these circumstances, however, would connote a much deeper level of psychopathology than was the case here.

In a somewhat different vein, an Indian man related to me that for a very long time he would be extremely sensitive to the moods and feel-

---

[3] The same search for intimacy and friendship, and the same frustration of finding them hard to come by in their relationships with Americans, also characterize the more male sample of Desai and Coelho's study (1980, 363–386).

ings of his analyst, trying not to be silent for too long so as not to hurt him—and implicitly so as not to have any rupture in the relationship. Then there was a graduate psychology student whom I supervised, who requested a change of hours. I had to tell her that for the time being the hour she wanted was not available, but that I would let her know as soon as there was any possibility of changing it. For the next few months, she repeatedly asked me in a charming way if that hour was now becoming available—far more often than any American supervisee would ever ask. As an Indian she felt free to presume upon our relationship to ask repeatedly for something she wanted.[4]

In contrast to this mode of being and relating in Indian intimacy relationships, two Indian women married to Americans, who are thus involved in a basically American life style, experience the American self as being much more independent and autonomous in functioning, more assertive and highly individualistic, with far more defined boundaries around oneself and between oneself and others. These women experience these two modes of being in the world as highly dichotomous and contradictory. They say it's like being two different persons. One of these women related that it took many years of psychoanalysis with a warm, supportive analyst gradually to be able to have a more individualized self; and when she did, reactions from Indian relatives were that she had become selfish to become so involved with herself. During that time, she found it impossible to be with her Indian relatives or other Indians, or once with them for any period, to be with Americans; the strain of the difference between the two modes of functioning and being was just too great. It was only after some fifteen years in America that she was able to feel perfectly comfortable with either Americans or Indians, to be able to switch back and forth with some ease, and gradually to integrate the two. Although most Indians relate that they are pained by the lack of emotional intimacy in American relationships, they find that once they are here for some time and then visit home, they experience themselves as being swallowed up in familial relationships with too little sense of a self or their own boundaries.

There is still another side to Indian intimacy relationships that Indians in psychoanalytic therapy are particularly aware of when they are in

---

[4]Conversations with a number of Americans who have had contact with Indians frequently elicit their sense of annoyance at the degree of asking, since Americans experience this as a profound infringement upon their autonomy. Indians, on the other hand, usually experience this as a confirmation of intimacy and caring, and of according the other respect—unless it is another with whom there are no ties, in which case it can be manipulative.

American relationships. An Indian woman married to an American related that although her husband sometimes has difficulty expressing his feelings, particularly angry ones when there is a disagreement between them, she frequently finds herself to be completely unaware that there is any disagreement, and is therefore completely out of touch with any anger over it. Her need to deny any issues of dissension becomes highlighted in a particular American life style where issues of conflict are to be talked about. She realizes that in her Indian family and those of her relatives any disagreement or conflict is usually swept under the rug; agreements are made even when there is no real agreement, and any anger is contained, swallowed, or denied. She herself gradually recognized through her own therapy that even though she strongly tends to deny any issues of conflict with her husband and is therefore unaware of any anger, her annoyance unconsciously does get expressed nonverbally and indirectly, occasionally building up to an outburst. The point of all this is that conflict or anger must be contained so that it should never interfere with or disrupt the strong mutual emotional connectedness and the pleasant ambiance of Indian familial relationships.

In psychoanalytic terms, internalized structures in the Indian conscience, in both the superego and ego-ideal, severely inhibit the direct verbal expression and sometimes even awareness of any kind of ambivalence, anger, annoyance, or hostility. The cultural codes of conduct around the inhibition of anger are deeply internalized, so that anger doesn't disrupt the close, familial intimacy relationships. Ego-ideal values assert the primacy of harmony and emotional connectedness to be preserved at all cost. Thus, the American saying, "Sticks and stones will break my bones but words will never hurt me," becomes transformed in Gujerati to, "the wounds of physical abuse will heal, but the wounds of words will never heal." (Desai and Coelho 1980, 369)

For Indian women married to Americans, marital and family relationships can sometimes seem quite paradoxical. According to three Indian women, the marital relationship itself is much more intimate in America in the earlier years, with a much greater verbal sharing of one's inner life than is characteristic of an Indian marriage—which tends to become closer after some years together. For one of these women, an artist, it was more difficult preserving a private self around her art since everything is more verbally shared than it would have been in an Indian marriage, which she felt would have accorded her more private space as differentiated from privacy. This confirms another key facet of the Indian familial self: as deeply emotionally enmeshed as Indians are in their intimacy relationships, they keep a profoundly private self.

199

Another of these women related that Indian women, once they are married and have children, look much more to the women of their husband's family, including their mother-in-law, for emotional intimacy than American women characteristically do. In her particular case, her mother-in-law was not nearly enough involved with her or her children, which deeply pained her; whereas the third woman mentioned that her Jewish mother-in-law was indeed similar to an Indian one emotionally. These profoundly internalized expectations by Indian women for emotional involvement with their female in-laws, including their mothers-in-law, have been overlooked in the anthropological and psychoanalytic literature that so emphasizes daughter-in-law/mother-in-law conflict (Kakar 1978, 73–74).

There is still another important facet to Indian intimacy relationships as they contrast with American ones, involving the dimension of communication. Indian communication is subtle and frequently nonverbal, in terms of the emotional closeness which one has with another—which Indians seem constantly attuned to. This contrasts with the American life style where, as one woman put it, "everything is out in the open, it's all expressed, hashed out, and worked out." But for her, when there is something missing on the subtle level of emotional intimacy, this verbalizing of the problem only makes it more painful. She feels Indians are more attuned to remedying the situation without expressing anything about it.

In a related vein, one woman said that she and her friends find American superficial talk—the "how are you?"—a strain. They find that this kind of communication never really takes into account the real nature of the intimacy relationship that is going on. If they answer honestly, they either feel that the American isn't really interested, or that they are being inauthentic because they are answering on a level that the relationship isn't really on. In terms of the Indian self, the remarks of both these women—and men have mentioned similar feelings—convey a greatly heightened empathic capacity for sensing the degree of emotional bondedness and flow between persons.

There is a paradoxical communicative situation that between Indian friends there can be a much more passionate arguing of views on various matters than seems characteristic of Americans. In fact, it was observed that Americans sometimes become appalled at the intensity with which Indians will present their views. First one person will occupy center stage, and then another. In an American social setting, an Indian can easily take over the conversation. This contrasts with typical American interchange, where one usually doesn't attempt to foist one's own view on another but rather to have a give and take between equals, no one person monopolizing the stage. In Indian relationships, however, it is assumed and accepted through internalized values that one or another person may be clearly influential over another.

Narcissism and the Indian Conscience

All of my subjects report that on the whole they adapt very quickly to the norms of American life, whether in college, work, or social situations. One woman recounted her American college days as a seventeen-year-old fresh from New Delhi. The other students marveled at how quickly she had become Americanized in her manner and in her participation in all of the college activities—the involvement in various extra-curricular activities being far greater than at her previous college in New Delhi. She related that in typical Indian manner she quickly sensed what it was to be like an American student and was able to act accordingly. But every few weeks she took a couple of days off and simply stayed in bed all day. She was exhausted from becoming involved in an American life style and demeanor that stemmed from totally different motivation and inner psychological makeup than her own. She had remained totally Indian.

What enables her and other Indians to adapt so quickly? In part, the ability derives from the highly developed astute sensitivity to relationships and awareness of the norms of particular situations. This adaptive behavior also unfolds from a profoundly internalized ego-ideal that is strongly oriented toward having appropriate attitudes and actions in different social contexts and relationships, enhancing feelings of inner esteem by gaining approval from others for acting appropriately. Some of my women subjects assert that Indians have a constant need for confirmation, appreciation, and approbation to have a good sense of self and self-worth. The constant mutual, subtle mirroring becomes central in confirming that one is living up to inner images of the ego-ideal and idealized self, and greatly enhances feelings of self-esteem. Since this need for self-esteem maintenance through continual, greatly heightened mirroring in everyday relationships tends to transcend the degree of mirroring present in American relationships, it can then become a real strain for Indians adapting to the American life style.

The Indian ego-ideal to act appropriately and differentially depending on the social context—even when the norms for one situation may be totally different from those for another—is far different from the American one, which tends toward a greater consistency, though American women are inclined to be more socially contextual in their norms than American men (Gilligan 1980; Bernstein 1983). To Americans, this behavior of Indians can sometimes appear to be two-faced or unprincipled, if they do not realize that it is an internalization of cultural norms that are far more socially contextual in the well-defined categories and boundaries of relationships in Indian society than is true in Western society, ruled by the categorical imperative.

The differences between the Indian and American ego-ideals emerge even more saliently in American competitive school and work situations. One Indian woman in graduate school was running to be head of the student organization, a highly important and influential body. She ran her campaign on the basis of being modest, self-effacing, and dedicated to working hard and serving the other students—reflecting Gandhian influence in her family. She became simply appalled by the aggressive, self-promoting tactics of her American opponents, mainly women. Her nonaggressive demeanor, however, was interpreted by her American fellow students as ineffectuality, which lost her the election. In like manner, another Indian graduate student reported that it was very difficult for her to write a curriculum vitae when she first came to America because of deeply internalized values of being self-effacing and not putting yourself forward. On this same theme, an Indian woman psychoanalyst reports that when she sees American patients, she always wears American clothes, in contrast to wearing a sari or kurta in other social situations. She finds that when she dresses as an American she can be far more assertive and confrontive with American patients, who often need it, whereas when she dresses in Indian clothes she finds herself being softer and more subtle in manner.

The paper by Desai and Coelho (1980, 367) amply confirms that male Indians also tend to avoid a competitive mode of behavior at work, instead trying to be loyal, cooperative, and agreeable—which is often misinterpreted as being too passive and compliant. What is appropriate behavior to the Indian ego-ideal in hierarchical intimacy relationships is seen by Americans as much too nonassertive for American-style individualism.

Internalized Indian ideals are further reflected in certain byways of the American life style. An Indian woman graduate student found her attitudes and behavior with her professors markedly different from those of her fellow students. She always feels professors are to be respected and deferred to, even if one doesn't think very highly of them—in contrast with American students, who tend to treat their professors on a more equal basis and with far less respect than she does. Then, when she really does think well of a professor, she will try to be as close as possible, to bring gifts, and in effect to share in this hierarchy by quality—thus enhancing her own esteem by identifying with the idealized teacher.

Indian internalized attitudes for proper behavior in hierarchical relationships are sometimes highlighted when the expected behavior is not present in an American life-style marriage. An Indian man married to an overtly assertive American woman believed she would probably leave him because she was not being properly deferential—thus conveying his internalized expectations of how a wife should conduct herself. In a similar vein, an Indian wife tends to be surprised when her American husband doesn't take over as much as she expects him to; and then finds it a struggle to assert openly what she wishes when he asks her what she wants to do. In these cases, the Indian spouses' expectations are for hierarchy, and the Americans' are for relative equality.

In a far more problematic situation, one Indian husband finds it extremely difficult to stay with his American wife and her child from another marriage. Complicated circumstances pushed him into the marriage, but his feelings of esteem are constantly threatened by being married to a divorced woman with a child, which by his internalized values reflects very poorly on his family in India, with whom he feels closely identified. This further exemplifies that Indians' inner feelings of esteem are deeply tied up with family reputation.

Experiential Sense of the Indian Self

Perceptive reflections from some of my subjects convey that the very experiential sense of self can be quite different in Indians and in Americans. They find, for instance, an ability on their own part to spend endless hours sitting around and being absorbed in their own thoughts, feelings, and fantasies, to chat with others and just putter around, without any compulsion whatsoever toward a goal-directed activity, such as they find with their American husbands and friends (cf. Kakar 1978, 136). This is even more striking since these subjects have doctorates and careers, and are obviously high achievers. They further document the point that the Indian's sense of self is far less identified with work and activity than is that of the American, who is constantly asserting and consolidating his or her identity through activity, work, and relationships. Work and activity have meaning for Indians primarily in the context of a relationship, rather than for maintaining their own identity. Perhaps another way of stating this is that the Indian self, when it is not involved in close emotional involvements with others, is more content to be; it is not constantly striving to become an individualized entity and identity.

Another experiential aspect of the self is expressed by some of my Indian subjects as being sensitive and receptive to one's personal destiny, to an unfolding of the self in life relationships and situations. One Indian professional woman, in fact, asked me if I knew of a good astrologer in New York City when she and her husband had some particularly difficult decisions to make on some mutual job opportunities. For her, there was a sense of personal destiny in the choice and decision that was central to the development of their selves. For an American, the characteristic attitudes are of creating one's own destiny, to be goal-directed, and to try to forge ahead to reach it. For an American, it is to be active; for an Indian, to be receptive. The sense of an evolving self over many lives is a major part of an Indian acceptance of a wider range of eccentricities and inclinations in each other than Americans tend to tolerate—another observation conveyed by some of my subjects.

Career and Motherhood:
Indian and American

Some years ago, I was stimulated by personal experiences at home, social ones with friends and colleagues, and clinical ones with patients to investigate the intrapsychic sources of the enormous guilt and anxiety expressed by American women who were combining a career with having a family. Their guilt over not being home enough with the children, and their anxiety over not adequately fulfilling their career standards, seemed to go appreciably beyond the considerable social constraints and reality factors they had to deal with. To probe this subject both psychoanalytically and historically, I organized a symposium which was later published (Roland and Harris 1978).

In the intervening years I have worked with a few Indian women in short-term psychoanalytic therapy who combined careers with having a family. Although these women had at times inner problems and struggles, if suitable child care could be arranged they had almost none of the inner conflict in this area characteristic of similar American women. What accounts for this startling difference?

If an Indian woman is to have a career, almost inevitably her extended family has decided that the daughters or certain particular daughters of the family are to go on for advanced education and have a career; and then her family, in arranging her marriage, negotiates in advance with her future husband and in-laws that they accept and support her in her career. If there is not this support, first from her original family and then her in-laws, in India it is virtually impossible for a woman to have a career. When children come along, arrangements are usually made that either her in-laws or servants will help take care of the children.

Assuming, then, that this necessary family social support exists, what are the internalized cultural ideals and intrapsychic patterns that enable her to combine career and motherhood so easily? In terms of values, having a career is fundamentally a family endeavor; her ego-ideal for achievement and success is basically related to the family. It is not that the career does not offer her considerable personal satisfaction; but it is also overwhelmingly connected to how it reflects on the family—both her original family and her husband's. Career is thus experienced as much for the family as for herself.

This relates to another aspect of her ego-ideal as well as the makeup of the self. An Indian woman, especially after having children, considers herself to be far more integrated into her in-laws' family than does an American woman. Perhaps even more important, the experiential sense of self for both Indian women and men is much more of a we-self that includes others in the extended family; whereas the American self is implicitly a highly individualistic I-self. Thus, having a we-self makes it experientially much easier for an Indian woman to experience her career as being for the family, rather like having children.

There are still other crucial differences in the ego-ideal and structuring of the self that are central to the issue of career and motherhood. The Indian moral code, always to act appropriately in terms of the social context, goes much further than American women's orientation in this direction (Gilligan 1980; Bernstein 1983). Thus, for an Indian woman, differences in norms and behavior between career and family create far less dissonance than they do for an American because of this contextual ethic.

Moreover, Indians' inner sense of self is felt as being far more relational and situational than is an American's. As the artist who was my subject stated, "Americans seem to have to be one thing. I and my Indian friends are able to be many different kinds of persons in different situations. I feel very comfortable slipping back and forth from being a professor to being a painter to being a mother and wife. I can't understand these American women who are conflicted between having a ca-

205

reer and a family. I don't have to be one set self or have a single identity. In fact I avoid like the plague having a set identity." She was expressing both a contextual ethic and an experiential structuring of the self that is highly relational. The inner consistency of self and identity that Americans strive for creates more of a potential for conflict between different spheres of life such as career and family.

To give still another example of this contextual ethic and relational self, an Indian psychoanalyst recounted that she was a member of two private psychoanalytic seminars with completely different orientations as well as leaders;[5] but that she felt perfectly comfortable in both groups, with no conflict whatsoever, and learned a great deal in each. No American psychoanalyst I know of would consider being a member of these two particular seminars simultaneously, because they would experience them as far too dissonant and too disruptive of a consistent inner professional identity.

What light does this Indian background shed on the anxieties and guilts of American women in a similar position? American women's traditional ego-ideal, in a way like that of Indian women, is to be there for others, particularly husband, children, and others of the family. But a career signifies the dominant cultural ideal of Westerners, that of individualism, of being there for oneself—hitherto reserved almost entirely for men. Thus, to have a family draws upon the traditional female ego-ideal, usually incorporated early in childhood, while having a career draws on an ego-ideal generally incorporated by females in later childhood, or often not till adolescence or even young adulthood. I would submit that it is this clash of cultural ideals, profoundly incorporated into American women's ego-ideal, in the context of a self and identity overwhelmingly oriented toward inner integration and consistency, that generates such feelings of guilt and anxiety in even women of considerable maturity and highly competent functioning.

[5] One group is very much more traditional, whereas the other emphasizes the personal exploration of countertransference, mainly using object-relations theory. The two leaders' personalities also reflect this traditional-innovative dichotomy.

PART TWO

The Indian and Japanese Self: Theoretical Perspectives

The Indian Familial Self in
Its Social and Cultural Contexts

The Extended Family

I would now like to reshape the data gleaned from the psychoanalytic case material of the last five chapters into a comprehensive formulation of the Indian self, and then move on to a similar conceptualization of the Japanese self in Chapter Eight. In this endeavor, I shall also rely on extensive discussions with Indian psychoanalytic therapists and social scientists. In this and the following chapter, I shall refine my clinical observations into a formulation of various major dimensions of the familial self as functioning within extended family hierarchical relationships; in Chapter Nine, I shall discuss the spiritual self and its complex psychological interrelationships with the familial self.

Even to begin to understand the subtleties and complexities of the inner psychological makeup of the Indian familial self, it is essential to elucidate the soil and climate in which it grows and functions: the Indian extended family, and the richly complex hierarchical relationships that constitute it and other *jati* and group relationships. Although the caste system is undoubtedly the most striking feature of Hindu society—investigated and analyzed by a variety of social scientists with various views of it—undeniably it is the kinship system, or the extended family, that is the social and psychological locus throughout life of the vast majority of Indians. Social, personal, economic, status, and sexual needs of the person are traditionally played out and fulfilled overwhelmingly within the extended family. To a great extent this is still true even in contemporary urban society. Even relationships with friends, professionals, or others, when they become personalized and significant, become assimilated into the extended family.[1] Similarly, relationships in other groups outside the family tend to become modeled after personalized familial relationships rather than impersonal contractual ones.

Perhaps the dominant images of the Indian extended family are its corporate and corporeal nature. It is sometimes viewed as a living cohesive body, growing, developing, expanding, and at times contracting or even withering when struck by major calamities; in effect, it is always in process (Das 1976b; Dube 1955; Hanchette 1988; Inden and Nicholas 1977; Kapadia 1966). Another image is that of a banyan tree, which expands by sending down new roots (individual families) into the ground from its branches (Hanchette 1988). Others define the extended family in a more philosophical and mythological way as consisting of shared bodily substance with an inherent code for conduct, with further sharing of other substances like food, wealth, or land conducive to the prosperity of the family—all in the family being transformed by these transactions (Inden and Nicholas 1977). "One's own people" becomes an important experiential phrase expressing this cultural principal of shared substance. In a more pragmatic vein, still others emphasize the corporate nature of the patrilineal extended family, citing the joint ownership by the males of the family resources; the formal decision-making process by which all economic and social decisions are made by the male elders of the family, frequently through consultation and consensus, for its younger members and the family as a whole; and the over all economic and social security that the extended family affords to all its members (Dube 1955; Kapadia 1966; Mandelbaum 1970). Then there are others who cite the extended family as the locus for a plethora of Hindu religious rituals and festivals, usually arranged by the women of the family, which are intrinsically related to the auspicious and prosperous growth and development of the family (Dube 1955; Hanchette 1988; Srinivas 1966; Wadley 1980).

A family is constantly striving to protect and enhance its reputation and rank as a family within its own *jati,* as well as to insure the welfare of its members, through alliances and connections with other families.

---

[1] The outsider, for example, becomes auntie or uncle for the children (Inden and Nicholas 1977).

Its reputation greatly affects its ability to develop these alliances, which are generally accomplished through the arranged marriages primarily of its daughters but also its sons. Through these marriages the family attempts to gain higher rank within its own *jati*. This seems true of families from all the *jatis,* from the upper to the scheduled castes (Inden 1976; Moffatt 1979). Even the establishment of hierarchical rankings among the different *jati* in the rural areas takes place primarily through the interactions of families, not individuals (Mandelbaum 1970).

Members of a given family are all responsible for the reputation and honor of their family, are profoundly identified with the family by others and themselves, and in turn are all affected by family reputation (Das 1976b; Kapadia 1966; Mandelbaum 1970). Therefore, it is imperative to keep family matters, particularly any problems, strictly secret within the family (Dube 1955; Kapadia 1966; Srinivas 1976). This has profound psychological import, and clearly manifested itself in the cases of Ashis and Shakuntala around the suicide of Ashis's father and Shakuntala's astrological chart, which predicted problems in her getting married. A further corollary is the development of public and private spheres of behavior, where proper public behavior becomes inculcated at a very early age so as to enhance, or at least not draw criticism, on the family.

The extended family can live in either unitary or joint households, but maintains its basic structures in both; frequently there is an alternation in types of household depending on the stage of the family life cycle. Family members will frequently live in a unitary household, which becomes joint again when one or more of the sons marries and stays with his parents, such as Joan's and Saida's husbands. Living together jointly is usually predicated on a certain amount of land or wealth, and where there is a considerable amount of either, the extended family living together may become very large (Beteille 1964). Joint households can become unitary again as a result of the not infrequent and sometimes bitter partitioning of family property by the sons after the father or both parents have died; or simply when one of the sons wants to establish a unitary household. Or extended-family decisions may call for one son to set up a unitary household elsewhere because of a position that will benefit the family as a whole.

In the basic patrilineal structural paradigm of the extended family—though as with everything in India exceptions can be easily cited—the whole is not only greater than the sum of its component parts but, far more important, the paradigm significantly transforms its component parts, especially in a joint household. That is, a joint household is not simply a number of unitary families living together but rather a structure of various hierarchical relationships governed by the overall needs of the extended family, as will be described in some detail below.

Moreover, these norms and strong extended family ties have traditionally been kept up when the family is living in unitary households. They may, for instance, still share or jointly own many of their resources, rely on family elders for major decisions, and keep up mutual obligations to each other; meet together on important ritual occasions such as births, marriages, and deaths as well as certain festivals; feel profoundly affected by the reputation of other branches of the family, and maintain close family relationships through a great deal of mutual visiting. Moreover, the hierarchical relationships within the unitary households are usually all modeled after the basic structural paradigm of the extended family.

Psychosocial Dimensions of Familial Hierarchical Relationships

The nature of hierarchical relationships within the Indian extended family is a profoundly complex subject—from a psychological standpoint, much more intricate than the current social science literature would have it. Yet, only to the extent that we comprehend Indian hierarchical relationships in their fullest and subtlest nature can we gain insight into the Indian familial self, as well as some of its inner transformations into a spiritual self; conversely, through the observations of psychoanalytic therapy, we can gain new ethnographic insights into some of the intricacies of hierarchical relationships. Thus, Indian hierarchical relationships have anthropological, social psychological, and intrapsychic dimensions, when looked at from different angles. I shall try to integrate all three perspectives, realizing that the subject needs ever more perceptive and fuller analysis.

In this section, I shall elaborate three essential psychosocial dimensions to Indian hierarchical relationships that interact in differing kinds of asymmetrical balances with each other; in the next, I shall delineate various intrapsychic structures of the familial self congruent with these psychosocial dimensions. I should stress that the total gestalt of Indian hierarchical relationships differs radically from that of Western hierarchical ones, as does the congruent psychological makeup.

STRUCTURAL HIERARCHY

The first essential psychosocial dimension of hierarchical relationships is the structural one, described at length by innumerable social scientists. Within the extended family, structural hierarchy is primarily governed by kinship position and relationship, and gender. Thus, a man may have grown children to whom he is the hierarchical superior; but if his father is still alive, the latter will be the hierarchical superior in the family, who may well make the major decisions for his grandchildren. As an example, one woman patient described her mother as wanting postgraduate education in one of the sciences, which the mother's father would have sanctioned and supported; but the mother's grandfather vetoed the idea, since he believed that women should not go into science. This had profound consequences for my patient: her mother fulfilled her own ambitions through her daughter, who later became a major scientist in India.

Hierarchical position is established for all members of the extended family. Hierarchy prevails among brothers by birth order when viewed as related to their father, but are seen as equals in relation to their mothers (Das and Nicholas 1979); hierarchy prevails among the various wives in terms of the seniority of their husbands, and in relation to their mother-in-law; between the wife and her husband and in relation to all the males in the family older than her husband—a more informal, joking relationship usually being allowed to the husband's younger brothers (Roy 1975); and, of course, between all children and their elders. The mother will frequently mediate between the children and their father, and between younger and older brothers, harmonizing many of the male hierarchical relationships (pers. com. Anjali Apte).

These multiple hierarchical relationships are given expression through kinship terms that are much more precise than those in the West (Das 1976b). For example, a specific term will be used for a given aunt and a different one for another aunt to indicate where each is located in the hierarchical order. These complex hierarchical relationships are also given symbolic definition and expression through myriad exchanges of gifts, foods, and such, as well as through rituals, and are marked by different kinds of property that cannot be reduced to fair market value (Das and Nicholas 1979).

From a psychological standpoint, there are specific expectations in the structural hierarchy for certain attitudes and behavior in both subordinates and superiors that are strongly internalized. Deference, loyalty, and subordination are deeply ingrained in the former; whereas nurturance, concern, and responsibility are expressed by the latter. It is just this normal set of behavioral expectations in the subordinate that is frequently misunderstood by American superiors as passivity and compliance (Desai and Coelho 1980). Expectations for deference are stronger for children toward their fathers and their paternal grandfathers and uncles than toward their maternal uncles and other maternally related men, with whom they are allowed a more relaxed, intimate relationship.

Moreover, these internalized sets of expectations for subordinate and superior are also reciprocal. Subordinates fully expect superiors to fulfill certain responsibilities to them. The father and oldest brother, for example, are expected to fulfill obligations for the marriage and education of the various children; brothers assume a lifelong responsibility for their sisters. Meena, for instance, was bitter toward her brothers for not assuming the degree of responsibility she felt they should in finding her a husband. Musafer commented that his most difficult adjustment problem in a good position in a major American corporation was his repeated disappointment and hurt that his superiors did not respond knowingly and with concern to his needs after he had worked so loyally and well. He had to adopt the American saying, "You have to look out for yourself, no one else will"—which is directly antithetical to Indian expectations of reciprocity.

These hierarchical relationships are fundamentally oriented toward the well-being of the extended family as a whole. Hierarchical values orient the husband and wife, who are drawn together privately in a more equal relationship by the powerful forces of sexuality and procreation, to participate significantly and fully in the extended family, subordinating any tendency to becoming a system closed to the needs of the larger family (Das 1976b; Inden and Nicholas 1977). In a joint household, husband and wife spend little time together and make no overt displays of affection to each other in the presence of others; they are not expected to exhibit any favoritism or possessiveness toward their own children, but share and raise their nieces and nephews as others help raise their children. Occasionally, a mother will even give up one of her children to a childless couple of the family.[2]

A dimension of kinship morality termed modesty/shame (Das and Nicholas 1979) is also oriented toward the primacy of the extended family. It calls for the wives to be distant and extremely circumspect in their

[2] Although socially this practice seems to be readily accepted, there may be negative repercussions in the child. Dr. B. K. Ramanujam reports from psychotherapeutic work with several adults originally raised by other members of the family that they are indeed disturbed as to why their mothers gave them away.

behavior toward their husband's older brothers, father, and uncles, as well as toward their husbands when others are present. Together with the cultural principle that women's and men's natures are significantly different, this results in quite separate social spheres for men and women in a joint household, and more so in north than south India. Men and women traditionally rely a great deal on same-sex relationships for their intimacy needs—with certain exceptions such as the wife's relationship with younger brothers-in-law, and that between a mother and her children.

The young wife is at the very bottom rung of the hierarchical ladder, expected to fit in to her new family, learning and adhering to its customs and norms rather than to those of her natal family, and gradually learning to consider this family as her own. She is expected to be extremely submissive and deferent, expressing little to the female in-laws and her husband in the first few years, while containing almost all of her feelings. It is culturally recognized that her husband is more attached to his mother than to her, since maternal nurturance is viewed as transcending sexual intimacy; nevertheless, it is understood that he and his wife will gradually become increasingly involved over the years (Das 1976b), and that he will give due to the needs of both wife and mother to maintain harmony.

Adjustment is primarily on the young wife's shoulders both in the marital relationship and in relation to her in-laws; but her anxiety is much more focused on her mother-in-law and sisters-in-law, to whom she is an outsider, than on her husband (as in the case of Joan, Chapter Four). I have been struck in clinical work by the relative lack of anxiety over the actual marital adjustment, even to someone the woman hardly knows.

Correct behavior (*dharma*) is much more oriented toward what is expected in the specific contexts of a variety of hierarchical relationships than on any unchanging norm for all situations. A person's *dharma* also depends in good part on the particular norms and customs of the family, which are related in a broader way to its *jati;* and is modified by situational variables such as the inner natures of each, and the specific time and place. Self-respect and honor are very much at stake in observing correct behavior in these various social contexts, and feelings of shame are evoked for not living up to expectations (Das 1976b). The implications for the development and functioning of conscience in Indians are enormous.

A central underpinning of these complex hierarchical relationships is the traditional cultural value system conveyed to the young mainly by the older women of the family—mothers, grandmothers, aunts, servants, and others. This value system calls for an ideal of solidarity and cooperation, affection and understanding, observation of the traditional norms and customs of the family, and mediation and conciliation for the resolution of the inevitable problems and conflicts that arise. The ideal goal for the person is to live in harmony within the multiple hierarchical relationships of the extended family. These older women recite the vitally alive mythology from the two major epics, the *Ramayana* and *Mahabharata,* and a variety of Puranas, as well as a plethora of proverbs and folktales appropriate for a great variety of relationships and situations, thus giving meaning to the myriad hierarchical relationships through clear images of good and bad. Timeless models become crucial for living in traditionally defined, multiple hierarchical relationships in the extended family and other groups.

Another central value orientation is formed by the Hindu world views of the life cycle and the four goals of life. The life cycle ideally encompasses four stages, the first two especially orienting the person in a broad way toward the fulfillment of extended family hierarchical responsibilities. The beginning stage is preparation during childhood and adolescence for the next stage of the householder, whose *dharma* encompasses pleasure (*kama*) and wealth and power (*artha*) in the procreation and fulfillment of family responsibilities. When these responsibilities are largely fulfilled and the children are grown up, married, and have their own children, in the traditional ideal of the third stage, the parents gradually relinquish many of their responsibilities to their grown sons and daughters-in-law to turn increasingly to more spiritual pursuits. This occasionally culminates in the final stage of renouncer, who devotes total energy in the direction of spiritual realization. As the parents turn over their responsibilities, they become increasingly dependent on having their needs fulfilled by their sons and daughters-in-law, particularly the latter, who will serve them most directly (Vatuk 1981).

From the psychological standpoint of normal social functioning, the first two stages of life and the first three goals of life—*dharma, artha,* and *kama*—primarily involve the familial self. Fulfillment of these is seen as a necessary basis for most people for the realization of the spiritual self in the last two stages of life.

Although it is essential to emphasize the continuing influence of the pervasive, cultural value system, one must also note the considerable tensions, strains, and conflicts that often exist. These sometimes manifest themselves in complicated family feuds. Tensions are created when fathers are reluctant to turn more inward and are ambivalent in turning over their responsibilities to their sons—as portrayed in Satyat Ray's film *Devi;* or in examples one hears of in which the son is given increasing responsibility in the family enterprise, only to be thwarted at every turn when he needs to make a decision. Or different problems may result when sons and daughters-in-law do not particularly want to take care of aging parents—a prime source of anxiety in older people in India (Vatuk 1981).

If we focus our lens for a more intimate look at the hierarchical structures of the extended family, other significant phenomena begin to emerge. What becomes increasingly striking are subtle balances between a number of polarities, calling to mind the image of a see-saw. A see-saw, to balance properly, does not always have to be symmetrical. That is, a person of heavier weight on one side will have to sit closer to the fulcrum to effect a proper balance. These asymmetrical balances, as well as symmetrical ones, also seem to be true of the structures of the Indian family.

There is, for instance, the balance of overt and more covert structures involving Hindu men and women. The overt hierarchical structure of the Hindu family is completely male-oriented, inasmuch as the family resources have traditionally been controlled by the men of the family, decisions are ostensibly made by the male elders, and the women are deferential and subordinate to the men. In more covert or less noticed structures such as Das (1976b) has described, the women do most of the work in arranging marriages, and therefore work out new family alliances and connections—of enormous importance to the social position of the family. Moreover, family honor depends a great deal on women's sexuality, particularly the daughter's chasteness before marriage and her behavior in the in-law's family. Women not only manage internal family affairs, but it is mainly the women of the family who participate in and take care of various family festivals, giving definition to and preserving various family hierarchical relationships through ritual practices (Hanchette 1988; Wadley 1980). In this sense, women are perceived as agents of the supernatural or aspects of the divine, aspiring to powers of the goddesses to further the growth and process of development of the family. As the main conveyers of the multiple myths and prolific proverbs to the children, they are also keepers of the culture. This is not even to mention the enormous power of the mother both overtly with her sons and covertly within the male psyche. Over all, the overt hierarchical structure of male dominance which is so evident in any number of ways in the family and other social structures is balanced by the enormous, covert structural powers of the women.

Hierarchy by Quality

As intricate as structural hierarchical relationships are within the extended family, a further significant level of complexity is added by the second essential psychosocial dimension: hierarchical relationships governed by the particular qualities of the person.[3] In hierarchy by quality, it is the particular qualities and abilities of the person that establish the hierarchical relationship in contrast to kinship or organizational position. Whereas in structural hierarchy, deference, subordination, and loyalty are called for toward the superior, in hierarchy by quality, respect, idealization, and veneration toward the superior is present. Hierarchy by quality can be fully congruent with structural hierarchy—that is, the superior person can be in a superior position. But not always. It not infrequently occurs that someone younger and/or female, or of lower social position such as servants or lower-caste persons, may have qualities or abilities of personality that are far more valued than those of the superior in the hierarchy. It can happen in a marriage for instance, that the wife has the superior qualities. In such an instance, a complex hierarchical relationship is established with subtle balances, such that the wife is duly deferent and subordinate to her husband, observing the etiquette of the structural hierarchy, but the latter deeply respects and looks up to her in the less socially visible hierarchy by quality.

To cite a pertinent example of the social range of these two types of hierarchy, the oldest son of the (Subhas) Bose family in Calcutta was always shown due deference; but the real responsibility and respect was conferred on Sarat, the second oldest, by his father and the other family members because of his clearly superior abilities in handling family responsibilities (pers. com. Leonard Gordon). Another example from a more Westernized family demonstrates how complex the situation can become within a family. The oldest of three sons, a psychologist, reported that he will be shown due deference on all major family matters, as well as on psychological problems, if others don't feel too threatened. On any financial decision, however, he and the middle brother will consult his youngest brother, who is in management, and for any publishing decisions he consults his middle brother, a well-known writer. One can surmise then that hierarchy by structure and by quality are always in a potentially dynamic, complex interaction, where the range may be from

[3] This observation was stimulated by discussions with McKim Marriott and B. K. Ramanujam, and is implicit in some of Kakar's (1978) formulations. Discussions with Ramanujam greatly helped to clarify psychological attitudes involved in these two types of hierarchical relationships.

full congruence to a division whereby one or the other type of hierarchical relationship tends to predominate, sometimes quite sharply, to each being equally present and honored.

To render cultural support to the everyday recognition of hierarchy by quality, there is the highly particularistic assumption that members of the family are indeed quite different in their natures as a result of past actions (*karma*) and present qualities (*gunas*) and powers (*shakti*). The proper fulfillment of *dharma* and the display of deference toward those higher in the structural hierarchy by those who are lower but have superior qualities that are venerated is depicted over and over again in the mythology. Thus Rama, an incarnation of Vishnu, willingly obeys his father and goes to a long period of banishment in the forest at the insistance of one of his father's envious wives.

Another salient psychosocial difference between hierarchy by structure and that by quality is that in the former there are frequently varying degrees of differences between the inner feelings of the person and the public attitudes and behavior displayed, whereas in the latter inner feelings and the overt behavior are far more congruent. Of course, subordinates in structural hierarchical relationships can genuinely feel loyalty and deference, as superiors may also feel responsibility and nurturance. But in other circumstances the actor and action are by no means one.[4] Clinical work with Indian patients not infrequently elicits bitter, angry feelings about a superior in the hierarchical relationship, although the overt behavior remains highly deferential, conforming to the expectations of the situation. Or quite frequently the overt attitude is deferential but the actions are less than cooperative.

Clinical case material well illustrates the relationship between private feelings and public attitudes and behavior as this relationship differs between hierarchy by structure and one by quality. When Ashis was working for a hierarchical superior whom he idealized, he was able to work highly effectively and creatively, his overt behavior fully reflecting his inner feelings and attitudes; with other organizational superiors for whom he felt minimal respect, he was deferential in attitude, but accomplished very little. Another pertinent example emerged from a personal experience at N.I.M.H.A.N.S. when I requested an interview with Dr. Murthy, the highly revered, retired former head of the Psychology Department. When he arrived for our meeting, many psychologists unex-

[4]Ethnosociologists cite the oneness of actor and action in Indian cultural concepts, particularly where one's nature is seen as in good part a result of past actions (Marriott 1976). But in social interaction, there is not infrequently a sharp separation between the actor and action, or at least between inner feelings and overt behavior.

pectedly emerged from their offices and came to the doorway of the room where we met. Spontaneously, one of them asked me in a deferential tone if it would be all right for them to sit in on the interview. When I nodded assent, almost the entire department entered, sitting on chairs and on the floor, engrossed in listening to Dr. Murthy. I had the distinct impression that their deferential request of me to be allowed to sit in was an honoring of the structural hierarchical relationship, while their attitudes of veneration toward Dr. Murthy conveyed a sense of having *darshan* with him in what was clearly a hierarchical relationship by quality.[5]

QUALITATIVE MODE OF
HIERARCHICAL RELATIONSHIPS

This brings us to the third major psychosocial dimension of Indian hierarchical relationships, the qualitative mode of hierarchical relationships. This encompasses the actual emotional or affective quality of the hierarchical intimacy relationship, which Francis L. K. Hsu (1971) has repeatedly emphasized in his anthropological work on Eastern societies, criticizing Western anthropologists for overemphasizing the structural aspects of hierarchical relationships. Hsu sees these Eastern emotional intimacy relationships as being of a very different quality and order than any in the northern European/American culture belt.[6]

The qualitative mode of these highly personalized extended family hierarchical relationships can be characterized by an intense emotional connectedness and interdependence with a constant flow of affect and responsiveness between persons; by a strong mutual caring and dependence, with an intensely heightened asking and giving in an emotional atmosphere usually of affection and warmth, with full expectations for reciprocity;[7] and by highly empathic sensitivity to one another's feelings and needs without explicit expression them (Das and Nicholas 1979; Sinha 1980). I should emphasize that this qualitative mode primarily takes place on a nonverbal level and has to be felt empathically to be

[5] This example also strikingly illustrates a very different sense of privacy among Indians. No American would consider asking to sit in on another's interview.

[6] This dimension has recently received some attention in Indian studies, especially in the work of Sudhir Kakar (1978), B. K. Ramanujam (1980a), and Jai Sinha (1980).

[7] Francis L. K. Hsu (1963) drew attention to this same quality of relationship in India, labeling it "unilateral dependence," relating it as I shall to the quality of the mother-child relationship. The phrase, however, is inaccurate because of the strong reciprocity and interdependence involved in Indian dependency relationships.

understood. When intense expectations are not fulfilled, considerable hurt and anger are experienced. However, emotional connectedness is always central, and any feelings disruptive to the hierarchical relationship, especially ambivalent ones that may be experienced by the subordinate, are most often contained, inhibited, or defended against through a variety of unconscious defense mechanisms in order not to disturb the relationship.

These highly personalized hierarchical relationships become models for other relationships outside of the extended family, particularly within one's own community or *jati* (cf. Sakala 1981), where there is also a feeling of being at home, and even within some organizational hierarchies. B. K. Ramanujam (1986) has emphasized that Indians are constantly guaging and testing the level of intimacy they may have with someone outside of the extended family. On the whole, however, there is a sharp division between one's own people of family and community, and others from other communities (Sinha 1980). The qualitative mode as well as the norms of the hierarchical relationship can change radically between own and other, or insider and outsider. If more personalized familial type of hierarchical relationships are not established outside of family and *jati*, then these relationships can be characterized by very little caring of the other person, and in fact considerable manipulation of the other may take place for one's own ends.

STRUCTURAL HIERARCHY
AND THE QUALITATIVE MODE

Indian relationships and communication are often overwhelmingly governed by varying subtle balances between the intense, emotional intimacy needs and wishes of the qualitative mode and the deeply internalized expectations of superior and subordinate in the structural hierarchy. Both of these psychosocial dimensions must constantly be taken into account to assess any given situation, relationship, or communication. In the daughter-in-law/mother-in-law relationship, structural hierarchical expectations of deference and subordination strongly predominate over emotional intimacy in the early years of a young woman's marriage. Witness Saida's bitter feelings that her mother-in-law greatly favored her own daughters over Saida, while expecting total subordination from the latter. Yet the profound expectation of eventual intimacy with the mother-in-law was revealed by Menakshi, who expressed intense anguish when her English mother-in-law did not accord her and her infant son anywhere near the degree of emotional involvement and attention she would normally expect from an Indian mother-in-law. Thus what starts out to be a relationship heavily weighted by structural hierarchical considerations eventually becomes more evenly balanced by the emotional intimacy of the qualitative mode once the daughter-in-law becomes older and has children.

The asymmetrical balance between structural hierarchical relationships and the qualitative mode of the hierarchical relationship are major factors in the fact that Indian communication is always conducted on at least two levels: the nonverbal and verbal, or the affective and cognitive. The overt verbal communication is generally dictated by considerations of structural hierarchy, but verbal communication itself is frequently indirect, implicit, and ambiguous so that one is not put into a position where there is little room for maneuvering; alternatively, one might want to test out the level of intimacy and concern with another person. But the nonverbal affective communication by facial expression or by actual actions may be quite different: it can be either more positive or more negative than what is communicated verbally. Since there is a constant flow of affect in the qualitative mode, the nature of it is always noted. Indians are always attuned to these different levels of communication, as well as making considerable efforts at interpreting the frequent implicit and ambiguous verbal communication, even if they are not always able to resolve the ambiguities. The complexities involved in Indian communication can also be viewed from the cultural perspective of cultivating intentional ambiguity (Egnor 1980).

When Joan's assistant principal, for instance, was unnecessarily upbraiding some students and their parents, she observed the structural hierarchy by not directly opposing him, but through staring at him she effectively communicated her reproach. A striking example of these different levels of communication is cited by Das (1976b): a man beat his wife in accordance with the complaints of his mother and sister, thus fulfilling structural hierarchical expectations within the family, but that night made love to her in such an indiscreet way that he clearly communicated to the others that his deeper loyalty and love was to his wife, not to his mother and sister. From reports of his wife, his mother and sister were crestfallen the next morning.

In the extended family, all members become astutely sensitive to observing proper etiquette while maneuvering indirectly for what they want. Since multiple authority figures are present in the extended family, particularly in a joint household, children develop into minor politicians to fulfill their wishes, playing on the fact that no one authority is totally responsible (pers. com. Ramasthray Roy). A simple example of communication by indirection for getting what one wants occurred when I attended a case conference at a major psychiatric center where the head of psychiatry was extremely ambivalent toward psychoanalysis and did not want my influence to rub off. A senior staff member who was psychoanalytically oriented wanted very much to meet me, but knew the head would never introduce her. Nor could she approach me directly, as this would have expressed disloyalty to him, which would have resulted in untoward consequences for her. Instead, she used a number of the latest psychoanalytic concepts in a meaningful way during the discussion period. I naturally became interested in her comments and requested the head psychiatrist for an introduction, which he graciously agreed to. I later realized this was exactly what she was counting on.

In other cases, an interpersonal situation is subtly set up so that the other person volunteers. There is thus no threat either to one's own or the other's self-regard over any refusal. I have found myself in different situations volunteering to help out one or another person without being asked for anything, then realizing later that the whole situation had been set up that way. It is not that the "demands" were unreasonable or that I wouldn't have agreed to help if I were asked directly, but even so, the communication was indirect. Thus at one psychiatric facility I visited, the head of psychiatry wanted me to hear a case one of the staff had treated in psychotherapy. The woman who presented displayed a most unusual sensitivity to do psychoanalytically oriented psychotherapy with very little training. I then suggested to the head psychiatrist the possibility that she might get a couple of years of training abroad, which I might be able to arrange, and which he agreed was an excellent idea. From a later remark he made, it dawned on me that that was exactly what he had had in mind in the first place, which was why he wanted me to hear this woman.

The tension between the strong wishing of the qualitative mode with the firm expectancies of the structural hierarchy is sometimes manifested through choosing someone favored by the superior to ask for what one wants. In the family this is frequently the mother, but can also be a favored sibling. Saida had often been used by her older siblings to request various things of their parents, since she was their favorite.

The Familial Self: Symbiosis-Reciprocity

Up to this point I have endeavored to survey the major contours and forms of extended family and other hierarchical relationships from anthropological and psychosocial perspectives. I shall now elaborate the inner landscape of the familial self that enables the person to function well within the psychosocial dimensions of these familial hierarchical relationships. There are four major suborganizations of the familial self that I shall investigate in this and the following chapter: *symbiosis-reciprocity*, or the affective and experiential dimension of the self; the narcissistic dimension of *we-self regard*; the Indian conscience in terms of its *superego and a socially contextual ego-ideal*; and *cognitive aspects of ego functioning*. I should emphasize that although I am investigating each of these suborganizations separately, they are obviously all closely intertwined and function as a whole. By outlining the development of each of these suborganizations of the familial self through child rearing relationships and practices, I shall endeavor to formulate a psychoanalytic developmental psychology appropriate to Indian familial hierarchical relationships, in contrast to our current psychoanalytic developmental psychology, which is overwhelmingly oriented toward Western individualism.

The congruent inner psychological makeup that enables a person to be enmeshed in the emotionally intense intimacy relationships or the qualitative mode of hierarchical relationships I term *symbiosis-reciprocity*. It is a new concept for an important area of Indian psychological functioning in which the psychological realities are strikingly different from those of Westerners; thus there is no available psychoanalytic concept or phrase. In fact, I have joined together two psychoanalytic concepts that are usually considered antithetical, but are highly relevant to Indian psychological reality.[8] Takeo Doi (1973) approached this same problem of describing Japanese psychological functioning in hierarchical intimacy relationships by discarding psychoanalytic theorizing as implicitly too Western to fit Japanese psychological and interpersonal reality. Instead, he relied on a subtle psychological exegesis of indigenous Japanese linguistic concepts, particularly of *amae*. My approach here will be to use Western psychoanalytic concepts, but to "Indianize" them.

Central to symbiosis-reciprocity is the Indian sense of a "we-self." Current psychoanalytic discourse on the self, regardless of theoretical

[8] Thus, symbiosis connotes not only a very early developmental stage of infancy, but also an intense one-way clinging dependency that is viewed pejoratively as psychopathology in adult relationships because of the strong emphasis on autonomy and separation in American psychoanalysis (Mahler et al. 1975). Reciprocity connotes not only a later developmental stage, but also the mutuality of interdependent giving (Erikson 1950). In the Indian context, and Japanese one too, symbiosis-reciprocity conveys both the intense dependency and the reciprocity of adult mutuality.

224

orientation, always implicitly and unreflectively assumes an individual-istic "I-self"—the predominant experiential self of Westerners. But the inner representational world of Indians is much more organized around images of "we," "our," "us" (pers. com. B. K. Ramanujam); or around an "I" that is always relational to a "you," (pers. com. A. K. Ramanu-jan), usually in one or another kind of hierarchical relationship. This is in contrast, for instance, with the American highly individualistic sense of "I" and "me," with its inherent duality between "I" and "you," the "you" frequently being implicitly a more or less equal other in egalitar-ian relationships or even hierarchical ones.[9]

Indians rarely think and feel in terms of an independent, self-con-tained I-ness, but rather experience a constant "we-ness" in having the other in mind as intrinsically related to the self in a superior or subor-dinate way and in varying degrees of intimacy. Or the we-ness may be experienced as the self enmeshed and allied with the extended family, *jati*, or other groups as a whole. Since Indians are oriented to a multi-plicity of hierarchical relationships, the inner images of a we-self are far more multifaceted and relational than the self of Americans, who strive for a more inner integrated unity.

One can hypothesize a differently accentuated inner representational world in Indians from Americans. Normality is based in the latter on a strong differentiation between inner images of self and other; whereas in Indians, inner images of self and other are much more interconnected and suffused with affect. As an example of this different inner reality, some Indian psychoanalysts were seriously considering starting a psy-choanalytic journal, "The Feeling Mind," a title no American psychoan-alyst would ever dream of.

It is difficult to cite specific clinical material to illustrate the above points since so much of it is highly subtle and has to be empathically sensed. Or at other times it comes from self-reflective reports of Indian therapists and patients, especially those with considerable contacts with Westerners. However, this inner sense of we-ness implicitly subsumes all of my patients' relationships.

Strong identifications on the part of both women and men with their families and *jatis* often lead to feelings that others of another community

---

[9] The sharply dualisitc "I" and "you" of Western relationships has entered psychoanal-ysis in its concepts of self- and object-representations with an emphatic differentiation between the two in the person's inner representational world, strongly reflecting the basic Cartesian dualistic philosophical position in psychoanalysis as well as in social reality. More recently, psychoanalysts such as Erikson (1968) and the Menakers (1965), influ-enced by ethology, have emphasized reciprocity and mutuality in relationships.

may be tremendously different—which indeed they are in terms of customs, ethos, traditions, and norms—whereas the inner psychological structures and modes of relationship may actually be overwhelmingly similar. The experiential sense of we-ness and a we-self in the close identifications with one's own family and community thus enhances the perception of enormous differences in others. As a result, a person coming from a very different tradition in marriage may become extremely jarring to extended family relationships.

Indian ego boundaries are also significantly differently constituted, and have a totally different balance from the dominant American mode. Outer ego boundaries are far more permeable to others, especially to those of the extended family, and are decidedly less self-contained and rigorously drawn. Affective exchanges and flows of all shades of feelings constantly go on through these more permeable outer ego boundaries in the highly personalized relationships of the extended family. The psychological space around oneself is also far less contained in Indian familial relationships than in the dominant mode of American psychological functioning. Indians who have returned home after a long sojourn in the West, or Americans who have lived in an Indian family, experience themselves as being "swallowed up" in Indian relationships, feeling any well-set boundaries between self and other as gradually dissolving and disappearing. One American woman professor related how she and her family fled after a few months from living with an Indian family they dearly love while she had a year's grant in India: they felt extremely threatened when their own well-set boundaries began to dissolve while living in Indian family-style relationships.[10] The normal separation, privacy, and autonomy of Western-style relationships and the psychological space around oneself disappear into the more symbiotic mode of giving and asking, of caring for and depending on, of influencing and being influenced, of close, warm emotional connectedness and interdependence. The centrality of relationships completely transcends any other considerations of the separate or individualized self.

Similarly, the innermost ego boundaries—those in touch with inner feelings, fantasies, and wishes—also seem on the whole more flexible and permeable than in most Westerners. I have found in psychoanalytic therapy that once one gets by the deliberate caution and circumspection involved in proper behavior by establishing a relationship of confidentiality and trust, Indian patients tend to be much more in touch with

---

[10] A relevant Indian proverb is that a door is a door only when it is open; otherwise, it is a wall (pers. com. A. K. Ramanujan).

the intense feelings and fantasies of their inner world, especially sexual ones, than my American patients.[11] Witness both Joan and Shakuntala, the former expressing strong angry feelings about her assistant principal and the latter revealing highly passionate sexual feelings around her lover, all within a relatively short period of psychoanalytic therapy. All kinds of feelings and fantasies that must be consciously contained within the exingencies and etiquette of structural hierarchical relationships are usually kept quite accessible within the private self. Other feelings, however, particularly ones of anger and ambivalence, are frequently subject to unconscious defensive processes and may be precluded from awareness.

As a counterpoint to permeable outer ego boundaries in the intense familial intimacy relationships where there is little if any privacy, Indians establish another inner ego boundary to protect and enhance a highly private self with its rich feelings and fantasies—thus creating inner psychological space. This kind of ego boundary is as yet unformulated in psychoanalysis in the West—mainly because Western individualism, with its emphasis on strong outer ego boundaries and individual autonomy, precludes the necessity of developing such an inner boundary and private self as central psychological structures. But three rather than two kinds of ego boundaries must be taken into account to understand Indian psychological makeup.

This commentary on an inner, private self is further extended by the observation of an Indian woman therapist who lives in the United States, but who shuttles regularly to Bombay. She relates that her Indian women friends chatter endlessly together with warmer exchanges of feelings than her American friends, but reveal much less of their inner world than the more self-expressive Americans (pers. com. Niti Seth). Another illustration of the private psychological space Indians create for themselves was related by A. K. Ramanujan about his father, a noted mathematician, who wrote almost half of his 120 published papers with his children actively playing about in the same room.

Another major facet of symbiosis-reciprocity is the cultivation of strong dependency needs within the hierarchical intimacy relationships. Intimacy to a considerable extent connotes the extent to which one may depend on another, and Indians by report constantly gauge both within the extended family and without the degree of intimacy and dependency

[11]This point has been confirmed by Indian psychoanalytic therapists who have also worked in the West, such as B. K. Ramanujam. He relates that in his thirteen years of clinical experience at the B. M. Institute in Ahmedabad, intense sexual fantasies and feelings have usually been expressed from the beginning of therapy by Indian patients.

they may attain with others (Ramanujam 1986). To give clinical examples of this, Ashis felt very free to arrange to see me in psychoanalytic therapy on a financial basis in which payment might never occur; while Manisha experienced intense anguish over my not being available for her to depend on, and broke off treatment after she could not reach me by phone one week because of a phone strike while I was on vacation. Most Americans react critically to this more open expression of dependency needs than they are used to; they feel it impinges on their autonomy. And, in fact, Japanese who have contact with Indians also react negatively to this overt expression of wishes in non-intimate relationships: Japanese strongly reserve the same kind of dependency to a closed inner circle of relationships, showing considerable self-restraint in extrafamilial ones.

Correlated with highly interdependent relationships is a lack of regard for and at times definite discouragement of both physical and psychological separation, as well as strivings for autonomy in the social sphere—the hallmark and ideal of American psychological development (Erikson 1950; Mahler et al. 1975). A case in point is Amal, who was simply not allowed by his father to go to Germany for advanced electrical training and who, psychologically, was totally unable to consider doing it on his own even though it would have been financially feasible.

With regard to individuation—in American psychoanalysis considered to be intrinsically related to separation processes (Mahler et al. 1975)—Indian culture stresses individuation apart from society as much if not more than social individuation (pers. com. J. S. Neki). The indigenous cultural principle of particularism is extended much more to the person's inner psychological makeup in the area of spiritual strivings and their related disciplines than in his or her functioning in familial hierarchical relationships. Social individuation, on the other hand, is much more geared to the level of skills and development relevant to one's particular family culture, which also includes various norms of the *jati* of which the family is a part.

Another major facet of symbiosis-reciprocity is an unusually strong wishing, wanting, expecting self—in psychoanalytic terms, a self intensely oriented toward libidinal strivings and fulfillment. Indians tend to be very much in touch with what they want, while simultaneously keeping in mind the etiquette of the structural hierarchy and the similar needs of others. The late Kamalini Sarabhai, a psychoanalyst, commented that there is a constant polarity and tension within everyone between sensitivity to the needs of others and of the group, and one's own wishes. This results in the intensely heightened wanting being fulfilled through very subtle maneuvering. Since expectations for reciprocity and fulfillment are high, disappointments small and large are not infrequent in the hierarchical intimacy relationships, resulting in hurt feelings and at times considerable anger.

Another aspect of this libidinal self is a degree of sensuality in both women and men that again tends to transcend what is present in contemporary American personality. This sensual self operates in a context of extremely rigorous codes of conduct involving a relative separation of the sexes, and modesty/shame wherein the wife must avoid too close contact with any other older men in the extended family. Sensuality is communicated socially almost entirely on an affective, nonverbal level, often through subtle eye movements; but is also clearly to be perceived through various Indian art forms—sculptures and paintings, and particularly in *bhakti* poetry and the classic dance forms such as Bharat Natyam, Kathak, and Manapuri.

To function well within the qualitative mode of personalized, hierarchical relationships requires an unusual degree of interpersonal sensitivity, which is again mutually expected. Ego capacities are highly developed from early childhood for a radar-sensitive, empathic awareness of others' feelings, moods, and needs for closeness, affection, dependency and esteem. However, there is little sensitivity to any striving for autonomy or to many of the person's more individualized needs. Sensitivity is particularly acute to the norms of any new situation or group, as well as to how receptive others may be to fulfilling one's needs. Indians usually have tremendous sensitivity to the effects of what one says or does on another, that is, whether it will hurt another's feelings or make them feel better. This inner stance an Indian generally takes toward others is far more ego-receptive than ego-assertive—receptiveness being dynamically very different from passivity.[12] Pertinent is the spontaneous comment of an Indian psychoanalytic colleague who has lived many years in New York City: "If you find an American who is highly sensitive and empathic to others, you comment on it. In Indians it is the normal and necessary mode of relating" (pers. com. Loveleen Posmentier).

In summary, major dimensions of symbiosis-reciprocity, a key suborganization of the familial self, encompass the experiential sense of a we-self with its own inner representational world; ego boundaries that on the outside are highly permeable, with a constant interchange of affect between persons and on the inside protect a highly private self, while

[12] The psychoanalytic viewpoint tends to see passivity as the opposite of assertiveness. However, receptiveness is the truer opposite.

on the innermost side are unusually open to fantasy and feelings; heightened dependency needs in interdependent relationships, with a strong wishing, sensual, libidinal self; and strong empathic awareness of the other.

A Developmental Schema
for the Indian Self

Central to psychoanalytic thinking are developmental schemas that trace psychological development from infancy through early childhood and sometimes into later childhood and adolescence. These developmental schemas began with Freud's stages of psychosexual development; continued with Klein's notions of object-relations development in early childhood, followed by Erikson's and Mahler's stages of psychosocial development; and most recently appeared in Kohut's views of developmental needs and deficits involving narcissism in his newly formulated self psychology. One or a combination of these developmental schemas are essential theoretical frameworks for a psychoanalyst for understanding the way his patient's current difficulties derive from past conflicts and deficits in development. Although all of these developmental schemas have been formulated only on Western clinical and observational data, there has nevertheless been an explicit assumption that they are universal. They have thus been used as a yardstick to evaluate development and normality in persons from all other cultures.[13]

Although there is not nearly the extensive psychological and psychoanalytic research on Indian development that there is in the West, particularly in the United States and England, nevertheless there seems so strong a consensus on various issues of child rearing and child development by anthropologists, psychoanalysts, and psychologists that a new developmental schema for the Indian familial self can be conceptualized.

---

[13] This assumption is rooted in the psychoanalytic formulations of the primacy of psychic reality and psychic determinism, which usually read that the character formation brought about through the particular vicissitudes of universal early childhood psychosexual and psychosocial stages is a strong determinant on the sociocultural patterns of a given society. For an example of this point of view on India, where social and cultural factors are completely ignored and large leaps are made between the effects of child rearing and so-called later observations, such as Indians' lack of truthfulness and ambition, see Sylvan 1981. By neglecting social and cultural factors, Sylvan's paper, like others of its kind, becomes highly reductionistic, more than a little colonial in its attitudes, and fundamentally interferes with a useful integration of psychoanalysis with South Asian social science research.

Further research will supplement and refine what is currently known. Formulating this developmental schema will obviate invidious comparisons on a yardstick of Western psychological development, whereby Indians (and most other Asian and African peoples) must inevitably come out on the short end because the developmental norms are stacked in favor of a Western individualized self. I shall now focus on child rearing and developmental issues related to various facets of symbiosis-reciprocity, and in the next chapter I shall delineate development as related to other major dimensions of the familial self such as we-self regard and the Indian conscience.

Central to child rearing are cultural notions and social patterning of women's place in the extended family. Although there has been considerable emphasis in the literature on the young bride going to her in-laws' family and being treated very much as an outsider at the bottom rung of the hierarchy (this is more true in the north than in the south), she is also seen as essential to the continuity, development, and prospering of the family. Hindu culture places overwhelming emphasis on the woman attaining her main identity, position, and recognition as mother, and as mother preserving and passing on the various cultural traditions to the children—essential to family cohesion and continuity. Social patterning is quite congruent with these cultural notions.

Where there is a traditionally deemphasized conjugal marital relationship, especially in a joint household where the husband is strongly emotionally involved with his own mother, and where there are separate social spheres for the sexes, the wife turns to the other women, sometimes a younger brother-in-law, and particularly her children, both sons and daughters, to satisfy her intimacy needs. Her bond to her sons in particular becomes enormously strong over the years and is a major source for gaining an increasingly superior position within the family hierarchy as they grow up (Roy 1975; Kakar 1978).

Innumerable writers have noted that mothering persons—and these often include the infant's grandmother, aunts, older siblings, cousins, and servants besides the mother in the extended family—are tremendously physically and emotionally gratifying to the infant and young child, often through the fourth year of life. As Kakar (1978, 85–87) rightly stresses, the degree of maternal gratification and close mother-child relationship are of a completely different magnitude from normal mothering in the northern European-American culture belt.[14] What has been universally

[14] In America, there are obviously ethnic and national groups that differ from this dom-

231

noted is an extraordinarily close tie of the developing child, male and female, to the mothering person(s).

Cultural conceptions view the infant and mother as being of the same substance and therefore intrinsically connected. Some writers emphasize indulgence, but that is clearly from a more Western perspective. Weaning often does not take place until the second or third year. There is a great deal of sensuous, physical closeness in the ways of handling and carrying the child, and the child is rarely left alone. This is especially true of the sleeping arrangements—even where there is a lot of room, which there often isn't—for the infant and toddler is in the mother's or parental bed until being displaced by the next sibling, or until being several years of age. The youngest child may sleep with her mother for a number of years, and especially if a girl, well into her teens and even until marriage. One woman patient who is now a physician was the youngest of five children and slept in her mother's bed until she was thirteen. When the child leaves the maternal bed, it is to sleep with another sibling, aunt, or uncle, but almost never alone. This is equally true of Japanese child rearing (Caudhill and Plath 1974). Separation and aloneness are to be avoided at all costs in Indian family relationships. Dependence and interdependence are far more valued and cultivated than autonomy and separation.

To the extent that the mothering person is able—and various responsibilities at times prevent her—she will handle her infant's or young child's frustrations, anxieties, and unhappiness by instant gratification, assisting and closely protecting the toddler whenever possible. The young child is also distracted through gratification from any potential conflict with or willful assertiveness toward the mothering figure, even during the period of toilet training, which is relatively free of anal conflicts.[15] As Menakshi related to me in session one day, her English mother-in-law chided her for not setting limits on her two-and-a-half-year-old. "How can you not set limits! He will run out into the street and be run over." Menakshi exclaimed, "But how can a mother set limits!" What Menakshi didn't tell her was that the moment her son would get into a potentially dangerous situation, she would distract him by gratification.

It is readily apparent how this enormously gratifying mothering relationship develops the various inner psychological structures involved in symbiosis-reciprocity. This prolonged maternal matrix fosters a sense of

---

inant mode of child rearing—such as those from southern Europe and Africa, as well as Jews and Armenians.

[15] This seems to be much less true among urban Indians, according to the observations of Loveleen Posmentier, a psychoanalyst.

self which is much more inclusive of we-ness, with a closer interconnection of inner images of self and other; outer ego boundaries that remain much more permeable to constant affective exchanges and emotional connectedness with others, while simultaneously a private self is allowed to develop; and a heightened empathic awareness of others with considerable sensitivity to nonverbal communication. The constant physical closeness and gratification also foster intense dependency needs and a strong libidinal, sensuous self, with clear-cut characteristics of orality. The ubiquitous mothering presence results in the child having much less need of transitional objects[16]—an essential element in the developing separation and individuation of the Western child. Instead, this intense mothering creates an inner core of well-being and a profound sense of protection, with the expectation that others will somehow come through for you, inuring the person against great struggles and deprivation (Kakar 1978).

Simultaneously, there is a subtle inhibition of too great self-other differentiation and separation through the amount of gratification and closeness an Indian child experiences. This decidely contrasts with the "optimal" frustrations of the Western child, which foster the inner separation process of the child from the mother.[17] While there is a great deal of affection, emotional and physical gratification, and empathic awareness of the child's dependency needs, there is often very little empathy with the more autonomous and individualized strivings of the child (pers. com. Dr. Bhutta and Erna Hoch)—again central to both the separation and individuation processes in Western children.

Individuation in the social sphere is fostered in Indian child rearing in two ways. The first is the explicit, particularistic recognition in Indian culture of persons having very different natures, which encourages parental acceptance of greatly varied proclivities in Indian children (Anandalakshmi 1978), even when the child is older and is expected to observe fully the social etiquette of hierarchical relationships. This results in a striking asymmetrical balance between conforming to the social hierarchy and expressing personal variation. The second mode of individuation is the general fostering of ego skills involving sensitivity to relationship, context, and affective exchanges; and the more specific

[16] For a discussion of transitional objects and the separation and individuation process, see Grolnick and Barkin 1978.

[17] It is basic to psychoanalytic developmental psychology that a child must be raised with optimal frustrations; otherwise, psychopathology will result. However, it has never been questioned whether optimal frustrations vary cross-culturally; and if they do, how this is adaptive to the society in which the child is raised.

occupational and other skills congruent with a particular family and *jati* (community). In more modern, urbanized families individuation also encompasses a high degree of education and technological or professional skills; whereas in a traditional craft community the technical and interpersonal skills appropriate to families in that particular *jati* are involved (Anandalakshmi 1978).

From cultural expectations and actual social patterns, a profound inner connectedness in the Indian man to his mother lasts throughout life. The strong pull to the maternal matrix seems to stem from intense sensuous gratification, feelings of an omnipotent alliance with an all-powerful mother, and vulnerability to either the mothering person's intrusiveness or narcissistic use of the child. As a clinical example, a talented patient, Ravi, found it extremely difficult to organize himself to write a series of articles. His difficulties in self-discipline and organization were in part traced to mothering that was always sensuously gratifying, with few or no limits set. Associations to a dream led to memories of taking baths with his mother till age eight, and rubbing her foot and legs till age eleven. As he then recalled a memory in another session of a grandmother he visited who did set firm limits on him, he was gradually able to write.

A psychopathological dimension of this intense mother-son relationship tends to emerge when there are feelings of an omnipotent alliance on *both* sides; that is, both son and mother may have strong inner feelings of powerfulness with little or no constraints on what they want and/or should do as long as they feel deeply connected to each other. To give an example, in certain *bania* or business communities in Bombay where there are extremely sharp business practices, no guilt is experienced by the man as long as he remains in an omnipotent symbiotic alliance with his mother. The mother seems to revel in her son's success and looks the other way on the dishonest business practices, while the son feels confirmed and powerful in what he does. As long as this inner alliance is maintained, anything goes (pers. com. Sailesh Kapadia and Udayan Patel).

Although the anthropological and psychological literature emphasize the enormously close mother-son relationship, my own clinical experience indicates that the daughter can also be intensely emotionally close to her mother in a similar symbiotic mode of relating. This seems to be particularly true if the daughter is the youngest or only girl. Saida and Shakuntala are good examples of this, but it also occurred among some other of my women patients such as Sunita and Rashi. Sunita, the youngest of five children, slept in her mother's bed until she was thirteen, experiencing intense separation anxiety when she later went away to medical school. Rashi, a married Muslim woman with three children, still finds it difficult to live apart from her mother. She was clearly the mother's favorite of seven children, and experiences herself as a carbon copy of her mother.

Mothers have profound emotional expectations of their daughters as the carriers not only of the family culture but also of the customs and traditions of the *jati*. Thus, Shakuntala ruled out a love marriage with a man from another community, in good part because it would interfere with the passing on of traditions from her own. The girl is less gratified than the boy and more trained for responsibility so that she can leave her own family to live in another one to carry on their traditions and customs at a relatively early age. However, the close tie to the mother and the natal family certainly continues after marriage, and may inevitably be carried over to her mother-in-law, as in Saida's case. Her vulnerability to her mother-in-law in part stemmed from the expectation of the same emotional gratification that she had had with her own mother, with whom she was the youngest and favorite. This unconscious dynamic may be present to varying degrees in much daughter-in-law/mother-in-law conflict.

Developmental Models:
Indian and American

In comparing child rearing and its effects in India and America, we must assume that the attitudes and ways of relating in the early maternal matrix play upon very different chords of childhood potential, organizing these chords into very different patterns and themes. We cannot assert that one pattern is necessarily more universal or better than another; rather that each is profoundly adaptive and congruent within its sociocultural milieu. From a cross-civilizational perspective, separation-individuation and a relative inhibition of gratification and dependence can be seen as fundamentally geared to the individualized self of American individualism. On the other hand, the various developmental facets involved in symbiosis-reciprocity are basically oriented toward the qualitative mode of highly personalized hierarchical relationships in India and other Asian countries such as Japan. Although I have emphasized these dominant developmental chords, this is emphatically not to negate the minor chords of development in each society: Indian infants and toddlers do develop some degree of self-differentiation from the mater-

235

nal matrix while remaining deeply embedded; whereas American ones must keep a certain degree of emotional connectedness throughout life even with their highly autonomous functioning—a point that Kohut (1984) and his associates have recently emphasized (Goldberg 1980). Thus, each culture unwittingly sets its own optimal range of psychological development through its early child rearing.

We must further take into account a developmental matter that is generally overlooked: the striking congruence between the themes of early childhood potential that are strongly played upon through the early maternal matrix, and the variations on these basic themes that are sounded during adolescence as it is socially and culturally structured. Thus, the dominant themes of American early child rearing around self-other differentiation, autonomy, and individuation are played out in the increasing separation of the adolescent from his family. Indian early child rearing, on the other hand, which so fosters we-ness, affective exchange, and empathic sensitivity, imperceptibly leads into an adolescence in which the boy or girl remains a highly interdependent part of the extended family. The we-self is further enhanced by the child and adolescent being constantly with their parents and other parental figures, since there is no real separation of age groups in adolescence, as in the West (Anandalakshmi 1978). When parents visit other families for dinner or such, even in modern urban families, children and adolescents are almost invariably taken with them. All major life decisions for the adolescent, including education, vocation, and marriage are arrived at through the guidance and decisions of the elders strongly influenced by (*jati*) norms. These greatly enhanced identifications for adolescents are not only with parental figures, but also with the particular customs, traditions, ritual observances, values, and life style of their extended family and community.

While the American adolescent is psychologically involved with the *sturm und drang* of self-creating and integrating an identity, with all of the conflicts, moratoria, and resolutions that go with it, the Indian adolescent in traditional society gradually moves from childhood into adult responsibilities with little if any conflict. The primary source of stress is the adaptation to new positions of young adulthood where there are considerable pressures from the social hierarchy. B. K. Ramanujam has observed that adolescence in traditional Indian society simply does not constitute the separate psychological stage that it does in the West. Thus, Indian adolescence continues to be oriented toward the development of a relational, familial self, and also toward self-transformation through

236

the growth of more subtle qualities and enhanced inner powers—sometimes expressed in everyday language as becoming a better person.

It is instructive to note the observations of Mrs. Bim Bissel, director of The Playhouse School, a progressive nursery school and kindergarten in New Delhi for upper middle-class families, consisting of some 80 percent Indian and some 15 percent Western children, the remainder being Japanese. She observed that the Indian children, even at ages two and a half, are far more sensitive to relationships within the group, to each other, and to the teacher than Western children, who are more autonomous in approaching tasks with greater initiative and independence; whereas Japanese children are far more oriented toward task performance and skills than Western or Indian children.

On a more informal level, consider the comments by sixteen-year-old girl college students at Jai Hind College in Bombay, upon seeing a Canadian film of two- and three-year olds in a nursery school and at home. These students found these children to be far more exploratory of their environment and involved with toys than corresponding Indian children, while the nursery school teacher and mother seemed far less involved and protective than the typical Indian mothering person. It is apparent from both their observations and Mrs. Bissel's what some of the effects of this early child rearing are, and how they are basically adaptive to functioning in very different sociocultural milieux.

Coming closer to home, I can give a more specific example of the effects of differential child rearing on boundary-formation between self and others, citing the vicissitudes of our five-and-a-half-year-old boy in Bombay. After an initial happy period of some three months in India, he suddenly began to have nightmares of monsters in his favorite swimming pool, and increasing compulsive symptoms of touching his face—which aroused considerable parental anxiety. One day I noticed that he built a fort out of blocks between his bed and that of the *ayah* (housekeeper) on the other side of the room. A few days later, his fort had retreated to a small corner of the room, the fighters now having their backs to the wall. Nothing that he or his older sister could say gave us any clue to his increasing disturbance, nor did psychological tests I gave reveal anything other than a considerable inner state of anxiety. It was more than a month later, when we went to Mount Abu for a weekend without our *ayah,* that the children spontaneously called our *ayah* Shirpurnika, a love demoness.[18]

[18] Shirpurnika is a demoness sister of Ravanna, the evil demon king of the *Ramayana.* She unsuccessfully tried to seduce first Laxman and then Rama, the heroes of this epic. The children had become familiar with the *Ramayana.*

237

They then related how she, like the teen-age girls in the flat next door, would constantly scoop our son up and hug him when we weren't around. Some attempt was made to do this with our daughter, too, but her boundaries were so firm that she would fight off anyone who attempted it. Our *ayah* came highly recommended and was an extremely responsible person with four children of her own. It was clear that this was normal Indian mothering, with no attempt at any sexual seduction. It was only when we returned to Bombay and I explicitly told her and the teen-age girls in the most diplomatic manner that I could muster not to touch him that all of the symptoms began to disappear. Our *ayah* had clearly penetrated our son's outer ego boundaries, evoking considerable anxiety in him, and provoking unconscious defensive maneuvers to contain his anxiety and reset his boundaries. Her mothering would have aroused no anxiety in an Indian child whose outer boundaries would have been much more permeable, while an inner one would have been more firmly set.

In this modal type of Indian mothering it is obvious that symbiotic modes of relating and gratification are continued far beyond what American psychoanalysis considers to be optimal for "normal" development: "an omnipotent mother who interferes with the child's innate striving for individuation . . . may retard the development of the child's full awareness of self-other differentiation" therefore promoting borderline or psychotic psychopathology (Mahler et al. 1975, 3).

Warner Muensterberger (1969), a psychoanalyst anthropologically trained, continues this line of reasoning on a number of non-Western cultures, including India. Muensterberger asserts that the type of child rearing in these societies interferes with all of the processes involved in separation and individuation, ranging from the formation of normal ego boundaries to cognitive development, differentiation of images of self and other, reality testing, superego regulatory functions, ego autonomy, and optimal frustration tolerance, and concludes that there is simply "not good-enough mothering"—in contrast to Winnicott's (1965) concept of "good enough mothering" that takes place in normal development. Muensterberger thus utilizes the psychoanalytic developmental models of Western personality as the measuring stick against which psychological development from a variety of non-Western societies is assessed. Child rearing and development from these other societies uniformally emerge as inferior. More to the point, Muensterberger does not recognize that there can be other kinds of intrapsychic structures and cognitive abilities with their own developmental stages and schedules, which may indeed strongly contrast with predominant Western ones,

238

but which are highly adaptive to the different social and cultural contexts of Asian societies such as India.

The question nevertheless remains as to why the highly symbiotic mode of mothering in India develops different psychological structures and an experiental sense of self, but not the severe borderline or psychotic psychopathology that occurs in American mothering of this type, according to contemporary psychoanalytic ego psychology (Blancks 1974; Jacobson 1964; Mahler et al. 1975). An important part of the answer lies in the nature of American child rearing and the personality of the American mother. In normal American child rearing, the mothering person must have a dual attitude of subtly encouraging and being involved in her toddler's distancing behavior and explorations, while simultaneously being emotionally available and supportive as her child constantly returns for reassurance over his or her separateness. These attitudes of a supportive maternal presence are then internalized by the toddler.

For an American woman to raise her child in the more Indian mode of prolonged symbiotic mothering—assuming she was not from a Mediterranean or black ethnic group, where early child rearing tends to approach the Indian mode—would usually indicate a quite emotionally disturbed woman, departing drastically from the child rearing norms of American society. It would further imply that she could not differentiate her child as being other than a narcissistic emotional extension of herself, thus generating severe psychopathology.

The normal Indian woman, on the other hand, prepares her child for intense familial interdependencies through her symbiotic mothering, while still being able gradually to differentiate her child from herself. The assumption of the psychoanalytic ego psychologists that prolonged, highly intense symbiotic modes of mothering will of itself result in severe psychopathology results from their underemphasis of the psychological makeup of the mothering person, while unreflectively assuming that Western modes of child rearing and development are the only normal ones.

Individualism, Individuality,
and Individuation

Some psychoanalytically oriented social scientists (e.g. Rudolphs 1976) have assumed to varying degrees that collectively organized societies with extended families create underdeveloped, immature, and incomplete personalities who are strongly dependent and passive, unable to deal objectively and competently with reality, and have little or no achievement motivation. Their ranks have been joined by the scathing criticisms of V. S. Naipaul (1978, 107–109), indicting the Indian familial self—as well as the self of other Asian and African peoples—as inferior to the Western psyche. This viewpoint bolsters feelings of Western superiority with scientific embellishment.

A careful analysis of the issues around individualism, individuality, individuation, and the individualized self will put this whole matter in perspective. Competitive individualism is severely frowned upon in Indian society because it can so disrupt relationships by hurting others' feelings, though it is now promoted by some urban institutions, especially the school system. Even so, an Indian colleague, one of the most brilliant in his field and enormously productive, attested to inner feelings of uneasiness and guilt over always having been at the very top of his class.

Competitive individualism was originally the prerogative of American men, but is now being increasingly assimilated by American women. A source of American-style individuality as well as anxiety, it is rarely present in the traditional Indian familial self or even in any predominant way in the urban educated. Even the contemporary variations of American individualism, that of doing one's own thing, fulfilling and actualizing various aspects of oneself and one's potentials, are quite foreign to the Indian familial self, basically oriented as it is to personalized familial concerns.

Individuality, on the other hand is richly developed in certain ways in Indians. Their individuality is first fostered by the prolonged symbiotic, nurturing maternal relationships. Where close affectional ties and emotional responsiveness are present, and strong identification processes are at work, rich individuality usually develops. Moveover, Hindu culture not only recognizes the particular proclivities of a person, but also accords a remarkable degree of freedom in feeling, thinking, and maintaining a private self, while greatly encouraging the cultivation of one's inner life, in counterpoint to the considerable constraints in behavior in the social hierarchy. Even the formal hierarchical relationships may be played out with wide variations in nuance and style, affording considerable scope for a highly developed individuality (Anandalakshmi 1981; Rudolphs 1976; pers. com. Bharati Mukerjee and Clark Blaise).

In her more recent reflections, Anandalakshmi (1981) cogently argues for a three-dimensional model of Indians. A more usual two-dimensional model stresses the greater emotional enmeshment in relationships than the more individualized, autonomous self of Westerners. But a three-dimensional model emphasizes that there is also a richly developed inner world of feelings, thoughts, and fantasies, and an unusual ability to create an inner private space where there is little if any social privacy. These are central to Indian individuality. However, when the hierarchical relationships are not sufficiently nurturant, or may even be sadistic, the inner world may then become a depressed one.

It should be patently clear that the bases of individuality in Indians is of a quite different order from those in Americans. Thus, those who place such a negative valuation on the Indian familial self are obviously writing from the unspoken assumption of universal standards deriving from the Western individualized self, highly developed social individuation, and various forms of individualism. Indian culture emphasizes a completely different type of individuation and even separation, which I shall turn to in Chapter Nine.

The Indian and Japanese Familial Self

The Indian Familial Self: We-Self Regard

Two other central patterns of the familial self are narcissistic structures, or structures of self-regard, and the conscience. As before, I shall interweave discussion of these with the psychosocial patterns of familial hierarchical relationships into their distinctly Indian design, and shall then show how these configurations orient cognitive functioning in a uniquely Indian way.

The particular organization of narcissistic needs and structures requisite for functioning in familial hierarchical relationships is *we-self regard*. That is, the feelings of inner regard or esteem are experienced not only around oneself and one's body-image, but equally around the "we" of the extended family, the particular community (*jati*) and other groups one belongs to, and the other(s) at either end of the hierarchical relationships. Moreover, the narcissistic dimension involving inner esteem is, from my clinical and social experience, much more intense in Indians than in Americans, and pervades familial hierarchical relationships to a much more significant degree and in a different way than in American-style relationships.

Since there are powerful and pervasive feelings of esteem around the honor and reputation of one's family, particularly in relation to other families in one's community, public behavior always reflects on family reputation and affects other family members. Rashi, a Muslim woman patient in her late twenties, experienced her husband's criticism of any member of her original family as being a criticism of herself, her we-self regard clearly including her original family. In another vein, some of the vague social anxieties of female college students derived from their internalized fears of how strangers would evaluate or criticize their demeanor and behavior in public, and how this would reflect on family reputation and affect their own and their sisters' marriageability.

The interdependence of esteem and family reputation is particularly true of the father-son relationship, where each expects the other to reflect well on one another continuously, and where the son even as an adult strives to gain the respect of his father. In Ashis's case, although his father had expectations and values of achievement and success very different from Ashis's more natural literary-meditative inclinations, Ashis as a teenager went completely along with his father to gain his respect and to reflect well on him. This was similarly true of Sunil, who endured great hardships in college in Boston, feeling that he was doing it all for his father.

On the other hand, where the son feels the father has seriously let him down, this profoundly effects the son's we-self regard. Thus, Ashis responded with an excrutiating inner sense of shame to his father's scandal-motivated suicide. Undoubtedly, this event would be traumatic for an American youth, too, but the inner sense of regard in a nineteen-year-old would not have been so closely interwoven with the father and family reputation, and he would therefore not have been so utterly shaken. In self psychology, it is assumed that although idealizations continue throughout life, by American developmental norms the idealization-identification process of the son with his father will be more or less completed and internalized by late adolescence. But the Indian son-father dyad tends to continue throughout life.

Another variation on father-son we-self regard is the case in which the son gets back at the father by reflecting poorly on him through failure after he feels the father has seriously let him down by interfering with his ambitions and wishes. Amal is an excellent example of this, when he failed in the electrical shop his father had set up for him. This kind of reaction is by no means absent from American male patients, but again usually stems from much earlier periods of interference by the father than in late adolescence or young adulthood.

I have also come upon this same dynamic of we-self regard in the daughter-father and daughter-mother relationship. When Sunita barely missed the highest distinction on the Cambridge examination upon graduating from high school, even though she did substantially better than her older brothers, her educator father became deeply chagrined;

243

the highest distinction would have tremendously enhanced his and their family reputation. In the case of Manisha, an internationally outstanding scientist in her field, an important motivation of her achievement was to reflect extremely well on a mother who had become heavily invested in her. Another portion of her psychological baggage of we-self regard was to carry on over a century of outstanding accomplishment by various forebears of her extended family.

Fear of the evil eye by women is also related to issues of their we-self regard in the extended family, according to B. K. Ramanujam. Where women's position and standing are so related to their being mothers, envy is easily generated among the sisters-in-law and aunts over each other's children. Therefore, when a child is born, a black spot is put on the child's face to protect it from the evil eye or the other women's envy; and as the child grows up, the mother will not give any overt praise directly to the child nor speak to others in glowing terms about her own children, in good part to avoid the other women's envy.

The centrality of we-self regard in the very core of the Indian psyche emerged in clinical material around the whole issue of arranging a marriage, where the reputation of the family and status within the *jati* are so overwhelmingly important. Meena, a brilliant career woman at the very top of her field, had originally turned down an arranged marriage in her early twenties so that she could have a career, to which her parents agreed. Her father in the meantime had died, and her elder brothers and mother were at a loss to find someone suitable for her because she was so highly placed. With the help of a male friend she ran marriage ads in the leading Bombay newspapers and got a good response. What was striking was her profound concern for how a man would reflect on her and enhance her inner regard: his appearance, his education—with particular attention to his going to just the right boarding schools in India and colleges and graduate schools abroad—his family and caste background, his job and position in his field, how well he would fit into her urban social-occupational group (which she referred to as a new kind of caste), and how well and sophisticatedly he spoke English. Other than one central concern that he be totally supportive of her career, there was almost no anxiety whatsoever about how they would get along. She assumed her sensitivity and willingness to adjust would insure that everything would work out perfectly well once the status considerations were satisfied.

I do not mean to convey that these status and self-esteem considerations are absent from American marital choices; far from it. But the balance is different. Considerations of how well you get along are infinitely more important and therefore more fragile in the American marital relationship, whereas the consideration of enhancing we-self regard of the persons and families involved becomes overwhelmingly important in the Indian context.

Also reflecting the relationship of we-self regard to family reputation are the observations of an Indian psychoanalytic colleague. She commented on the long time that urban Indian women will spend on personal grooming and dress, including putting on much of their best jewelry, to reflect well on the family when they go out in public—far more time and effort than she spends in New York City on any similar occasion (pers. com. Loveleen Posmentier). In a similar vein, it seemed rather remarkable to my wife and me how very young children would sit for hours, quiet and well-behaved, in an urban restaurant—in embarrassing contrast to our own children.[1] We know, of course, through other families we were friendly with that these young children were perfectly capable of being hellions at home, where family reputation would not be at stake. What is communicated to them from a very early age is that their behavior in public will reflect on the family, that every stranger around them is an auntie or uncle who won't like their misbehavior and will think poorly of the family (pers. com. Anandalakshmi).

A further important manifestation of we-self regard in Indian psychological makeup is its relationship to life space. Bassa (1978), for example, observes that even in the most squalid and abject conditions in a mud hut slum, personal grooming is relatively good, and the inside of the small huts are invariably neat and clean. Oddly enough, the same observation can be made about persons of the middle and upper-middle classes and their living conditions. The public areas in luxury buildings are frequently a striking contrast to the family areas of the flats and to personal grooming. There are, of course, certain social and environmental factors that are partly responsible for these conditions, not the least of which is the monsoon. Nevertheless, I would strongly suggest that these striking contrasts reflect persons' narcissistic investment of esteem as extending overwhelmingly to the "we" of the extended family and to the personal body-ego and self-image; outside the family space is a no-man's land.[2]

---

[1] I am certain that there are children from other groups from the highly heterogeneous American society who would much more closely approximate the public behavior of Indian children than our own. There may also be other factors in the restrained behavior of the Indian children at a restaurant, such as the importance of how food is eaten.

[2] This lack of interest in public space is confirmed by still another anecdote. In one building in a well-to-do neighborhood in Bombay, a wealthy paint manufacturer as well

We-Self Regard and Hierarchical Relationships

The particular inner patterning of we-self regard changes significantly as it becomes interwoven with either structural hierarchical relationships or hierarchical relationships governed by the quality of the person. In structural hierarchical familial relationships, I have found extraordinary sensitivity to whatever one says or does in its effects on the we-self regard and pride of the other; and conversely, what the other says or does on oneself. A subtly constant, but mainly nonverbal approbation and confirmation go on from both ends of the hierarchical relationship, maintaining and enhancing each other's we-self regard. I sense that this ongoing mirroring in Indian relationships, and Japanese ones too, goes way beyond mirroring in adult American relationships. It is from these empathic observations that I conclude that the narcissistic dimension is more pervasive, more intense, and in general of more paramount importance in Indian and Japanese psychological and social functioning than in American (Spratt 1966).

In organizational settings where familial-type relationships predominate, there can be considerable fragility in the we-self regard of superior and subordinate. There are tremendous need and expectations on one hand, and on the other, vulnerability to the other's approval or rejection, no matter which end of the hierarchy one is on. Slights are quickly registered, and anger easily evoked even if infrequently expressed. Steven Hoffman (1981) noted that notwithstanding long-term, close working relationships between leader and followers in Indian political factions, on any serious disruption of either's we-self regard by the other, hurt and mistrust frequently ends the relationship.

I have found in conferences that what is conveyed, or even more importantly, what is *not* said is more often governed by how it will affect the other person's esteem than by the issues at hand. In one conference I attended, sharp disagreements were kept to themselves by my Indian colleagues so as not to challenge the other's esteem and seriously disrupt the relationship; whereas disagreements were frequently voiced by my American ones. In still another instance, a highly esteemed Indian colleague pleaded illness so that he would not have to attend an important talk of another esteemed but more junior colleague, because the former felt he would have to disagree openly with the latter. Thus, narcissistic

---

as the other well-to-do occupants were completely uninterested in repainting the delapidated hallways and lobby, even though the cost would have been minimal and of no consequence to them.

considerations of we-self esteem are always more central in Indian hierarchical relationships than in American-style ones.

This point is further illustrated by Indian colleagues who always attended presentations I gave at major meetings in America even though they were familiar with my views, in contrast to many of my American colleagues, who politely excused themselves to hear other papers they were more interested in. For my Indian colleagues, this was clearly a way of expressing their support for my feelings of esteem, and in turn, they expected me to attend their own papers to enhance their own feelings of regard. At any Indian presentation, a good number who attend are there to enhance the we-self regard of the presenter rather than because they are necessarily interested in the particular subject. This is equally true of Japanese.

Still another striking part of we-self regard and structural hierarchical relationships is subtle maneuvering to enhance the esteem of the superior to get what one wants, or at least not to threaten it. Women, for instance, are overtly deferent and subordinate in public to their husbands and male superiors at work, but by playing upon male esteem constantly angle for what they want—something I heard from Indian women over and over again.[3] An example is the psychoanalytically oriented therapist who maneuvered to get around her head psychiatrist who was opposed to her meeting me, well knowing she had to be extremely careful not to slight his self-regard. A year previously she had done so, and the consequences had been harsh.

One particular aspect of we-self regard and structural hierarchical relationships is profoundly related to caste. As Bhaskar Sripada (1981) has noted from reflections on his own psychoanalysis, the particular ego-ideal internalizations of a Brahmin enhance his or her own self, we-self regard being further supported by unconsciously splitting off and projecting any poor aspects of self-esteem onto the lower castes. In turn, the lower castes split off certain idealized aspects of their own self and project them onto the upper castes, further supporting the we-self regard of the upper castes.

We-self regard becomes interrelated with sharply different attitudes and feelings in hierarchical relationships governed by the superior qualities of the other. Here, feelings of respect, veneration, and idealization tend to predominate. There is further a wish to be as close to the superior

___

[3] Obviously, this is present in American social life as well, but not to the degree present in Indian relationships.

person as possible, in effect to sit at his or her feet, have *darshan*. By identifying with and sharing in the qualities of a revered other, the subordinate hopes to enhance his or her own we-self regard and to become inwardly transformed into a better person with more refined qualities and greater inner power. The other thus becomes a highly idealized model for the further development and fulfillment of one's ego-ideal. In effect, whereas hierarchy by structure looks more toward the approbation of mirroring processes in its promotion of we-self regard, hierarchy by quality depends primarily on the idealization process in enhancing we-self regard.

This idealization process is amply evident in Ashis's case. By reading and rereading the works of Gandhi, Tagore, and Coomaraswamy, he tried to associate himself with these highly revered nationally recognized figures. He also enhanced his we-self regard by working closely with two heads of agencies who were deeply respected both for their abilities and spiritual presence.

Some of the complex patterns of we-self regard, when they are interwoven simultaneously with hierarchy by both structure and quality, can seem to be as intricate and ornate as the designs of some traditional Indian textiles and ritual drawings for festivals. The search for the idealized figure can sometimes be an unconscious effort to defend against considerable ambivalences generated by the everyday stresses of structural hierarchical relationships (pers. com. B. Desai and Udayan Patel). Persons in the structural hierarchy may become endowed with highly idealized qualities that they do not necessarily have (Kakar 1978, 138–139), in part confirming the profound psychological need of Hindus for idealized models, and in part indicating a possible unconscious defense against ambivalent feelings.

A Developmental Schema for We-Self Regard

How does this intricate patterning of we-self regard develop? And to what extent does it differ from the predominant mode of child development in America? Self psychology posits the significant emotional investment and empathic resonance that mothers have with their children as being central to an infant's and young child's basic sense of inner esteem; and Indian mothers in particular seem to make an extraordinary investment in their children. The Indian woman is a mother of sons to carry on family continuity and support, and of daughters to be the carriers and preservers of traditions, customs, and norms, as well as of the family honor. Intense, prolonged maternal involvement in the first four or five years with the young child, with adoration of the young child to the extent of treating him or her as godlike (Das 1976b; Sakala 1977), develops a central core of heightened narcissistic well-being in the child. Mothers, grandmothers, aunts, servants, older sisters and cousin-sisters[4] are all involved in the pervasive mirroring that is incorporated into an inner core of extremely high feelings of esteem. But it is clear that the subtle expectations and valuing are not for the increasingly autonomous, exploratory behavior of the American toddler (Mahler et al. 1975), but rather for the child's growing emotional interdependence and sensitivity to others.

These intensified feelings of inner regard—which gradually manifest themselves as we-self regard in the child's experiential sense of a we-self—are further enhanced by powerful idealization and identification processes that are culturally promoted. Indian culture inculcates veneration and respect from an early age for all who are superior in kinship rank, particularly the elders—these attitudes continuing throughout life. The subtle interweaving of mythological images with those of individuals to be idealized greatly reinforces this process: parental figures, for instance, become associated with god-images. We-self regard then profoundly partakes of the idealizations attached to the reputation and honor of the extended family as well as of the community. This is as true of untouchables or the scheduled castes as of Brahmins (Moffatt 1979).

The high level of we-self regard develops in a very particular way between sons and fathers. Since the father is overtly distant, though usually intensely emotionally attached to his son, any sign of his confirmation is greatly sought after by the son. Clinical case material and reports of Indian psychoanalytic therapists amply confirm that sons are extremely sensitive to and eager to gain their father's respect, treasure any sign of recognition and approval, and in turn try to reflect well on their father, to enhance his regard by their own behavior. This is not only while the son is growing up, but throughout life, and by reports even after the father's death (pers. com. B. K. Ramanujam and Jai Sinha). Having his father's respect is central to a mature man's esteem, no matter how well respected he is by others and now successful he is in his own endeavors.

With daughters, my impression is that an important segment of their we-self regard consists of profoundly internalized attitudes of carrying

---

[4] First cousins are referred to in English as cousin-sisters and cousin-brothers to convey their familial closeness and the ethos of the extended family that nieces and nephews are to be treated as one's own children.

on family and *jati* customs, culture, and traditions, not wanting to hurt or let down their mothers in particular and family in general by breaking them, and upholding family honor by adapting well in their in-laws' family.

Indian child rearing and the inner structuralization of heightened esteem are profoundly psychologically congruent with the basic Hindu concept that the individual soul is essentially the godhead (*Atman-Brahman*) (Spratt 1966). A heightened sense of inner regard and the premise that a person can strive to become godlike are strongly connected. Such a premise was indeed profoundly important to the inner sense of esteem of both Ashis and Shakuntala, who were both deeply involved in spiritual pursuits. This is in contrast to the Western Christian premise of original sin, whereby the individual must ultimately be saved by a god quite removed from within oneself.

This elaboration of the narcissistic dimension gives some idea of its central place in the Indian familial self. Yet the subject is even more complex, since these same components play an absolutely crucial role in the Indian conscience, where the ego-ideal is of fundamental importance.

The Familial Self: A Socially Contextual Ego-Ideal

Possibly no other structure of the Indian familial self is so patently different from Western psychological makeup than the Indian conscience. It has therefore been almost ubiquitously misunderstood and often maligned as either unprincipled or inferior to a Western conscience and morality. In reality, the Indian conscience as oriented around *dharma* is extremely highly developed and is eminently suited to function within the complex hierarchical relationships of the extended family, *jati*, and other groups that are so different from Western-style relationships.

According to psychoanalysis, the conscience consists of two inner organizations: the superego and ego-ideal. The former more generally regulates the drives and affects, and frequently functions more unconsciously; whereas the latter is oriented around the more conscious inner effort to live up to certain ideals and idealized images of oneself. In contrast to the makeup of the Western conscience, where the unconscious superego tends to predominate, the dominant structure of the Indian conscience is the ego-ideal. It is, moreover, an ego-ideal that is constituted differently from the Western one, and has in many respects significantly different norms and ideals.

250

It is a socially contextual ego-ideal, in Hindus one that is also myth-ologically oriented. What is correct conduct (*dharma*) in one situation and relationship is not in another, depending not only on one's position in the hierarchical relationship and one's stage in the life cycle, but also on the specificities of the person, time, and place involved. *Dharma* is modeled after the conduct of highly venerated persons (pers. com. McKim Marriott) as well as the cues received from elders in the family or group. Thus, what is said about a given issue to one person in one situation may be quite different from what is said to another person in another situation, both statements being quite appropriate to the context. It is just this socially contextual way of functioning that appears so unprincipled or hypocritical to a Westerner. Moreover, the context itself is often more complex than the typical American dyadic and triadic relationships, since Indian family and group hierarchical relationships tend to be multiple.

Giving a cultural frame for the Indian ego-ideal, A. K. Ramanujan (1980) stresses this context-oriented ethic, as contrasted to Western universalistic ethics: "One has only to read Manu after a bit of Kant to be struck by Manu's extraordinary lack of universality. He seems to have no clear notion of a universal *human* nature from which one can deduce ethical decrees like, 'Man shall not kill,' or 'Man shall not tell an untruth.' One is aware of no notion of a 'state,' no unitary law of all men. . . . Even truth-telling is not an unconditional imperative. . . . Universalization means putting oneself in another's place—it is the golden rule of the *New Testament*. . . . The main tradition of Western/Christian ethics is based on such a premise of universalization—Manu will not understand such a premise. To be moral, for Manu, is to particularize—to ask who did what, to whom and when. . . . Each class (*jati*) of man has his own laws, his own proper ethic not to be universalized" (pp. 10–11).

Another fundamental aspect of the Indian ego-ideal is reciprocity in varied hierarchical relationships. While a person becomes well grounded in his or her own responsibilities, obligations, proper behavior, and such in a relationship, there are equally strong expectations that the others will live up to their obligations and responsibilities. As either side does, there is considerable nonverbal approbation. If, on the other hand, reciprocity is not forthcoming, angry—sometimes bitter—feelings may result. A simple example of this are Meena and Laxmi, who were bitterly angry at their brothers for not fulfilling certain expected responsibilities.

Open rebellion, which is very rare, occurs almost only when there is complete disappointment in the expected nurturance and responsibility of those superior. In an unusual case, one college girl in a psychotherapy session was openly and vehemently angry at her mother. It gradually emerged that her mother was such an anxious and insecure woman that she could not fulfill the expected nurturance of her daughter. Another example involved the subordinates of Ashis's father, who were apparently so angry at him for identifying with British notions of authority and abandoning the nurturance and protection they had expected that they brought him up on charges of what was then quite normal corruption.

A relevant metaphor for the Indian ego-ideal is radar, in contrast to the gyroscope for a Western conscience. A gyroscope enables the Westerner to sail the seas of innumerable social situations by keeping his balance around more universalistic principles of behavior, even while perceiving and partly identifying with various group norms. It suits the autonomous, mobile individual, who must participate in any number of extra-familial groups and relationships, ones that in America may be shifted about relatively frequently—friends, neighbors, and jobs, not to mention lovers and spouses. Radar, on the other hand, enables Indians to be extraordinarily sensitive to the norms of responsibilities and proper behavior, as well as the customs in complex familial and extra-familial hierarchical relationships, enabling them to act appropriately in these very specific situations. Thus, Indians will constantly sense what is expected of them, acutely aware of how others are reacting to them.[5]

Even in a Western setting, Indians adapt very quickly through sensitively picking up the cues for appropriate behavior. Dina, who attended an American college at age seventeen, immediately picked up the cues and norms and was complimented by her American friends for fitting right in and becoming American—they did not perceive that she was very differently motivated. When a new situation or relationship occurs, Indians frequently act with considerable circumspection and caution until they are more certain of what is expected. How one's behavior will be regarded by others, particularly by those superior, and how this pro-

---

[5] David Reissman (1951) uses the same metaphor of radar for the change in the American conscience toward being strongly oriented to the specific social or work group norms the person is functioning in, tending to identify with the values and goals of each of these groups. However, as Francis L. K. Hsu (1972) has rightly emphasized, the American ego-ideal in identifying with group norms is still far more individualistic than that of the person in Eastern cultures. Qualitatively, American "radar" is nowhere nearly as oriented to a subtle sensing of others' feelings, moods, and expectations, as well as approbation and criticism, as is Indian "radar."

motes or undermines one's we-self regard, are always of the most central concern to Indians.

The Ego-Ideal and Mythic Orientation

Integral to the socially contextual ego-ideal for Hindu Indians is a strong mythic orientation. Adults have deeply incorporated into their preconscious powerful emotional-cognitive images of the vitally alive, richly complex mythology told by various mothering figures during their childhood. The plethora of mythic models and relationships are not only suitable for ego-ideal identifications, but also give norms for correct reciprocal behavior in the complex hierarchical relationships, where the *dharma* of each is elaborated in the myth. Not only are these norms elaborated upon endlessly in the mythology, but negative images of what to avoid are equally stressed. For every god there is a demon, and for every virtuous man or woman an equally evil one. Thus, the powerful incorporation of mythic stories helps to orient the person throughout life.

Although psychoanalysts have extensively investigated the psychological meaning of individual myths, including Indian ones (Kakar 1978, 140–159), how these mythic models function psychologically in Indians and others on an everyday basis has been almost totally ignored.[6] It is a subject needing extensive exploration. In one of the only papers devoted to this exploration, Manisha Roy (1979) poignantly recounts how she finally dealt with an unrequited love relationship by recalling the myth of Shiva swallowing the poison that would destroy the gods, and holding and neutralizing it in his throat. Through her memory of this myth, she realized how she had to resolve her own bitter feelings of disappointment and not let them destroy her.

In Indian cognition, it must be noted that the mythic is experienced as contiguous or metonymic with the other person or idol or even everyday objects, and not as a symbol or representation of it (Ramanujan 1980). A simple example of this occurred when we were having dinner at an Indian friend's apartment in New York City, and our son, then nine, had taken off his sneakers and rested them on a book he had

---

[6]Undoubtedly, the major reason that psychoanalysts have not explored everyday mythic functioning is that myth (in the Indian sense of a story integrating the divine and the mundane) does not occupy any significant mental space in the vast majority of Westerners. Even Jungian analysts rely on dreams to reach a mythic level in their patients, since the latter have no mythic vocabulary readily available.

brought so as not to get their couch dirty. Their Western-educated daughter commented matter-of-factly that an Indian would never put shoes on a book, for the book was a manifestation of the goddess of learning, Saraswati.

It unexpectedly emerged in a discussion that women in Professor Narayanan's therapy groups at N.I.M.H.A.N.S. use mythic images in everyday relationships far more than men—a point confirmed by others. As an instance, a young woman of seventeen who was having hysterical fits brought in a dream of a black snake coming to rest on a lotus. While Professor Narayanan was trying to puzzle out the meaning of this dream, one of the older women in the group immediately responded that this girl must be tremendously upset because her family was arranging a marriage to a man much more dark-skinned than she wanted. The girl confirmed this, and for the first time began to vent her feelings about the proposed marriage. The older woman had realized from the mythology that a lotus can symbolically represent a woman's breast, and the snake of course was a phallic symbol representing the male, a black snake thus being a dark-skinned man. The men in his groups are more oriented to the philosophical doctrines of the *Upanishads* and *Bhagavad Gita* than to mythology.

By constantly referring everyday relationships and situations back to the web of mythic images, women call up a host of associative memories and connections about a person, and invest meaning in any and all situations. "Ah, he is like Duryodhana" (a major antagonist in the *Mahabharata*) will immediately bring up images of an envious, ambitious man; or conversely, "he is like Laxman" (Rama's devoted brother in the *Ramayana*) conveys images of loyalty and faithfulness in the most trying of circumstances (pers. com. Dr. Satyavathy). When I asked the head of a psychology department and her assistant whether they use mythic images in their highly modernized hospital setting as well as at home, they paused for a moment, looked at each other, smiled, and then answered, "only in private." Thus, traditional Indian women can relate everything on an everyday basis to mythic stories. The relationship of this mythic orientation to the spiritual self I shall discuss at length in the following chapter.

THE EGO-IDEAL AND GOSSIPING

Gossiping and the constant comparison of women with each other, a pervasive form of social behavior that has been cited both in anthropological and psychological studies (Anandalakshmi 1978; Das 1977), is also related in a major way to Indian women's ego-ideals. In one counseling group of college girls, it became evident that the compulsive gossiping about each other always involved criticizing the other for acting in a way that was forbidden to oneself, thus unconsciously projecting the forbidden part of oneself onto the other and then criticizing it. Projecting the negative images of a deeply internalized ego-ideal onto the other reinforces the positive images of how one should be, and deflects the anxiety that one is not fully living up to these good images and will be found out. This need to enhance inner regard through constant comparison may become particularly important since there is a lack of overt praise for good behavior but instant criticism and shaming for what is forbidden.

THE EGO-IDEAL, DEPENDENCY, AND WE-SELF REGARD

There is a highly subtle but central interaction of the Indian ego-ideal with intense dependency needs and heightened we-self regard. In the strong wishing, wanting, and asking of the other, there is the unspoken recognition that the person from whom you are requesting something is accorded a superior position, thereby enhancing the other's we-self regard. Thus, asking of another is very subtly a giving. When not reciprocated, it can evoke hurt, angry feelings. In turn, dependence also triggers an ego-ideal response in the other of wanting to live up to his or her inner ideal of being the nurturing, sustaining hierarchical superior, also enhancing the giver's esteem. It is this kind of expectation that in all probability enabled Ashis to enter psychoanalytic therapy with me, well knowing that I might never come to India to be reimbursed monetarily. This is a kind of subtle exchange, enhancing intimacy, that Westerners find hard to grasp: they often experience it as intrusive and presumptive.

The Familial Self: The Superego

Not to be underemphasized in the Indian conscience is a powerful superego, profoundly oriented around the conscious containment and often unconscious repression or dissociation of angry feelings, and to a lesser extent, sexuality, through a number of defense mechanisms. Where dependency and narcissistic needs are so intensified in familial and group relationships, considerable anger and ambivalence can be generated by disappointed expectations, slights, and lack of reciprocity, on the one

255

hand, and on the other, by the elder or superior sometimes being exceedingly strict or making decisions that may go completely against the
grain of what the subordinate or younger person wishes. Moreover,
there are certain stages of the life cycle that may generate more conflict
and anger than others, such as the early years of a married young woman's life in her in-laws' household.

At the same time, there is a strong superego response to contain if not
to suppress and repress these ambivalent reactions in order to function
harmoniously within the close-knit familial hierarchical relationships from
which there is no exit. Erna Hoch once put it as "not to spoil the atmosphere within which one lives," nor to disrupt the strong emotional
relatedness and connectedness between family members. The psychoanalytic work with Joan clearly gives evidence of an extremely strict
superego that resulted in her becoming jittery and upset once she began
expressing the full brunt of her anger in sessions. There is widespread
agreement among Indian psychoanalytic therapists that the superego's
control and containment of angry feelings lead to the main psychological problems of Indians and are undoubtedly the major unconscious
motivation in causing psychopathology.

Clinical psychoanalysis also clearly indicates that intense anxiety is
generated by strict superego reactions to any direct expression of anger
toward a superior in either male or female hierarchical relationships. In
the confidentiality of the psychoanalytic relationship, patients can indeed express anger and hostility toward all kinds of people, including
superiors, but it is extremely difficult for the patient to voice any of
these feelings at all directly toward the therapist (like Japanese but unlike Americans).

A telling example of this difficulty in expressing ambivalence toward
superiors emerged when a senior psychiatrist asked my assistance for
what had been a highly problematic self-exploration group with first-
year residents. After the psychiatrist encouraged the residents to be self-
expressive, the moment the residents even raised the possibility of expressing their ambivalence toward male authority, they unconsciously
began to panic and miss sessions out of an unconscious fear of punishment. Upon further encouragement, they began to express some gripes
but defensively deflected all of them toward his assistant, a much less
threatening male authority. After still further interpretation enabled the
residents to express their criticisms increasingly openly, the two psychi-
atrist-leaders experienced such anxiety of their own that they went to
the head of psychiatry out of fear that the residents were getting out of
hand, wanting him to discipline them. Thus, direct expressions of criti-

cism from subordinates to superiors arouse considerable anxiety in both subordinates and in superiors, even psychologically sophisticated ones.

The vicissitudes of superego control of anger in the Indian psyche are legion. Like a bubble under plastic, anger can be shifted around here and there, but sooner or later it surfaces. On a more conscious level, the superego allows hurt and angry feelings to be conveyed nonverbally by suddenly stopping talking, or leaving the room, or not eating the next meal while conveying that you are feeling perfectly fine, or simply walking around with an unhappy look. Or the subordinate may agree to what the superior asks for but then simply not do it.

Note that these indirect expressions of hurt and anger are often attempts to shame the other person into realizing what he or she has done. Such nonverbal cues are readily apprehended and sometimes responded to. It was only after I became more cognizant of these methods of shaming that I realized that Gandhi had ingeniously elevated these everyday methods of coping with being wronged into effective political tactics against the British through such means as hunger strikes and noncooperation.

On a more unconscious level, there are various defensive maneuvers and compromise symptom formations to deal with superego anxiety over anger and ambivalence.[7] The panoply of symptoms, particularly among more traditonal families, in many respects resembles that of Freud's early twentieth-century Vienna, in his classic descriptions of hysteria, obsessive and compulsive symptoms, amnesias, and such; it is completely different from what is now present in American patients.[8] What accounts for these striking differences both cross-culturally and historically?

The key dimension is the kind of superego generated by cultural codes and family structures, where the close-knit, hierarchically oriented family of turn-of-the-century Vienna and contemporary India and Japan necessitates a strong containment of unacceptable aggressive and sexual feelings and impulses, resulting in psychological symptomotology. This contrasts with the contemporary American superego, where internalized cultural values allow for a much freer expression of anger and sexuality

[7] Unconscious defenses such as repression do not really get rid of the undesireable affect, such as hostility, but rather separate it from its source. Thus, someone can be angry at another but will then unconsciously express the anger at someone else, displacing it from its source to another.

[8] The Viennese symptom picture also characterizes Japanese as well as certain ethnic groups in the United States such as Hispanics.

within the more mobile and partially estranged nuclear American families.[9]

The most salient symptoms are compulsive, repetitive handwashing and somatization or physical ailments, both frequently resulting from suppressed anger. The former is religiously sanctioned, while the latter is frequently socially accepted: for example, a young wife might be excused from some of her chores because of a splitting headache or backache. Perhaps a majority of patients come to psychoanalytic therapy because of somatic complaints that do not yield to any kind of medical treatment, foreign or indigenous.

Indians seem highly cognizant of the connection between the emotional stresses of extended family living and somatic problems, especially in women. Astute psychotherapists are often able to pinpoint quite quickly the sources of emotional stress by being familiar with the particular patterns of kinship relationships in the locality, and the stage of the life cycle and kinship position that the patient is in (Hoch 1977). Indians further have the congruent cultural notion of intrinsically monistic mind-body interactions—mind and body being simply gradations of subtle and gross matter—in contrast to the usual mind-body duality of Western thought (Marriott 1976). In fact, my Indian patients would generally relate almost *all* physical problems to their emotional state of mind, coming curiously close to the attitudes of many patients in New York City, who in recent decades have been almost brainwashed to think of all physical ailments as psychosomatic. Joan, for instance, recounted that her previous therapist had been extremely helpful in enabling her to get in touch with and express all kinds of feelings, which had the salutary effect that her frequent colds and other minor illnesses completely subsided.

Still another symptom is hysterical amnesia. Personal outbursts of rage are extremely rare, and when they do occur, there is frequently total amnesia afterward, as in the case of Amal. On the other hand, persons consciously participate in group outbursts of rage and violence because the sense of we-ness with the group relieves these persons from their own strong superego strictures (pers. com. B. K. Ramanujam).

Unconscious defenses are also used to inhibit awareness of the sources of aggressive feelings because of superego prohibitions. Unconscious displacement is almost ubiquitously used. Children and adolescents unwittingly displace ambivalent feelings from parental figures to younger sib-

---

[9] On the other hand, one does not usually encounter the early emotional deficits and self-fragmentation in Indian and Japanese patients that one so frequently sees in American ones today (Kohut 1971, 1977).

lings or cousins. Boys in particular may be overtly obedient with elders, but covertly bullying toward siblings, cousins, and playmates. Adults displace much of their aggression to those lower in the hierarchy, those younger or of lower caste, including servants when they have them.

Displacement of anger from original family members to others was rife with my patients. Rustum blew up at his brother-in-law when the latter suggested how Rustum should approach an exam he was about to take—a clear displacement from his intense anger at his father who constantly lectured him. In women, the unconscious displacements occurred primarily from their original families to their in-laws and occasionally to persons at work. Joan reacted with overly intense rage (the sign of an unconscious displacement) when she felt her mother-in-law favored some of her children over others. Girls seem more forbidden to express anger and rebellion than boys—not unlike Americans.

A more subtle and complex displacement occurs when families in an unconscious conspiracy dump their ambivalences to each other on one child, who then, like Joan, becomes quite disturbed while the several other siblings in these large families seem to grow up perfectly fine. The role of black sheep is usually accepted by the child who, being so emotionally enmeshed within the family, is vulnerable to its overall mood and underlying dynamics.

Another form of displacement occurs in protracted family feuds. Since family partitioning among brothers is a not unusual part of the extended family life cycle, and the division of property being quite complicated, there can be ample opportunity for all kinds of alliances and bitter feuds to develop. Alternatively, the space outside the family is frequently an arena for conflicts generated within the family which cannot be expressed there (pers. com. Kamalini Sarabhai). This displacement often involves an ideology of we-other ethics. Where ethical norms must be carefully observed within familial hierarchical relationships, situations involving others who are not part of one's own people may result in all kinds of aggressive and callous manipulations. Unless a personalized relationship is formed, the displacement of all that is forbidden within the extended family and community may take place (Sinha 1980).

There are still other major defenses to handle the considerable ambivalences generated within familial hierarchical relationships. Idealization can be used unconsciously to defend against anger. Still another defense is reaction-formation, where the person may feel loving, concerned feelings toward someone in order unconsciously to keep in check underlying negative ones. Jai took a most benign, pseudo-Gandhian stance toward his highly sadistic father who was trying to cheat Jai out of his inheritance, but was unconsciously defending against considerable fear and rage.

A discussion of ambivalence and its attendant defenses would not be complete without mentioning the presence of sado-masochism in Indian familial relationships. When the more prevalent concern, love, sensitivity, and responsibility are absent and the elders become sadistic, relationships can easily degenerate into sado-masochism, since the subordinate is so emotionally enmeshed with his or her superiors.[10] The younger person unconsciously incorporates the sadism as a way of getting along, and identifies with the aggressor.

Four of the male patients I saw had fathers who were sadistic to varying degrees. I interpreted to Ashis his nastiness to family and subordinates as an unconscious identification with his father as the aggressor. In the more dramatic case of Krishna, a foreman in a factory who on a number of occasions had life-threatening accidents—such as driving his scooter at full speed into a factory gate that was closed—he had incorporated his father's sadism, expressed by frequent, crushing beatings of Krishna as a child. At other times, Krishna was highly sadistic with subordinates, unconsciously identifying with his father.

SEXUALITY AND THE INDIAN CONSCIENCE

Sexuality I have reserved for last because it is very much related to both ego-ideal and superego structures. One of the more striking polarities that pervades Indian psychological functioning, social relationships, and cultural expressions is that between intense sensuality and strict social controls. There is culturally a profound acceptance of the instinctive, the sensual and sexual, in striking contrast with Western attitudes (Roy 1975). In psychoanalytic therapy, Indian patients more readily and easily than Americans express sexual fantasies, including ones toward the therapist (pers. com. B. K. Ramanujam), in sharp contrast to their inhibition of any ambivalent feelings toward the analyst.

One aspect of this is the familial acceptance of the young wife's intense sexuality. She is treated for some time as an outsider in her in-law's family, in part so that her sexuality can be differentiated from that of the women of the family. When she is too easily accepted, as sometimes happens, she may become an incestuous image in her husband's

[10] For an elaboration of this viewpoint of masochism within ego psychology and object-relations rather than drive theory in psychoanalysis, see Berliner (1947) and Menaker (1952). Kakar (1978, 120) gives an example of this masochistic incorporation of attitudes of those superior in the hierarchy.

unconscious, who will then experience sexual inhibitions (pers. com. Niti Seth). That her sexuality is also almost her only leverage in a situation where she is the lowest in the hierarchy can also be perceived as a profound source of danger, especially in a joint household.

Social controls around sexuality are equally strong and are profoundly internalized into the Indian conscience. Where incestuous fantasies are present—as clearly emerged in the dreams of Joan, Saida, and Shakuntala—there are also strict superego reactions. The modesty/shame morality, where wives of the extended family are to keep considerable distance and act circumspectly with the family men older than their husbands, is an active part of women's ego-ideal.

Strictures over the control of sexuality outside the family are also deeply internalized into the ego-ideal. Counseling sessions with college girls clearly evidence how powerful are ego-ideal strictures over proper dress, demeanor, and behavior in public. Ego-ideal values of shyness and modesty in these girls, as well as gossiping and pointing fingers at others, reinforce irreproachable behavior in public. Yet, the dialectic continues between their intense sexuality and strict controls. Girls and boys will stay in separate groups at college and not talk to each other, but nevertheless communicate in a highly sensuous manner through subtle eye movements and facial gestures (pers. com. Udayan Patel).

Although the unmarried girl must avoid outside relationships with boys, she does have close contacts with cousin-brothers and uncles. Infatuations or romantic involvements with them are not infrequent and parents usually respond by turning their heads the other way (pers. com. Anjali Apte and Krishna Kumar). The point is that what is kept within the family will not hurt its reputation. Thus sexuality, in contrast to aggression, is kept within the family, especially with girls—quite the opposite of Western social patterns. This point is further substantiated by an anthropological study that documented an unusual number of affairs that women had, all with the men of their joint households—brothers-in-law, uncles-in-law, fathers-in-law, and such.[11] The sexual politics of these families is something needing combined anthropological and psychoanalytic study, which might clarify more of the underlying dynamics of extended family functioning.

It has been repeatedly noted in anthropological studies that Indian

[11] The anthropologist who conducted this study is a woman who discussed some of the data with me on women of some fifty interrelated families of one *jati*. I am extremely doubtful whether a male anthropologist would have been able to get this kind of data, as Indian women can be extremely circumspect in speech and behavior when talking to a man.

men often have appreciable anxiety over their sexuality and potency. The cultural concept is that too much discharge of semen will be debilitating to a man's health and vitality, so that moderation in normal sexual relationships is to be followed. Indian men, on the other hand, often perceive Indian women to be sexually voracious, seductive, and powerful, constantly tempting him to depart from a course of moderation, and thereby arousing his anxiety (Carstairs 1957; Das 1975; Kakar 1978; O'Flaherty 1973). Psychodynamically, the Indian man tends unconsciously to project his inner image of the sensuously stimulating mothering figures of childhood onto his wife and other women, thereby perceiving the latter as highly seductive and dangerous. From clinical work, men's sexual anxiety seems related more to their unconscious fear of a symbiotic, sensual envelopment by the powerful women of childhood than from oedipal castration anxiety (Kakar 1980; Roy 1975), as in the case of Ravi, where there was clear evidence of a highly sensuous tie to his mother.

Indian culture oscillates between the erotic and ascetic. Sexuality and sensuality pervade the religious dimension through *bhakti* practices, whereas its total opposite is expressed through renunciation and asceticism. I was particularly struck one day while attending rehearsals at a major Bharat Natyam school in Bombay that the dancer was at times extraordinarily sensuous in her subtle eye and facial movements, while at other times not at all. I assumed, approaching it as I did through my Western lens, that the striking sensuality related to secular dances. In actuality, the more devotional the theme, the more utterly sensual the dancer became. Sensuality was thus given full release in the service of aesthetic religiosity, while being properly contained in the aesthetics of the social sphere. As Barbara Stoler Miller (1977, 17) aptly puts it in her introduction to Jayadeva's *Gitagovinda*, "Jayadeva's verses . . . are explicitly sensual, and celebrate the sensual joy of divine love."

A Developmental Schema for the Indian Conscience

How does the Indian conscience develop?[12] In both conscious social attitudes and classical texts, the Indian child up to the age of four or five is regarded as an innocent, pure and godlike, whose actions have

[12] I shall again rely on the observations of Indian psychoanalysts, child and adolescent psychiatrists, and psychologists, who express surprising agreement on the developmental stages.

little or no karmic influence for the future because of ignorance, and is therefore to be gratified, not yet ready to be trained as a member of the social community (Sakala 1977). Psychoanalytic observations of child rearing indicate that the formation of the Indian conscience takes place in two basic ways that are congruent with these cultural formulations. While the mothering person frequently distracts her very young children from any wrongdoing or unwanted behavior through gratification, certain limits can be reached. When children sense that their mother is unduly upset by what they are doing, which she will rarely convey verbally, they will frequently desist in order to have her in a better mood.[13]

This acute sensitivity to the moods and emotional states of the mothering person derives from the more prolonged symbiotic mode of mothering, and becomes the bedrock for the later sensitivity to nonverbal communication, and to approbation and criticism from others—all crucial to the Indian conscience. Thus, early on, the Indian conscience develops in relation to close familial interdependence, whereas the developing American superego is trained for eventual autonomous adaptation in extrafamilial relationships.

To digress momentarily, the benevolent and fierce forms of the powerful mother goddesses seem far more related to early child rearing involving intense maternal gratification and protective angry moods than to the usual psychoanalytic explanation, which posits a defensive splitting of the goddess into good and bad objects because of unacceptable aggression toward the mother (Kakar 1978; O'Flaherty 1976).[14] This latter view overlooks the facts that the goddess-mother only becomes fierce when the devotee-child departs too much from acceptable behavior or *dharma;* and the devotee does not shun the wrathful goddess, as would occur if defensive splitting were present.

Following this early period of enormous affective and narcissistic gratification comes a severe crackdown for proper behavior in hierarchical relationships through later childhood and well into adolescence (Bassa 1978; Kakar 1978; Ramanujam 1977). This crackdown often occurs suddenly, especially for boys, and sometimes occurs dramatically

---

[13] This observation emerged from close watching of mother-infant interactions over a prolonged period by psychoanalytic students in Bombay under the leadership of Udayan Patel; the process was similar to what the students of the British Psychoanalytic Society do.

[14] Gananath Obeyesekere (1984, 442–446) offers an alternative anthropological explanation that Kali is much more prevalent in north India, where the wife must live in her unfamiliar in-law's family and is far more frustrated than in the south, and is therefore an angrier mother.

at the birth of a younger sibling, when the child simultaneously has to give up the mother's bed and her security. This loss of an initial state of heightened narcissistic well-being with a corresponding great increase in anxiety are what Bassa terms "the cardinal crisis of Indian childhood"; what Ramanujam describes as "the main and only developmental conflict of Indian children"; what Udayan Patel calls a "severe latency superego"; and what Kakar (1978, 126–133) also describes. The Indian superego is developmentally in dramatic contrast to a Western-style one, which is considered to be consolidated during the oedipal period of development—four to six years of age—before latency even begins. The considerable anxiety that is generated is frequently channeled into culturally sanctioned rituals such as frequent handwashing to maintain purity, which may become defensively compulsive (pers. com. B. K. Ramanujam).

Both Bassa (1978) and Ramanujam (1977) have commented from clinical work in child-guidance centers that parental figures do not institute any firm, consistent controls on aggression—which is central to the internalized regulatory controls of the Western superego for autonomous functioning. Where distraction by gratification and angry moods are used for control in the early childhood years, shaming, scolding, and physical punishment are instituted in the later ones. Parental strictures are on behavior in specific hierarchical relationships, with anger toward the superior simply not being countenanced in later childhood. The child gradually learns to become extremely circumspect around his or her elders, but away from them can be quite expressive if he feels no one will learn about it, displacing angry feelings to a variety of others who cannot punish. Thus how he will be regarded by others becomes a central inner dynamic, rather than a feeling of inner guilt over aggressive impulses per se, which is more characteristic of the Western superego.

Where proper behavior is extremely well defined in a traditional society, both socially and in text (Sakala 1977), the child and adolescent are gradually grounded in their *dharma*. The child is expected to be obedient and respectful of elders, to contain aggressive reactions, and to conform to traditionally well-defined responsibilities in Indian extended family life. Adults are ready and willing to exert a great deal of effort to convey what is proper, and to give continual guidance and admonishment not only to family members but neighbors' children as well. "A girl must have a thousand eyes on her body" is a saying expressing the need to be constantly on the alert for others observing her behavior; I suspect it also represents her experience that there are a thousand eyes on her.

Whereas bad behavior is immediately met with shame and punishment, good behavior is only confirmed with subtle, nonverbal expressions. Overt praise is assiduously avoided for three major reasons, according to the child rearing observations of Anandalakshmi (1978, 1981). It is extremely immodest to praise your child when your child's and your own self are so closely interlinked. Moreover, praise ultimately deflects a child from realizing his or her real self (*Atman*) by having an inflated notion of the phenomenal self or I (*ahamkara*). Finally, praise might draw untoward consequences in the form of the evil eye, or envy from others.

Shaming is used as one of the paramount means of instituting controls in child rearing, and seems to be very effective. Children are highly susceptible to shaming because they are so dependent on others (Lewis 1971), and because they wish to regain their early childhood sense of high regard. Further, the child is extremely sensitive as to how his or her behavior reflects upon and affects the we-self regard of others of the extended family. Parental figures frequently convey a tone of real concern and affection for the child when the shaming criticism or guidance is being made. The ego-ideal is obviously appealed to: "How can you possibly do this?" or "We wouldn't expect this of you." An older child is told to be protective of a younger one, or siblings are told not to fight because members of the same family love one another. The well-being of the family may be appealed to as a reason for the child to mend his or her behavior. In public, shaming statements may include: "Auntie or uncle (nonfamilial adults) would not like your doing this" (pers. com. Anandalakshmi); or "what will they say about us (the family)?"; or sometimes shaming is effectively done indirectly by the parental person talking about a neighbor's child, someone with whom the child or teenager easily identifies, doing something reprehensible. Not living up to familial expectations is to experience an intense, inner sense of shame (Das 1976b).

Ego-Ideal Development and Mythic Orientation

The strong mythic orientation in the Hindu ego-ideal derives not only from the frequent recital of the myths by mothering persons in childhood, but also from other social and psychological processes. Families will emphasize different mythic models and stories for their children to identify with, depending on the norms of their *jati;* for example, heroic military myths will be stressed to a child of Rajput background (pers.

265

com. Dr. Parmar). Parental figures may also invest a child with mythic associations of their own, referring to the child by the name of one or another mythic figure, depending on the child's nature, which image is then incorporated by the child into his or her ego-ideal. Children are encouraged to venerate parents and other family elders as living manifestations of the gods and goddesses, more easily incorporating these mythic idealizations into the ego-ideal when the elder is truly a superior person.

Children also actively identify with one or another mythic figure on the basis of temperament, inclination, and cognitive style. For girls there is not only the model of Sita from one version of the *Ramayana,* totally faithful and loyal to her husband, Rama, under the most trying of circumstances; but in another version, the emphasis is on a more assertive Sita. There is also the more dynamic, wily Savitri, who dramatically wrests her husband from the hands of Yama, the god of death. There is, in effect, a plethora of models for ego-ideal identifications not only for girls but obviously for boys as well.[15]

THE INDIAN OEDIPUS

In contrast to the Western familial situation, the Indian male is expected to remain closely involved with his mother throughout life, and his relationship with her is far more intense in the first several years of childhood than is customary in the northwest European-American culture belt. The power of this tie is further reinforced by the mother frequently mediating between father and son for anything the boy might want. Sexual impulses on the male's part are frequently associated with the underlying anxieties over engulfment in the maternal relationship, with a regressive pull toward the affective-sensuous gratifications of these first several years of life. Sexuality is not associated by Indian men with freedom and separation from the original family, as it is for Westerners, but is overwhelmingly associated with intense extended family emotional involvements and responsibilities (Grey 1973).

Within the oedipal context, the Indian son identifies with the father as the ego-ideal and leader of the family (if a grandfather is not fulfilling that role), needs the father to give him inner structure and organization, and is interdependent with the father in mutually enhancing each other's we-self regard. The father, paternal uncles, and grandfather gradually

[15] This viewpoint of multiple models differs from Kakar (1978, 63–70), who conveys that for girls there is primarily the one model of Sita (pers. com. Anandalakshmi).

become an important intrapsychic balance to the intense mother-son relationship (Grey 1973; Kakar 1980; Ramanujam 1981a; pers. com. Kanwal Mehra). This balance reflects the socially asymmetrical one between structural hierarchy and the qualitative mode of hierarchical relationships. These men teach the son during later childhood and adolescence the strict observances of the structural hierarchy in an overtly distant, authoritative manner, in which deference and containment of feelings on the son's part predominates. This contrasts with the more informal relationship with the maternal uncles and grandfather, more reminiscent of the qualitative mode of hierarchical relationships in which the boy relates more on the basis of his intimacy needs.

Psychoanalysts in India who have worked with both Indian and European patients have observed that Indian men have less castration anxiety than European men and, correspondingly, Indian women have less penis envy.[16] I would strongly suspect that this results from two interrelated factors. Competitive individualism among males, which is a major factor in the intense castration anxiety in Western countries, is profoundly frowned upon in the Indian milieu. Instead, there is a decided emphasis on nurturant, caring attitudes in Indian male authority, which evidences far more incorporation of feminine-maternal principles from the early years of the intense mother-son relationship than occurs in Western men (Erikson 1969; Kakar 1978; Nandy 1980b, 32–46). Moreover, the son needs the sustenance of the male superior. Although competitive feelings are often present among brothers and cousin-brothers close in age, even here the ideology of the extended family still stresses cooperation and harmony. Envy of others' positions and accomplishments is readily observable in Indian men, but seems to stem from envy of the other's better connections and nurturance from a superior—for instance if the other has a mentor who more effectively promotes his advancement. Thus, the Oedipus complex in Indian males revolves less around castration anxiety than around the need for the structuring identification with the father and other male elders of the family, this structuring identification only beginning in the later phase of the oedipal period and lasting through adolescence (Kakar 1980).[17]

It would appear that daughters are more strictly brought up from an earlier age by their mothers and the other female elders, but seem to be

[16] This point was made by T. C. Sinha, then president of the Indian Psychoanalytic Society in Calcutta, in a talk given to the National Psychological Association for Psychoanalysis in New York City, October 1964.

[17] The primacy of the structuring identification with the parent of the same sex for both sons and daughters is increasingly being stressed among Western psychoanalysts.

allowed a close relationship with their fathers. In some milieus, it can be openly close (Roy 1977), while in others, the father maintains overt distance while having a covert close relationship, enabling her to effect some separation from the mother.[18] Joan's relationship with her father is an excellent example of the latter.

The threat in the Indian oedipal situation is not from the boy who wants to get rid of his father and have his mother, as the Greek myth emphasizes. In Indian mythology it comes primarily from fathers who are intensely jealous of their sons and do them in, while being highly attracted to their daughters; whereas mothers are intensely jealous of daughters-in-law and attack them, being strongly attached to their sons (Ramanujan 1983). This makes perfect sense, given the structure of relationships and the modes of child rearing in the Indian extended family. Intergenerational conflict and rebellion by the sons are largely absent in Indian mythology, as well as in the social milieu—again a sharp contrast to oedipal resolutions in many Western men.

THE INDIAN CONSCIENCE AND PSYCHOSEXUAL THEORY

The particular development of the Indian ego-ideal and superego, as they differ from the Western conscience, raises questions concerning classic psychoanalytic formulations of psychosexual development. In classical drive theory, the patterning of gratification and frustration of drives, with conflicts thus engendered in each of the psychosexual stages, result in the particular structuring of character formation and later adult behavior: oral, anal, phallic, and genital character. It is pertinent to cite Mark Sylvan's (1981) application of classical formulations on oral character to his elaboration of Indian character and behavior. His application incisively illustrates serious problems in the classic psychoanalytic theory of psychosexual development when the theory does not take into account the specific development and functioning of the ego-ideal and superego as it is culturally influenced in specific societies and historical eras, as well as of early object-relations involving the mother-child dyad.

To quote Sylvan, "the Hindu child generally experiences an *extremely* gratifying oral phase, characterized by tactile as well as oral/intestinal stimulation and pleasure. . . . What do we know of the oral character

---

[18] Doris Bernstein (1978, 1983) stresses the importance of the American father-daughter relationship in enabling the girl to effect an inner separation from the close mother-daughter tie.

and reactive oral sadism? The oral character may, as Abraham (1924) puts it, have 'a deeply rooted conviction that everything will always be well . . . always some kind person . . . to care for them and give them everything they need. This optimistic belief condemns them to inactivity' (p. 399). Now indeed the Hindu tends to leave things not only to family but to God and fate. He tends not to anticipate bad things. Dependency, too, is considered a significant oral trait. Where an excessive fixation has occurred, the 'general behavior' of the individual in Fenichel's (1945) words, 'presents a disinclination to care for himself and requires others to look after him' . . . 'this demand for care, may be expressed through extreme passivity or through highly active oral-sadistic behavior' (p. 489). Another facet of Indian character—generosity, the importance of giving and being given to—is also often connected with oral character structure, as is intense sociability and the wish not to be alone" (pp. 95–96).

Sylvan then goes on to write, "I should like to propose some additional . . . psychodynamic formulations with respect to Indian personality. First, that there is a dominance of oral sadism in a reactive form that is pervasive in interpersonal dealings. From this expression of oral sadism emerges the typical placating or apparently compliant attitude that has been amply—and often disparagingly—described by Western students, visitors, empire builders, etc. . . . And here I come to one of the most outstanding characteristics of Indian interpersonal relationships: the extreme difficulty of saying "no" and the virtual impossibility of refusing to do what someone has requested. *Overt* refusal is very, very hard. . . . And I think that the apparent compliance, the need to say 'yes,' not 'no,' the need to please at all times reflects not so much 'empathy' as a reaction-formation against oral aggression. Like all such mechanisms, however, it tends to gratify the repressed wish, for often that 'yes' causes great inconvenience" (pp. 95–96, 128).

I have quoted Sylvan at some length to demonstrate how psychoanalytic formulations of the oral stage are applied to Indian character and behavior, illustrating the kinds of leaps that the classical drive theorist makes between intrapsychic, psychosexual development and interpersonal relationships. I shall leave aside some of Sylvan's more Western-colonial pejorative attitudes, as well as some gross inaccuracies, such as Indians tending "not to anticipate bad things," "leaving things . . . to God and fate," and being condemned "to inactivity." What a drive theorist such as Sylvan profoundly misses is the whole nature and development of the Indian conscience, on the one hand, and many aspects of the early mother-child relationship as it is internalized into the child's psyche, on the other. He has not taken Freud's structural theory seriously as it is involved in cross-cultural work.

Far more relevant than reactive oral sadism to the patterns of interpersonal behavior he mentions, such as compliance and never directly saying "no," is the Indian child's internalization of strong social values in his ego-ideal and superego during the latency and adolescent periods. Reaction-formation is indeed frequently present, as Sylvan noted, but it is far more related to the strict latency-age superego resulting from the crackdown for proper behavior in hierarchical relationships than it is to the oral phase and oral sadism. The specific dictates and development of the conscience are thus much more central to subordination and related aspects of Indian character development and later behavior, as well as to the emphasis on certain defenses such as displacement and reaction-formation, than simply the vicissitudes of the drives.

In like manner, the pejorative ring to "pronounced oral traits" that seemingly condemn the person to inactivity or extreme passivity derives more from a kind of Western symbiotic mothering that is highly incongruent to the predominant dictates of separation-individuation and individualism, and thus is usually psychopathological, than to intense early libidinal gratification. In contrast to Sylvan (who was never in India), I have not particularly observed these negative oral traits in Indians, nor for that matter in Japanese, for both of whom there is normally much more prolonged symbiotic mothering with much greater libidinal gratification than in the northern European-American culture belt. Rather than passivity and inactivity, they have a highly sensitized receptivity to others.

In Western cultures, this classical psychoanalytic model has a certain degree of clinical explanatory power. But largely, I would submit, this is because child rearing has been relatively of one piece, with but minor variations; that is, the intrapsychic internalizations of the early maternal relationship, as well as superego development, have been quite similar in Western societies. Classical psychoanalysts have not usually realized that their generalizations made on the gratification-frustration patterns of the drives at each of the psychosexual stages are closely related to the complex nature of the mother-child emotional relationship and superego dictates.

In conclusion, from cross-civilizational psychoanalytic work it is evident that psychoanalytic drive theory needs serious amending. The vicissitudes of superego and ego-ideal development and early object-relations are as or more central to character development, later behavior, and the kinds of defenses that are emphasized than those of the drives alone.

THE INDIAN CONSCIENCE AND INTERNALIZATION

An important issue within cross-cultural psychoanalysis and psychoanalytically oriented anthropology is whether the Indian conscience—as well as related types of conscience in those from Asian and African societies—lacks the internalized psychological structures of the Western superego, and is basically dependent on externalized controls and guides such as elders of the family. Muensterberger's (1969) summary paper on psychoanalytic anthropology forcefully supports this point of view, which Kakar (1978, 135–136) agrees with. This becomes one more nail in the coffin of the inferiority of Eastern psychological makeup versus the Western.

As I have already amply delineated from psychoanalytic case material, the Indian conscience is profoundly internalized, but into psychic structures that develop and function significantly differently from those of Westerners, as well as having a different value orientation. Various aspects of the ego-ideal of Indians, such as its unwavering orientation to the reciprocities of specific hierarchical relationships in varying social contexts, its radar sensitivity to the cues and norms of a given situation and others' reactions, and its mythic orientation are all deeply internalized into psychic structures and an inner representational world. Even more obvious is the nature of the Indian superego that renders unacceptable the expression of all kinds of negative feelings in hierarchical relationships, and copes with them through a variety of conscious and unconscious defense mechanisms.

What tends to mislead the psychoanalytically oriented observer is that Indians are constantly sensitive to how others regard them and seem quite open to be guided and directed by an elder or other superior in their hierarchical relationships. I was constantly being asked in sessions, and usually quite sincerely, for direction and guidance, for what would make one a better person, or how to handle specific situations. But looking to others for approbation and guidance is also a deeply internalized structure of the Indian conscience. This way of reacting cannot easily be jettisoned, as is evidenced from Indians in the United States, where relationships do not call for this type of psychological functioning.

The Familial Self: Cognition

One of the more profound contributions of clinical psychoanalysis is the close relationship that has been shown between the internalization process and the resulting inner representational world on the one hand and ego functioning on the other. The kinds of psychological structures that are developed basically affect how one thinks, feels, and perceives relationships (Segal 1964). This fundamental insight, while highly relevant to psychoanalytic therapy, has never been utilized in cross-cultural psychoanalytic work, where differing contents and structures deriving from the internalization process can be related to differing kinds of ego functioning and cognition, depending on the civilizational context.

I would first like to illustrate how startingly different cognitive functioning can be as related to internalizations. My wife gave me directions to meet her at one of her Indian colleagues' home in a suburb of Bombay. In good American spatial terms, she told me first which road to take, then to make a sharp right turn to another road, and then to go to the fifth house from the corner. I had some difficulty finding it only because it was the third, not the fifth house from the corner. Whereupon our Indian hosts declared that there would have been no difficulty whatsoever finding their flat if only she had told me that it was in the building immediately adjacent to the burned-out house. It dawned on me then that almost every direction I had ever been given in India was in terms of relation to another building or landmark. Nothing was given in geometrical, objective space, but rather in relationship to another place—with the exception of those Westernized New Delhi planners who have taken extra pains to lay out their housing colonies in the most systematic, geometric way imaginable. Indians relate to so-called "objective space" in a Western sense in terms of personal relations and contexts. I would submit that this is a profound Indian perception of reality and the world as based on internalized personal relationships that are contextualized; and that one relates oneself to so-called objective reality in terms of these inner contextualized relationships, not as an individual monad in an impersonal geometric space (such as the third house from the corner), as in America. You are thus *always* located in relationship to others.

This insight was dramatically confirmed when an Indian family moved to the United States and first lived with us for a few weeks in New York City. I initially used American-style directions for their extremely bright, graduate school-educated daughter to go to New York University from our house in Greenwich Village. The directions in geometric space were quite simple: when you go out of our front door, turn right and go down our street for five blocks to University Place, then turn right for four blocks and you are there. She simply couldn't do it. It was only when I began citing mailboxes, St. Vincent's Hospital, the clocktower, and other Greenwich Village landmarks large and small *in relationship to each other* that she successfully negotiated the trip. They all formed a pattern of relationships that she could then relate herself to, each landmark becoming personalized or invested with affect.

Contextualizing, rather than universalizing, is central to Indian cognition as contrasted to Western (Ramanujam 1980). This is not only in areas I have already referred to, such as conscience, *dharma*, hierarchical relationships, space, and such, but also time, aesthetics, medicine, the various schools of Indian philosophy, and in fact almost everything, whether material or cultural. Thus, musical ragas are only to be played at certain times of day or seasons. Culturally speaking, nothing is quite equal: everything from the specific time of day, which has its own particular moods and flow, to specific houses, landscapes, whatever, all have their own substances, gross or subtle, which flow from their context to those around through permeable ego boundaries, thus affecting those in their proximity (Marriott 1976). Context is therefore very much affected by the substances involved in particular things. Psychologically, this seems to be experienced through everything in one's environment becoming personalized. Even so-called "impersonal" things or objects are related to on a personal basis, affecting one through being absorbed through permeable outer ego boundaries.

Related to contextualization is another major Indian cognitive mode, that of metonymic thinking (Ramanujan 1980), which posits, for instance, a profound interlinking between cosmic influences and/or past lives and the present life. Shakuntala easily assumed a congruence between attachments from past lives, planetary influences, unconscious fantasies from childhood, and her current love relationship with Kumar. In Ashis's case, his coming to see me for psychoanalytic therapy was related metonymically to astrological predictions from the Brighu *shastras*. Metonymic thinking does not imply a passive attitude to fate or destiny, but rather an orientation to working with destiny through ritual or action.

Metonymic thinking also relates to Hindus' mythic orientation and worship. Seeing another person or situation as belonging to a mythic context actually establishes them as being part of the myth, not simply

273

similar to the myth. Thus, a person can be seen as a partial manifestation of a particular god, goddess, or demon. Similarly, an idol that is being worshiped is not so much a symbol of a particular divinity as a partial manifestation.

Indian cognition is strongly oriented to the high-level abstractions of secondary process thinking in terms of contextualization, as well as mathematical and philosophical deliberations, and is less involved in self-reflection, universalistic abstractions, and critical, causal thinking (Ramanujan 1980). The Indian ego is also intensely involved in the imagistic thinking of the primary process. This makes complete sense from the work of Pinchas Noy (1969), who views the primary process as essentially related to the integrations and expressions of the self. In a culture that so emphasizes living in harmony within complex hierarchical relationships, with a highly cultivated subjectivity involved in mythology, ritual, and aesthetics, primary process thinking is highly adaptive.

Entitlement, the *Amae* Psychology, and the Japanese Self

There is a central issue in all of the cases I supervised in Japan that has important ramifications for an understanding of the Japanese familial self. In Mrs. K's case, it surfaced in her intense feelings of entitlement that husband, therapist, and mother should all sense and take care of her needs—in this case her painful feelings of childlessness—while she assumed little or no responsibility for communicating any of her feelings, and openly blamed her husband when she felt he didn't meet what she felt she was entitled to. These strong feelings of entitlement and blame were equally present in Kiyoshi's and Hiroshi's cases, as they were with two other cases I supervised, and with cases of a young man and young woman in Tokyo presented to me by Miss Yamagami. The entitlement is of a completely different magnitude and emphasis from that of not only my American patients but of my Indian ones as well. This is not normal dependence or even interdependence, but rather a highly passive demandingness with considerable underlying resentment if not rage when it is not fulfilled.

From what does this very particular kind of Japanese syndrome derive? And how is it related to the psychology of dependence (*amae*), which is accounted to be so central to the Japanese psyche? Further, what light does an analysis of entitlement shed on the overall development, structuralization, and functioning of the Japanese familial self? I shall attempt to answer these questions by utilizing my clinical understanding of the data of these patients in a cross-cultural perspective: not simply from the usual Japanese-Western psychoanalytic comparison, but much more from a Japanese-Indian one.

My impression is that there are three major interrelated factors in the Japanese maternal child rearing relationship that can generate such intense feelings of entitlement, resentment, and blame, and that all three have to be present for this to occur. The first is prolonged symbiotic mothering, where there is enormous emotional involvement and devotion with considerable physical closeness, caring, and affection. This results in both son and daughter being intensely emotionally tied to the mother in a relationship of dependence and interdependence, with diffuse outer ego boundaries, an inner representational world with images of self and other being closely interrelated, and a developmental emphasis on symbiosis rather than separation or autonomy. While this is very different from the dominant mode of American maternal care and child development, it is remarkably similar to the Indian mode. Thus the development of dependence with its various concommitants is as much Indian as Japanese. It is only in a Japanese-Western comparison, or for that matter an Indian-Western one, that it appears unique.[19]

The second factor revolves around the high degree of maternal empathy with the child's inner feelings, needs, wishes, temperament, and inclinations. In the close, emotionally involved mother-infant relationship, where the two are together throughout the day and night, the mother remains constantly and silently in tune with her child. As in the case of Indians, the empathic emphasis is oriented toward the child's moods, feelings, and wishes, and particularly toward needs of dependence, self-esteem, and affiliation rather than toward those for self-assertion, independence, and self-expression of the will, as is more the case with American mothering. This develops a high level of inner esteem in the child, which in later life is supported by constant social mirroring. Here, however, I must emphasize that it is crucial to differentiate maternal empathy from caring, affection, and emotional involvement. The

---

[19] Many traits that are considered unique to the Japanese are, I find, essentially similar to those of Indians and I suspect of other Asians as well. The emphasis on the uniqueness of the Japanese seems to derive from two sources: Japanese compare themselves more with Westerners than with other Asians, as they feel superior to the latter in their successful modernization; and part of the Japanese cultural heritage stresses Japanese uniqueness.

latter was almost always present in good measure in the Japanese case material, but the former was frequently insufficent or out of kilter.

The third factor is indeed more specific to the Japanese and involves intense maternal expectations for a very high degree of performance and skill in both relationships and tasks (DeVos 1973; White 1987). The mother uses her empathy with her child's particular makeup to encourage her child to be sensitively aware of others' feelings, moods, and needs so that she or he can be a cooperative, engaged, and harmonious group member; and as the child becomes older, gradually to observe strictly the detailed formal etiquette of numerous family and group hierarchical relationships through the proper respect language, appropriate gestures, and attitudes of compliance and deference. In this sense, there is much in common with the Indian mode of functioning in formal hierarchical relationships, although the social etiquette of Japanese hierarchy is more detailed and more rigorously observed.

What is more specifically Japanese is that the mother uses her empathic understanding to encourage and guide her growing children in persisting and concentrating in their work, in becoming fully emotionally engaged in doing something as well as possible, in enduring all kinds of hardships and overcoming obstacles, in examining themselves for faults and correcting them (White 1987), and for boys in competitively achieving in school. All of these are strong cultural ideals and values that the mother helps to inculcate in her child's character through utilizing her empathic sensing of her particular child's individuality, while using the leverage of the child's intense bondedness with her for his cooperation.

These maternal expectations are deeply incorporated into the ego-ideal of Japanese, and become a major source of esteem in performing on such a high level—as well as a major threat when any criticism or failure looms. This narcissistic dimension is further developed and reinforced by culturally promoted idealizations of elders and mentors, as well as in children's identifications with the self-idealizations of both parents. As another key part in living up to high levels of performance and being empathic with others, Japanese children are discouraged from dwelling on their own wishes and making them known. Instead, they initially rely wholly on their mother to sense their needs correctly; and on the basis of this paradigm later rely on others, ranging from the father, to teachers and mentors, to superiors at work to have concerned empathy with their needs and feelings, and to respond in a nurturing way.

Returning to the case material, in Mrs. K's, Kiyoshi's, and Hiyoshi's cases, the mother was indeed caring, affectionate, and deeply emotionally involved, had the culturally normal high expectations, but was in some way too much out of touch empathically with her child's inner world. This might be from being completely out of touch with herself as well, as with Mrs. K's mother; or from using her son too much for her own needs, as with Hiroshi's mother; or even from rejecting her son's inner world, as in Kiyoshi's case. Thus, in all three of these cases, as well as in others I have heard, the concerned empathic sensing which is so central to Japanese relationships was seriously out of kilter.

How then does this empathic failure result in such strong feelings of entitlement and blame in Japanese, whereas it rarely results in these reactions in Indians and Americans? It evidently is not due to frustrated *amae,* as a patient such as Mrs. K even complained of being overly indulged by her mother. "My mother is still overprotective of me, she even infantilizes me. All I want from her is for her to listen to me." Rather entitlement results from failure in empathy combined with the intense dependency relationship on one hand, and the internalization of very high maternal expectations for performance—the dependency relationship being quite different from that of Americans, while the maternal expectations are of another order from those of Indians.

It is as if these patients are implicitly saying, "I have tried so hard to live up to your high expectations of me, but in some way I have failed. (In Mrs. K's case it was her childlessness, while for Hiroshi and Kiyoshi it was poor performance in school.) You are to blame for my failure by being so out of tune with me and letting me down. But I am so dependent on you I cannot do anything myself. I am therefore deeply resentful and feel thoroughly entitled to be taken care of."[20] The other—in Mrs. K's case, her husband—is then supposed to make up for the failure without any initiative or communication on the suffering person's part. This sense of entitlement can well include the therapist, who is expected to remedy the patient's situation with little effort on the latter's part. In another sense, the feelings of failure, so painful to Japanese, become unconsciously reversed by experiencing the other as having failed oneself.

Another aspect of this syndrome is the development of a false self, with no awareness of any authentic feelings or wishes. When there is insufficient maternal empathy to recognize the child's inner individual-

---

[20] Of course blaming the other for insensitivity or nonrecognition does not always lead to these feelings of deep resentment and entitlement. The feelings can, for instance, be modified by culturally patterned attitudes of resignation or by reaction-formations generated by feelings of gratitude for the mother's sacrifices (pers. com. Nobuko Meaders).

ity, then all authenticity is given up to meet the high maternal expectations for performance. Mrs. K mentioned, "So far I use mother's responses as the major criteria to evaluate myself; therefore, unfortunately, I do not even know what kind of person I am." And at another time she related that she fulfilled her mother's expectations in learning a handicraft skill rather than becoming a schoolteacher, as she had originally wanted. In Kiyoshi's and Hiroshi's cases, they struggled to maintain a modicum of self-integrity by either doing poorly in or refusing to go to school.

It is significant to note that the major problem of those patients involved in Naikan Therapy (Reynolds 1983) is just those feelings of resentment and blaming of the mother that seriously interfere with the person's relationships. Naikan Therapy deals with these negative feelings toward the mother by reminding patients of how great her sacrifices and devotion were to them. This draws upon a major Japanese ethic of repaying one's debt to one's mother, as well as having remorse over any negative feelings toward her because of her great sacrifices; this enables feelings of gratitude to overcome those of resentment, blame, and entitlement. Psychoanalytic therapy, on the other hand, enables the patient to come more in touch with her own feelings and wishes as well as those of others, to alleviate a driven conscience, gradually to work out more satisfying relationships, and to begin developing a real sense of an authentic inner self. With these changes, entitlement and blame gradually subside rather than being suppressed. Like Naikan Therapy, psychoanalytic therapy in Japan helps to reintegrate the person within family and group relationships, but on a much different basis of resolving inner conflicts and deficits.

It is important to reiterate that the syndrome of passively demanding entitlement was not present in my clinical work with Indians. Two of the same factors are present with them as with Japanese: the highly prolonged mother-child, emotionally interdependent relationship, and the strong emphasis that the mother and others of the extended family be empathic with the child's emotional life and needs. But there is not the maternal expectations for a high level of performance that highlights failures and tends to inhibit persons' awareness of their own wishes, resulting in their being extremely dependent on the hierarchical superior's correct sensing of their needs. Indians seem far more in touch with their own wishes and wants, and are much freer to ask or maneuver to fulfill them, while still keeping in mind group needs.

In more normal Japanese functioning, persons are well grounded in fulfilling the intricate social etiquette of family and group hierarchical

278

relationships, at the same time performing at high standards of accomplishment. Simultaneously, the Japanese are still in touch with an inner authentic self (*hara*) that has been silently mirrored in their development. This polarity of meeting high social expectations while remaining in touch with oneself is always in a complex, dialectical relationship in Japanese. Inner individuality may well manifest itself subtly through the style in which the person enacts the formal etiquette (Doi 1986, 23–47). But it is only more directly communicated in trusted, insider intimacy relationships.

What, then, are the theoretical implications of this syndrome of entitlement, blame, and resentment for the *amae* psychology? Doi (1973), in effect, first drew attention to the central importance of emotional dependency (*amae*) in Japanese relationships. This not only occurs in the mother-child relationship and the intimacy relationships of friends and marriage, but also in various hierarchical relationships, where the fulfillment of obligations (*on*) through the performance of proper social etiquette is a vehicle for the gratification of dependency—the relationship between the two obviously varying according to the kind of relationship and persons involved.[21] Doi believed motivation in Japanese relationships to be primarily centered on this need for being passively loved and nurtured, and derived this need in adult life from the prolonged nurturing mother-child relationship, where the latter's wish to be passively loved denies any feelings of separation. Doi's emphasis on *amae* is closely related to Francis L. K. Hsu's (1971) stress on the qualitative or emotional nature of intimacy relationships in societies such as China, India, and Japan, and to my own focus on symbiosis-reciprocity.

Later writers (Kumagai 1981; Lebra 1976; and Taketomo 1985) have critiqued Doi's theory of *amae* on several points. Particularly cogent is the criticism that Doi's theory, like much of psychoanalysis, is far too individualistic in focusing on individual motivation only (for being passively loved) rather than on a profound interdependence and intimacy between two persons. That is, the motivation of the person who gratifies the one who wants gratification is equally central; thus *amae* should be seen as a "metalanguage," as Taketomo (1984) proposes, to connote this interdependent interaction with its complementary motivations, rather than as the motivation of the dependent person alone. These three au-

---

[21] Thus, in a traditional mother-in-law/daughter-in-law relationship, as in India, in the early years the formalities of an apprenticeship relationship predominate, but as the daughter-in-law has children and grows older, intimacy and dependency usually develop between the two.

thors further differentiate the *amae* interdependence in various social interactions.

From my understanding, the person who gratifies the other is also being given to, so that certain narcissistic needs are satisfied and intimacy is heightened by mutual gratification. Someone who becomes dependent immediately reinforces the other as superior in the hierarchical relationship, thus enhancing the latter's inner esteem by giving a sense of being needed and of being idealized, as well as by enabling the superior to live up to his or her inner ideals of nurturing the subordinate.

Two brief examples will illustrate this highly subtle exchange of dependency and narcissistic needs in Japanese hierarchical intimacy relationships; in the first case the process becomes short-circuited, in the other fulfilled. A patient reported in session that although he worked assiduously in his stepfather's business, he felt wounded because his stepfather didn't give him sufficient recognition. He therefore refused to ask the stepfather for all kinds of expensive material goods that his siblings requested, and which the stepfather as a successful businessman happily gave (pers. com. Yoshiko Idei). Because of the patient's deep resentment over being insufficiently appreciated, he refused to be dependent on the stepfather, well knowing that he would hurt the stepfather's feelings and esteem by not allowing the latter to give anything to him.

In the second example, a twenty-six-year-old Japanese woman in psychoanalytic therapy remarked, "My mother has never said she was lonely because I am living away from her in New York. However, I would write to her in the pose of *amae,* intending to be supportive of her desire to feel that I need her. . . . In order to express my indebtedness to her, I let her think with me. There is an aspect of her living through me" (Taketomo 1983). Although this woman was perfectly capable of making her own decisions, she wrote to her mother in a pose of being dependent (*amae*) in order to gratify her mother's sense of esteem through being needed, thereby enhancing their intimacy relationship.

Still another important critique is that Doi does not distinguish sufficiently between normal and pathological *amae* (pers. com. Hiroshi Wagatsuma and Mikihachiro Tatara), that is, between the passive fulfillment of dependency needs and a demanding, dependent entitlement. Doi seems to convey that psychopathology in Japanese is primarily due to an inability to *amaeru* or seek fulfillment of dependency wishes, which in turn derives from frustrated childhood *amae* relationships. In actuality, pathological *amae* or entitlement is more complex, as I have described above.

Even normal adult *amae* relationships, according to Lebra and especially Taketomo, must be viewed within a subtle interaction with strong ego-ideal demands for appropriate behavior—the indulgence of dependency needs being a mutually agreed upon deviation from internally expected social behavior. Or in other circumstances, *amae* can only be fulfilled as ego-ideal and social etiquette demands are being met. I would strongly suspect that in normal *amae* interdependency relationships, what has been crucial in childhood and still continues to be so is that the giver is not only willing to indulge the asker, but equally important is empathically in tune.

In conclusion, the amae psychology must expand from its present more exclusive stress on individual's passive dependency strivings to include complex interactions in interdependent hierarchical relationships, where issues of others' empathy and inner feelings of esteem are accounted for as well as an ego-ideal so oriented toward high standards of performance.

The Self in Japan and India:
A Psychoanalytic Comparison

Psychoanalytic cross-cultural analyses in India and Japan have always been in relation to the West, highlighting the unique psychological characteristics of Indians and Japanese as compared to Westerners (Doi 1973; Kakar 1978). A depth psychoanalytic comparison, however, has never been attempted between Indians and Japanese, nor for that matter with persons from any other Asian society.[22] The reasons for this are not difficult to ascertain. Key Indian and Japanese psychoanalytic therapists have been trained in the West and then returned home. It is from their intense personal experience of living in an entirely different life style while undergoing training by Western therapists on Western patients that they have probed self-reflectively their own psychological makeup. And in the process, they have forged meaningful cross-cultural psychoanalytic comparisons of their own countrymen with Westerners. None of these psychoanalytic therapists has, however, worked in another Asian country—thus the absence of any intra-Asian cross-cultural psychoanalytic analysis.

It would seem plausible simply to emphasize the psychological uniqueness of Japanese or Indians—as compared to Westerners—since

[22] There is now a psychological (in contrast to psychoanalytic) comparison on the self between Chinese, Indians, and Japanese (Marsella, DeVos, and Hsu 1985).

social science analyses evaluate their social structures as being radically different, not to mention important dimensions of their culture (Hoffman 1981; Nakane 1970). On closer scrutiny, however, there are profound psychological and psychosocial commonalities among Japanese and Indians that emerge from clinical psychoanalytic work. By comparing persons in these two Asian societies psychologically, it becomes feasible to evaluate what is truly unique to the Indian and Japanese self, and what are the important commonalities when predominant sociocultural patterns are hierarchical in nature. This comparative analysis can then be extended to encompass how Indians and Japanese have reacted psychologically to Westernizing/modernizing trends through an expanding self.

SIMILARITIES IN PSYCHOSOCIAL DIMENSIONS OF HIERARCHICAL RELATIONSHIPS

Certain broad similarities emerge from the clinical data in the structuralization of the familial-group self in Japan and the familial-communal self in India, as these selves function in family and group hierarchical relationships, although strikingly different balances between psychosocial dimensions of hierarchical relationships and the self also stand out. My clinical research in Japan has more than ever confirmed that there are three essential psychosocial dimensions to Eastern hierarchical relationships—structural hierarchy, the qualitative mode of hierarchical relationships, and hierarchy by quality—that are profoundly different from those of Western individualism. Further, various facets of the Japanese and Indian familial selves must be seen as congruent and interrelated with these three psychosocial dimensions as they vary in those societies.

In the qualitative mode encompassing intense emotional enmeshments, there is considerable similarity between Japanese and Indians inasmuch as both have far more open outer ego boundaries with less psychological space around themselves than in Westerners; a we-self that is far more relational; a strongly set inner ego boundary that preserves a much more private self; and a more developed interpersonal sensitivity and interdependence. The Japanese variant is that their outer boundaries are even more permeable or vaguer than Indian ones in the closer emotional enmeshment Japanese have in either the family or work group, which can result in a stronger inclination toward merger with the other and less *overt* individuality.[23] The Japanese private self seems

[23] These cross-cultural clinical observations accord with the more anthropological ones

even more distinctly private than that of Indians, and is usually communicated only by innuendo, whereas if Indians sense that the other is receptive and in tune, they can pour out immediately all kinds of personal feelings and thoughts. In terms of interpersonal sensitivity, Japanese seem to rely even more than Indians do on an empathic sensing of the other(s), with less overt verbal and nonverbal expressiveness.

The structural hierarchy in Japan is more vertical and pyramidal in nature (Nakane 1970), and is more governed by seniority and position in the group than it is in India. Although the female is overtly subordinate to the male in both cultures, there is a greater polarity in the balance between the two in Japan, where men are even more dominant than Indian men in the public sphere and Japanese women are even more controlling of the household and child rearing. Japanese follow more rigorously than Indians a traditional social etiquette through a complex respect language with proper proprietary behavior and gestures, whereas Indians will more readily convey by behavior or gesture underlying feelings of disagreement or resentment over unfair hierarchical expectations—while still observing proper etiquette on a more verbal level.

Various facets of the familial self relate to structural hierarchy in both societies. Japanese and Indians internalize into their consciences a greater sense of reciprocal responsibilities enacted through their public selves and a far more contextually-oriented ethic than Westerners have, while inhibiting any direct expression of anger or ambivalence to the superior. Although we-self regard is greatly fostered in both Japanese and Indians through constant mirroring and idealizations, the Japanese place even greater emphasis than Indians on the particular school, college, and work group that a male is involved in, whereas the Indian emphasis is somewhat more on the standing of the extended family in its particular *jati*. Japanese assume a posture of greater modesty and humility while praising the other than Indians do; but reciprocity is fully expected (Miyamoto 1983).

Both Japanese and Indians are constantly aware of the degree of intimacy and the nature of formal hierarchical expectations in any relationship, as well as distinguishing between insider and outsider relationships in which intimacy and interdependence are fulfilled through the former, and formal social etiquette predominates in the latter. Japanese

---

on India and Japan of Chie Nakane (pers. com.). It is much more difficult to be admitted into a Japanese group or family than to an Indian one, not only because of the firmer boundaries of the Japanese group, but also due to the greater enmeshment of persons within the group.

men usually reserve insider relationships (*uchi*) for family, friends, and close associates from the work group; outsider ones (*soto*) usually involve other members of one's group, neighbors, and such. For women, insider relationships are with family and friends. Similarly, Indians clearly distinguish between one's own people and others, the former being limited to members of the extended family and community, the latter including persons from other communities. Further variations occur inasmuch as Japanese are far more restrained in their dependency wishes in outsider relationships than Indians are, whereas Indians seem far freer to test out the possibilities of intimacy in what are initially outsider relationships, then bringing a responsive outsider into extended family insider relationships.

In the multi-leveled communication of Indians and Japanese that is related to social etiquette and private feelings, Indians have far more latitude in expressing their inner reactions both verbally and nonverbally.[24] Thus Indian modes of communication operate more overtly on more levels simultaneously than do the Japanese.

Hierarchy by quality is readily observeable in both India and Japan, where the particular qualities of a person may be idealized to the point of veneration, and where the superior person may or may not be the superior in the structural hierarchy—though in Japan the master-disciple relationship is greatly emphasized. In both cultures, idealization and identification with a qualitatively superior person aid in inner transformation toward the gradual realization of a spiritual self. In Indians, this transformation is formulated as attaining a more refined quality (*sattva*) and enhanced inner powers (*shakti*); in Japanese, it is considered as becoming more mature, wiser, and more natural.[25]

Broad aspects of child rearing are remarkably alike in both countries as they work to develop various facets of the familial self. Both societies

---

[24] A number of Japanese who have attended various conferences with Indians have commented on this. In an informal social situation at a meeting I attended, an Indian panelist who was chatting with his American colleagues suddenly turned to the Japanese panelist and commented that he seemed very quiet. There was a pause, after which the Japanese replied, "Silent yes, quiet no"—alluding to his restrained public self and his bustling inner private world.

[25] I became increasingly aware while in Dr. Tatara's group of psychoanalytic therapists that I was being evaluated not only on the basis of my psychoanalytic expertise, but also on my personal qualities and relationships—just as the group commented on these qualities in other psychoanalysts both Japanese and American. This attitude toward the idealized superior manifested itself in one Japanese psychoanalyst by his having a picture of his analyst in an honored place in his house—something I have not yet observed among any American colleague.

have prolonged, intense mother-child emotional involvement for fostering dependence, interdependence, and inner esteem, with the child sleeping by the mother far longer than in most Western societies (Caudhill and Plath 1974). After this prolonged period of early childhood gratification, there is a crackdown on the child, a requirement of proper behavior in hierarchical relationships from the ages of four or five through adolescence, leading to the devleopment of a strict conscience that starts far later than the American superego. The Indian and Japanese father, who tends to be overtly distant and reticent but covertly attached to his children, becomes a structuring counterpoint to the mother-child symbiosis. The Japanese variant is that the mother plays a more major role in grounding sons in the requisites of hierarchical relationships, and seems to start this training at a somewhat earlier age.

Differing Balances of Japanese and Indian Hierarchical Relationships and Familial Selves

Although the three essential psychosocial dimensions of hierarchical relationships are common to Japanese and Indians, together with similar congruent facets of the familial self, there are profound differences in the balances of the qualitative mode of hierarchical relationships with the structural hierarchy and with important dimensions of the familial self. In other words, the elements of hierarchical relationships and the familial self are often remarkably similar, but the balances are significantly different. The closer emotional enmeshment of Japanese in family and group hierarchical relationships, with vaguer and less defined outer ego boundaries, is balanced on the one hand by a stronger inner ego boundary preserving a more private, secretive self, and on the other by more rigorous observation of formally structured hierarchical relationships, with a much stricter and more complex social etiquette.

It is as if semi-merger with others in tight-knit family and work-group relationships has to be balanced in the Japanese by a more structured hierarchy, and by a more private self that maintains individuality. Conversely, Indians, being less emotionally enmeshed and having a socially sanctioned greater overt individuality, have a less secretive private self, and their public self observes the etiquette and obligations of the structural hierarchy less rigorously. Thus, the enmeshment of the qualitative mode is in balance with the formal hierarchy (the greater the enmeshment, the greater the need for formal structure) as well as with the inner, private self (the greater the enmeshment, the more secret the private self).

Psychologically speaking, neither the qualitative mode of hierarchical relationships nor the structural hierarchy can be meaningfully discussed without the other, nor for that matter without the private and public selves. These differing balances in hierarchical relationships and private and public selves are also centrally related to other key structures of the familial self: particularly the ego-ideal and we-self regard.

The stricter Japanese ego-ideal that derives considerably enhanced inner esteem from living up to extremely high internalized standards for social and task performance is centrally related to the much more rigorously observed etiquette of structural hierarchical relationships on the one hand, and to the need for a more secretive, private self, on the other. Without very strong inner standards of personal conduct in a public self, the strict, formalized etiquette of the structural hierarchy could never be realized. And because of these strict standards, less can be openly expressed or sometimes even felt.

Constant tension is generated in living up to these inner ideals in one's performance within the family and group (pers. com. Mikihachiro Tatara). Where hierarchical relationships are problematic in terms of the superior's expectations or behavior, Japanese have an inner standard of enduring in the face of adversity and persisting in one's position. At least for men, time out is granted through the vast entertainment and pleasure quarters of the cities, perhaps the largest in the world, in a townsman tradition that goes well back into the seventeenth century of the Tokugawa era (Plath 1980, 84–94). And in the reciprocities of structural hierarchical relationships, Japanese are acutely aware of the need for the other to be as perfect as possible in their performance, and of the vulnerability of the other to any criticism or intimation of failure. Thus, we-self regard is constantly supported in the other in reciprocal exchanges.

This strict Japanese ego-ideal is culturally congruent with little social sanction for entertaining different ideas and opinions from those of the head of the family or community (Nakane 1970), whereas Indians have a greater social lattitude for individualistic expression and for openly stating a variety of views. This is in part due to the constant exposure in India to much greater cultural and social diversity than in Japan, to Indian particularistic cultural notions that persons are born with certain characteristics and qualities that must be lived out (Anandalakshmi

1978),[26] and to more easy acceptance of ideological diversity within extended family insider relationships, which is the central psychological locus of an Indian's life.

HIERARCHY BY QUALITY AND THE SPIRITUAL SELF

My comparative analysis so far holds that two of the psychosocial dimensions of hierarchical relationships—the qualitative mode of intimacy relationships and the structural hierarchy with its formal social etiquette—are in differing balances in Indians and Japanese with a private self, with the kind of ego-ideal being the most salient factor related to the differing balances. One can view these balances and interactions on a two-dimensional spatial plane: the structural hierarchy, the degree of emotional enmeshment in intimacy relationships, and the private self are on one continuum; and the nature and strictness of the ego-ideal are on the other.

Where, then, does the third psychosocial dimension, hierarchy by the particular qualities of a person, enter? It is at this point that the spatial perspective becomes three-dimensional. It is with this person whom they deeply respect that they attempt to have as close a relationship as possible, to share in and identify with his or her superior qualities, and in the process to become inwardly transformed into superior persons themselves. It is in this transformational process, in which the other becomes a highly idealized selfobject, even at later periods in life, that there enters the third dimension of a spiritual self that psychologically affects all of the other dimensions.

By closely identifying with a person of superior qualities, Japanese and Indians can on the one hand fulfill the reciprocal responsibilities of hierarchical relationships with greater mastery and poise, respond to the inevitable narcissistic wounds and emotional frustrations of intimacy relationships with greater equanimity, and have a more stabilized private self with less anxiety and conflict. Further, the cultivation of a spiritual self through various disciplines enhances empathic capacities so central to functioning within Indian and Japanese society. Failure to recognize these aspirations and transformational processes in Indians and Japanese leaves only a very flat, two-dimensional view of their functioning.

[26] The Japanese also recognize an intrinsic self (*hara*) that is fundamental to a person's individuality.

287

Within each society, there are various modes to aid in this inner transformational process. Japanese modes range from a particularly strong emphasis on aesthetic disciplines[27]—tea ceremony, flower arranging, calligraphy, painting, poetry, and especially communing with nature[28]—to some of the martial arts such as judo and archery, to various forms of Zen meditation, to devotional forms of Buddhism. The concentrated manner of Japanese work and craftsmanship must also be viewed from this perspective of self-transformation. Involvement in aesthetic and other activities are not simply serious hobbies or recreation, as would frequently tend to be the case with Americans, but are much more a way of life geared to the inner cultivation of a spiritual self.[29] As with Indians, in most of these activities there is almost inevitably a hierarchical superior with superior qualities that the subordinate is not only deferent to but usually venerates as well.

Indian involvement in overlapping approaches toward self-realization will be discussed in the following chapter.

[27] Internalized values of perfectionism in Japanese, according to Yasuhiko Taketomo, are related to Japanese aesthetic norms and disciplines (pers. com.).

[28] Japanese aesthetic modes of self-transformation have historically been considerably influenced by Chinese Taoism.

[29] These activities end with "do," (e.g. judo), which connotes that the activity is a discipline for cultivating the inner self through a whole way of life (pers. com. Mikihachiro Tatara).

The Spiritual Self:
Continuity and Counterpoint
to the Familial Self

Without positing the realization of an inner spiritual self (*Atman*)—a self considered to be one with the godhead (*Brahman*)—as the basic and ultimate goal of life (*moksha*), it is virtually impossible to comprehend Indian psychological makeup, society, and culture.[1] The assumption of an inner spiritual reality within everyone and the possibility of spiritual realization through many paths are fundamental to the consciousness and preconscious of Indians. Within an Indian context, these assumptions have to be explicitly denied when they are not implicitly adhered to—in contrast to the dominant rational-scientific culture of the contemporary secular West, where they are usually ignored or denigrated.[2]

This is not to say that all Indians are actively engaged or even interested in spiritual pursuits and disciplines. Nor is this meant to minimize the increasing numbers of Americans seriously involved in one or an-

---

[1] This particular way of expressing the spiritual self is that of Advaita Vedanta philosophy.

[2] There are, of course, numerous exceptions to the dominant positivistic, scientific world view in the West, ranging from groups mystically oriented within Catholicism, Protestantism, and Judaism to others in the arts.

other form of Eastern discipline. I am simply emphasizing the prevailing views of reality in contemporary Indian and American consciousness.

To give an idea of how deeply these assumptions are ingrained, one woman patient, Rashi, with two very young children bemusedly commented one session, "I know if I get up at 4 A.M. every morning and meditate and pray, sooner or later I shall experience God. But I am just too tired to get up so early." Or on a more serious note, some highly respected social scientists with doctorates from major American and English universities commented, "no matter what position you are in life, it (the spiritual self) kind of tugs at your coattails."[3] I have not yet heard anything close to these kinds of comments from patients, colleagues, or friends in America, regardless of ethnic or religious background, unless they are themselves seriously involved in a spiritual quest.

With three of my eighteen Indian patients, unless I took their spiritual aspirations seriously, psychoanalytic therapy would have been adversely affected. To have ignored or denigrated Ashis's frequent associations around his involvements with spiritual persons and his own practices as regressive or psychopathological would have resulted in serious problems in working together. Even more to the point, when Shakuntala sensed the unreceptiveness of her former therapist to her spiritual life, she simply left her inner struggles around this major dimension out of her free associations. Yet psychoanalytic therapy was highly relevant in both cases in helping them toward some partial resolution of inner conflicts and deficits that were having a stultifying effect on their spiritual pursuits: Ashis's inner conflicts with his father needed to be ameliorated for him to pursue his writing as *sadhana;* whereas Shakuntala had to resolve her lack of discipline resulting from paternal indulgence, which interfered with the assiduous practice of daily meditation.

The spiritual dimension was even more central in the psychoanalytic therapy of Rashmi, a Hindu woman artist who had arranged her own marriage in the modernized circles of Bombay. Rashmi experienced intense anxiety that her strong spiritual strivings involving her painting had no place whatsoever in this marriage, as her husband, though a substantial man, was not at all oriented in this direction. Through dream analysis, the roots of Rashmi's intense anxiety became clarified. A maternal uncle, a highly venerated holy man, had greatly encouraged Rashmi in her childhood in spiritual pursuits and painting, but unfortunately had died when she was eleven. When her family then spent their time with her father's family, Rashmi felt stultified by them, as they seemed

---

[3] Comments made at the Centre for the Study of Developing Societies in Delhi.

to lack any genuine spiritual presence. Later she was able to resume cultivation of her inner life through art with a couple of unusual teachers. By interpreting an unconscious displacement wherein she unwittingly perceived her husband as being as threatening to her inner development as her father's family, her anxiety subsided appreciably, and she was able to continue reasonably comfortably with both her painting and her marriage.

It is further assumed in the Indian cultural context that everyone is at different stages along the road, inwardly evolved and involved to varying degrees, and that only the extremely rare person has attained a high degree of self-realization. In the Indian cultural context, it is that person, or ones actively engaged in the search, who are profoundly respected at all levels of society. As an instance, a highly respected Indian psychologist related that as she got off her train in Delhi in the early hours of the morning, the taxi drivers were rather sour over the prospect of getting up and driving her home—until she said, "Oh, come on, I've just returned from a pilgrimage and I'm exhausted." One immediately took her home.

To discuss the spiritual self meaningfully one must immediately confront two major issues. First, it is impossible to write about the spiritual self perceptively unless one has undergone various practices for extended periods of time. Haas (1956) has cogently asserted that there is nothing mystical in mysticism: one simply has to be intensely involved—and have both talent and inclination in this direction—in various disciplines such as breathing and meditation, prayer and worship, and to be so involved over extended periods of time under the tutelage of an instructor to have some idea of what it is all about. (The same, of course, is true for psychoanalysis, where it is extremely difficult to have any real sense of unconscious motivation, defenses and conflict, as well as transference, resistances, and dream analysis without going through one's own psychoanalysis.) What various writers and others have described is that these spiritual practices are generally geared toward a calming and concentrating of the mind and emotions, so as to permit an inner transformation, allowing the emergence of other levels of consciousness and being.

The second major difficulty resides in the issue of terminology: there are no truly accurate concepts for what are ineffable inner experiences. Thus myths and metaphors, parables, and other imagery have inevitably been used by those who have realized the spiritual self to convey some sense of their experiences. I am fully aware that my concept of the spiritual self is no better than other concepts traditionally used. From a psychological standpoint, what I am trying to convey is that phenomenologically there is a different inner experiential ego state or kind of consciousness separate from everyday waking and dream consciousness, with a different sense of inner being. Perhaps aesthetic experiences are experientially closest to the kinds of inner ego states present in various centering and meditative practices. The spiritual self is also immanent in that these inner states of consciousness and being are actually experienced and are not transcendent in the way spoken of by Kant and other Western philosophers.[4] Further, that there are inner psychological structures and inclinations of a very different kind from what we encounter in psychoanalytic work that may be actualized through various spiritual disciplines, or allowed to remain nascent and quiescent.

There is the still further difficulty in addressing a Western psychoanalytic audience on various aspects of the spiritual self. The spiritual self is certainly a topic that has never received any welcome reception within the psychoanalytic community, with important exceptions in the Jungian group and certain segments of neo-Freudian psychoanalysis. Although Freud (1927, 1930) was somewhat wary of making definitive valuations in this area, instead directing his attention to the role of religion within the psyche of the Western common man, he and other psychoanalysts have approached any spiritual search as being essentially reducible to some form of compensation or psychopathology. In our more sophisticated psychoanalysis of today, the spiritual self is usually relegated to an unconscious effort to reassert symbiotic union with the mother—a newer version of the oceanic feeling. In its place, Freud and psychoanalysis has posited the ideal of the rational, scientific man (Meltzer 1978).

This reductionistic strategy of psychoanalysis—which Leon Edel (1966), the literary critic, referred to as leaving muddied footprints in other disciplines—has been taken over by other psychoanalytic writers about Indian personality. Carstairs (1957), coming from a Kleinian viewpoint, has rendered the spiritual path as motivated by unconscious infantile fantasies of trying to regain infantile omnipotence, repossession of the early gratifying mother and intense gratification of infantile sexuality, and the symbiotic togetherness of prenatal existence. More recently, J. Moussaieff Masson (1976, 1980), a Sanskrit scholar later trained in

[4]Kant used the concept of the transcendent self as a reality that transcends human cognition and the categories of the mind, but is essentially unknowable and beyond experience. The first part of his conception is similar to the Indian notion of *Atman*, but the last part is definitely not.

psychoanalysis, has asserted reductionistic strategies *ad absurdum* in the area of Indian studies by drawing upon the full psychoanalytic armamentarium of psychopathology. His seemingly meticulous Sanskrit and psychoanalytic scholarship are unfortunately flawed by his wild methodology of speculating loosely on ancient Indian texts as well as modern Indian biography without any effort whatsoever to ground his speculations in any actual clinical data of Indian patients who are involved in spiritual disciplines.[5] Finally, Edward Shils (1961), a sociologist, simply agrees with the standard psychoanalytic formulation that the striving for *moksha* is for symbiotic reunion or merger with the mother. One can thus be Kleinian or classical or even contemporary Freudian in outlook, but the overwhelming reductionism on the spiritual self in Indian personality remains.

On the other hand, there are occasional psychoanalysts who indicate a different position. The English psychoanalyst and artist, Marion Milner, cites her personal meditation experiences in an unpublished paper, while also reviewing the more explicit mystic positions of Bion (1977)— the latter being one of the only psychoanalysts besides Jung and his followers to introduce this dimension into psychoanalytic thinking. R. D. Laing, involved in Buddhism, also belongs to this group, though he was omitted from Milner's paper. More forthright involvement in American psychoanalytic circles has come mainly from the Karen Horney group, Erich Fromm, and Erik Erikson. Karen Horney, Harold Kelman, David Shainberg, Antonio Wenkert, and others of this group, originally inclined in this direction from their interest in Hassidic Judaism and Martin Buber, later became involved in Zen Buddhism through Dr. Akihisa Kondo, who was in training with them. Kondo introduced Horney and Fromm to D. T. Suzuki, the renowned teacher of Zen Buddhism; Fromm then influenced a number of members of the William Alanson White Institute in New York City. Erikson (1958, 1969) has, of course, a longstanding interest in "homo religiosus" through his work on Martin Luther and Gandhi. In recent years, other American Freudian psychoanalysts have become deeply interested in the spiritual self: Margaret Brenman-Gibson, an associate of Erikson;[6] Harmon Ephron, cofounder of the Flower Fifth Avenue Psychoanalytic Institute, with his wife, Pat Carrington, and a few other associates;[7] and Elsa First, trained

[5] There is also criticism of Massons's scholarship and methodological approach by Sanskritists. See Wilhelm Halbfass's (1982) review of *The Oceanic Feeling*.

[6] Dr. Brenmen-Gibson's interest has mainly centered in Transcendental Meditation.

[7] Patricia Carrington's (1977) book summarizes the results of numerous research projects in America on various forms of simple meditation or centering techniques. In one

at Hampstead in London, and currently practicing and writing in New York City.[8] Morris Carstairs himself has in recent years become involved in Tibetan Buddhism.

The Familial and Spiritual Selves: Continuity

The interrelationship between the Indian familial self and the spiritual self is psychologically far more complex and paradoxical than meets the eye. The spiritual self simultaneously encompasses both continuity with and counterpoint to various aspects of the familial self. Hindu thought recognizes the psychological phenomenon or experiential duality of the phenomenological self (*jiva atman*), particularly in the everyday consciousness of I-ness (*ahamkara*) versus the inner experience of spirit or *Atman*. Simultaneously, Hindu philosophy is profoundly monistic—in contrast to Western thought, which emphasizes dualities between spirit and matter, sacred and secular—in its positing various aspects of the phenomenological world, including the phenomenological self, as essentially manifestations of spirit (*Brahman*).[9] Experientially, a person may not be aware of this. Further, the fundamental goal of all relationships and living is the gradual self-transformation toward finer and subtler qualities and refined aspects of power in the quest for self-realization.[10] Thus, my paradoxical assertion that the spiritual self is simultaneously on a continuum with the familial self and in counterpoint to it spells out psychologically both the Hindu monistic position and the dualistic, experiential one.

Continuity is present in a variety of ways that are quite different from what has been imagined and implied by psychological writers, particularly those in the reductionistic stance of psychoanalysis (Carstairs 1957; Masson 1976, 1980; Shils 1961), while the strong counterpoint between the two is completely overlooked. There appear to be five major categories of continuity, all interrelated in a variety of ways. Broadly speaking, these bridges between the two selves are: the presence and utiliza-

---

chapter she recounts the interesting results of a small group of psychoanalytic therapists who have used simple meditation techniques themselves and with their patients.

[8] Elsa First, like Morris Carstairs, follows Tibetan Buddhism. I know of at least three therapists who have become interested in various aspects of meditation through being introduced to it by their children.

[9] Again, this is the position of the Advaita Vedanta school of philosophy.

[10] This cultural view is formalized in Sankyan philosophy, particularly in its emphasis on the different qualities (*gunas*).

tion of certain psychosocial dimensions of hierarchical relationships in realizing the spiritual self; a Hindu cultural world view giving spiritual meaning to interpersonal transactions and the various goals and stages of life; a mythic orientation to everyday relationships; a magic-cosmic involvement with destiny; and the practice of a wide variety of rituals frequently associated with both myths and magic-cosmic correspondances.

HIERARCHICAL RELATIONSHIPS AND THE SPIRITUAL SELF

One can readily observe that certain central structures of the familial self, ones especially oriented around hierarchical relationships by quality and the qualitative mode of hierarchical relationships, are frequently intensely involved in ongoing efforts to realize the spiritual self. In hierarchical relationships governed by the quality of the person, there is a marked veneration of the superior, with strong efforts to subordinate oneself, to be as close as possible, to have *darshan*, in order to incorporate, identify with, and share in the superior qualities of the other for inner self-transformations. These focal attitudes of hierarchy by quality, originating in childhood, are later extended to more and more venerated beings—from highly respected familial and community members to gurus and to the worship of various gods, goddesses, and avatars or incarnations—in a continuity between the familial self and spiritual self. As an example, Ashis in his devoted readings of Tagore, Gandhi, and Coomaraswamy was trying to associate himself as closely as possible to share in their superior qualities, as he did even more with two outstanding benefactors at work.

In *bhakti* devotional worship, various facets of symbiosis-reciprocity involved in hierarchical intimacy relationships become clearly accentuated. Intense emotional connectedness and reciprocal affective exchanges, a sense of we-ness, and permeable ego boundaries are all intensely involved in *bhakti* worship. The devotee seeks through intense emotionality to be merged with the god, goddess, or incarnation—whether Shiva, Durga, Krishna, or whomever—and in turn through the merger expects the reciprocity of divine bliss. Sensuality becomes intensely heightened, and becomes an important facet of *bhakti* religious experience (Miller 1977). In the worship of Krishna, the most frequent form of the *bhakti* cults, men draw upon their early identification with the maternal-feminine to identify consciously with Radha in her divine passion for Krishna.

295

It is not difficult to see why psychologically these modes of religious worship, which so stress longings for and experiences of merging with the god, are overwhelmingly reduced in psychological writing to a regressive pull to the elation and omnipotent union in the early mother-infant symbiotic tie (Carstairs 1957; Kakar 1983, 151–190; Masson 1976, 1980; Shils 1961). The psychological reality is, however, not that the path of *bhakti* is a regression to more symbiotic modes of relating, but that the aspirants use their internalized symbiotic modes in the service of their spiritual practices. Further, the imagery of a symbiotic, familial mode of relating becomes a metaphor for another level of union, or at minimum a complex interplay of different levels of a monistic reality in intentional ambiguity.[11]

What has been profoundly overlooked is that however much these religious modes of worship and experience are related to the intense mother-child symbiotic relationship, the actual religious experience enables the person to become increasingly individuated, differentiated, and separated from the intensely emotional, familial involvements. This experience thus becomes an essential counterpoint to the familial self.

Transactions, Transformations, and the Spiritual Self

Another major category of continuity between the familial self and the spiritual self is the Hindu world view that gives meaning to the reciprocal exchanges so fundamental to hierarchical relationships as self-transformations. As Marriott and other ethnosociologists have increasingly spelled out, all kinds of transactions and exchanges, as well as the directionality of how much and what one gives and receives, are utilized or avoided to enable the person to move toward the more subtle and purer substances and qualities and more refined power, and away from the grosser ones in their inner transformations. Profound cultural assumptions are present that everything transacted and exchanged between people from food to words are substances of grosser or finer nature, that through permeable boundaries they enter and help transform a person's nature, and that anyone's nature is a particular composite of a variety of substances and qualities, and is therefore different

---

[11] Margaret Egnor (1980) elaborates the notion of intentional ambiguity as central to Hindu culture, particularly in its playfulness with different levels of reality. Ambiguity is emphasized and embraced in the subtle, multiple levels of communication, in the acceptance of opposing models of the universe, in the double nature of many Indian deities, in the social position of women, and in many other aspects of Indian culture and society.

from another's. Those persons and/or groups who deal in subtler substances (such as teachers) have traditionally been accorded greater respect and hierarchical rank socially.

Another part of this internalized Hindu world view involving self-transformation are basic orienting concepts around *dharma, karma,* and *samskara.* These give meaning to various aspects of the familial self in its multiple relationships and experiences in a monistic continuum with the spiritual self, and are really concerned with a soul in pilgrimage to its ultimate spiritual realization throughout a multitude of lives. Thus, by living correctly according to one's *dharma,* a person also moves along his or her spiritual path. How one life is lived affects the circumstances in another (*karma*), which in turn will affect the future life. And the kinds of relationships, experiences, and deeds constantly leave imprints (*samskaras*) that effect inner transformations. Not only is meaning given, but all kinds of practices are attended to that will, it is hoped, further inner transformation—such as eating certain foods and avoiding others.

The life cycle is seen in a similar light. If the first two stages—that of student and householder, examples par excellence of the familial self—are lived properly according to one's *dharma,* which also encompasses the proper fulfillment of desire (*kama*) and wealth and power (*artha*), then there are inner transformations that help the person toward realization of the spiritual self in the third and fourth stages of life. To whatever extent these cultural orientations are implemented, they lend symbolic significance for interconnecting the familial and spiritual selves in a monistic cultural style.

MYTHIC ORIENTATION AND THE SPIRITUAL SELF

One of the strongest lynchpins linking the familial and spiritual selves in Hindus is their mythic orientation, an essential part of their conscience. Women, especially, traditionally experience everyday relationships within the framework of myths, which are a guide to the complex familial hierarchical relationships and situations.

Simultaneously, the myth also conveys the presence in everyday relationships of the divine and the demonic through metonymic thinking (Ramanujan 1980) that links these relationships with mythic images in a monistic view of reality. Thus, aspects of another reality may manifest themselves through relative, friend, or stranger. The myth always allows for the interplay of a spiritual level of reality and self in what is seemingly the most mundane and prosaic of persons and relationships. In the myths themselves, although some are much more oriented toward varied aspects of hierarchical relationships and the familial self, and others stress more the spiritual self and reality, the two levels are almost always intertwined (O'Flaherty 1980). The myth therefore constantly orients the person toward the continuity of the familial and spiritual selves in everyday life, while at times it is a strong counterpoint to both the familial self and hierarchical relationships. Hanchette (1982) and Wadley (1975) report that mothers aspire to embody characteristics of one or another mother goddess in their everyday mothering relationships, thus using mythic models to integrate aspects of a familial with a spiritual self.

A strikingly moving personal example of this mythic orientation was related to me by an Indian psychologist. She was visiting her family at a time when her sister had just undergone an operation, when life-threatening postoperative complications set in. "I suddenly awakened after midnight and felt I just must go to the hospital. My parents didn't stop me though it was very late. . . . When I got there, I found a few nurses in her room. She seemed in a terrible state. I could just sense the vibrations that the nurses expected her to die and that she soon could. I immediately sent them all out and said I would take care of her. I began to pace up and down the room, always looking at my sister and keeping in mind images of the Himalayas from my recent pilgrimage. I was absolutely determined not to let her die. I had become Savitri to wrest her from the hands of death. A couple of hours later I somehow knew there was a turning point and she would be all right. The next morning after she awakened, my sister told me that she had a dream that night of slowly and uncontrollably sinking into a morass, when suddenly a hand reached out and pulled her out. She now felt much better, and soon recovered." It became evident how this woman drew upon a lifelong childhood identification with the mythic figure, Savitri—a wily and determined woman who tricked Yama, the god of death, from taking her husband as was fated—to help rescue her sister.

From this perspective there is no opposition in Indian culture between myth as social charter (Malinowski 1954, 108)—that is, as guideline to extended family and communal hierarchical relationships—and myth as indicative of a spiritual reality and self.[12] Both are always implicitly present. Very little study has been made, however, of the everyday psychological use of myths in this dual perspective.[13] Western psychoanalysts of whatever persuasion are faced with the situation that their patients simply do not have an everyday mythic orientation to life because

[12] This opposition has been posited by O'Flaherty 1980.
[13] Exceptions to this are Roy 1979, B. K. Ramanujam 1980b, and Obeyesekere 1981, 1984.

there is no vitally alive mythic culture, except perhaps in isolated pockets. Jungians, by the use of dreams and various products of the imagination, do dredge up mythic and archetypal themes that they then relate
to the person's life. But even here, Western persons are not psychologically functioning with the myth as a pervasive part of their mental space
from childhood. Since there is almost nothing written on an everyday
mythic orientation in Western psychoanalysis and psychology, and since
these are the theoretical models for Indian therapists and psychologists,
the latter are rarely oriented toward research in this area—even when
some of them are personally highly involved in a mythic orientation.
Instead they take for granted their own mythic functioning; or as Kakar
(1978) does, follow the traditional path of psychoanalysis in simply using myths to elucidate psychological makeup.

MAGIC-COSMIC INVOLVEMENT WITH DESTINY
AND THE SPIRITUAL SELF

Profoundly linking the familial and spiritual selves is the fourth category
of a magic-cosmic involvement with destiny.[14] Indians are deeply concerned with the unfolding of destiny, not only of persons, but also of
families, *jatis,* and now political parties and leaders. Implicit are the
gradual inner transformations of the familial self as they take place through
destiny in the vicissitudes of everyday relationships. Indians tend to be
constantly on the look-out for signs and predictors, relying a great deal
on the magic-cosmic to arrange and manage their practical affairs and
relationships—marriage, education, career, children, health, wealth, and
power—as auspiciously as possible. This everyday conscious and preconscious awareness of the magic-cosmic involvement with destiny is
profoundly ingrained as a major dimension in the Hindu psyche in a
way that it simply is not true of the overwhelming majority of contemporary Westerners.

Culturally speaking, destiny is essentially linked to the unfolding of a
person and/or group's moral actions and experiences and attachments
from past lives, and to the influence of celestial bodies in the present—

---

[14]I am here using magic-cosmic as Haas (1956) does, not in its pejorative sense within
the current Western rationalist-scientific world view, but rather as a nonrational, noncausal monistic relationship between planetary and other celestial bodies with past lives on
one hand, and with everyday relationships and events on the other, through correspondances, identities, and emanations that are metonymically understood. Philosophically, this
is based on the idea that human beings constitute a microcosm with a number of inner
correspondances and identities with the forces of the macrocosm or cosmos.

all of these influences being played out in everyday relationships and situations metonymically, and varying considerably with the particular person and situation (Pugh 1977, 1978). This unfolding of human destiny can be revealed through astrology and palmistry, clairvoyant and telepathic dreams, premonitions, contact with the spirit world, and such. It is evident that the magic-cosmic world is by no means a unitary one; rather it encompasses a variety of dimensions and methods.

The magic-cosmic world was referred to at one point or another by all of my Indian patients, and seemed to constitute an important area of their cognitive map of reality, particularly for my Hindu patients. Ashis, more than any of the others, was constantly using readings from the magic-cosmic world in the form of palmistry consultations with Professor Mukerjee to gain direction in his career. But the directions suggested by Professor Mukerjee were not simply to achieve some kind of career success; they were much more to develop and utilize Ashis's literary-meditative or spiritual side of himself in his work—something Ashis could only do to a limited extent because of inner conflicts with his father's values. His mode of working with Professor Mukerjee seems analogous to what was reported in an anthropological investigation into astrological advisory sessions.[15]

Shakuntala and Meena, like most women, used predictions from astrology and/or palmistry regarding their prospects for marriage—the latter maintaining hope from them in her thirties that she would finally be married. Shakuntala also had premonitions a family member would die. Rustum and Ashis, like most men, used readings from astrology and palmistry for direction and advancement in career. The former's engineering education in the United States was arranged solely on the basis of an astrological consultation, although his family are highly Westernized Parsees.

Clairvoyant dreams were reported in detail by Shakuntala and Laxmi, as well as by others on social occasions. The openness toward having clairvoyant dreams is not only infinitely greater than what I have encountered in New York City, but Hindus also have a decided penchant to act on a dream they believe to be clairvoyant—thus fulfilling their destiny. As an example, a psychoanalyst offhandedly related the following dream and its sequel: "I dreamt of a holy man or *sadhu* staying in

---

[15] Through mutual collaboration, astrologer and client establish a contextual framework for celestial readings and influences in everyday problems and relationships, which are then understood metonymically in terms of correspondances and identities between the two—with advice then being given as to how to handle these problems through certain actions and rituals (Perinbanayagam 1981).

a room on the third floor of a building on Grant Road (Bombay). The next morning after having the dream, I got in my car and drove over to Grant Road. There was a building just like the one in my dream. I got out of the car, went to that room on the third floor, knocked on the door and went in. There was the *sadhu*. I said to him, 'You appeared in my dream, so I thought I would come over to meet you.' "

Still another dimension of the magic-cosmic world related to the unfolding of destiny is the spirit world. In counseling sessions with three different groups of female college students, there was a recurrent theme: they were all involved in trying to contact the spirit world for advice and predictions as to what would happen to them. Both a social worker and a psychoanalyst gave the following psychodynamic explanation: these sixteen- and seventeen-year-old adolescent girls would have arranged marriages in only a few years with absolutely no say on their part as to who the husband or the husband's family would be, and would carry the whole burden of adjustment on their shoulders. They were therefore trying to contact the spirits as a common adolescent way of trying to assert control over their lives and destiny. But what was even more striking is that both of my colleagues, in voicing their psychological insight, did not in the least deny the existence of the spirit world—that is, souls between reincarnations—or the possibility that the spirits could shed light on these girls' destiny.

It also emerged from the case data that there is an active stance toward altering or shaping destiny through counteracting adverse influences and maximizing good ones. This sharply contrasts with the usual Western stereotype of Indians' passive resignation and acceptance of fate. Thus, Ashis asserted himself in a number of directions to try to fulfill Professor Mukerjee's guidance to develop the more literary-meditative side of his talents; as did Meena in trying to arrange her own marriage through putting marital ads in the newspaper and contacting her social network for potential spouses. Viewed from one angle, their actions were in many respects similar to what many Americans would do. But from another angle, their inner sense of themselves was much more connected to larger forces and influences than is that of Americans; they feel connected to a much longer time perspective, to a sense of inner evolution through life events and relationships, and to an ultimate sense that their efforts would only prove fruitful if they were in accord with their destiny.

For Shakuntala, a ritual was used to maximize an auspicious time and offset adverse planetary influences, the assumption being that through the self-transformations involved in performing the ritual, her marital destiny might be partially altered. Anthropological studies report other methods that are used, ranging from alms-giving, taking vows, and going on pilgrimages to using appropriate gems, charms, and concoctions, to observing auspicious or inauspicious times and cycles for undertaking various ventures, to associating with persons of counteracting influences. All of these methods are to aid in inner transformations that will reverse or mitigate adverse celestial influences and/or *karma*. This integral connection between remedial measures and astrology was matter-of-factly expressed by a woman educated in a British-style boarding school, who related that she had little use for astrology because she was away from home so much that she could not learn the necessary rituals to counteract adverse celestial influences as revealed through astrological readings (Mehta 1970).

As psychologically important as the magic-cosmic involvement with destiny is to the Hindu, it is anathema to the scientifically educated Western mind. Westerners, with but rare exceptions, respond to the magic-cosmic in Indians as superstition and ignorance. It is simply too much for the Western mind, grounded in well over a century and a half of rationalism, science, empiricism, and positivism to take very seriously. Nor are American South Asian specialists necessarily exempt from these reactions.

According to Haas (1956), the objectivization of phenomena and the fundamental split between subject and object in the Western mind has all but obliterated the magic-cosmic world from Western consciousness; it has survived only in rare pockets, and has been resurrected in certain artistic and philosophical circles over the last hundred years or so by Theosophy and Anthroposophy (Washton-Long 1980), and now in the "counterculture" by a host of Eastern teachers. But since the magic-cosmic world is still perceived so negatively by the dominant world view of modern Western culture, many of its current manifestations are shadow reactions occurring in highly commercialized, degenerative forms (pers. com. Manisha Roy).

In an interview, Professor Mukerjee commented, "The West has investigated issues of causality and time, place and person, but not of destiny. In the sense of destiny, time becomes extremely complicated; it is not a linear sense of time at all. There are issues of premonitions as to what will happen in the future, what part one will have and what part one can play. This concern with human destiny is deeply tied in with the ultimate goal of spiritual realization. The ability to see destiny and cosmic influences is related to yogic practices and a person's spiritual development."

The magic-cosmic involvement with destiny and self-transformation is as much present among highly educated, scientifically trained Indians as it is among the uneducated. Scientists generally experience little if any conflict between objectivization and analysis of phenomena in the scientific approach and their concern with destiny. They simply view these two endeavors as related to different layers of reality, each valid on its own level; they have a wide toleration of the ambiguity involving different levels of reality, as is central to Hindu culture (Egnor 1980; Nandy 1980a).

How are we to understand Indian involvement in the magic-cosmic world from a psychological standpoint? It is apparent that Indians, from illiterate villagers to educated urbanites, live in a highly peopled world, not only the social world of kinsmen and other groups, but with a whole inner host of more invisible powers, influences, and spirits that can affect them through permeable ego boundaries. In turn, the person can exert influence on this invisible world through rituals and other means.

Can a psychoanalyst comment meaningfully on the magic-cosmic, including psychic phenomena and the spirit world? Freud (1922) gradually recognized the validity of phenomena like telepathy; but he focused primarily on telepathic occurrences as relating to patients' unconscious motivations and processes of distortion, rather than on the nature of psychic phenomena themselves. Since Freud, there has been remarkable indifference and resistance on the part of Freudian psychoanalysts to examine psychic phenomena. As an exception, Eisenbud (1953) perceptively noted that telepathy in the psychoanalytic relationship invariably involves the unconscious of the analyst as well as the patient.

Kakar (1978, 20) sees a strong tendency toward magical and animistic thinking just beneath the surface in most Indians. He asserts that reality for Indians "emanates from the deeper and phylogenetically much older structural layer of personality—the id, the mental representative of the organism's instinctual drives. Reality, according to Hindu belief, can be apprehended or known only through those archaic, unconscious, preverbal processes of sensing and feeling (like intuition, or what is known as extrasensory perception) which are thought to be in touch with the fundamental rhythms and harmonies of the universe." After noting that Hindu culture relies a great deal on primary process thinking involving representational and affective visual and sensual images to convey abstract points, he writes, "The projection of one's own emotions onto others, the tendency to see neutral and human 'objects' predominantly as extensions of oneself, the belief in spirits animating the world outside and the shuttling back and forth between secondary and primary process modes are common features of daily intercourse. The emphasis on primary thought processes finds cultural expression in innumerable Hindu folk-tales in which trees speak and birds and animals are all too human, in the widespread Hindu belief in astrology and planetary influence on individual lives, and in the attribution of benign or baleful emanations to certain precious and semi-precious stones" (1978, 105).

Then Kakar continues, "The widespread (conscious and preconscious) conviction that knowledge gained through ordering, categorizing, logical reasoning, is *avidya,* the not-knowledge, and real knowledge is only attainable through direct, primary process thinking and perception; the imperative that inspires the yogi's meditation and the artist's *sadhana,* namely that to reach their avowed goals they must enlarge the inner world rather than act on the outer one; . . . the indifferent respect given to eminent scientists and professionals, compared with the unequivocal reverence for . . . spiritual preceptors . . . are a few of the indicators of the emphasis on the primary processes of mental life" (1978, 107). Kakar then relates this mode of thinking to the ego configurations generated through the prolonged mother-child symbiotic relationship.

I have quoted Kakar at length because of the fundamental question as to whether the striving for the realization of the spiritual self and the orientation to the magic-cosmic preoccupation with destiny can be basically subsumed under the primary process, as he apparently does. There is no question that primary process thinking is overwhelmingly present in Indian culture and the Indian mind, and is quite adaptive in a society that is so oriented toward relationships and inner feelings. There is also no question that a major component of the thinking involved in the mass of Indians' relationship to all kinds of psychic and magic-cosmic phenomena is replete with fantasy, externalization, and wish-fulfillment, which is constitutive of the primary process.

However, unless one totally rejects any validity to the striving for the realization of the spiritual self, to the powers (*siddhis*) that sometimes accrue in the process, and to the varied facets of the magic-cosmic involvement with destiny, as related in the case data reported above (including Kakar's own first-hand observation of a group of persons carrying burning hot coals with no ill effects as a religious ritual in a village festival), then these phenomena simply cannot be subsumed under the primary process. The primary process works by *symbolic* expressions of displacements, condensations, and symbolism, not by actual influences over external phenomena, extrasensory perception, or emanations and correspondances.

Perhaps we can take a cue from some of the recent work on cognitive modes involved in artistic creativity. There has never been any question of the strong presence of the primary process in artistic creativity, later elaborated in the more sophisticated theories of Ehrenzweig (1967), Kris (1952), and Noy (1968), to involve an integration of primary and secondary process thinking. However, the more recent research of Rothenberg (1979) with outstanding writers and artists indicates that there are essential translogical modes of thinking in artistic creativity involving antithetical conceptualizations and metaphor formation, which are not present either in the primary process or in the usual rational, conceptual secondary processes. In my own work (Roland 1972, 1981), I have demonstrated how primary process thinking is integrated within the artist's work and governed by these translogical modes of thought, the former giving emotional power to the artistic vision of the latter.

I think other modes of thinking and being must inevitably be present in those genuine instances of clairvoyant dreams, contacts with the spirit world, and accurate predictions from astrology, palmistry, and such. I do not think these can be subsumed under the guise of the usual psychoanalytic definitions of primary and secondary process thinking, in whatever combinations. I suspect that they must be related more to yogic observations that through various forms of breathing exercises, rituals, prayer, meditation and such, there is some kind of inner transformation of energies, qualities, perception, knowledge, and control. Certainly, some of this has already been documented by certain medical experiments at the Menninger Foundation on Swami Rama (Rama et al. 1976), who has control of certain bodily processes that are usually considered involuntary. There are also the experiments involving beta, alpha, and theta EEG waves, cited by Kakar (1978, 18), but also conducted in Japan on states of consciousness. At the very least, Freudian psychoanalysts would do well to be modest with regard to understanding these phenomena. The contemporary culture of science, which they have profoundly internalized into their own ego-ideal, could well be examined critically so that they might expand their horizons to investigate some of these phenomena. Jungian psychology, on the other hand, is far more receptive to the magic-cosmic, psychic phenomena, and issues of self-transformation (Jung 1968). There is no question that through their concept of synchronicity, originally gleaned from Chinese Taoist philosophy and practices, Jungians are attuned to a noncausal concantenation of inner psychological and outer social and physical events; some Jungian analysts are seriously involved in astrology and palmistry.

305

Rituals and the Spiritual Self

The fifth and final category mediating the familial and spiritual selves is the extensive use of rituals, frequently interrelated with the Hindu mythic orientation and sometimes the magic-cosmic continuity in human affairs. While these three cultural categories are often closely interwoven in actual practice, I think it heuristically valuable from a psychological perspective to treat them as relatively separate, since they mediate the continuity between the familial and spiritual selves in recognizably different ways. Rituals are frequently performed around extended family concerns and needs, such as the occurrence of illness, the wish for a child, the concern for a good marriage, or the reasonable prosperity of the family (Hanchette 1988; Srinivas 1978).

The efficacy of the ritual in attaining these family-related goals are through subtle mutual actions and attitudes that help transform the performer and others closely associated (Raheja 1976). Self-transformation is thus central to the psychology of ritualistic performance (Marriott 1976; Wadley 1975). As the ritual is properly performed and the person becomes transformed from *tamasic* and *rajasic* to more *sattvic* qualities,[16] these more subtle and refined qualities then effect changes in grosser substance, thus fulfilling the needs of the familial-social world.

Cognitively, rituals express the constant interchange and interpenetration of the divine with the mundane (pers. com. Kapila Vatsyayan). Hindus, Vatsyayan observes, are particularly oriented toward the symbolic transformation of everyday household and other objects into sacred items for ritual and worship, the items than regaining their more prosaic meaning after the *puja* or ritual worship is over. She cites as an example a rectangular eyeglass case that one may put on the ground and draw certain geometric shapes around; then by reciting certain mantras, one uses the eyeglass case as an object of worship. When the worship is finished, one will pick it up and relate to it once again simply as an eyeglass case. Thus, all kinds of objects can be utilized for ritual worship in the service of self-transformation.

Indian scientists who have this monistic view of reality emphasizing continuity from subtle to gross substance experience no conflict in being involved in both scientific investigation and in the performance of various rituals.[17] Thus, at the very time of this writing, an internationally

---

[16] The philosophical suppositions of ritual efficacy are based on Sankyan philosophy.

[17] This seems similar to certain Catholic scientists in the West, although the philosophical premises are different.

noted Indian chemist performs daily rituals to aid his teen-age grandson abroad afflicted with childhood diabetes.

The Familial and Spiritual Selves:
Counterpoint

It is a profound paradox that the realization of the spiritual self by Hindus is in experiential counterpoint to their familial self, even while the spiritual self is in continuity with the familial self as elaborated above. Counterpoint is nowhere more clearly seen psychologically than around the issues of detachment and *maya* (illusion). In the intense emotional involvement in familial hierarchical intimacy relationships, while there are considerable gratifications of dependency and esteem needs, there are equally potent possibilities and actualities for disappointment, frustration, hurt, and anger.

In Hindu religious philosophy, these intense emotional attachments with their disappointments and hurt can only be loosened through efforts to realize the spiritual self, through effecting a new bonding on a spiritual level of reality. *Maya* can be viewed from this perspective not simply as illusion, as it usually is, but rather as the strong emotional attachments of the familial self that profoundly distract the person from his or her real nature, or the spiritual self. As the person becomes increasingly involved in the realization of the spiritual self, he or she still relates to others and fulfills responsibilities, but without the intense looking to the other for the fulfillment of wishes, esteem, and the desire to be needed. What is termed detachment can be viewed psychologically as increasing involvement in the spiritual self and a loosening of the powerful emotional bonds in familial-social relationships (pers. com. B. K. Ramanujam).

This theme of detachment is beautifully expressed in R. K. Narayan's novel, *The Vendor of Sweets.*[18] The father, Jagan, is intensely attached to and easily manipulated by his increasingly Westernized son until he finally becomes involved in the mythological figure of the goddess. Turning more to this spiritual reality, he then fulfills his responsibilities to his son, but handles him in a firmer, more appropriate way, since his attachment and wish to be needed by the son have been loosened. The

---

[18] This analysis of *The Vendor of Sweets* emerged from the astute comments of Bharati Mukerjee and B. K. Ramanujam at a seminar on "The Indian Self in Its Social and Cultural Contexts," Southern Asian Institute, Columbia University, March 1980.

novel thus humorously revels in the traditional Hindu theme of self-realization and detachment—not escapism, as V. S. Naipaul (1977) would have it.

The simultaneity of continuity and counterpoint by detachment clearly emerges in the biography of Justice Ranade by his wife (Sakala 1981). Continuity is present in his *bhakti* worship, while counterpoint and detachment are strikingly present as his wife experiences his being far less emotionally involved with her as he becomes increasingly involved in the spiritual self.

Still another aspect of counterpoint by detachment involves the pervasively intense sensuality and sexuality of Indians. In the West, sexuality is increasingly associated with personal autonomy and separation from the parents as a child grows older; whereas in India, sexuality connotes greatly increased familial obligations and enmeshments (Grey 1973). Thus, the striving for *brahmacharya,* or sexual abstinence and renunciation in adulthood in the service of spiritual disciplines (in adolescence it is considered appropriate for the preparation for becoming a householder) can also be viewed as a step in the loosening of the intense personal attachments and obligations in extended family-communal relationships and a reaching toward personal autonomy in the spiritual sphere. In the case of Gandhi's striving for *brahmacharya,* Grey (1973) is appropriately critical of Erikson's (1969) emphasis on defensive motivation rather than a striving for competency and autonomy.

Viewing the counterpoint of the spiritual self to the familial self from still another angle is A. K. Ramanujan's (1980) grammatical perspective of context-sensitive and context-free cultural ideals. Citing the overwhelming contextual emphasis of Indian culture and social patterns, he then emphasizes the strong context-free counterpoints involving the four goals of life, the four stages (*ashramas*) of the life cycle, and religious movements, particularly *bhakti:* "Where *kama, artha,* and *dharma* are all relational in their values, tied to place, time, personal character and social role, *moksa* is the release from all relations. If *brahmacharya* (celibate studentship) is preparation for a fully relational life, *grhasthashrama* (householder stage) is a full realization of it. . . . *Vanaprastha* (the retiring forest-dweller stage) loosens the bonds, and *sannyasa* (renunciation) cremates all one's past and present relationships. . . . In each of these the pattern is the same: a necessary sequence in time with strict rules of phase and context, ending in a free state. . . . *Bhakti* defies all contextual structures: every pigeonhole of caste, ritual, gender, appropriate clothing and custom, stage of life, the whole system of homo hierarchicus ('everything in its place') is the target of its irony" (p. 26).

Similarly, pilgrimage institutionalizes a strong counterpoint to the familial self, as the pilgrim, like the renouncer, becomes dead to the contextual enmeshments, responsibilities, and obligations of family and *jati* in the quest for the spiritual self. From a more psychological perspective, through a series of rituals and inner disciplines, the pilgrim strives to transcend the intense emotional involvements of the familial self to attain more illumined qualities and powers (Daniel 1976).

In a still further variation of counterpoint, there is far more room for individuation, individualized instruction, privacy, and separation in the spiritual quest than in the rest of the culture, and greatly enhanced individuality (Dhairyam 1961). The cultural particularistic view of one's personal nature is given only limited accord in the social sphere, since the expectations of the etiquette of hierarchical relationships are given equal if not considerably more weight. On the other hand, considerably more choice and differentiation is accorded for a person's spiritual practices and beliefs, including the choice of a guru, of whom there are a great variety. The practice of one or another kind of yoga is based to a considerable extent on individual cognitive style, temperament, emotional makeup, inclinations, motivation and aspiration, talent and capacity, and level of attainment.[19] There is a basic supposition of inborn spiritual-psychic structures. Thus, when I asked a recognized guru how she decided on the mantra she would assign to a disciple, she answered that through her own meditation she could perceive the spiritual makeup of that disciple and so assign the suitable mantra (pers. com. Mattarji). The mantra is thus chosen on a highly individualized basis and may differ from that of other family members or even the guru.

There is also considerable privacy and often secrecy involved in individual spiritual practices, key ingredients in the separation process. As one long-term Western observer put it, "They will far more readily discuss all kinds of sexual practices and personal problems with you than their spiritual practices. Only upon the closest intimacy will anyone tell you what they are doing" (pers. com. Arthur Eisenberg). This is corroborated by social scientists who upon being asked how many educated persons still practice meditation, answered that you will frequently not know who is or isn't involved even if you may know the person quite well. Moreover, many gurus may not be very visible, in contrast to the

[19]The four basic categories of yoga are generally acknowledged as devotional (*bhakti yoga*), work and service to others (*karma yoga*), inner discrimination and knowledge (*jñana yoga*), and the various postures, breathing exercises, and meditative practices of *raja yoga* (Vivekananda 1949). These yogas, suitable to different temperaments, are seemingly related to Freud's (1931) concept of libidinal types.

better known ones who give lectures, hold classes, have ashrams, or even fly around the world. The point is that Indians are extremely reticent on the subject unless they perceive the other to be readily receptive and noncondescending.

Congruence and counterpoint coexist in the context of daily life. Efforts to realize the spiritual self are not simply confined to the renouncer, as Dumont (1970) implies (thus counterpointing the renouncer with the caste-bound man).[20] The effort to realize the spiritual self is present at various stages in the life cycle in any number of Indians I met, so that I must posit it as the central theme of Indian individuation throughout life. That it tends to become much stronger at later stages of life, from the time one's children have grown up and married according to the traditional schema of the life cycle, does not negate its central psychological position throughout life.

Conclusion

I would like to ascend once more to my imaginary platform in psychological space, and see if we can make out the major contours of the ultimate ideals of Indian and American civilizations that give a spoken or unspoken shape to the self in each society. In this perspective, I see the holy man and the artist as the contrasting ideals, not Dumont's (1970) collective man and renouncer or Marriott's (1976) dividual versus individual. I am using the artist in the Rankian and Eriksonian sense of a person analogous to the hero who creates his or her own personality and identity out of different components of the self, who is motivated by the actualization of his own potentialities, and creates in order to change the identity of his audience and ultimately society (Erikson 1950, 1968; Brenman-Gibson 1981; Menaker 1982; Rank 1932). The holy man, on the other hand—and I use this word advisedly instead of the renouncer, as the holy man may be within society or renounce it— realizes a state of profound consciousness and being, becomes transformed into a different kind of social being who is a model for others, without ties to anyone, and helps others to effect this same inner transformation. This is without necessarily attempting to make any fundamental change in society.[21]

---

[20] Veena Das (1977) questions the soundness of this structural opposition, instead seeing the Brahmin as mediator between the caste-bound man and the renouncer.

[21] Obviously, some spiritual leaders did who were involved in the Indian struggle with British colonialism, including Gandhi, Tagore, Aurobindo, and Vivekananda.

What about the Indian artist? Traditionally, the artist in India has aspired to states similar to those of the holy man in his striving to depict them, and is therefore far more in the vein of the holy man than the Western self-creating artist. Today, however, the Indian artist frequently mediates between the more traditional familial-spiritual self and strong individualizing changes (pers. com. Meena Alexander).

Conclusions: Psychoanalysis in Civilizational Perspective

The Integration of Psychoanalysis with History and the Social Sciences

For anyone endeavoring to integrate psychoanalysis with history and the social sciences, it is highly instructive to note how to glue back together one of those large, old Bennington clay pots that has been broken into a number of fragments. The most logical method is to glue first two or three fragments together as exactly as possible into a section, then to take another few fragments and do likewise, and so on. The next day, after each section has thoroughly dried, these few sections can then be glued together. It makes perfect sense. Only it doesn't work. The sections don't really fit together. The slight amount by which one is inevitably off in gluing the fragments into a section—no matter how precisely one tries—results in serious problems when one tries to fit all the sections together.

What is the solution? To glue every fragment together at the same time, and to hold them in place until the glue dries (it helps to use 5−minute epoxy). One then notices something quite remarkable. Although the individual fragments do not fit together nearly as exactly as when glued in sections, nevertheless the pot holds together quite nicely; it is not pristine, to be sure, but it is still quite serviceable. There are numerous cracks and even slight holes all around, but all of the pieces are completely interrelated to each other. It is as if there had to be some sacrifice on the lower level of organization for all of the pieces to be related to the whole, and thus reconstitute the reality of an old Bennington clay pot.

How is this model and metaphor related to the integration of psychoanalytic with historical, social, and cultural dimensions? The disciplines of each, that is, of psychoanalysis, history, sociology, and anthropology have all developed on their own, have formed their own internal consistencies of theory connected to specific methodologies and to particular data bases. Each of these disciplines forms, so to speak, the different sections of the broken clay pot. The several fragments of each kind of reality studied—whether a psychological reality, or social institutions and patterns, or cultural symbol systems and meanings, or historical change—are firmly glued together in a tightly organized system. This is not to say that there is only one system or theory for psychoanalysis, sociology, anthropology, and history; but all of the theories in each of these disciplines strive for an internal consistency and rigorous systematization.

It is my contention that to try to fit these disciplines together in their original, highly organized system is to court failure if not disaster—or at very best, limited integrations. To cite one of the more egregious examples of this approach—that of applying psychoanalysis to anthropology and history—the result is that social, cultural, and historical realities are seen much as Steinberg's New Yorker views the rest of the United States.[1] That is, these realities are thoroughly bent out of shape to fit with the psychological dimension, since the psychoanalytic researcher is unwilling to accord these other realities parity with the psychological. In similar fashion, some of the anthropologists oriented toward cultural relativism, or others toward historical evolutionism, treat the psychological as but an expression of cultural or historical patterns, bending the psychological dimension out of kilter to fit with their own disciplines (LeVine 1982, 52–55). This kind of approach results in a one-sided theoretical pot that doesn't hold water.

There has fortunately occurred among some psychoanalysts such as

[1] In the famous drawing of Steinberg's New Yorker's view of the United States, Manhattan is in the foreground and occupies a highly disproportionate portion of the composition, while the rest of the United States fills in the background. In similar fashion, applied psychoanalysis, particularly in the United States, puts the psychological dimension disproportionately in the foreground, and the rest of social, cultural, and historical reality as much smaller background elements.

Kardiner (1945) and social scientists such as Hallowell (1955) and Parsons (1964)—to mention a few—a different approach to applied psychoanalysis whereby the other sections of the pot—historical, social, and cultural realities—are indeed accorded their necessary reality, but all of the sections are still to be glued together intact.[2] Thus, Erik Erikson interrelates social, cultural, and historical dimensions with the varied needs and challenges of the psychosocial dimensions of development throughout the life cycle, as he has systematically elaborated these in his developmental schema. There is much to commend in this approach. The only problem is that in cross-cultural and psychohistorical interdisciplinary work in India and Japan it doesn't fully work. The tightly organized sections don't fit together.

Why? Because Erikson systematized and universalized a developmental schema that is completely based on the data of Western personality. Strivings for autonomy and initiative in young children, or the identity crises, moratoria, and syntheses of adolescence and young adulthood may be central to American, and even Western development, but they certainly are not to Indian and Japanese development. His schema not only emphasizes what is not central to their development, but completely omits what is paramount—such as the child's reactions to the active encouragement of dependency needs in the earlier phases of childhood, and the child's negotiation of the severe crackdown on behavior in familial hierarchical relationships from ages four or five through adolescence. In effect, Erikson has kept his section of the pot too intact to fit in with the cultural, social, and historical dimensions of these societies. In psychohistorical and cross-cultural work in India and Japan, the psychological section has to be considerably modified in order to interrelate with other dimensions of reality. Kenneth Kenniston (1974), a disciple of Erikson, realized this when he recognized that developmental stages, as contrasted to maturation, must differ in other historical eras as well as across cultures.

In the last decade or so, beginning with two major theoretical works in psychoanalytic sociology (Weinstein and Platt 1973) and psychoanalytic anthropology (LeVine 1973), a surge of interest has developed in integrating psychoanalysis with anthropology and sociology. But the problem of trying to integrate the highly organized sections of these individual disciplines to reconstitute reality still remains. A favorite way is to accept classical Freudian metapsychology concerning psychosexual

---

[2] Hallowell is a partial exception in his assertions that the self must vary significantly according to its cultural and behavioral environment.

development and the vicissitudes of the drives (libido theory), and/or the conflictual nature of the psyche between the drives, defenses, and super-ego (the structural theory), or more rarely various aspects of ego psy-chology; and then to relate these tightly organized theoretical systems to other social, cultural, and historical realities.[3] But once again, since the psychological organization is kept completely organized and unal-tered, analyses of social and cultural realities become overwhelmingly involved with culturally constituted defenses,[4] with how behavior is controlled and fantasy is expressed, and with displacements of anxiety and stress from particular social institutions to culturally more expres-sive forms. Occasionally, psychological modes of defense and adapta-tion are related to cultural styles. I am not gainsaying the important insights of such approaches. But it ends up as a pot not simply with some cracks and crevices, but with major holes in it, since a number of fragments of psychological, social, and cultural reality end up on the floor rather than being glued together into the whole. The integration is very limited because, once again, the psychological section is kept intact.

There are indeed glimmers of another approach, starting with Erik-son's (1950) and Hallowell's (1955) emphasis on the individual's inter-nalization of the cultural maps of time and space and the cultural value system; including the citation by Parin, Morgenthaler, and Parin-Matthey (1980) of a different kind of superego—a clan conscience in the Africans they studied—as well as voicing uneasiness over whether traditional me-tapsychology fully encompassed their observations; and Weinstein and Platt's (1973) theoretical statement that all levels of personality are af-fected by the social system, that implicitly psychological makeup must be different in other societies, and that a more suitable mode for inte-grating psychoanalysis with the social sciences is to emphasize the inter-nalization process and object-relations theory, especially in the internal-ization of the symbolic codes and meanings of the culture.[5] But Erikson, as noted above, relies on his tightly organized schema of psychosocial development; Parin, Morgenthaler, and Parin-Matthey are all too will-ing to fall back on the rigorous system of traditional Freudian metap-

---

[3] Some of the more relevant researchers in this vein are Boyer (1979); Devereux (1978, 1980); Endleman (1981); Kakar (1978, 1982); R. LeVine (1982); S. LeVine (1979); Ob-eyesekere (1981, 1984); Parin, Morgenthaler, and Parin-Matthey (1980); and Spiro (1965).

[4] Culturally constituted defenses relate to cultural patterns that prohibit privately moti-vated satisfaction in one domain, but sanction it in another with a cognitive pattern that maintains this separation.

[5] Weinstein and Platt in this aspect of their work are utilizing the contributions of Par-sons (1964).

sychology as universal; and Weinstein and Platt repeatedly cite statements from ego psychology as universals in development and functioning when they are really quite Western-centric. Again, these are significant advances in trying to interrelate the psychological, historical, social, and cultural, but they do not really get the pot together as a workable, holistic reality.

From a social science perspective, this need to alter a highly systematized theoretical approach in a particular discipline to accommodate a broader interdisciplinary integration surfaced in the recent anthropological work of Charles Lindholm (1982) on the Puthuks of Pakistan. A structural-functional analysis of that society simply couldn't encompass certain ideals and social patterns of friendship and hospitality in Puthuk men. Lindholm then posited that a society must accommodate certain universal emotions that are developed in childhood, no matter how out of tune these are with the basic structures and functions of that society. Thus, his theoretical analysis went beyond current anthropological-sociological orientations to include fundamental psychological issues, thereby partially altering his original discipline.

Perhaps the main stumbling block to abandoning this older approach of gluing one thoroughly organized theoretical discipline to another is a methodological one: psychoanalytic theory has only developed through the clinical data of psychoanalytic therapy, but in all of these studies with African, Asian, Melanesian, Eskimo, or even American Indian, with only the very rarest of exceptions, psychoanalytic therapy is simply not in evidence. Thus, psychoanalytic theory has been used to encompass all kinds of ethnographic observations, sometimes in a carefully considered way, much too often in the ways of wild analysis wherein it seems that once one leaves the couch and consulting room anything goes methodologically. There have even been earnest attempts on the part of Parin, Morgenthaler, and Parin-Matthey (1980) and L. Bryce Boyer (1979) to pay native informants to free associate; but this is in effect one-way psychoanalysis, where the informants mainly cooperate because of the directives of the tribal elders, and are in no real sense analysands.

This is not to negate that much can be learned by these sensitive, essentially *ethnographic* approaches to the individual; obviously, empathic observations are by no means the monopoly of psychoanalysts in their consulting rooms. But the method and process of psychoanalytic therapy are completely different from the ethnographic one. Not only are there unique frames for evaluation in psychoanalytic therapy that are carefully set up and observed (LeVine 1982a, 185–202); but confidentiality is established, with no third party present (as so frequently occurs in ethnographic interviews), so that through free association and the analysis of resistances the analyst can attain a more profound and extensive view of the inner landscape of a person's mind. Even more to the point, it is through the effects of the analyst's interventions and the process of change that the analyst can begin to ascertain which of his suppositions are on target, and which, though they seem perfectly plausible, are completely inaccurate or irrelevant.[6]

To return to my main metaphor and thesis of this chapter, it can only be through actual psychoanalytic therapy with persons from other than Western cultures that one can begin to abandon the tightly organized section of current psychoanalytic theory of whichever persuasion, and begin to interrelate this new clinical data with the particular culture, social patterns, and historical development of the society in which that person resides. This is not to say that a change in methodology to doing psychoanalytic therapy in Asian and African societies will necessarily guarantee gluing the pot of psychological and social reality together so that it holds water, but it would seem a necessary beginning to change the overall approach.

The second solution to putting the old Bennington clay pot together is, I suggested, simply to glue all of the fragments together more or less simultaneously, shifting individual fragments here and there as needed so that all will be interrelated in a way that holds the pot together. To utilize this method for interconnecting psychoanalytic, sociological, anthropological, and historical realities is necessarily to do some violence to each of these disciplines as currently constituted. One cannot make room for interrelationships with other disciplines without changing each one, at least to some extent.[7]

In attempting this kind of integration using specific psychoanalytic case material in India and Japan one is struck by two unexpected phenomena. The first is that sociohistorical factors involving social change are closely intertwined with social and cultural ones. That is, a person's inner conflicts, struggles, makeup, and aspirations not only reflect significant aspects of the dominant social and cultural patterns of that society—as well as the idiosyncratic in his or her own familial background—but also important aspects of social change. This contrasts with

---

[6] As Freud noted early on, it makes little difference whether or not a patient agrees with the analyst's interpretations; it is only on the basis of a patient's subsequent reactions and actions that the analyst truly gains some idea of the accuracy of his understanding and interventions.

[7] This critique accords with Clifford Geertz's (1973, 33–54).

some of the work in psychoanalytic anthropology, where case material is discussed from the standpoint of cross-cultural understandings, but where sociohistorical factors centrally involved in the informants' conflicts cry out for recognition and analysis.

It is evident that this phenomenon is equally present in Western countries. However, this kind of integrative approach in psychoanalysis has only rarely been used for understanding analysands within Western history, society, and culture in any *theoretical* perspective.[8] In actual practice, psychoanalysts constantly draw upon their implicit understandings of their own culture, social patterns, and history, but they rarely do it in any explicit way. A psychoanalyst is constantly guaging how a patient is reacting to different relationships, including the analytic one, in terms of the known norms of the social, cultural, and developmental patterns of the analyst's own particular culture and the patient's ethnic subculture. Psychoanalysts in Western societies do on occasion get into trouble when they are unfamiliar with certain ethnic subcultures, such as the Hispanic—unless, of course, the analyst makes a particular effort to understand a patient from a very different subculture from his or her own.

The second unexpected phenomenon that comes more sharply into focus encompasses the subtle patterns of emotional relatedness characteristic of persons in a given society—patterns that are loaded with specific cultural meanings and embedded within various institutional settings.[9] More specifically, when one delves more deeply psychologically through psychoanalytic therapy in India and Japan, subtle psychosocial dimensions of family and group hierarchical relationships in differing balances emerge in a way they usually have not in anthropological studies.[10] These dimensions then complement the anthropological formulations of Eastern hierarchical relationships.

[8] Erik Erikson (1946), Esther and William Menaker (1965), and Otto Rank (Menaker 1982) are among the only psychoanalysts within the Freudian framework who have even begun to attempt to integrate social, cultural, historical, and psychological factors in their theoretical analyses of their analysands. Neo-Freudian psychoanalysts, however, have been more disposed in this direction.

[9] My position that varying patterns of emotional relatedness in different societies are centrally related to the makeup of the self in those societies is in accord with the recent work of Marsella, DeVos, and Hsu (1985), who stress the experiential self in social interaction rather than in social role structures.

[10] Psychoanalytic therapy in a cross-cultural context through comparativity can not only illuminate the culturally related inner psychological makeup of the person, but it can also function in an ethnographic mode by delineating subtle emotional patterns of relatedness in that society.

It is just these kinds of fragments of psychosocial reality that connect, so to speak, the intrapsychic makeup of the self with the social institutions and social role patterns, the cultural symbol code, and social change. To omit these intermediary links of emotional relatedness is to leave too large a gap between the psychological and the sociocultural. Psychoanalytically, the focus shifts from a conflictual model of the mind to a multi-faceted view of the self that enables the person to function well in these highly complex hierarchical intimacy relationships in India and Japan, which in turn can frequently generate considerable inner conflict in the person. Similarly, an integrative analysis in Western societies would also need to interrelate the individualized self to broader social and cultural patterns and historical change by highlighting the modes of emotional relatedness in the varied forms of individualism and egalitarian-contractual relationships.

There is still another way to play upon the metaphor of the old Bennington pot, by looking upon the different fragments as a whole repertoire of models and observations from each of the relevant disciplines. In any given discipline, after all, there are a number of theoretical perspectives, each attempting to integrate specific kinds of data. What I am proposing is to use as many of these different theoretical perspectives as possible from each of the fields, meanwhile adjusting the differing fragments so that they gradually interrelate. It is an argument for complexity and open-endedness—not a superficial eclecticism, but rather multi-facetedness and interrelatedness in depth. This orientation leaves open for future integrations new contributions and theoretical perspectives from each and all of the disciplines involved. From this perspective, the pot will never be complete. The fragments on hand will be interrelated holistically into the approximate shape of the pot. But there must inevitably be various gaps that can only be filled as major new contributions to the relevant disciplines emerge. And as these are later incorporated into a new analysis, the shape of the pot will unfailingly become somewhat altered.

This approach contrasts with what I consider to be the highly useful, but single-dimensional models of integrations cited above. I find that the more models of psychoanalysis that I have drawn upon, ranging from the various traditional Freudian models, including ego psychology, to other newer models within Freudian psychoanalysis, such as Erikson's work on self-identity, self psychology, object-relations theory, and Rank's and the Menaker's work on individuation, the more I can address a complexity of personality dimensions. But this must always be done by de-Westernizing the specific content of these models. That is, one must always assume that these models are built on the clinical data of Western personality, and must therefore be decontextualized to allow for a new contextualization based on the data of Indians and Japanese.

Similarly, the more one is acquainted with the varied contributions of anthropologists and other social scientists and historians in India and Japan, the richer can be the integration of the psychoanalytic dimension with the social, cultural, and historical. This orientation carries forward an informal attitude of psychoanalysts in their clinical work, where they use a variety of models, recognizing that no one theory can encompass the overwhelming and at times bewildering variety of clinical data one encounters with different patients or even with the same one at differing stages in the analysis. This integrative approach is very much in accord with Clifford Geertz's (1973) call for a synthetic integration of the cultural, social, psychological, and biological, using findings from these various fields in a unitary analysis that sees systematic relationships among diverse phenomena.

Finally, we must face the delicate issue that psychoanalytic theory draws upon and expresses itself within Western cultural categories and philosophical assumptions—one of which is a strongly rational, positivistic view of reality. With the exception of Jungian psychology and very occasionally Freudian and neo-Freudian psychoanalysts, almost the entire field of psychoanalysis subscribes to these rational, positivistic assumptions. This is firmly carried over to psychoanalytic anthropology, sociology, and psychohistory where, with only rare exceptions,[11] the spiritual dimension and magic-cosmic orientation are constantly being reduced to one or another kind of unconscious defensive maneuver of coping with stress, of psychopathology, or of regression to infantile states of development. Psychoanalysts and psychoanalytically oriented social scientists and historians have simply not realized the extent to which their views of reality stem from a modern Western positivistic culture of science (Nandy 1980a; Uberoi 1978). To hold to this highly systematized psychoanalytic view that approaches the spiritual and the magic-cosmic in India and Japan in a pervasively reductionistic manner is to leave out large fragments of the psyche and of social and cultural realities, and thus to leave the pot of reality with a gaping hole.

[11] Two of the exceptions among the psychoanalytic and psychological anthropologists are Gananath Obeyesekere (1981, 1984) and Manisha Roy (1975), the former from Sri Lanka, the latter from Calcutta.

Case Illustrated by
an Integrative Model: Ashis

To illustrate the complexity of integrating the psychological dimension with the cultural, social, and historical in a holistic manner, I shall return to the case data of Ashis. In capsule form, Ashis's father strongly identified with British social and cultural values while simultaneously denigrating Indian ones, a not unusual identification for those who try to advance themselves with a colonial power that inevitably asserts the superiority of its own *Weltanschauung* and the gross inferiority of those it rules. Similarly, his father identified with the British social pattern of hierarchical relationships at work, but at home with his sons he related through more Indian hierarchical expectations. To act so differently probably stemmed from an Indian psychological mode of contextualizing situations, whereby acting appropriately in a given situation is much more in accord with an internalized conscience based on the Indian cultural code of *dharma* rather than the Western cultural code of universal principles and consistancy in all situations. Ashis, in growing up, related to his father in social and emotional patterns that were completely Indian, including the strong idealizations, the profound need for gaining his father's respect for his self-esteem, and the covert intense emotional connectedness whereby the father's expectations for the oldest son are paramount; but within this totally Indian father-son relationship, strong Western cultural norms and values were internalized and more Indian ones denigrated. This strongly conflicted with the cultural values and outlook, usually internalized earlier, from the mother in particular, from various members of the extended family and servants, and from the ever-present mythology and festivals.

Theoretically, to effect an integration, we must take account of the historical dimension of British colonialism with its loaded value orientation, and the social pattern of a limited number of educated Indians becoming cogs in the colonial administration for Indian social purposes of advancing family standing and status in their community. The psychosocial dimensions of Western and Indian hierarchical relationships at work and at home, respectively, must also be attended to. Highly relevant is the psychological dimension encompassing: the identification of these Indians with the colonial *Weltanschauung;* the nature of the Indian conscience and the cultural code for proper behavior that is internalized; profound differences in adolescence as a developmental stage between Indians and Westerners, in which struggles for identity and autonomy are simply not at stake for Indians, but rather the profound narcissistic need to gain the respect of father and family, as well as to reflect well on them; a powerful superego that severely inhibits any direct expressions of ambivalence to a father; and the internalization of cultural values of a colonial presence that are deeply incorporated into the son's psyche through the extremely important relationship with the father, thus severely denigrating earlier internalized values from a more maternal matrix. From a psychoanalytic standpoint alone, I have had to use models encompassing the categories of ego-ideal and superego, psychosocial stages of development and identity theory, self psychology and the category of narcissism, object-relations theory and the internalization of cultural values from different stages of development, and the structural hypothesis; while simultaneously I have had to de-Westernize the contents of all of these to fit Indian psychological data, and then to interrelate these newly contextualized categories to Indian historical, cultural, and social realities.

Ashis also serves to illustrate what has happened to many sons from educated families in a colonial setting not only in India but, I strongly suspect, in other countries as well. His father's suicide when Ashis was nineteen derived from the differences between Western and Indian social patterns of hierarchical relationships and the historical circumstance of Indian Independence. This suicide resulted for Ashis in a devastating narcissistic blow and the loss of meaning, evoking unusual narcissistic rage openly expressed at the father; a profound search for meaning and cultural roots with new idealized images of male Hindu religious reform leaders of his grandfather's generation, and of major Hindu leaders who asserted an Indian world view while integrating various aspects of Western culture with it; a turn to writing and spiritual disciplines to implement his new views and meanings; and an intense identity struggle between his earlier Westernization through his father and English-style boarding schools, and his about-face turn to a Hindu world view.

From a standpoint of theoretical integration, one has to take into account narcissistic structures and the needs of the self, but from an indigenous Indian standpoint; other psychological issues involving depression and mourning; Indian cultural and social reactions to British colonialism and Western culture through such national leaders as Gandhi and Tagore, and a major cultural spokesman, Coomaraswamy—all of whom Ashis idealized; the nature of identity struggles in Indian men, which are between Western and indigenous values, both of which are anchored emotionally through familial relationships rather than from the developmental needs of Western adolescents; and the individuation struggles of the artist to articulate for a relevant audience some of the same identity struggles he is experiencing.

Ashis's case, then, is a model for what happened to many Indian men in a colonial setting where Western norms were profoundly inculcated in the son through the father, denigrating more indigenous cultural values from an earlier maternal-extended family matrix, which resulted in a major part of the self being depreciated. There is then an anguished search for indigenous values and meanings of self-respect and parity once there is disillusionment with the father, and an intense identity struggle to integrate both Western and Indian world views because cultural meanings and values from both have been deeply internalized. It is instructive to note that in the case of major national leaders such as Jawaharlal Nehru and Subhash Chandra Bose, their fathers directed them to be Western-educated, but also communicated a deep respect for Hindu culture.

Finally, we must take into account a differing integration of psychological, social, cultural, and historical realities to understand Ashis's work conflicts and strivings. In terms of Indian hierarchical social patterns of work, a subordinate must have a superior as a benefactor, who will protect and nurture in a reciprocal exchange for loyalty and subordination. Psychologically, Ashis could indeed only work in this way, but needed a superior he could profoundly respect and one who deeply respected him—a particular mode of hierarchy by the quality of the person, by no means always present in Indian work situations. However, in terms of historical change, Ashis is one of an increasing number of Indians educated in college and graduate school in the United States or in other Western countries. Like these other Indians educated in the West, he is used to a much more individualized way of working, in which the American cultural values of autonomy, initiative, and individuation or self-actualization through work are implemented in hierarchical work patterns in a way often radically different from the Indian situation.

Thus, Indians such as Ashis, upon returning home, feel stifled as junior members of their organization, where an Indian hierarchical order traditionally gives little recognition or scope to the junior member, in contrast to many American organizations. However, with a hierarchical superior whom Ashis respects, and who also respects Ashis, giving him free scope for his unusual literary-technological skills and talents, Ashis has performed in an outstandingly creative way. In this paradigm of increasing education and work experience in the West for so many educated Indians now, if creative work is to be done in India there apparently must occur a significant change in the psychosocial patterns of the hierarchical relationship; there is a continuation of the traditional reciprocities and emotional connectedness on the one hand, but the superior must give the subordinate far greater scope and recognition for more individualized and creative functioning, on the other. In this way there can occur a cultural, social, and psychological integration between Indian modes of hierarchical functioning at work with more Western and particularly American ones that could foster more creative work for those Indians educated in the West who have returned to India.

Individuation, Psychopathology, and Developmental Schemas: A Cross-Civilizational View

To assess the greater range of the development of human potentialities as well as of psychopathology, and their relationship with each other, one must look to a depth psychological comparison of persons from living civilizations with longstanding literate traditions and highly complex cultures and social institutions. Even though there have been psychoanalytic movements for some decades in both India and Japan, with substantial contributions from psychoanalysts in both societies, Freudian psychoanalysis has not been concerned with any cross-civilizational perspective. Nor, with two important exceptions,[12] has psychoanalytic anthropology, which has retained its almost exclusive preoccupation with persons from less complex, nonliterate cultures; whereas psychoanalytic sociology has been involved only with Western cultures.

It is apparent from psychoanalytic work in India, Japan, and the United States that the kinds of potentialities persons actually develop, how they function and communicate in society, what their mode of being and experience is in the world and within themselves, and what their ideals and actualities of individuation are depend overwhelmingly on the given culture and society to which they belong.[13] And when these cultures are embedded in distinctly different civilizations, the psychological differences can be considerable. The cultural ideals and symbol systems that

---

[12] See Crapanzano (1980) and Obeyesekere (1981, 1984) for studies that concern themselves with persons in longstanding, literate, religious traditions and institutions.

[13] These observations are very much in accord with Clifford Geertz's (1973: 33–54) assertion that human nature completes itself through particular cultures. Further, he asserts that since there is such great diversity, a search for universals loses any substantive meaning since the universals of human nature constitute the lowest common denominator in man.

324

give meaning and form to the social patterns and child rearing ultimately shape the development of potentiality and range of individuation
in a given society.

Persons in these varied cultures all obviously have the common threads
of humanity within them, which enables the psychoanalyst and anthropologist from another society to be able gradually to empathize and
understand. In more conceptual terms, the psychic unity of mankind
seems well established: that all humans are endowed with more or less
the same range of potentialities. Moreover, the categories—rather than
the contents of these categories—of psychoanalysis seem relevant to persons from a great variety of cultures. But how these common threads of
humanity are colored, and how they are interwoven with each other
varies enormously in persons from cultures that are civilizationally distinct.

From an evolutionary perspective, since the ultimate cultural ideals
and meanings are so enormously different in such major complex societies as India, Japan, and the United States—as are the social systems,
social role structures, subtle emotional patterns of interpersonal interactions, and personality development—it is impossible to speak of any
unitary evolutionary schema. That is, the kind of potentialities developed in persons in a given society cannot be said to be inherently superior to any others. All too often, any evolutionary schema contains
implicit assumptions that the kind of human being that is considered
the latest outcome of evolution comes from just the kind of background
the author is from—which is usually a Western culture. When one is
dealing with major complex cultures rooted in different civilizational
configurations, it is more accurate to speak of significantly different strands
of evolutionary potential that have been developed and realized than of
any unitary thread.

It is also apparent from clinical psychoanalytic work in India, Japan,
and America that in each society there are distinct kinds of psychopathology, structural deficits, and unconscious conflicts—a finding that is
generally congruent with anthropological work relating mental illness
to specific cultural and social patterns. These particular kinds of psychopathology are, however, far more interrelated to the potentialities
developed in a given society through its social and cultural patterns and
historical development than has heretofore been recognized and conceptualized. In effect, the actualization of potential always has a price.

For a theoretical analysis, one must investigate both the particular
potentialities and the psychopathologies present in persons in a given
culture to assess their interrelationships. This kind of analysis ap-

proaches the interrelationship of potentiality and psychopathology differently from the path pursued by a number of psychoanalytic anthropologists, sociologists, and psychohistorians who simply use the current Western norms of psychoanalysis and its developmental schemas as a universal measuring stick to gauge individuation and psychopathology in all other societies.

The perspective I am using obviously relates individuation, ego functioning, psychic structures, intrapsychic conflict, the internalization process, and psychopathology a great deal more to varying cultural and social patterns and social change than is characteristic of Freudian psychoanalysis. In particular, I find that the structure and contents of the ego-ideal and superego must be explicitly explored to understand the nature of psychopathology as well as of developed potentialities—an investigation that lends itself more to a clinical psychoanalytic than an ethnographic methodology, since the superego in particular largely functions on an unconscious level. Although psychoanalysts and psychoanalytic anthropologists (Boyer 1979; Devereux 1978, 1980; LeVine 1982a; Spiro 1965) adhere to the structural theory and the importance of the superego and ego-ideal, with but occasional exceptions (Doi 1985; Kondo 1975; Parin, Morgenthaler, and Parin-Matthey 1980), they rarely focus on differences in these structures, or even the contents of them from a cross-cultural or sociohistorical perspective.

Let me be more specific about the interrelationship of development and psychopathology. Child rearing in India and Japan foster capacities for intense dependence and interdependence; for an unusually high degree of empathy to others and receptivity to the norms of any given situation; for a we-self that is highly emotionally enmeshed with others but maintains a very private self; for unusually strong we-self esteem that must be constantly enhanced through ongoing mirroring and idealizing relationships throughout life; and a conscience that is particularly attuned to reciprocities in varying contexts, and the containment of ambivalences and anger.

On the one hand, the development of these potentialities enables Indians and Japanese to function extremely well in family and group hierarchical intimacy relationships. On the other hand, where there are such strong expectations of being given to—as well as of giving to others—hurt and anger are easily evoked. In Indians with a highly developed wishing, wanting, libidinal self, persons inevitably meet with disappointed expectations and slights in everyday relationships. In Japan, the junior person may feel deeply hurt and angry if the superior has not correctly sensed and responded to all kinds of needs that cannot be expressed openly because of the internalized ego-ideal of self-restraint. Countering these hurts and anger in both societies is a very strict super-ego that prohibits anger from being expressed directly, especially to someone hierarchically superior; rather it must be contained for rela-tively harmonious living within the tightly knit, extended family and group. Since there is no exit from these "long engagements," and the we-self is so emotionally enmeshed with others, if particular relation-ships engender so much anger that it cannot be handled by simple con-scious containment or suppression, a number of symptoms may take over—somatization being a very frequent one in Japanese and Indians. Thus, the very high level of dependency and narcissistic needs that are cultivated along with an emotionally enmeshed we-self and a highly developed superego and ego-ideal not only enables the person to func-tion adaptively, but almost inevitably results in the predominant kinds of psychopathology that are present.

In Japan, where the ego-ideal for a very high level of performance and skill is cultivated by the mother from early childhood, one not only attains the capacity for high levels of skill and performance in adult-hood, but one also may have psychopathology involving perfectionism, intense self-criticism, and extreme social shyness, or a false self struc-ture, that is in good part related to the tensions generated in the person to realize these particularly exacting ego-ideals.[14]

To reflect on the realization of psychological potential and psycho-pathology in the United States, a great many capacities are developed for the individual to be able to function relatively autonomously in a highly mobile society, where extrafamilial relationships are central and where there is a considerable shifting of job, social relationships, mar-riage, and place of residence, and where the individual must evolve his or her own value system. The individual is more or less on his or her own—at least as compared to Indians and Japanese. Thus, development emphasizes separation-individuation, autonomy, and initiative, with the uses of transitional objects in early childhood to help effect this—as contrasted with intense dependence and interdependence; an ego-orien-tation toward assertiveness, mastery, ambition, and competitiveness—as contrasted with receptivity and sensitivity to the other; a strong sense of an I-self in which initiative and responsibility are located, with sharply differentiated inner images of self and other, and firmly set outer ego

[14] Another result of extremely close maternal involvement that fosters high expectations is anorexia as the predominant form of psychopathology in teen-age girls (pers. com. K. Ogura)—anorexia being integrally related to problems in ego boundary formation vis-à-vis the mother.

boundaries—in contrast to a we-self with permeable outer boundaries and a highly private self; a conscience in men that tends to revolve more around the pole of abstract, universal principles than particular situational or contextual norms; empathy that is more oriented toward individual needs for autonomy, privacy, and self-actualization than to needs for dependence and self-esteem; and identity formation that grants the person autonomy to create himself or herself through integrating major and minor life decisions, roles, and value systems with earlier identifications and self-images—in contrast to familial and group interdependence with the careful fulfillment of reciprocal responsibilities.

If these are some of the major potentialities that are realized in an individualized self to enable the individual to function well in an American life style, then the obverse appears in the serious deficits in the emotional quality of relationships, with deleterious effects on self-esteem and self-integration. The advent of self psychology in the United States specifically addresses the issues of self-esteem and self-fragmentation and alienation as related to relational emotional deficits in childhood and adolescence with the concommitant developmental arrests. But self psychology does not realize that this major strand of psychopathology in Americans is intimately related to just those social and emotional patterns and cultural ideals that promote the dominant forms of the realization of psychological potentialities in American personality. Social mobility and psychological actualization can come at the cost of deeply entwined human relationships and a solid sense of self.

For this conceptualization of the interrelationships of potentiality and psychopathology in persons from major cultures in different civilizations, it is essential to reformulate the developmental schemas of psychoanalysis. Developmental schemas have been essential to both the psychoanalytic clinician and the theoretician for understanding the various lines of personality development and psychopathology. These range from the historically early formulations of the psychosexual stages of libidinal development, to somewhat later ones around superego and ego development, to still later ones around psychosocial stages of development, to object-relations, and to recently formulated narcissistic stages of development. One or more of these schemas are the working vocabulary of any practicing psychoanalyst.

These schemas are also the working vocabulary of psychoanalytic anthropologists, psychoanalytic sociologists, and psychohistorians. When applied to persons from Asian or African cultures, the Western norms that have been built into these schemas result in these persons emerging as inferior or pathological.

The conceptual framework of developmental schemas that deal with the differing lines of development within the child and adolescent is obviously valuable. But it will need very serious amending to formulate the actualities of psychological development, individuation, and psychopathology in persons from India and Japan—as well, I might add, as in persons from almost every other culture that is not European or North American. Even the psychosexual schema will have to be reexamined because it basically assumes a certain kind of child rearing, early maternal relationships, and superego formation that is broadly characteristic of Western child rearing patterns. Oral, anal, phallic, and genital character as currently delineated are far more Western-centric than is now appreciated. Thus, one can keep a schema for libidinal development, but its contents will have to be altered to be able to relate it to character development in persons in Asian and African societies. Even more striking are the psychosocial developmental schemas, which are so reflective of functioning and conflicts in Western and particularly American society. Developmental lines of ego and superego development, narcissism, and of object-relations will clearly all need major reformulation, as well.

Although I have initiated aspects of this task, the major work of reconceptualizing developmental schemas is obviously one that will have to be done by psychoanalysts and child psychologists in such countries as India and Japan. These new schemas can then reflect major stages of development in those societies, such as the cultivation of *amae* or dependency strivings in early childhood; the crackdown on behavior at ages four or five through adolescence, with its implications for superego and ego-ideal structuralization and functioning; the development of cognitive capacities for contextualization and metonymic thinking; the enhanced early mirroring and the culturally sanctioned intense idealizations for the development of narcissistic structures; and constant exposure in early childhood to mythic images as related to ego-ideal development. Until these reformulations take place, however, extreme caution should be used in utilizing the contents of the current developmental schemas of psychoanalysis in any analysis of persons from different civilizations or cultures.

INDIVIDUATION: IDEALS AND ACTUALITIES

Perhaps nowhere are the ideals and actualities of psychological individuation so differently shaped by culture as between Eastern and Western societies. In contemporary America, the central ideal of psychological individuation revolves around predominant cultural values of individualism: that the individual through autonomous choice can actualize and realize a variety of inherent potentialities and capabilities first through education, then through various jobs, activities, and relationships throughout life. Thus, the person evolves a highly distinct and differentiated personality with specific ambitions, skills, and ideals; all of these to be more or less centrally organized around the person's evolving identity, and actualized through a variety of activities and relationships. That these ideals of individuation may encompass considerable variation—from, for instance, the competitive individualism of an establishment ethic to a counterculture ethic of doing one's own thing—or that they may only be partially realized, with a casualty list of those fallen by the wayside through alienation or failure, or that the ideals may be those of the more educated middle and upper-middle classes, do not detract from their predominant influence in American life.

It has frequently been asserted that such ideals and actualities of individuation are the result of an advanced industrial, urban society, and that as other societies approach a more complex industrialization and urbanization these ideals and actualities will predominate there as well. In this perspective, Western cultural ideals and social patterns are taken to be the measuring stick of sociocultural and even psychological evolution for the rest of the world. It is evident that in Japan, however, where there is also a very high degree of industrialization and urbanization, individuation both in ideals and actualities does not in the least follow the American pattern. Throughout life, as in India, the person is guided by elders and mentors in every major life decision, from education to vocation to marriage, and is not accorded the full autonomy of choice and evolving of identity that are so central to American individuation. There is no question that Japanese acquire a very high level of skills in positions ranging from housewives and mothers to various jobs and professions. But such achievement is rarely experienced as the basic fulfillment of inner potentialities or self-actualization, but more in terms of functioning as a we-self for the family and/or group, and living up to one's inner ideals of high performance.

In Japan, the central ideal of individuation is the cultivation of the inner self through a variety of aesthetic and other activities, which are considered ways of life. These activities are pursued not simply to develop various skills and actualize potentialities but to cultivate various aspects of an inner self. Again, particular Japanese may be involved in a quite limited way in any of these activities, but this does not mean

330

they do not have a predominant psychological influence on individuation in Japan.

In a similar vein, Indians in their increasing urbanization and industrialization have acquired considerable skills through an advanced educational system and various technological and other positions in an urban industrial economy. Nevertheless, such skills and even motives for achievement tend to be subsumed under a we-self and familial embeddedness rather than acquired for self-actualization. The central cultural ideals of individuation revolve around the gradual realization of the spiritual self, wherein subtle differences and nuances in inner make-up, temperament, and inclinations are all utilized in the spiritual quest. It is again the cultivation of the inner self through various disciplines such as yoga that is more central to individuation than the realization of various potentialities through activities.

Individuation and Psychopathology: An Historical Perspective

I have so far discussed individuation and psychopathology from a cross-cultural or, more accurately, cross-civilizational perspective. But to account for the actualities of psychological change in these areas, one must turn to a more historical analysis of cultural, social, and ultimately psychological change. To cite one example, in the United States, through the greatly increased advanced education of women from the 1930s on, and from increased entry into the work force from World War II on, American women in the era of social reform in the 1960s evolved a movement sanctioning and encouraging a dual role of career and family. This has led to greatly increased individuation and functioning in American women along the predominant lines of American ideals of individuation and self-actualization through education, work, and relationships—leading to a greater sense of individual identity and accomplishment. The change has been so profound since the 1960s that no American young woman can go on to higher education now without seriously considering the option of having a career.

On the other hand, considerable inner conflict has been introduced into many of these women between an older ego-ideal, formed from childhood identifications with traditional mothers, of being there predominantly for others, particularly those of the family, and the later incorporation of an ego-ideal more derived from male-oriented individualism of being there for oneself in work and career. Thus, sociohistorical change once again results in developing new potentialities into an expanding self as well as fostering new inner conflicts. That these conflicts are rooted in the particular ego-ideals of women in contemporary American culture and the change in ideals brought about by specific sociohistorical circumstances—as contrasted to some universal psychological principle—emerged from my earlier analysis which indicates that Indian women with differing ideals combine career and family with far less inner conflict.

To turn to another example, the nineteenth-century Meiji Restoration, which modernized Japan sufficiently to fend off Western colonialism, gradually and increasingly enabled male youths from various social classes for the first time to advance into new positions through a competitive educational system and bureaucracy. A new ego-ideal was fostered of being highly competitive in school and work, side by side with the older ideals of always acting harmoniously and cooperatively in the work group. Pressure was particularly put on the oldest son to achieve a good position. Psychologically, this opened the way for many youths to acquire new kinds of skills and function in new kinds of ways in an expanding self. On the other hand, the inner conflict between antithetical ego-ideals—to be harmonious within the group and competitive, simultaneously—resulted in a whole new syndrome of symptomatology, *shinkeishitsu*.

Then we can see in India, through the case of Ashis, that British colonialism in its denigration of Indian culture resulted in enormous identity conflicts in Indian, Western-educated men with considerable self-deprecation, and in some cases, psychological paralysis. On the other hand, it also resulted in a major nineteenth- and twentieth-century cultural movement, the Indian Renaissance in Bengal, and the later National Movement, whereby Indians began to reassert their Indian identity and cultural values; and to a new identity synthesis whereby Indians incorporate a great deal of Western culture with their Indian heritage. To this very day, especially in Indian men, these kinds of identity issues with their opportunities for a larger integration into an expanding self and their pulls toward inner conflict remain strikingly alive.

One of the most noticeable, pervasive psychological changes that is taking place in the modernization process in India and Japan is an increasing individualization. There is no question that this thrust toward greater consideration of the adolescents' and young adults' wishes and inclinations in a number of areas by the elders, and the imbibing of an ego-ideal by youth to be somewhat more independent of familial, community, and group enmeshment, have come from exposure to Western

332

culture and values. This movement will hardly lead to the type of individualism that prevails in the West; rather it is gradually being incorporated into a broader "familialism" in India and Japan. It is one of the cornerstones of an expanding self in Indians and Japanese; but at the same time, it can generate considerable conflict.

Turning again to the United States, it is evident that there is an increasingly serious interest and intent on the part of a number of Americans toward the realization of the spiritual self. What had accelerated in the 1960s as an involvement with Eastern cults and movements that was at times commercialized and superficial has become gradually transformed into deeper involvements on the part of many with highly reputable Indian gurus, Tibetan lamas, Japanese Zen Buddhists, Sufi pirs, and such. This more serious and less ostentatious involvement heralds an expanding self in Americans, whereby a totally different psychological paradigm for individuation is being followed from what is predominant in contemporary Western secular culture. It is less obvious because it is now taking place on a quieter level. This striving by Americans to realize the spiritual self will result in a totally different gestalt from what is present in Indians and Japanese, where the spiritual self is in a complex relationship to the familial self. In Americans there will have to be a new integration between their individualized self and the spiritual self. At present, however, this new paradigm for individuation is frequently in conflict with the predominant cultural maps of reality around rationalism and positivism that are so deeply ingrained in the American psyche.

From the foregoing analyses, it is more than apparent that the human race has not been moving along any simple line of evolution of human potential. But rather humanity has developed a few major strands of individuation through complex cultures that are civilizationally distinct. These strands are now being further developed and altered through far-reaching sociohistorical change generated both from within these societies and from increasing contact with each other. That psychological conflict can sometimes result from these profound changes does not negate the movement toward new integrations and an expanding self.

GLOSSARY

ahamkara: ego or I-ness that distracts from awareness of the inner Spirit (*Atman*).

amae: behavior or attitudes expressive of passive dependent wishes.

amaeru: to try to fulfill *amae* through another.

amayakasu: to indulge another's *amae*.

anal character: a personality type characterized by orderliness, obstinacy, and frugality, which stems from exaggerated significance of the anal phase of development: when defenses are less adequate, there is heightened ambivalence, untidiness, and defiance.

anal phase: the stage of psychosexual development that lasts from about one to three years of age, marked by the recognizeable emergence of the aggressive drive, voluntary sphincter control, a shift from passive to active modes, and ambivalence toward the mother in a struggle for separation, individuation, and independence.

applied psychoanalysis: the application of psychoanalytic theory to a number of other fields, including literature, art, history, anthropology, and religion.

artha: the pursuit of material gain and power as one of the four goals in life; encompassed by the first goal, *dharma*.

Arya Samaj: a major nineteenth-century Hindu reform movement started in the Punjab by Swami Dayananda: among its many reforms, it emphasized women's education.

ashram: a residence or hermitage of a saint, sadhu, or guru engaged in some form of religious instruction.

ashrama: the four stages of life for males of the three upper castes: the first stage is *brahmacharya*, or a period of education and discipline. The second is *garhasthya*, or the time of householding and active production in society. The third stage, *vanaprasthya*, or partial retreat from worldly ties, comes after one's children are grown and married. The last stage, *sannyasa*, involves total immersion in spiritual pursuits.

Atman: the true or spiritual Self, Supreme Existence, essentially undefinable.

ayah: a housekeeper who takes care of the children.

bhadralok: community of Western-educated Bengali Hindu men and their

335

families from whom came many of the intelligentsia during British colonial rule; they were especially strong during the nineteenth and early twentieth centuries.

Bhagavad Gita: "The Song of the Lord," a highly popular sacred book, consisting of a long dialogue between Krishna, an incarnation of Vishnu, and Arjuna, a noble warrior: it is both an independent work and part of the epic, the *Mahabharata*.

Bhagavata Purana: the leading *Purana*, composed in south India in the ninth or tenth century A.D., which tells the story of Krishna, an incarnation of Vishnu, and is a major text for *bhakti* worship.

bhajan: a religious hymn chanted or sung in the local language in honor of a deity—often Shiva, Vishnu, or Krishna—as part of various *bhakti* cults, and carried to a high pitch of ecstatic emotion, often through dancing.

bhakti: a popular path of devotion and love for God manifested as a major deity or incarnation: music, songs, poetry, and the dance are all used. The *Bhagavad Gita* and the *Bhagavad Purana* are the main *bhakti* texts.

bhakti yoga: a discipline of yoga using devotion and love for God.

bipolar internalization process: the two processes of developing self-regard: identifying with others whom one has idealized, and internalizing empathic responses from others. *See* idealized selfobject, mirroring.

Brahman: the Supreme Reality conceived as one and undifferentiated, static and dynamic, the ultimate principle or reality, yet above all definitions.

brahmin: the priestly caste, highest in the *varna* hierarchy of castes.

castration anxiety: fear of genital loss or injury; an integral part of the Oedipus complex and a major source of conflict in child development, playing a large role in the formation of symptoms and character traits.

confidentiality: in psychoanalysis, not revealing to others what a patient has communicated to the psychoanalyst.

countertransference: the analyst's own feelings, reactions, and attitudes toward the patient as they relate either to the analyst's own unresolved problems or to what is subtly evoked by the patient; gives important clues to the underlying meanings of the patient's way of relating to the analyst.

cultural relativism: an anthropological theory that societies vary widely in cultural values, and that cultures different from one's own require examination from the indigenous point of view: personality

336

patterns are seen as integral parts of pervasive, culturally distinctive configurations.

darshan: literally, sight or vision: having *darshan* of a saint, sage, or deity means being in his or her presence and receiving a blessing by being there.

defenses: painful feelings of anxiety, guilt, or shame that impel the ego unconsciously to ward off forbidden wishes, drives, or feelings.

defense mechanisms: specific methods of the ego to ward off forbidden wishes, drives, and feelings that activate painful feelings of anxiety, guilt, or shame.

developmental arrests: experiences that an individual legitimately needed at a certain childhood stage of development, but which were insufficiently present: for example, an unempathic maternal relationship, or insufficient qualities to idealize in parental figures.

developmental deficits: these result from developmental arrests and constitute what is missing inside a person's psychic structures, such as insufficient self-esteem.

developmental models: models to describe the development of different psychological structures, functions, and behavior in childhood and adolescence in terms of the interaction between maturation of inherent human capacities and familial relationships.

developmental schemas: *see* developmental models.

developmental stages: the varying phases of the development, particularly in childhood but also in adolescence, of different dimensions of psychological structures and functions.

dharma: the traditional established order, which includes all duties—individual, moral, social, and religious: everyone has his or her individual *dharma* (*svadharma*), which is determined less by abstract moral principles than by contextual factors such as stage in the life cycle, particular hierarchical relationships, caste, and individual temperament.

displacement: the unconscious association of feelings with a different image (as in dreams) or a different person (as in transference) from the original situation or person that evoked them.

drive theory: a theory that considers the vicissitudes of the sexual (libidinal) and aggressive drives to be motivational forces that initiate behavior, and that studies the interaction of the drives with defenses in inner conflict.

ego: the theory of what the ego is has varied in psychoanalytic formulations: in Freud's theory, the ego encompassed both the internalization of early relationships and various functions. In ego psychology as first developed by Hartmann, the ego was defined in terms of function only. Some functions, such as perception, language, thinking, and such are relatively free of conflict. Other functions, such as defenses, are much more involved in unconscious conflict.

ego boundaries: a phenomenological concept formulated by Federn (1952) to denote the kinds of emotional boundaries between self and other, and between the conscious self and one's inner emotional and fantasy life.

ego functions: most relevant to psychoanalysis among numerous ego functions are reality testing and adaptation to reality, regulation and control of drives, relationships with others, thought processes, defenses, and synthetic or integrative abilities.

ego-ideal: the image of the self to which individuals aspire both consciously and unconsciously, and against which they measure themselves, based on childhood and adolescent identifications with parents and other figures, or idealized images of them, and parental expectations of the child.

ego-identity: the ego's ability to integrate various experiences into an identity, maintaining continuity and sameness.

ego psychology: a major dimension in psychoanalytic theory, beginning with Freud's structural theory (1923, 1926): its focus has been on different facets of the ego, ranging from its various functions (including those involved in psychological conflict as well as those that are conflict-free) to its adaptation to the social environment, its development (including a strong emphasis on developmental models), and its role in individuation.

ego states: a concept formulated by Federn (1952) for experiential states of mind that differ during varying activities of a person's day as well as through the person's life cycle.

English school of psychoanalysis: a group of major theorists with varied viewpoints, such as Bion (1977), Klein (Segal 1964), Fairbairn (1952), Guntrip (1968), and Winnicott (1951, 1965), all of whom subscribe to some version of object-relations theory, which emphasizes the central importance of the early mother-child relationship, its internalization, and its role in psychological development and psychopathology.

epigenetic stages: in Erikson's (1950) developmental model, stages of development that overlap and encompass the preceding one(s).

ethnosociology: an anthropological theory, developed chiefly in South Asian studies, which gives the cultural values and philosophic as-

338

sumptions of a culture central importance in any theoretical analysis of that society.

false self: the unconscious submission to parents' and others' expectations when such expectations do not accord with an inner authentic sense of one's own self (Winnicott 1960).

functions: these are grouped under the id, ego, and superego in classical psychoanalysis. (*See* id, ego, ego-ideal, *and* superego.)

genital phase: the final phase of psychosexual development: at puberty, component sexual drives from earlier stages of psychosexual development have been organized in the service of ultimate genital satisfaction. Successful resolution of this phase implies the ability to love others and achieve intimacy.

giri: social obligation.

guna: the three properties or aspects of *prakriti* or primordial matter: *sattva*, or the quality of harmony and luminosity; *rajas*, or energy, activity, and passion; and *tamas*, or inertia, torpor, and pleasure-seeking: the three *gunas* are in everyone in different balances, with one or another predominant.

historical evolutionism: a theory that presupposes the superiority of one culture over another in an evolutionary scale that inevitably places Western societies at the top.

id: a totally unconscious part of the mental apparatus representing the sum total of wishes arising from the individual's needs, which are indicated by their mental representations, that is, the instinctual drives.

idealized selfobject: the psychological meaning a deeply respected other has for oneself, particularly in terms of someone to identify with and enhance one's self-regard. Kohut (1971) originally saw this as a developmental need of childhood and adolescence, but he later (1984) formulated this need as existing throughout life.

idealizing transference: in self psychology, a patient's perception of the analyst as an idealized selfobject as a reparative experience for damaged self-esteem from the past. In other more borderline kinds of psychopathology, the therapist may be idealized as an unconscious defense against rage, which is split off to another person who is denigrated, or the therapist may be denigrated and another idealized.

identification: a normal, usually unconscious developmental process whereby an individual becomes like another person in one or several aspects. Identification aids in the learning process as well as in the acquisition of interests, ideals, and such.

ie stem family: a family structure in which the oldest or only son inherits in the main house (*honke*), with younger sons setting up their own households (*bunke*) under the male authority of the main house. The *ie* has also been a corporate household with occupational specialization, in which adopted sons or sons-in-law, employees, and servants are integral members of the *ie*, while larger organizational structures are formed through intermarriage (*shinseku*), building on the main and branch houses (*dozoku*).

imago: inner image derived from childhood familial relationships.

individualization: a psychological process in Indians and Japanese by which wishes, inclinations, and talents of children, adolescents, and young adults are given greater recognition and scope than previously accorded in the realms of education, vocation, marital choice, and familial relationships.

individuation: a term used in different ways by different psychoanalysts. Mahler et al. (1975) use it as the development of ego skills from six months to three years of age to effect inner separation of the self from the love object, thus hyphenating this process as separation-individuation. Menaker 1980, 1982) sees individuation as the progressive development, differentiation, and new integrations of the self accomplished through the will in constant interaction with one's social and cultural environment throughout life.

intentional ambiguity: a multi-leveled view of reality that is cultivated in Hindu ways of thinking and communication.

internal objects: from the perspective of Melanie Klein (Segal 1964), inner enduring schemas of others modeled by experiences, images, fantasy, and projections.

internal representational world: stable images of self and other derived from childhood interaction with family members, colored to varying extents by fantasy and projections.

internalization process: a progressive process by which external interactions between the self and others are replaced by inner representations of these interactions and their end results.

jati: caste, in the sense of communities traditionally sharing an occupation within which marriages are arranged. This use of caste is different from *varna* or the ranking of the four major castes.

jñana yoga: the path of discrimination, knowledge, and rigorous self-discipline that leads to the Divine.

juku: in contemporary usage, a cram school for entrance examinations usually preparatory to college but sometimes to high school.

kama: sexual desire as one of the four goals of life; encompassed by the first goal, *dharma*.

karma: a complex concept indicating the effect of any action upon the doer, whether man or god, in the past, present, or future life.

karma yoga: the path of discriminating, selfless action that leads to the Divine.

kayastha: a high-ranking caste originally consisting of scribes.

kshatriya: the administrative-military caste, second in ranking in the *varna* system of caste.

Kundalini: the Supreme Power, sometimes called the "Serpent Power," located at the base of the spinal column. When aroused by certain forms of yoga, it travels through certain centers higher in the spinal column to yield spiritual experiences.

latency: the state of relative inactivity of the sexual drive during the period from the resolution of the Oedipus complex to pubescence (from five or six years old to eleven, twelve, or thirteen). Drive energy is channeled into learning and the acquistion of basic cultural skills; latency is thus a period of considerable ego development and differentiation.

latent content: the underlying meanings of a dream.

libidinal self: the self as infused with sensuality and wishing.

libido theory: the theoretical description of a characteristic biological maturational sequence of phases from the oral to the mature genital phase, deriving from an extensive exploration of the origin, development, and vicissitudes of sexual drive influences from birth to old age, interrelating sexual drive organization with total personality development. Libido theory dominated psychoanalytic thinking until the early 1920s, after which there was increasing interest in the ego and its development.

Mahabharata: one of the two major Indian epic poems. It tells of the battle between two branches of a royal family, and includes the *Bhagavad Gita*.

manifest content: the dream as remembered and reported.

maya: a concept that the world and one's emotional attachments in it are but appearances that mask a deeper reality; God's creative energy and cosmic illusion.

metapsychology: the highest level of abstraction in establishing a systematizing framework around which clinical data and various psychoanalytic propositions are organized. Metapsychology encompasses viewpoints that include the dynamic (psychological forces in conflict), the economic (the deployment of psychological energies), the structural (id, ego, and superego), the genetic (relating to the individual's history and development), and the adaptive (inner psychological changes and modifications of the social environment to bring about a harmonious relationship between the individual and others).

metonymic thinking: a mode of thought that places signifier and signified in the same context, making an object or event continuous with another reality rather than symbolic of it: for example, a book as a partial manifestation of the goddess Saraswati.

mirroring: developmentally, the quality of empathic and valuing responses, as well as emotional relatedness, that a parental figure gives to a child, with the child reading his or her self-image and self-regard from these responses. In adulthood, it is the empathic responsiveness one person has for another.

mirroring transference: process by which the analyst serves as an empathic selfobject to remedy past deficits in empathic relationships.

moksha: one of the four goals and highest aim of human life, the liberation from the bondage of *karma* and rebirth, and the attainment of unity in the Supreme through various forms of yoga.

moratorium: a concept of Erikson (1968: 156–158) denoting a period of delay of adult commitments to work or school, to allow the individual to work out further his or her identity.

narcissism: a highly complex subject full of healthy controversy in psychoanalysis, quite different from its more popular, pejorative meaning of self-centeredness (Lasch 1979). From a self psychological perspective (Kohut 1971, 1977; Stolorow and Lachmann 1980), everyday psychological activity is narcissistic to the degree that it functions to help develop, structure, and maintain self-regard (in Westerners) or we-self regard (in Indians, Japanese, and other Asian and African people), and thus to foster a positive inner image in the person. This building up of inner esteem takes place through two major processes of internalization: idealization and mirroring. Healthy narcissism or positive feelings of esteem derive from good mirroring and idealization experiences, whereas narcissistic wounds and the psychopathology of developmental arrests and deficits are caused by idealization and/or mirroring experiences gone awry.

narcissistic injury: a wound to a person's self-esteem from something hurtful communicated through words or actions.

narcissistic rage: an angry reaction to narcissistic injury.

ninjo: human emotions, emotional responsiveness, and relatedness to another.

342

object-relations theory: a major psychoanalytic theory of the effect of relationships with familial figures, primarily in early childhood, and to a much lesser extent in later childhood and adolescence, examining how relationships are internalized into the growing child's psyche, their aid in development, and the role these internalized images play both in normal and psychopathological adult functioning.

object-representation: an enduring schema of images of another person derived from a multitude of impressions and experiences with that person, sometimes colored by fantasy or projections.

oedipal phase: the period during which the Oedipus complex occurs.

Oedipus complex: a characteristic group of sexual drives, relationships, and fears found at the height of the phallic phase of psychosexual development (three to six years). The child strives in a limited way for sexual union with the parent of the opposite sex and for the death or disappearance of the parent of the same sex. The specific fear for these forbidden wishes is castration in the male and fear of penetration and damage in the female.

omoiyari: concerned empathic kindness.

on: a social debt or obligation.

oral character: a personality type developed through strong gratification of oral needs in early infancy, consisting of later optimistic attitudes to the world, altruistic feelings toward others, and strong expectations of having one's needs fulfilled in dependency relationships.

parameter: a term conceptualizing departures from classical psychoanalytic technique in which interpretation is the exclusive technical tool.

particularism: in anthropology, a differential occurrence of a certain type of behavior as relative to, because determined by, differential sociocultural conditions. In South Asian theory, it refers to the idiosyncratic makeup of the person.

phallic character: a personality type characterized by recklessness and resoluteness, pride and courage, bashfulness and timidity, traits developed around the conflicts of the castration complex during the phallic phase.

prakriti: primordial matter or nature consisting of three qualities or *gunas* in a state of equilibrium.

primacy of psychic reality: the psychoanalytic assumption that psychic reality takes precedence over all other realities.

primary process: both a mode of psychic energy discharge and a type of thought process. The latter applies to a nonrational type of wishful thought, dominated by the emotions, close to the drives, and characterized by condensation (one image encompassing different associations and meanings), displacement (affects belonging to one image but attached to another), and symbolism. Primary process thinking has been characteristically conceptualized as disguising forbidden wishes, but in recent years it has also been viewed as expressing various aspects of the self (Noy 1968).

projection: a process whereby a painful impulse or idea that cannot be tolerated is unconsciously attributed to others.

projective identification: the unconscious projection of some aspect of one's own self, frequently a forbidden aspect, onto another person, and subsequently to relate to the other on the basis of that projection.

psychic determinism: the doctrine that all present events are influenced and largely shaped by the past, all psychic events and processes following strict laws so that the determining factors for current human behavior and symptomatology can be understood in psychological terms.

psychic structures: usually the id, ego, and superego, each of which is composed of groups of mental contents (memories, affects, fantasies, organized thoughts, and body images) and processes that are functionally related to each other.

psychic unity of mankind: the psychoanalytic assumption that all peoples have similar human potentialities.

psychological determinism: the theory that individual psychological factors are independent causes of cultural and social behavior.

psychoneurotic symptoms: compromise formations that derive from unconscious psychic conflict between the partial disguised gratification of unconscious fantasy wishes and psychic structures such as the ego and superego, which oppose the open expression of these wishes.

psychosexual theory: theory related to psychosexual development and the influence of this development on character formation.

psychosexual stages of development: a regular sequence of libidinal manifestations beginning in early infancy and continuing to adulthood. The early phases of infantile sexuality are organized sequentially around the oral, anal, and phallic. Besides physical pleasures associated with these phases, there are also psychic gratifications and frustrations with their accompanying conflicts.

psychosocial: a concept connecting the inner psychological world of the individual with social interaction.

psychosocial stages of development: stages of psychological development in childhood and adolescence, related to changing social interactions with parents and significant others.

puja: the common form of ceremonial worship of gods and goddesses, performed by both priest and individual.

Puranas: Narrative works dealing with ancient kings, sages, heroes, and the gods, in a synthesis of legends and myths. There are eighteen major and eighteen minor Puranas, constituting the main texts of popular Hinduism, particularly used in the *bhakti* cults.

raga: emotion; meaning can vary with the context. In music it denotes a mood related to a given time of day or season. Also the suffix of *anuraga*, meaning the first feelings of affection in a love affair. "Anger" in colloquial Bengali.

Ramayana: a large epic work centered around the noble king, Rama, an incarnation of Vishnu.

rationalism: a philosophical viewpoint emphasizing logic, causality, and reason.

reaction-formation: an unconscious defense whereby a painful idea or feeling is replaced in conscious awareness by its opposite.

resistances: strong counterforces to self-awareness and change, manifested in a variety of ways, which patients encounter during psychoanalytic treatment.

sadhana: any form of spiritual exercise from the simplest to the most complex, usually done under the guidance of a guru.

sado-masochism: a propensity both to inflict suffering on others and to seek physical or mental suffering oneself.

samskaras: purification rites for the various stages of life, to purify a temple, image, or ritual object; also, impressions or psychic traces remaining in the mind after an experience in the current or past life, indirectly influencing one's acts and thoughts.

sati: faithfulness; also the voluntary ritual burning of a widow on her husband's funeral pyre.

scheduled castes: castes formerly called untouchable because of occupations considered to be highly polluting.

secondary process: predominantly logical, controlled thinking characterized by the delay of immediate gratification as contrasted to the free fantasies and discharges of unbound energy in the primary process.

self-identity: a concept of Erikson (1968), referring to the actual contents and experiencing of one's identity.

selfobject: the psychological meaning one person has for another in terms of the development and maintenance of self-esteem and self-cohesiveness, particularly whether the other is experienced as mirroring (empathic) or idealized. Selfobject is a concept from self psychology.

self psychology: the theory formulated by Kohut (1971, 1977, 1984) to account for the narcissistic dimension of human experience in terms of self-regard and a cohesive self; how this is developed through bipolar internalization processes of mirroring and idealizations; and how developmental arrests and deficits manifest themselves in psychopathology and transferences.

separation-individuation: a developmental stage that Mahler et al. (1975) have formulated to describe the development of ego skills from age six months through three years, whereby the child differentiates inner images of self from the mother.

shadow: Jungian term for what is kept out of awareness, but nevertheless surfaces.

shakti: divine, creative energy; Supreme Power.

shinkeishitsu personality: a syndrome of psychopathology first described by Morita (Reynolds 1976), characterized by self-blame for symptoms of extreme perfectionism and hypersensitivity to oneself and others.

somatization: the tendency to react to disturbing stimuli with physical manifestations, such as headaches and stomach aches, rather than psychological ones. Actual physiological changes can take place in the body systems affected.

structural theory: advanced by Freud in 1923, the theory that the mind is divided into three functional groups called the ego, id, and superego. The groups are called structures because of the relative constancy of their objectives and consistency in modes of operation.

superego: those psychic functions which, in their manifest expression, represent moral attitudes, conscience, and the sense of guilt. The superego results from the internalization of the ethical standards of society, and develops by identification with the attitudes of parents and other significant persons in the child's life.

symbiosis: the interdependent condition of the human infant and mother; also a very early stage of development in which inner images of the self and mother have not yet been differentiated.

synchronicity: a Jungian term to describe parallel events in psychological and social or material reality with no causal relation; for example, a storm that occurs when there is a great personal tragedy.

topographical theory: the branch of psychoanalytic theory that attempts

346

to classify mental operations and contents according to their relationship to consciousness. Thus an idea, wish, or feeling that cannot be made conscious occurs in the unconscious, whereas if it can be brought to conscious awareness by an act of attention, it occurs in the preconscious. Other mental events occur in conscious awareness.

transference: the unconscious displacement of patterns of feeling and behavior, and the unconscious projection of inner images of self and other originally experienced with significant figures of one's childhood, to individuals in one's current relationships.

transference-analysis: the analysis of the transference as it is manifested in the relationship with both the psychoanalyst and others.

transitional objects: objects such as a blanket or toy on which a young child gradually depends when the relationship with the mothering person is only partially internalized, and which enable the child to withstand separation without undue anxiety. A seminal contribution of D. W. Winnicott (1951), further elaborated in Grolnick and Barkin (1978).

transmuting internalizations: the internalization of mirroring and idealizing selfobjects to develop and sustain necessary inner structures for a cohesive self and self-regard.

universalism: the idea that a particular belief or behavior pattern in one society occurs in all, or that one theory may be valid everywhere.

Upanishads: late Vedic treatises dealing with the Ultimate Reality of *Brahman* and *Atman*.

varna: the caste system in terms of ranking by occupations with four major castes: *brahmin*, or the priestly caste; *kshatriya*, or the administrative-military caste; *vaishya*, or merchant caste; and *sudra*, or artisan and peasant caste.

Vedas: the four *Vedas* are the earliest known Indian scriptures. The *Rig Veda* is a collection of praises in the form of hymns, the *Sama Veda* a collection of hymns, the *Yajur Veda* a collection of sacrificial formulas, and the *Artha Veda* a collection of charms and magic formulas: these texts are considered to have been revealed through seers.

Vaishya: Merchant or businessman, the third-ranking caste in the *varna* system of caste.

yoga: to yoke; various forms of spiritual disciplines to link the individual to an inner spiritual reality.

REFERENCES

Abraham, K. 1924. The influence of oral sadism on character-formation. In *Selected papers on psychoanalysis*, 393–406. London: Hogarth Press.

Alexander, F. 1950. Analysis of the therapeutic factors in psychoanalytic treatment. *Psychoanalytic Quarterly*. 19:482–500.

Alexander, V. K. 1979. Rural psychotherapeutic process. In *Psychotherapeutic processes*, edited by M. Kapur, V. N. Murthy, K. Sathyavathi, R. L. Kapur, 39–40. Bangalore: National Institute of Mental Health and Neuro Sciences.

Anandalakshmi. 1978. *Socialization for competence*. Delhi: Indian Council for Social Science Research.

———. 1981. Living in families: A holographic image of the Indian. Unpublished paper presented at the A.C.L.S./S.S.R.C. Workshop on Life Courses and Family Relationships in Alternative Psychologies of South Asia, Chicago, September.

Bailey, F. G. 1960. The joint family in India. *Economic Weekly*. February 20.

Bassa, D. M. 1978. From the traditional to the modern: Some observations on changes in Indian child rearing and parental attitudes. In *The child and his family in a changing world*, edited by E. Anthony and C. Chiland, 333–344. New York: John Wiley.

Bennett, J. W.; H. Passin; and R. K. McKnight. 1958. *In search of identity: The Japanese overseas scholar in America and Japan*. Minneapolis: University Minnesota Press.

Berliner, B. 1947. On some psychodynamics of masochism. *Psychoanalytic Review*. 16:459–471.

Bernstein, D. 1978. Female identity synthesis. In *Career and motherhood: Struggles for a new identity*, edited by A. Roland and B. Harris, 103–124. New York: Human Sciences Press.

———. 1983. The female superego: A different perspective. *International Journal of Psycho-Analysis*. 64:187–202.

Berry, J. W. 1980. Social and cultural change. In *Handbook of cross-cultural psychology*, volume 5, edited by H. Triandis and R. Brislin, 211–280. Boston: Allyn and Bacon.

349

Beteille, A. 1964. Family and social change in India and other South Asian countries. *Economic Weekly.* 16:237–244.

Bharati, A. 1965. *The tantric tradition.* London: Rider and Co.

Bhattacharya, S. 1981. Women in science and technology, some points to ponder. Unpublished paper presented at the National Conference on Women's Studies, SNDT College, Bombay, April.

Blanck, G., and R. Blanck. 1974. *Ego psychology: Theory and practice.* New York: Columbia University Press.

Bion, W. 1977. *Seven servants.* New York: Jason Aronson.

Bon Maharaj, Swami B. H. 1963. *Jiva atma or finite self.* Vrindavan: Institute of Oriental Philosophy.

Bose, G. 1966. A new theory of mental life. *Samiksa.* 20:1–105.

Boyer, L. B. 1979. *Childhood and folklore: A psychoanalytic study of Apache personality.* New York: Library of Psychological Anthropology.

Brenman-Gibson, M. 1981. *Clifford Odets: American playwright.* New York: Atheneum.

———. 1975. Transcendental meditation, psychoanalysis, and creativity. Unpublished paper presented as the Edmund Weil Memorial Lecture, Institute for Psychoanalytic Training and Research, New York City.

Burg, M. 1960. Cross-cultural psychotherapy of schizophrenics. *Transcultural Research in Mental Health Problems.* Montreal: McGill University Press.

———. 1969. A psychoanalytic study of Japanese linguistic symbolic processes: Relevance to Occidental schizophrenia. *Annual Journal of the Asia-Africa Cultural Research Institute.* March.

———. 1980. Aspects of life-space psychoanalytic therapy. *Annual Journal of the Asia-Africa Cultural Research Institute.* March; 69–78.

Burke, K. 1941. *The philosophy of literary form.* New York: Random House. 1957.

Carrington, P. 1977. *Freedom in meditation.* Garden City, New York: Anchor Press/Doubleday.

Carstairs, M. 1957. *The twice-born, a study of high-caste Hindus.* London: Hogarth Press.

Caudhill, W., and D. W. Plath. 1974. Who sleeps by whom? Parent-child involvement in urban Japanese families. In *Japanese culture and behavior,* edited by T. Lebra and W. Lebra, 277– 312. Honolulu: University Press of Hawaii.

Chaudhuri, N. C. 1930–1931. The "martial races" of India, I-IV. *Mod-*

ern Review (Calcutta). 48, no.1 (1930): 6–51; 48, no.3 (1930): 295–307; 49, no.1 (1931): 67–79; 49, no.2 (1931): 215–228.

Chhabra, R. 1981. Women and the media: What strategies for change. Unpublished paper presented at the National Conference on Women's Studies, SNDT College, Bombay, April.

Collins, A., and P. Desai. 1986. Selfhood and context. In *The cultural transitions, human experience and social transformations in the third world and Japan,* edited by M. White and S. Pollak. London: Routledge & Kegan Paul.

Condon, J. 1985. *A half step behind: Japanese women of the '80s.* New York: Dodd, Mead & Company.

Crapanzano, V. 1980. *Tuhami, portrait of a Moroccan.* Chicago: University of Chicago Press.

Daniel, E. V. 1976. A pilgrim's progress: A Peircean point of view. Unpublished paper presented at the A.C.L.S./S.S.R.C. Workshop on the Person and Interpersonal Relationships in South Asia: An Exploration of Indigenous Conceptual Systems, Chicago, May.

Das, V. 1975. Marriage among the Hindus. In *Indian women,* edited by D. Jain, 69–86. Delhi: Publications Division, Ministry of Information and Broadcasting, Government of India.

———. 1976a. Indian women: Work, power, and status. In *Indian women: From purdah to modernity,* edited by B. R. Nanda, 129–145. New Delhi: Vikas.

———. 1976b. Masks and faces: An essay on Punjabi kinship. *Contributions to Indian Sociology.* 10:1–30.

———. 1977. *Structure and cognition: Aspects of Hindu caste and ritual.* Delhi: Oxford University Press.

———. 1979. Reflections on the social construction of adulthood. In *Identity and adulthood in India,* edited by S. Kakar, 89–104. Delhi: Oxford University Press.

Das, V., and R. Nicholas. 1979. Family and "household": Differences and division in South Asian domestic life. Unpublished paper.

Desai, N. 1981. Reinforcing subordination of women: An analysis of media portrayal of women. Unpublished paper presented at the National Conference on Women's Studies, SNDT College, Bombay, April.

Desai, P., and G. Coelho. 1980. Indian immigrants in America: Some cultural aspects of psychological adaptation. In *The new ethnics: Asian Indians in the United States,* edited by P. Saran and E. Eames, 363–386. New York: Praeger.

351

Devereux, G. 1978. *Ethnopsychoanalysis*. Berkeley and Los Angeles: University of California Press.

———. 1980. *Basic problems of ethnopsychiatry*. Chicago: University of Chicago Press.

DeVos, G. 1973. *Socialization for achievement*. Berkeley and Los Angeles: University of California Press.

———. 1980. Afterword to *The quiet therapies*, by D. K. Reynolds 113–132. Honolulu: University Press of Hawaii.

———. 1985. Dimensions of the self in Japanese culture. In *Culture and self: Asian and Western perspectives*, edited by Marsella, A. J.; G. DeVos; and F.L.K. Hsu, 141–184. London: Tavistock Publishers.

Dhairyam, D. 1961. Research need for development of psychotherapy. In *Recent trends in psychotherapy*, edited by T. K. Menon. Bombay: Orient Longmans.

Doi, T. 1973. *The anatomy of dependence*. Tokyo: Kodansha International.

———. 1985. Psychotherapy: A cross-cultural perspective from Japan. In *Mental health services—the cross-cultural context. Cross-cultural research and methodology*, volume 7, edited by P. B. Pederson; N. Sartorius; and A. J. Marsella, 267–279. New York: Sage Publications.

———. 1986. *The anatomy of the self: The individual versus society*. Tokyo: Kodansha International.

Dore, R. P., ed. 1967. *Aspects of social change in Japan*. Princeton: Princeton University Press.

Dube, S. C. 1955. *Indian village*. London: Routledge and Kegan Paul.

Dumont, L. 1970. *Homo hierarchicus*. Chicago: University of Chicago Press.

Edel, L. 1966. Hawthorne's symbolism and psychoanalysis. In *Hidden patterns: Studies in psychoanalytic literary criticism*, edited by L. Manheim and E. Manheim, 93–111. New York: Macmillan.

Egnor, M. 1980. Ambiguity in the oral exegesis of a sacred text: *Tirukkovaiyar*. Unpublished paper.

Ehrenzweig, A. 1967. *The hidden order of art*. Berkeley and Los Angeles: University of California Press.

Eisenbud, J. 1953. Telepathy and problems of psychoanalysis. In *Psychoanalysis and the occult*, edited by G. Devereux, 223–261. New York: International Universities Press.

Eliade, M. 1959. *The sacred and the profane*. New York: Harcourt Brace.

Endleman, R. 1981. *Psyche and society: Explorations in psychoanalytic sociology.* New York: Columbia University Press.

Erikson, E. 1946. Ego development and historical change. In *Identity and the life cycle.* New York: International Universities Press. Reprint 1959.

———. 1950. *Childhood and society.* New York: W. W. Norton.

———. 1958. *Young man Luther.* New York: W. W. Norton.

———. 1963. *Childhood and society.* 2d ed. New York: W. W. Norton.

———. 1968. *Identity, youth and crisis.* New York: W. W. Norton.

———. 1969. *Gandhi's truth.* New York: W. W. Norton.

Fairbairn, W.R.D. 1972. *Psychoanalytic studies of the personality.* London: Tavistock Publishing.

Federn, P. 1952. *Ego psychology and the psychoses.* New York: Basic Books.

Fenichel, O. 1945. *The psychoanalytic theory of neurosis.* New York: Norton.

Freud, S. 1905. Three essays on the theory of sexuality. *Standard edition.* 7:135–243. London: Hogarth Press, 1953.

———. 1914. On narcissism: An introduction. *Standard edition.* 9:73–102. London: Hogarth Press, 1953.

———. 1917. A difficulty in the path of psycho-analysis. *Standard edition.* 17:135–144. London: Hogarth Press, 1953.

———. 1922. Dreams and telepathy. *Standard edition.* 18:195–220. London: Hogarth Press, 1953.

———. 1923. The ego and the id. *Standard edition.* 19:13–59. London: Hogarth Press, 1953.

———. 1925. Some psychological consequences of the anatomical distinction between the sexes. *Standard edition.* 19:248–260. London: Hogarth Press, 1953.

———. 1926. Inhibitions, symptoms and anxiety. *Standard edition.* 20:87–156.

———. 1927. Future of an illusion. *Standard edition.* 21:5–58. London: Hogarth Press, 1953.

———. 1930. Civilization and its discontents. *Standard edition.* 21:64–148. London: Hogarth Press, 1953.

———. 1931. Libidinal types. *Standard edition.* 21:215–220. London: Hogarth Press.

Fromm, E. and D. T. Suzuki. 1970. *Zen Buddhism and psychoanalysis.* New York: Harper and Row.

Gedo, J. 1979. *Beyond interpretation.* New York: International Universities Press.

————. 1981. *Advances in clinical psychoanalysis*. New York: International Universities Press.

Gedo, J., and A. Goldberg. 1973. *Models of the mind*. Chicago: University of Chicago Press.

Geertz, C. 1973. *The interpretation of cultures*. New York: Basic Books.

Gilligan, C. 1980. *In a different voice*. Cambridge: Harvard University Press.

Goffman, E. 1959. *The presentation of the self in everyday life*. Garden City, N.Y.: Doubleday.

Goldberg, A., ed. 1980. *Advances in self psychology*. New York: International Universities Press.

Goldman, R. P. 1978. Fathers, sons and gurus: Oedipal conflict in the Sanscrit epics. *Journal of Indian Philosophy*. 6:325–392.

Gordon, L. 1974. *Bengal: The nationalist movement, 1876–1940*. New York: Columbia University Press.

Gore, M. S. 1965. The traditional Indian family. In *Comparative family systems*, edited by M. Nimkoff, 209–231. New York: Houghton Mifflin.

————. 1978. Familial change and the process of socialization in India. In *The child and his family in social change*, edited by E. Anthony and C. Chiland, 365–374. New York: John Wiley.

Greenson, R. 1967. The working alliance. In *The technique and practice of psychoanalysis*, 190–223. New York: International Universities Press.

Greenson, R., and M. Wexler. 1969. The non-transference relationship in the psychoanalytic situation. *International Journal of Psycho-Analysis*. 50:27–39.

Grey, A. 1973. Oedipus in Hindu dreams. *Contemporary Psychoanalysis*. 9:327–355.

Grinker, R. 1957. On identification. *International Journal of Psycho-Analysis*. 38:379–390.

Grolnick, S., and L. Barkin, eds. 1978. *Between reality and fantasy*. New York: Jason Aronson.

Guntrip, H. 1968. *Schizoid phenomena, object relations and the self*. New York: International Universities Press.

Haas, W. 1956. *Destiny of the mind, East and West*. New York: Doubleday.

Halbfass, W. 1982. Book review: *The oceanic feeling* by J. M. Massson. *Journal of Asian Studies*. 41:387–388.

Hall, E. T. 1959. *The silent language*. Garden City, New York: Doubleday.

354

Hallowell, I. A. 1955. *Culture and experience.* Philadelphia: University of Pennsylvania Press.

Hanchette, S. 1975. Hindu potlaches: Communal reciprocity and prestige in Karnataka. In *Competition and modernization in South Asia,* edited by Helen Ullrich, 27–59. New Delhi: Abhinav Publishers.

———. 1988. *Coloured rice: Symbolic structure in Hindu family festivals.* Delhi: Hindustan Publishing Corporation.

Hartmann, H. 1939. *Ego psychology and the problem of adaptation.* New York: International Universities Press, 1958.

———. 1964. *Essays on ego psychology.* New York: International Universities Press.

Hoch, E. 1977. Psychotherapy for the illiterate. In *New dimensions in psychiatry: A world view.* Volume 2, edited by S. Arieti and G. Chrzanowski, 75–92. New York: John Wiley.

Hoffman, S. 1981. Faction behavior and cultural codes: India and Japan. *Journal of Asian Studies.* 41:231–254.

Hsu, F.L.K. 1963. *Clan, caste and club.* Princeton: Van Nostrand.

———. 1971. Psychological homeostasis and *jen:* Conceptual tools for advancing psychological anthropology. *American Anthropologist.* 73:23–44.

———. 1972. American core values and national character. In *Psychological anthropology: Approaches to culture and personality,* edited by F.L.K. Hsu, 209–230. Cambridge: Schankman.

———. 1985. The self in cross-cultural perspective. In *Culture and self: Asian and Western perspectives,* edited by Marsella, A. J.; G. DeVos; and F.L.K. Hsu, 24–55. London: Tavistock Publishers.

Hutchins, F. G. 1967. *The illusion of permanence: British imperialism in India.* Princeton: Princeton University Press.

Inden, R. 1976. *Marriage and rank in Bengali culture: A history of caste and clan in middle-period Bengal.* Berkeley and Los Angeles: University of California Press.

Inden, R., and R. Nicholas. 1977. *Kinship in Bengali culture.* Chicago: University of Chicago Press.

Inkeles, A., and D. Smith. 1974. *Becoming modern.* Cambridge: Harvard University Press.

Jacobson, E. 1964. *The self and object world.* New York: International Universities Press.

Jain, D. 1975. Introduction. In *Indian women,* edited by D. Jain, xi–xxii. Delhi: Publications Division, Ministry of Information and Broadcasting, Government of India.

Joshi, P. C. 1977. The value problem and the study of social change. In

Dimensions of social change in India, edited by M. N. Srivnivas, S. Seshaiah, and V. S. Parthasarathy, 59–81. New Delhi: Allied Publishers.

Jung, C. G. 1968. *Man and his symbols.* Edited by C. G. Jung. New York: Dell.

Kahn, M. 1974. *The privacy of the self.* New York: International Universities Press.

Kakar, S. 1978. *The inner world: A psychoanalytic study of childhood and society in India.* Delhi: Oxford University Press.

———, ed. 1979. *Identity and adulthood.* Delhi: Oxford University Press.

———. 1982. *Shamans, mystics, and doctors.* New York: Alfred A. Knopf.

———. 1980. Observations on "the Oedipal alliance" in a patient with a narcissistic personality disorder. *Samiksa.* 34:47–53.

Kapadia, K. M. 1966. *Marriage and family in India.* London: Oxford University Press.

Kapur, P. 1974. *The changing status of the working woman in India.* Delhi: Vikas.

Kardiner, A. 1945. *The psychological frontiers of society.* New York: Columbia University Press.

Karlekar, M. 1981. For women and employment—a perspective. Unpublished paper presented at the National Conference on Women's Studies, SNDT College, Bombay, April.

Kenniston, K. 1974. Psychological development and historical change. In *Explorations in psychohistory, the Wellfleet papers.* Edited by R. J. Lifton with E. Olson, 152–164. New York: Simon and Schuster.

Kernberg, O. 1975. *Borderline conditions and pathological narcissism.* New York: Jason Aronson.

Khare, R. S. 1978. *The Hindu hearth and home.* Durham, N. C.: Carolina Academic Press.

Kitayama, O. 1981. On the therapist's receptivity towards the patient's disclosure and shame experience. *Japanese Journal of Psycho-Analysis.* 25:317–328.

Klein, G. 1976. *Psychoanalytic theory: An exploration of essentials.* New York: International Universities Press.

Kohut, H. 1971. *Analysis of the self.* New York: International Universities Press.

———. 1977. *Restoration of the self.* New York: International Universities Press.

———. 1980. Summary to *Advances in self psychology,* edited by A. Goldberg. New York: International Universities Press.

———. 1984. *How does analysis cure?* Chicago: University of Chicago Press.

Kondo, A. 1975. Morita therapy: Its sociohistorical context. In *New dimensions in psychiatry: A world view,* edited by S. Arieti and G. Chrzanowski, 239–260. New York: John Wiley.

Kopf, D. 1969. *British Orientalism and the Bengal renaissance.* Berkeley and Los Angeles: University of California Press.

———. 1979. *The Brahmo Samaj and the shaping of the modern Indian mind.* Princeton: Princeton University Press.

Kothari, R.; B. G. Verghese; R. Thapar; R. Krishna; M. D. Chaudhary; B. Ahmed; and K. Nayar. 1981. *Agenda for India.* Unpublished manuscript, New Delhi.

Kris, E. 1952. *Psychoanalytic explorations in art.* New York: International Universities Press.

Kuhn, T. 1962. *The structure of scientific revolutions.* Chicago: University of Chicago Press.

Kumagai, H. A. 1981. A dissection of intimacy: A study of "bipolar posture" in Japanese social interaction—*amaeru* and *amayakasu,* indulgence and deference. *Culture, Medicine and Psychiatry.* 5:249–272.

Kuppuswamy, B. 1977. Psychological dimensions of social change. In *Dimensions of social change in India,* edited by M. N. Srinivas, S. Seshaiah, and V. S. Parthasarathy, 389–401. New Delhi: Allied Publishers.

Kurian, G. 1961. *The Indian family in transition.* The Hague: Mouton.

Langs, R. 1976. *The therapeutic interaction.* Volumes 1 and 2. New York: Jason Aronson.

Lannoy, R. 1971. *The speaking tree.* Delhi: Oxford University Press.

Lasch, C. 1979. *The culture of narcissism.* New York: W. W. Norton.

Lebra, T. S. 1974a. Reciprocity and the asymmetric principle: An analytic reappraisal of the Japanese concept of *"on."* In *Japanese culture and behavior,* edited by T. S. Lebra and W. Lebra, 192–207. Honolulu: University Press of Hawaii.

———. 1974b. Intergenerational continuity and discontinuity in moral values among Japanese. In *Japanese culture and behavior,* edited by T. S. Lebra and W. Lebra, 431–442. Honolulu: University Press of Hawaii.

———. 1976. *Japanese patterns of behavior.* Honolulu: University Press of Hawaii.

———. 1984. *Japanese women: Constraint and fulfillment*. Honolulu: University Press of Hawaii.

Leonard, K. 1976. Women and social change in modern India. *Feminist Studies*. Spring-Summer. 3:117–130.

Leowald, H. 1960. On the therapeutic action of psychoanalyis. *International Journal of Psycho-Analysis*, 41:16–33.

LeVine, R. 1973. *Culture, behavior, and personality: An introduction to the comparative study of psychosocial adaptation*. New York: Aldine.

———. 1982a. *Culture, behavior, and personality: An introduction to the comparative study of psychosocial adaptation*. 2d ed. New York: Aldine.

———. 1982b. The self and its development in an African society: A preliminary analysis. In *Psychosocial theories of the self,* edited by Benjamin Lee. New York: Plenum.

LeVine, S. 1979. *Mothers and wives: Gusii women of East Africa*. Chicago: University of Chicago Press.

Lewis, H. B. 1971. *Shame and guilt*. New York: International Universities Press.

Lichtenstein, H. 1977. *The dilemma of human identity*. New York: Jason Aronson.

Lindholm, C. 1982. *Generosity and jealousy: The Swat Pukhtun of northern Pakistan*. New York: Columbia University Press.

Leowald, H. 1960. On the therapeutic action of psychoanalysis. In *Papers on psychoanalysis,* 221–256. New Haven: Yale University Press, 1980.

Madan, T. N. 1976. The Hindu woman at home. In *Indian women, from purdah to modernity,* edited by B. R. Nanda, 67–86. New Delhi: Vikas.

Mahler, M. 1972. Rapprochement subphase of the separation-individuation process. *Psychoanalytic Quarterly*. 41:487–506.

Mahler, M.; F. Pine; and A. Bergman. 1975. *Psychological birth of the human infant*. New York: Basic Books.

Malinowski, B. 1954. Myth in primitive psychology. In *Magic, science and religion*. New York: Doubleday.

Mandelbaum, D. 1970. *Society in India, continuity and change*. Berkeley and Los Angeles: University of California Press.

Maritain, J. 1953. *Creative intuition in art and poetry*. New York: Bollingen Foundation.

Marriott, M. 1976. Hindu transactions: Diversity without dualism. In *Transaction and meaning, directions in the anthropology of ex-*

change and symbolic behavior, edited by B. Kapferer, 109–142. Philadelphia: ISHI Publishing.

———. 1978. Intimacy and rank in food. Unpublished paper presented at the I.C.A.E.S. Conference, New Delhi.

———. 1979a. Three processes in the Hindu flux. Unpublished paper.

———. 1979b. The open Hindu person and the humane sciences. Unpublished paper.

———. 1980a. *Samsara:* A game of Hindu rural life. Unpublished paper presented at the A.C.L.S./S.S.R.C. Workshop on Mythology and Hierarchy, Chicago, September.

———. 1980b. The open Hindu person and interpersonal fluidity. Unpublished paper presented at the Annual Meeting, Association of Asian Studies, Washington, D.C., March.

Marriott, M., and R. Inden. 1977. Towards an ethnosociology of South Asian caste systems. In *The new wind: Changing identities in South Asia,* edited by K. A. David. Chicago: Aldine.

Marsella, A. J.; G. DeVos; and F.L.K. Hsu, eds. 1985. *Culture and self: Asian and Western perspectives.* London: Tavistock Publishers.

Masson, J. M. 1976. The psychology of the ascetic. *Journal of Asian Studies.* 35:611–625.

———. 1980. *The oceanic feeling: The origins of religious sentiment in ancient India.* Dordrecht, Holland: D. Reidel.

Mazumdar, V. 1976. The social reform movement in India—from Ranade to Nehru. In *Indian women: From purdah to modernity,* edited by B. R. Nanda, 41–66. New Delhi: Vikas.

———. 1981. Education and women's development. Unpublished paper presented at the National Conference on Women's Studies, SNDT College, Bombay, April.

McClelland, D. C. 1961. *The achieving society.* Princeton: Van Nostrand.

Meaders, N. 1983. Japanese psychology of resignation and the works of Kawabata. Unpublished paper presented at the Annual Meeting of the Mid-Atlantic Association of Asian Studies, Philadelphia, October.

Mehta, R. 1970. *The Western educated Hindu woman.* Bombay: Asia Publishing House.

———. 1976. From Purdah to modernity. In *Indian women: From purdah to modernity,* edited by B. R. Nanda, 113–128. New Delhi: Vikas.

Meltzer, D. 1978. Part I, Freud's clinical development. In *The Kleinian development.* Perthshire: Clunie Press.

Menaker, E. 1942. Masochistic factors in the psychoanalytic situation. *Psychoanalytic Quarterly*. 11:171–186.

———. 1952. Masochism as a defence reaction of the ego. *Psychoanalytic Quarterly*. 21:205–220.

———. 1978. Some inner conflicts of women in a changing society. In *Career and motherhood*. Edited by A. Roland and B. Harris. New York: Human Sciences Press.

———. 1980. Some psychosocial factors in the development of ego and self: Individuation, identification, and identity. Unpublished paper.

———. 1982. *Otto Rank: A rediscovered legacy*. New York: Columbia University Press.

Menaker, E., and W. Menaker. 1965. *Ego in evolution*. New York: Grove Press.

Miller, B. S., trans. and ed. 1977. *Love song of the dark lord, Jayadeva's Gitagovinda*. New York: Columbia University Press.

Milner, M. Some notes on mysticism. Unpublished paper.

Minami, H. 1971. *Psychology of the Japanese people*. Toronto: University of Toronto Press.

Miyamoto, M. 1983. Reflexivity-mirroring process. Unpublished paper presented at the Annual Meeting of the Mid-Atlantic Association of Asian Studies, Philadelphia, October,.

Moffatt, M. 1979. *An untouchable community in South India*. Princeton: Princeton University Press.

Morioka, K. 1986. Ancestor worship in contemporary Japan: Continuity and change. In *Religion and the family in East Asia*, edited by G. DeVos and T. Sofue, 201–213. Berkeley and Los Angeles: University of California Press.

Muensterberger, W. 1969. Psyche and environment: Sociocultural variations in separation and individuation. *Psychoanalytic Quarterly*. 38:191–216.

Murthy, A. 1976. *Samskara*. Translated by A. K. Ramanujam. Delhi: Oxford University Press.

Myrdal, G. 1968. *Asian drama*. New York: Pantheon.

Naipaul, V. S. 1971. One out of many. In *In a free state*. New York: Alfred A. Knopf.

———. 1977. *India: A wounded civilization*. New York: Alfred A. Knopf.

Nakane, C. 1970. *Japanese society*. Berkeley and Los Angeles: University of California Press.

Nandi, D. N. 1979. Psychoanalysis in India. In *Psychotherapeutic processes*, edited by M. Kapur, V. N. Murthy, K. Sathyavathi, R. L.

Kapur, 21–32. Bangalore: National Institute for Mental Health and Neuro Sciences.

Nandy, A. 1979. The double in Hindi films. *Times of India*. October 14.

———. 1980a. *Alternative sciences*. New Delhi: Allied Publishers.

———. 1980b. *At the edge of psychology: Essays in politics and culture*. Delhi: Oxford University Press.

———. 1983. *The intimate enemy*. Delhi: Oxford University Press.

Narayan, R. K. 1967. *The vendor of sweets*. New York: Viking Press.

Neki, J. S. 1973. *Guru-chela* relationship: The possibility of a therapeutic paradigm. *American Journal Orthopsychiatry*. 43:755– 766.

———. 1975. Psychotherapy in India: Past, present, and future. *American Journal of Psychotherapy*. 79:92–100.

———. 1976a. An examination of the cultural relativism of dependence as a dynamic of social and therapeutic relationships I: Socio-developmental. *British Journal of Medical Psychology*. 49:1–10.

———. 1976b. An examination of the cultural relativism of dependency as a dynamic of social and therapeutic relationships II: Therapeutic. *British Journal of Medical Psychology*. 49:11–22.

———. 1977. Psychotherapy in India: An overview. Unpublished paper presented at the International Study Group on "Children and Parents in a Changing World," B. M. Institute, Ahmedabad, October.

Nishizono, M. 1969. Japanese characteristics of the doctor-patient relationship in psychotherapy. In *Psychotherapy—prevention and rehabilitation*, Part I, edited by T. Spoerri and W. T. Winkler, 46–51. Basel/New York: S. Karger.

———. 1980. Recent trend of psychoanalysis. *Inje Medical Journal*. 1:209–217.

———. Problems imposed on psychotherapeutic intervention in traditional milieux—acculturation in Japan and psychotherapy. Unpublished paper.

Noy, P. 1968. A theory of art and aesthetic experience. *Psychoanalytic Review*. 55:623–645.

Obeyesekere, G. 1981. *Medusa's hair*. Chicago: University of Chicago Press.

———. 1984. *The cult of the goddess Pattini*. Chicago: University of Chicago Press.

O'Flaherty, W. 1973. *Asceticism and eroticism in the mythology of Shiva*. London: Oxford University Press.

———. 1976. *The origins of evil in Hindu mythology*. Berkeley and Los Angeles: University of California Press.

361

―――. 1980. Inside and outside the mouth of God: The boundary between myth and reality. In *Intellect and imagination: The limits and presuppositions of intellectual inquiry. Daedalus.* 109:93–126.

Ogura, Ḱ. 1978. Children who attack their mothers. Unpublished paper presented at the International Association of Child and Adolescent Psychiatry, Melbourne, August.

Ohnuki-Tierney, E. 1984. *Illness and culture in contemporary Japan: An anthropological view.* Cambridge: Cambridge University Press.

Okonogi, K. 1978a. Age of the moratorium people. *Japan Echo.* 5:17–39.

―――. 1978b. The *Ajase* complex of the Japanese (1), the depth psychology of the moratorium people. *Japan Echo.* 5:88–105.

―――. 1979. The *Ajase* complex of the Japanese (2). *Japan Echo.* 6:104–118.

Pande, S. K. 1968. The mystique of "Western" psychotherapy: An Eastern interpretation. *Journal of Nervous and Mental Diseases.* 146:425–432.

Parin, P.; F. Morgenthaler; and G. Parin-Matthey. 1980. *Fear thy neighbor as thyself.* Chicago: University of Chicago Press.

Parsons, T. 1964. *Social structure and personality.* New York: Free Press.

Paul, R. A. 1982. *The Tibetan symbolic world: Psychoanalytic explorations.* Chicago: University of Chicago Press.

Perinbanayagam, R. S. 1981. Self, other, and astrology: Esoteric therapy in Sri Lanka. *Journal of Psychiatry.* 44:69–79.

Pharr, S. J. 1981. *Political women in Japan: The search for a place in public life.* Berkeley and Los Angeles: University of California Press.

Pine, F. 1984. *Developmental theory and clinical process.* New Haven: Yale University Press.

Plath, D. W. 1980. *Long engagements: Maturity in modern Japan.* Stanford: Stanford University Press.

Pugh, J. 1977. Fate and experience in the Hindu and Moslem cultures of North India: An astrological view, part I. Unpublished paper presented at the Annual Meeting of the American Anthropological Association, Houston, December.

―――. 1978. The astrological advisory session. Unpublished paper presented at the A.C.L.S./S.S.R.C. Workshop on the Person and Interpersonal Relationships in South Asia: An Exploration of Indigenous Conceptual Systems, Chicago, January.

Raheja, G. G. 1976. Transformational processes in Hindu ritual: Concepts of "person" and "action" in the performance of a *vrat.* Unpublished paper presented at the A.C.L.S./S.S.R.C. Workshop on the Person and Interpersonal Relationships in South Asia: An Exploration of Indigenous Conceptual Systems, Chicago, May.

Rama, S., R. Ballentine, and S. Ajaya. 1976. *Yoga and psychotherapy, the evolution of consciousness.* Glenview, Ill: Himalayan Institute.

Ramana, C. V. 1964. On the early history and development of psychoanalysis in India. *Journal of the American Psychoanalytic Association.* 12:110–134.

Ramanujam, B. K. 1977. Studies of change at the B. M. Institute of Mental Health. Unpublished paper presented at the Annual Meeting of the International Study Group of Child Psychiatry, Ahmedabad, October.

———. 1979. Toward maturity: Problems of identity seen in the Indian clinical setting. In *Identity and adulthood,* edited by S. Kakar, 37–55. Delhi: Oxford University Press.

———. 1980a. Technical factors in psychotherapy in India. Unpublished paper presented at Annual Meeting of the American Academy of Psychoanalysis, Puerto Rico, October.

———. 1980b. Odyssey of an Indian villager: Mythic orientations in psychotherapy. Unpublished paper presented at A.C.L.S./S.S.R.C. Workshop on Hierarchy and Mythology in South Asia, Chicago, September.

———. 1981a. The importance of fathers: An overview of Indian cases. Unpublished paper presented at the A.C.L.S./S.S.R.C. Workshop on Families and the Life Cycle in South Asia, Chicago, September.

———. 1981b. Response to change: adaptive and pathological seen in a clinical set-up in India. Unpublished paper presented at the Annual Meeting of the International Society for the Comparative Study of Civilizations, Bloomington, May.

———. 1986. Social change and personal crisis: A view from an Indian practice. In *The cultural transitions, human experience and social transformation in the third world and Japan,* edited by M. White and S. Pollak. London: Routledge, Kegan Paul.

Ramanujan, A. K. 1980. Is there an Indian way of thinking? Unpublished paper presented at A.C.L.S./S.S.R.C. Workshop on Mythology and Hierarchy, Chicago, September.

———. 1981. A comparison of *Samskara* and *Death in Venice.* Unpublished paper presented at A.C.L.S./S.S.R.C. Workshop on Families and the Life Cycle, Chicago, September.

———. 1983. The Indian Oedipus. In *Oedipus: A folklore casebook,* edited by L. Edmunds and A. Dundes, 234–261. London: Garland Publishing.

Rank, O. 1932. *Art and the artist*. New York: Alfred A. Knopf.

Reissman, D. 1951. *The lonely crowd*. New Haven: Yale University Press.

Reynolds, D. 1976. *Morita therapy*. Berkeley and Los Angeles: University of California Press.

————. 1980. *The quiet therapies*. Honolulu: University Press of Hawaii.

————. 1983. *Naikan psychotherapy: Meditation for self-development*. Chicago: University of Chicago Press.

Rieff, P. 1968. *The triumph of the therapeutic: The uses of faith after Freud*. New York: Harper and Row.

Roland, A. 1967. The reality of the psychoanalytic relationship and situation in the handling of transference-resistance. *International Journal of Psycho-Analysis*. 48:504–510.

————. 1971. The context and unique function of dreams in psychoanalytic therapy. *International Journal of Psycho-Analysis*. 52:431–439.

————. 1972. Imagery and symbolic expression in dreams and art. *International Journal of Psycho-Analysis*. 53:531–539.

————. 1974a. Pinter's *Homecoming:* Imagoes in dramatic action. *Psychoanalytic Review*. 60:415–427.

————. 1974b. Psychoanalysis and literature. *Book Forum*. 1:275–284.

————. 1978a. Psychoanalytic perspectives on personality development in India. *Samiksa*. 32:47–68. Also in *International Review of Psycho-Analysis*. 1980. 7:73–87.

————. 1978b. Towards a re-orientation of psychoanalytic literary criticism. In *Psychoanalysis, creativity, and literature: A French-American dialogue*, edited by A. Roland, 248–270. New York: Columbia University Press.

————. 1981a. Imagery and the self in artistic creativity and psychoanalytic criticism. *Psychoanalytic Review*. 68: 409–420.

————. 1981b. Induced emotional reactions and attitudes in the psychoanalyst as transference in actuality. *Psychoanalytic Review*. 68:45–74.

————. 1982. Towards a psychoanalytic psychology of hierarchical relationships in Hindu India. *Ethos*. 10:232–253.

————. 1983. Psychoanalysis without interpretation: Psychoanalytic therapy in Japan. *Contemporary Psychoanalysis*. 19:499–505.

————. 1987. The familial self, the individualized self and the transcendent self: Psychoanalytic reflections on India and America. *Psychoanalytic Review*. 74:239–252.

Roland, A., and B. Harris, eds. 1978. *Career and motherhood: Struggles for a new identity.* New York: Human Sciences Press.

Roland, A., and G. Rizzo. 1978. Psychoanalysis in search of Pirandello: *Six characters* and *Henry IV.* In *Psychoanalysis, creativity, and literature: A French-American dialogue,* edited by A. Roland, 323–351. New York: Columbia University Press.

Ross, E. 1961. *The Hindu family in its urban setting.* Toronto: University of Toronto Press.

Rothenberg, A. 1979. *Creativity, the emerging goddess.* Chicago: University of Chicago Press.

Roy, M. 1975. *Bengali women.* Chicago: University of Chicago Press.

———. 1979. Animus and Indian women. *Harvest.* 25:70–79.

Rudolph, L., and S. Rudolph. 1967. *The modernity of tradition.* Chicago: University of Chicago Press.

Rudolph, S., and L. Rudolph. 1976. Rajput adulthood: Reflections on the Amar Singh diary. *Adulthood, Daedalus.* Spring:145–168.

Sakala, C. 1977. A preliminary investigation of Hindu concepts of the child with special reference to rank. Unpublished paper.

———. 1980. Introduction: Resources and their uses. In *Women of South Asia, a guide to resources,* 3–13. Millwood, N. Y.: Kraus International Publications.

———. 1981. The stream of our lives: Self and interpersonal relationship in Chitpavin Brahmin personal narratives. Master's thesis, University of Chicago.

Satow, R. 1983. The convergence of cultural and individual intrapsychic factors. *Journal of the American Academy of Psychoanalysis.* 11:547–556.

Segal, H. 1964. *Introduction to the work of Melanie Klein.* New York: Basic Books.

Seth, N. 1980. Mixed paradigms and healing: Interviews with twelve analysands in Bombay. Unpublished paper.

Seth, V. 1980. Divali. *The Threepenny Review.* Summer.

Shils, E. 1961. *The intellectual between tradition and modernity: The Indian situation. Comparative Studies in Society and History,* Supplement I. The Hague: Mouton.

Singer, M. 1972. *When a great tradition modernizes: An anthropological approach to Indian civilization.* New York: Praeger.

———. 1981. On the semiotics of Indian identity. *American Journal of Semiotics.* 1:85–126.

Sinha, J. 1980. Power structure, perceptual frame, and behavioral strategies in dyadic relationships. Unpublished paper presented at the

International Association for Cross-Cultural Psychology, Bhubaneswar.

Sondhi, K. 1977. *Uprooted*. New Delhi: Arnold Heinemann.

Spear, P. 1970. *A history of India*. Volume 2. Middlesex: Penguin Books.

Spiro, M. E. 1965. Religious systems as culturally constituted defense mechanisms. In *Context and meaning in cultural anthropology*, edited by M. E. Spiro, 100–113. New York: Free Press.

Spratt, P. 1966. *Hindu culture and personality: A psychoanalytic study*. Bombay: Manaktalas.

Srinivas, M. N. 1966. *Social change in modern India*. Berkeley and Los Angeles: University of California Press.

———. 1976. *The remembered village*. Delhi: Oxford University Press.

———. 1977. *The dual cultures of independent India. Gandhi Memorial Lecture*. Bangalore: Raman Research Institute.

———. 1978. *The changing position of Indian women*. Delhi: Oxford University Press.

Sripada, B. 1981. Narcissistic personality disorders and the Hindu psyche. Unpublished paper.

Stolorow, R., and F. Lachmann. 1980. *Psychoanalysis of developmental arrests*. New York: International Universities Press.

Sullivan, H. S. 1953. *Interpersonal theory of psychiatry*. New York: W. W. Norton.

Surya, N. C. 1966. The ego structure in the Hindu joint family. Unpublished paper presented at the Conference on Mental Health in Asia and the Pacific, Honolulu.

Surya, N. C., and S. S. Jayaram. 1964. Some basic considerations of psychotherapy in India. *Indian Journal of Psychiatry*. 153–156.

Sylvan, M. 1981. Reply to Alan Roland's paper on "Psychoanalytic perspectives on personality development in India." *International Review of Psycho-Analysis*. 8:93–99.

Szaz, T. 1957. On the experiences of the analyst in the psychoanalytic situation: A contribution to the theory of psychoanalytic treatment. *Journal American Psychoanalytic Association*. 4:197–223.

Taketomo, Y. 1982. The reticent father: some thoughts on Japanese culture and conflict. *Journal of the American Academy of Psychoanalysis*. 26:12–14.

———. 1983. Towards a discovery of self: A transcultural perspective. Unpublished paper presented at the Annual Meeting of the Mid-Atlantic Association for Asian Studies, Philadelphia, October.

———. 1984. *Hiroshima mon amour* and persistence of memory. Unpublished paper presented at the Annual Meeting of the American Academy of Psychoanalysis, Los Angeles, May.

————. 1985. *Amae* as metalanguage: A critique of Doi's theory of *amae*. Unpublished paper presented at the Annual Meeting of the Association for Asian Studies, Philadelphia, March; and at the Annual Meeting of the American Psychoanalytic Association, Los Angeles, May.

Tanaka, M. 1986. Maternal authority in the Japanese family. In *Religion and the family in East Asia*, edited by G. DeVos and T. Sofue, 227–336. Berkeley and Los Angeles: University of California Press.

Tatara, M. 1974. Problem of separation and dependence: Some personality characteristics met in psychotherapy in Japan and some technical considerations. *Journal of the American Academy of Psychoanalysis*. 2:231–241.

————. 1981. Social change and its impact on family life in Japan: Some thoughts on parent abuse syndrome. Unpublished paper presented to the Board of Trustees Meeting, Austen Riggs Center, Stockbridge, May.

————. 1982. Psychoanalytic psychotherapy in Japan: The issue of dependency pattern and the resolution of psychopathology. *Journal of the American Academy of Psychoanalysis*. 10:225–239.

Thapar, R. 1966. *A history of India*. Volume 1. Middlesex: Penguin Books.

Turkle, S. 1978. *The politics of psychoanalysis: French Freud*. New York: Basic Books.

Uberoi, J.P.S. 1978. *Science and culture*. Delhi: Oxford University Press.

Vatsyayan, K. 1975. In the performing arts. In *Indian women*, edited by D. Jain, 291–300. Delhi: Publications Division, Ministry of Information and Broadcasting, Government of India.

————. 1979. Search for roots. *Sunday Standard*. September 23.

Vatuk, S. 1972. *Kinship and urbanization*. Berkeley and Los Angeles: University of California Press.

————. 1981. Cultural conceptions of aging and family relationships in a Delhi village. Unpublished paper presented at the A.C.L.S./S.S.R.C. Workshop on Life Crises and Family Relationships in Alternative Psychologies of South Asia, Chicago, September.

Vivekananda, S. 1949. *Collected papers*. New York: Ramakrishna-Vivekananda Center.

Vogel, E. 1967. Kinship structure, migration to the city, and modernization. In *Aspects of social change in Japan*, edited by R. P. Dore, 91–111. Princeton: Princeton University Press.

Vollrath, E.; J. N. Mohanty; and K. Dove. 1974. Colloquy on being: The Western versus the Indian traditions. *Graduate Faculty Philosophy Journal.* 4:1–18.

Wadley, S. 1975. *Shakti, power in the conceptual structure of Karimpur religion.* Chicago: Department of Anthropoplogy, University of Chicago.

———. 1980. Hindu women's family and household rites in a North Indian village. In *Unspoken worlds: Women's religious lives in non-Western cultures,* edited by R. Gross and N. Falk, 94–109. New York: Harper and Row.

Wagatsuma, H., and G. DeVos. 1984. *Heritage of endurance.* Berkeley and Los Angeles: University of California Press.

Walsh, J. 1982. *Growing up in British India.* New York: Holmes and Meier.

Washton-Long, R. C. 1980. *Kandinsky: The advent of an abstract style.* London: Oxford University Press.

Weber, M. 1958. *The religion of India: The sociology of Hinduism and Buddhism.* Glencoe, Ill.: Free Press.

Weil, E. 1956. Origins and vicissitudes of the self-image. *Psychoanalysis.* 6:3–19.

Weinstein F., and G. Platt. 1973. *Psychoanalytic sociology.* Baltimore: John Hopkins University Press.

White, M. 1987. *The Japanese educational challenge: A commitment to children.* New York: Free Press.

Winnicott, D. W. 1951. Transitional objects and transitional phenomena. In *Collected papers.* New York: Basic Books.

———. 1960. Ego distortion in terms of true and false self. In *The maturational processes and the facilitating environment.* London: Hogarth Press, 1965.

———. 1965. *The maturational processes and the facilitating environment.* London: Hogarth Press and The Institute of Psycho-Analysis.

Yalman, N. 1969. De Tocqueville in India: An essay on the caste system. *Man.* 4:123–131.

INDEX

identify resolutions (*continued*)
novators, 48-49; reaction to colonialism, 21-25
identity synthesis: Ashis, 28; Indian psychoanalysts and social sciences, 61-62
ie stem family: changes by American Occupation, 129, 135; in pre-Occupation Japan, 129, 182-183; structure of psychoanalysis in Japan, 75; structure and roles of the, 134-135; urban lower middle classes, 136n
incestuous fantasies: in Indian women, 118, 123, 261; Saida, 178; Shakuntala, 162, 168-169
Indian Council of Mental Health, 56
Indian culture: idealization processes and we-self regard, 249; erotic and ascetic, 262; respect for the spiritual person, 291. *See also* Hindu culture
Indian Institute of Technology, 103-104
Indian Psychoanalytic Society, 55-57, 61
Indian self: comparison with Japanese, 144-145; identity conflicts, 21-22; individualization, 58, 89; layering of indigenous and Western, 93; sociocultural contexts, xvii n
individualism: comparison of individual to dividual, 11; deconversion in America, 58; ego boundaries in, 227; in the West, 12; Indian-Western comparison, 240, 267; Japanese identity conflicts, 144; modernization models and India, 97; psychoanalysis and Japanese, 71-72, 80; Western ideal for women's careers, 206
individuality: Indian-American comparison, 240-241; Japanese private self and expressions of, 83, 189, 279; Japanese-Indian comparison, 282
individualization: Amal, 106-108; Ashis, 37, 104-105; development of psychoanalysis in India, 58; effects of Occupation, 134-137; Indian institutional innovation, 102; Indian familial conflict, 174; Indian women, 151-154; individuation and conflict, 332-333; Japanese psychoanalysts, 190; Japanese women, 184; Japanese-Indian comparison, 145; Joan, 112-113; Rustum, 124-125, 127;

Saida, 176; social change in India, 89, 98-100
individualized self: attitudes of Indian psychiatrists, 60-61; emotional relatedness as intermediary, 319; in Americans, 100-101, 328; organization of, 6, 8-9
individuation: in Indian child rearing, 233-234; Ashis, 34-35, 39, 104-105; Indian institutional innovation, 102; Indian spiritual practices and quest, 166, 309; Indian-American comparison, 100-102, 228; Joan, 112; reexamination in cross-civilizational research, xvi; social change in India, 89; Western-Japanese-Indian comparison, 329-331
insider/outsider relationships: in Japanese psychoanalysis, 189; Indian qualitative mode of hierarchical relationships, 221; Japanese Indian comparison, 283-284
intelligentsia (Indian): identity conflicts, 43, 45-46, 48; Westernization, 18-20
interdependence: revision of *amae* theory, 279-281. See also *amae;* dependence
interdisciplinary research, xii, 313-316
internalization process, xii, 272-274; of conscience in Indian female students, 181; integration of psychoanalysis with social sciences, 315-316. *See also* representational world
International Psychoanalytic Association, 55, 76, 78
interpersonal sensitivity, Japanese-Indian comparison, 282-283. *See also* empathy
interpretations: Amal's rage and hysterical attacks, 107-108; Ashis's anxiety over his artistic identity, 42; Ashis's literary creativity, 42; Ashis's unconscious identification with the aggressor, 44; Ashis's unfinished mourning, 39-40; Ashis's Westernization, 28' in Japanese psychoanalytic therapy, 88, 192; in psychoanalytic methodology, 317; Joan's conscience, 116, 118; Joan's identification with her mother, 120; Joan's projective identification, 111; Joan's rebellious feelings, 120-121; Joan's sibling rivalry, 114; Joan's unconscious guilt, 119; Mrs. K's communication, 193; Rashmi's

anxiety over her spiritual aspirations, 291; Rustum's unconscious rebellion, 125; Saida's displacement from her father to mother-in-law, 178; Saida's displacement from her mother to mother-in-law, 177; Shakuntala and her mother, 167; Shakuntala's dream, 163; Shakuntala's incestuous fantasies, 169; Shakuntala's rages at Kumar, 165

intimacy relationships: dependency in Indians, 227-228, 255; emotional exchange in Japanese hierarchical relationships, 8; empathy in Japanese, 189; Indian psychoanalytic relationships, 65-66, 68; Indian same-sex relationships, 215; Indian-American comparison, 196-200; Indian-Japanese-American comparison, 12; Japanese women's relationships, 182, 184-185; Japanese-Indian comparison, 283-284; qualitative mode of hierarchical relationships, 220-221

intrapsychic self, 3-4

I-self, 225

Japanese Psychoanalytic Association, 78

jiva, 5

Joan: anger, 110, 113-116, 120-121, 259; anxiety as a newlywed, 215; background and presenting problems, 108-110; communication, 222, 227; conscience and anger, 116-117, 256; dreams, 110, 114, 117, 119, 120; education and marriage, 112-113; guilt and projective identification, 111; identification with her mother, 120; incestuous fantasies, 261; mediator of in-laws' relationships, 116; palmistry, 118; relationships with father-figures, 117-118, 268; religious values, 118-119; scapegoating in Indian families, 111-112, 259; somatic symptoms, 258

joint household, Indian, 92, 211-212. *See also* family; extended family; *ie* stem family; kinship; unitary household

Jungian psychology, 299, 305

junior (Japanese), 74, 75. *See also* superior

Kakar, Sudhir, 50n, 93n

Kapadia, Sailesh, 234

Kapur, Ravi, 31-32

karma, 170, 297

kinship (Indian), 209-212; morality of modesty/shame, 214-215; somatization and stress, 258; terms for hierarchical relationships, 213. *See also* extended family; family; *ie* stem family; joint household; unitary household

Kiyoshi, 138-140, 276-277

knowledge, *see* cognition

Kondo, Akihisa, 77, 78, 80-81, 83, 86; individualization and social change, 137; Karen Horney Group and Zen Buddhism, 293

Kosawa, Heisaku, 76, 78-80

Krishna, 260

Krishnamurti, J., 61

kundalini, x n, 161

Laxmi, 251

life cycle (Indian), 216, 258, 297

life style, Indian-American comparison, 196-201

love affair, 156-57; Shakuntala, 160

love marriage: Indian, 99; Japanese, 135, 183-184. *See also* arranged marriage; Marriages

Maeda, Shigeharu, 76

magic-cosmic: 299-302; Ashis, 38-39; and destiny, 166, Indian Christians, 118; reductionism of, 320; Rustum, 124; subject-object relationship in, 10-11; V. S. Naipaul's critique, 49-50. *See also* astrology; clairvoyant dreams; destiny; palmistry

Main house in *ie* family structure, 134

mangal, Shakuntala, 165

Manisha: dependency, 228; we-self regard, 244

mantra, 30; Shakuntala's, 166

marriages: companionate marriage in India, 151-153; in Japan, 129, 134, 135; Indian structural hierarchy versus hierarchy by quality, 218; Indian women, 149-153, 158-159, 162; Indian-American comparison, 199-200, 203; individualization and modernization in India, 99; Japanese-Indian comparison, 73;

46-47; Indian-Western comparison, 66-67, 197-198; Japanese-Western comparison, 81-82; with Indians, 35, 63-66, 156, 256; with Japanese, 83-84, 87, 189-192, 194

psychoanalytic sociology, 314-316, 320

psychoanalytic therapy: and ethnography, 316-318; Ashis, 25-47; goals of in America and India, 62-63; hidden methodology of, xxiv-xxv; Hiroshi, 140-142; in cross-civilizational research, xxvi-xxviii; in India, xix, 290-291; in Japan, 81, 84-87, 278; Kiyoshi, 138-140; objections by Indian psychiatrists to, 63-64; real relationship in, xiii; universals versus Western-centrism, xvii

psychological make-up: Indian-Japanese-American comparison, 9

psychological space, 226, 227

psychological structures: effects of Indian mothering on, 232-233; of the Japanese self, 84, 85-86, 136; of the spiritual self, 292

psychopathology: and actualization of potentialities, 325-328, 331-333; in *amae* theory, 280; Indian superego reaction to anger, 256-257; Japanese-American comparison on, 138-139; modernization and Japanese kinds of, 132-133; relationship to spiritual self, 172-173. *See also* amnesia; anthrophobia; anxiety; hysteria; obsessive-compulsive; *Shinkeishitsu* personality; somatic symptoms; symptoms

psychosexual development: Indian-Western comparison, 268-271; need for reformulation of, 329. *See also* developmental schemas

psychosocial dimensions: Japanese-Indian comparison, 282-288; new concepts for Indians and Japanese, xvii; of hierarchical and psychoanalytic relationships, 64-67, 81-87

public self, 5, 219

puja, 171

qualitative mode of hierarchical relationships, 220-221; in continuity of familial and spiritual selves, 295-296; in hierar-chical and psychoanalytic relationships, 65-66, 81-84; interpersonal sensitivity, 229; Japanese-Indian comparison, 282-283. *See also* hierarchical relationships; hierarchy by quality; structural hierarchy

racism (India), 19-20

radar (Indian), 155, 252

rage: Amal and individualization, 107-108; Shakuntala, 165. *See also* ambivalence; anger

Rama, 219

Ramakrishna Order, 23-24, 29, 33

Ramanujam, B. K., 31-32, 57, 65, 67 n, 70-71, 97, 103, 111, 117, 152, 214 n, 218 n, 225, 227 n, 236, 244, 249, 258, 260, 307

Ramanujan, A. K., 225, 227

Ramanujan, Srinivasa, 24

Rank, Otto, xvi, 5

Rashi, 235, 242-243, 290

Rashmi, 290-291

rationalism in psychoanalysis, 59, 80-81

Ravanna, 96n

Ravi, 234, 262

reaction-formation: in Indians, 259-260, 269-270; in Japanese, 277n

real relationship, xiii, xxviii, 65, 67

reality, Indian-Western comparison on views of, 290

receptivity: in Indians and Japanese, 270; Indian interpersonal sensitivity, 229

reciprocity in Indian hierarchical relationships, 251

reductionism: historical and sociocultural with the psychological, xxvii n; psychoanalysis and religion, 296; psychoanalysis and the spiritual self, 292-293; psychoanalysis applied to literature and art, xii; psychoanalysis applied to the social sciences, xiii

reform: for Indian women, 147-148; movements and Indian identity, 22-24

reincarnation, 161

religion: and material goods, 118-119; psychoanalytic attitudes toward, 59, 296. *See also* meditation; spiritual aspirations; spiritual practices; yoga

385